SLOVENE:
A COMPREHENSIVE

MW01195336

Slovene: A Comprehensive Grammar is a complete reference guide to the contemporary language.

Since Slovenia gained independence in 1991, Slovene has grown steadily in importance. This is the first comprehensive grammar of the language to be published in English, and is an ideal reference source for learners and users of Slovene at every level: independent learners, university and college students, and professional linguists.

The volume is organized to enable students of the language to find the information they seek quickly and easily, and to promote a thorough understanding of Slovene grammar. Focusing on patterns of use among educated speakers in the Slovenian capital, Ljubljana, it indicates clearly where these conflict with the prescribed standard.

Features include:

- thorough description of all parts of speech
- jargon-free explanations
- numerous examples from contemporary sources
- clear distinction between written and spoken usage
- bibliography of works relating to Slovene
- full index

Slovene: A Comprehensive Grammar reflects the richness of the language and is an essential purchase for all students of Slovene.

Peter Herrity is Professor of Slavonic Languages and Head of Slavonic Studies at the University of Nottingham.

SLOVENE: A COMPREHENSIVE GRAMMAR

Peter Herrity

London and New York

First published 2000 by Routledge
2 Park Square, Milton Park, Abingdon, Oxon, OX14 4RN

Simultaneously published in the USA and Canada
by Routledge
270 Madison Ave, New York NY 10016

Routledge is an imprint of the Taylor & Francis Group

Transferred to Digital Printing 2006

Typeset in Times by RefineCatch Limited, Bungay, Suffolk

British Library Cataloguing in Publication Data
A catalogue record for this book is available from the British Library

Library of Congress Cataloging in Publication Data
Herrity, Peter.
 Slovene: a comprehensive grammar/Peter Herrity.
  p. cm.
 Includes bibliographical references and index.
 ISBN 0–415–23147–7 (hb)—ISBN 0–415–23148–5 (pb)
  1. Slovenian language—Textbooks for foreign speakers—English. 2. Slovenian
language—Grammar. I. Title.

PG1827.5.E5 H47 2000
491.8′482421—dc21

                                                    00–028085

ISBN 0–415–23147–7 (hbk)
ISBN 0–415–23148–5 (pbk)

CONTENTS

ACKNOWLEDGEMENTS

It is with sincere gratitude that I acknowledge the assistance which I have been fortunate enough to receive during the preparation of this grammar. First and foremost from Metka Čuk who encouraged me to undertake the writing of a Slovene grammar, Adriana Krstič who acted as an enthusiastic informant and Sabina Grahek who read the final draft of the manuscript from the point of view of a native speaker and made numerous useful comments and valuable suggestions. They and other native speakers too numerous to name here have patiently answered questions, given advice and often provided me with examples and other linguistic data. I am also indebted to Professor Jože Toporišič, who invited me to spend a semester at Ljubljana University to work on the grammar, and to his assistant Mateja Hočevar, who acted as my language mentor while I was there. I must also acknowledge my debt to the University of Nottingham for granting me study leave during this period. Finally my thanks go to Anne Johnson for her preparation of the manuscript for publication.

ABBREVIATIONS AND SYMBOLS

A./acc.	accusative	n./neut.	neuter
adj.	adjective	N./nom.	nominative
arch.	archaic	part.	participle
const.	constellation	pej.	pejorative
d.	dual	pers.	person
D./dat.	dative	pf.	perfective
det.	determinate	plur.	plural
f./fem.	feminine	pron.	pronounced
fin.	finance	sing.	singular
G./gen.	genitive	styl.	stylistic
imp.	imperfective		
indet.	indeterminate	ø	zero ending
I./instr.	instrumental	*	not attested
lit.	literally		reconstructed form
L./loc.	locative	>	changes into
m./masc.	masculine	<	comes from

INTRODUCTION

Slovene is a Slavonic language and is spoken in Slovenia and adjacent enclaves in Austria (Carinthia), Italy (Friuli–Venezia–Giulia) and Hungary (the Raba river basin). It is the native language of nearly two million Slovenes and it is also spoken by approximately 400,000 speakers in emigrant communities in the United States, Canada, Argentina, Australia, Germany and France. Considering the relatively small size of the Slovene speaking area (approx. 20,000 square kilometres), Slovene is remarkable for the heterogeneity of the dialects. These are conventionally divided into eight major geographical groups, within which there are numerous subdialects, giving a total of fifty dialects in all. Many of these dialects are distinctly different from one another, so much so that there can be some lack of mutual comprehension.

The official literary language of Slovenia is known as Contemporary Standard Slovene. It is a composite of several dialects, but is based mainly on the geographically central dialects of Upper and Lower Carniola (Gorenjska and Dolenjska). Ljubljana, the capital city, which is geographically just inside Upper Carniola, straddles the border between these two dialect areas.

As a result of its complicated historical development, Contemporary Standard Slovene is to a certain degree an artificial language. Not only is it not the same as any one Slovene dialect, but it also differs in many respects from the colloquial standard language used by educated people. Contemporary Standard Slovene is the language found in grammar books, taught in schools and universities and used in literature and the media on formal occasions. It is the written language of educated Slovenes and has to be learnt.

The colloquial standard language is on the other hand the language used in everyday life by educated speakers of urban areas. This colloquial standard language, affected by local speech habits, differs from the written standard in phonology, morphology, syntax and vocabulary. At the same time one must bear in mind that the colloquial standard of the capital, Ljubljana, will differ from the colloquial standard of other towns in other dialect regions, e.g. Maribor in Styria.

The difference between the written standard and the colloquial standard is the result of the long and complex history of the development of the written literary language. The Slav tribes who were the ancestors of the Slovenes settled in the eastern Alpine region in the sixth century AD. Although initially independent within a short-lived state called Carantanija, the Slovene lands from the eighth century onwards were controlled by Germanic speakers and in time they found themselves within the Austro-Hungarian Empire. In 1918, the Slovenes gained a measure of independence within the newly created Kingdom of Serbs, Croats and Slovenes, which in 1929 became known as Yugoslavia. Only in 1991, however, did the Slovenes finally achieve full independence for themselves. The ninth and tenth centuries saw the dissolution of Common Slavonic, the proto-language of all the Slavs, and the individualisation of a Slovene language. The earliest written records with Slovene features are the Freising Fragments, which were written between 972 and 1039. These are followed much later in the fourteenth and fifteenth centuries by a few religious manuscripts. The Reformation witnessed the publication of the first printed books by the Protestant reformers P. Trubar, S. Krelj, J. Dalmatin and A. Bohorič. These writers basically used the dialect of Lower Carniola with an admixture of Upper Carniolan and Inner Carniolan (Notranjsko) features. The dialect of Ljubljana was especially influential in this central dialect norm, which continued to be used even in the period of the Counter-Reformation, since when most Slovenes have remained Catholic. However, by the seventeenth and eighteenth centuries, the dialects of Carinthia, Styria and Prekmurje were also being used in writing as a result of the production of texts for individual diocesan needs. Writers from the central areas continued to follow the old Protestant norm, but it underwent certain changes in favour of Upper Carniolan phonology, due to the increase in the number of writers from this area in the eighteenth century. This broadened the dialectal base of the language and made it more accessible to speakers of other dialects. This adherence to a sixteenth-century written norm was very important in terms of continuity, because between the sixteenth and seventeenth centuries significant changes had occurred in the phonology and morphology of the central dialects and there was a gap between the spoken and written language. In 1808, J. Kopitar published his *Grammatik der slavischen Sprache in Krain, Kärnten und Steyermark*, which attempted to unite the speech of all Slovene regions based on a synthesis of Upper and Lower Carniolan features. Kopitar accepted the Protestant heritage as the basis for the literary language, but stressed the primacy of the vernacular purged of Germanisms. At the beginning of the nineteenth century debates on purism continued and new grammars appeared based on both Styrian and Lower Carniolan dialects. It was only at this time that Slovene became firmly established as the name of the language as opposed to the variety of terms previously used: Carniolan, Styrian, Carinthian, Windisch. In the second quarter of the nineteenth century there was a move by some Styrian and Carinthian writers to merge Slovene with Croatian and Serbian to create a new south Slavonic 'Illyrian' language, but the counter-efforts of the poet F. Prešeren and the great Slovene linguist F. Miklošič defeated these attempts and ensured the future of Slovene as an independent language.

Slovene grammarians and writers now accepted the idea of the integration of the Slovene dialects and concessions were made to Carinthian and Styrian in terms of morphological features. Newspapers and journals also adopted the new compromise norm which was still strongly linked to the Carniolan dialects. In the second half of the nineteenth century two further important linguistic processes took place – slavisation and archaisation. Slavisation introduced numerous words from the Slavonic languages, especially Serbo-Croat, in an attempt to eradicate Germanisms. Archaisation, with Church Slavonic as a model, affected the grammatical structure of the language, introducing categories which had long been lost or weakened long ago in the dialects, and indeed distinguish the literary standard from the colloquial variants in use today.

This reconstructive, diachronic approach to the language was superseded only at the turn of the century, when linguists embraced a more consistent synchronic approach, putting a check on borrowings from other Slavonic languages and limiting archaic forms to those actually attested in older Slovene. When Slovenia became part of Yugoslavia in 1918 a new influx of Serbo-Croat words entered the language, but this was followed later by a puristic tendency directed against Serbo-Croat words, not only current borrowings but also against previously admitted borrowings. After the Second World War the differences between the Slovene dialects diminished as a result of internal migration, urbanisation and industrialisation and the standard language has spread due to education and mass communication.

The problem of writing a grammar for English speakers is to what extent the Contemporary Standard, used only on formal occasions, should be presented. Many of its forms are archaic or it allows variant forms which are simply not used in the colloquial standard. The aim of this grammar therefore is to describe the standard language in terms of the most common usage and where appropriate indicate those forms that are archaic or little used. Where necessary reference will also be made to the colloquial standard particularly as reflected in the capital Ljubljana. It must, however, be remembered that even today there is a difference in approach by linguists. Some writers are more disposed to accept the spoken usage into the Contemporary Standard than others. A further problem is that there is still a hesitancy regarding the correctness or not of certain forms.

This is the first comprehensive Slovene grammar to be published in the UK and is based on personal research in Slovenia and a close study of reference materials by Slovene, European and American linguists. Its approach is descriptive and the rules of usage are illustrated by examples from contemporary literary and journalistic sources and native speakers. The grammar is presented in thirteen chapters which are further subdivided to take account of points of finer usage. The intention is to present the grammar in an easily comprehensible way, provide the essential facts, point out the subtleties of the language and explain clearly those areas of usage which create special difficulties for English speakers. When spoken and written usage diverge, this is explained as are forms which, though they may be regarded as grammatically correct, are felt to be stilted outside the most formal written registers. The vocabulary used in this grammar in the examples of usage is for the most part neutral. Therefore no attempt has been made to indicate the register of individual words. For details about register one should consult the Academy dictionary (*Slovar slovenskega knjižnega jezika*).

Contemporary Standard Slovene has two phonological systems which differ in respect of prosodic phenomena: a tonemic system and a non-tonemic system. The tonemic system has in fact been lost in most Slovene dialects and is now considered archaic. It is not considered obligatory in the standard norm. This grammar will therefore indicate accentuation as per the non-tonemic system, since this is the widely accepted norm and is the system currently used in dictionaries and prescriptive grammars of the language as well as in schools and universities. In Slovene the majority of words have just one stressed syllable. Only certain prefixed words and some compounds have two stressed syllables. The only words that are unstressed are proclitics and enclitics. Stress will be indicated in all Slovene words in this grammar. One feature of the modern Slovene language is that many words allow alternative stresses. In this grammar alternative stresses will not be indicated on words in the text or examples of usage. Only the most commonly accepted stress is given. For details on alternative stresses one can consult the Academy dictionary (*Slovar slovenskega knjižnega jezika*). Alternative stress, however, will be indicated in the grammar in those sections that specifically deal with this fact. In these cases the Slovene word(s) in question will be marked as follows with two stresses, e.g. **písáti** 'to write'. This will mean that both **písati** and **pisáti** are allowed in the modern language.

For ease of reference the grammar also includes an alphabetical index of grammatical topics.

1 PHONOLOGY

1.1 THE SLOVENE ALPHABET

There are twenty-five letters in the Slovene alphabet: five vowels and twenty
consonants. Three of the consonants have a superscript diacritic ˇ, i.e. **č, š, ž**.

	Approximate English equivalent	Slovene example	English translation
A a	a	**Amêrika**	America
		ávtobus	bus
B b	b	**Benétke**	Venice
		bràt	brother
C c	ts (as in bi<u>ts</u>)	**Cêlje**	Celje
		césta	road
Č č	ch (as in <u>ch</u>ur<u>ch</u>)	**Čéška**	Bohemia
		čáj	tea
D d	d (but dental e.g. as in French *dans* 'in')	**Dánska**	Denmark
		dán	day
E e	either e in 'get' or *é* in French *été* 'summer'	**Evrópa**	Europe
		êna	one
		Élba	Elbe
		étos	ethos
F f	f	**Fráncija**	France
		fànt	boy
G g	g	**Grčija**	Greece
		gledalíšče	theatre
H h	ch (as in lo<u>ch</u>)	**Holándska**	Holland
		híša	house
I i	i (as in mach<u>i</u>ne)	**Índija**	India
		igrálec	player
J j	y (as in <u>y</u>oung or bo<u>y</u>)	**Japónska**	Japan
		jêzik	language
K k	k	**Kitájska**	China
		krùh	bread
L l	l (or w see **1.7.4**)	**Ljubljána**	Ljubljana
		lép	beautiful
M m	m	**Máribor**	Maribor
		mléko	milk

see **1.3.3**

N n	n	**Nizozémska**	Holland
		nós	nose
O o	either o in 'got'	**Olímp**	Olympus
	or *o* in French *dos* 'back'	**ôče**	father
		Óhrid	Ohrid see **1.3.3**
		ópica	monkey
P p	p	**Prága**	Prague
		pótnik	traveller
R r	r (rolled as in Italian or Russian)	**Rúsija**	Russia
		ríba	fish
S s	s	**Slovénija**	Slovenia
		stòl	chair
Š š	sh (as in fi<u>sh</u>)	**Švíca**	Switzerland
		študènt	student
T t	t (but dental e.g. as in French *tomate* 'tomato')	**Témza**	Thames
		téden	week
U u	u	**Urál**	The Urals
		učítelj	teacher
V v	v (or w see **1.7.3**)	**Virgínija**	Virginia
		ví	you
Z z	z	**Zágreb**	Zagreb
		zíma	winter
Ž ž	s (as in mea<u>s</u>ure)	**Ženéva**	Geneva
		žénska	woman

The letters **q**, **w**, **x**, **y** are also sometimes found in Slovene but only in the spellings of foreign names or borrowed expressions, e.g. **New York**, **Quai d'Orsay**, **x žárki** 'x rays', **quidproquo**.

1.2   THE SLOVENE VOWEL SYSTEM

Standard Slovene has two phonological systems, which differ only as regards prosodic phenomena. One system is non-tonemic based on distinctive stress and vowel length, the other is tonemic based on stress, vowel length and pitch.

The system used in this grammar is the non-tonemic system based on stress and vowel length. This is the system used in the Slovene Academy Dictionary and the most up-to-date Slovene grammars. It is also the system taught in Slovene schools and universities, as well as on official Slovene language courses for foreigners and for Slovenes living outside Slovenia. From a historical viewpoint it is the more innovative system, based on the evolutionary tendencies of the non-central dialects. The tonemic system is the more conservative system and is based on the more archaic central dialects of Upper and Lower Carniola. Ljubljana, the capital of Slovenia, falls within those dialects with a tonemic system. Most educated people do not use tone distinctions and can hardly perceive them.

1.3   VOWELS

The standard language has seven long (stressed) vowels and six short vowels (stressed or unstressed). In the phonological system based on distinctive stress and vowel length three superscript diacritics are used to denote the quantity and quality of stressed vowels: ´, ˆ, ` .

The acute ´ is used to denote a long, close **e, o** or a long **a, i, u**
The circumflex ˆ is used to denote a long, open **e, o**
The grave ` is used to denote a short, open **e, o** or a short **a, i, u** or **ə**

Note: ə is an indistinct neutral vowel (schwa), which is pronounced like **e** in English 'butt<u>e</u>r'. Orthographically ə is always written as **e**.

In normal spelling in Slovene books, newspapers, etc. these diacritics are not used. They are, however, used in dictionaries and grammars.

In tabular form the Slovene vowel system appears as follows:

	Stressed				*Unstressed short*	
	long		*short*			
high	í	ú	ì	ù	i	u
high mid	é	ó				
mid			ə̀		ə	
low mid	ê	ô	è	ò	e	o
low	á		à		a	

1.3.1   The pronunciation of Slovene vowels

The following list gives the various vowel lengths possible in Slovene and examples of words containing the vowel lengths indicated, both stressed and unstressed. The International Phonetic Alphabet symbol indicates their exact pronunciation.

Conventional spelling	True length	I.P.A. symbol	Examples
a	á	'aː	káva, hvála, káj, vája
	à	'a	čàs, bràt, stàr, tàm
	a	a	vôda, híša, fakultéta, abecéda
i	í	'iː	govoríti, pívo, sín, ríba
	ì	'i	kìt, mìš, zanìč, sìt
	i	i	in, stanováti, mériti, Iréna
u	ú	'uː	kúhinja, lúknja, úra, korúza
	ù	'u	dùh, krùh, kljùč, tù
	u	u	ubíti, kupováti, turíst, poudárek
e	é	'eː	téden, pét, mésto, sedéti
	ê	'ɛː	pêta, êna, žêlja, mêdved
	è	'ɛ	kmèt, šepèt, pomèn, deklè
	e	ɛ	Evrópa, lepôta, medicína, sónce
	è	'ə	mègla, dèž, vès, pès
	e	ə	zvézek, Špánec, véter, čúden
o	ó	'oː	klóp, kokóš, teló, mórje
	ô	'ɔː	vôda, gôra, splôšno, rôka
	ò	'ɔ	otròk, nòž, stròp, gròb
	o	ɔ	obísk, popúst, krompír, obléka

I.P.A. symbols
' stressed vowel
ː long vowel

1.3.2 Stressed syllables

In Slovene words any syllable may bear the stress. Long stressed vowels may occur in any syllable while short stressed vowels normally only occur in monosyllabic words or final syllables. Exceptions to this latter rule are (a) a small number of nouns which allow an alternative final stress (e.g. **mèglà** 'mist'; **tèmà** 'darkness'; **čèbèr** 'pail') and (b) a small number of adverbs, pronouns and conjunctions (e.g. **sèmle** 'hither'; **kàkšen** 'some sort of'; **àmpak** 'but'). All unstressed vowels are short.

Note: A short stressed vowel in final position is automatically lengthened when the word is inflected and it no longer appears in final position.

bràt	brother	gen. sing. **bráta**
gròb	grave	gen. sing. **grôba**
deklè	girl	gen. sing. **dekléta**
gozdìč	grove	gen. sing. **gozdíča**
krùh	bread	gen. sing. **krúha**

1.3.3 The vowels e, o

(a) Phonetically é and ó are high-mid (close) vowels. The vowel é is pronounced like *é* in French *été* 'summer' and the vowel ó is pronounced like *o* in French *dos* 'back'. They are purely oral vowels and are not diphthongal like the English **a** and **o** in 'gate' and 'vote'. The low-mid (open) **e** and **o** are pronounced like **e** and **o** in English 'get' and 'got'.

In the modern language é and ó are pronounced as open **e** and **o** before 'j + vowel' and 'v + vowel', e.g. **sinóvi** 'sons' pron. **sinôvi**; **véja** 'branch' pron. **vêja**. The pronunciation of long close vowels in these positions is now considered archaic. When any é, ó, ê, ô, è, ò occur before tauto-syllabic -j(-) or -v(-), i.e. -j or -v at the end of a syllable before a consonant, or before -j or -v at the end of a word they are pronounced as a mid (central) or neutral **o**, **e**, e.g. **véjnat** 'branch'; **sôvji** 'owls'; **mêj** (gen. plur.) 'borders'; **nòv** 'new'; **sinóv** (gen. plur.) 'sons'.

(b) For a foreigner one great difficulty is distinguishing between the high (close) vowels é, ó and the low (open) vowels ê, ô, è, ò because normally the quality is not indicated except in grammars and dictionaries. Generally speaking é, ó occur more frequently than ê, ô, è, ò. Failure to distinguish between them can cause confusion, e.g.

péti	to sing	**pêti**	fifth
svét	world	**svèt**	council
móra	he must	**môra**	nightmare
otròk (nom. sing.)	child	**otrók** (gen. plur.)	children

The following hints will help to identify the quality of **e** and **o** in certain cases:

(i) é, ó nearly always occur in borrowed words, e.g. **zébra**, **tendénca** 'tendency'. Exceptions are foreign words where **e** appears before **r**, e.g. **šofêr** 'chauffeur'; **atmosfêra** 'atmosphere'.

(ii) ê always occurs before 'j + vowel' and ô always occurs before 'v + vowel', e.g. **mêja** 'boundary'; **sôva** 'owl'.

Note: In dictionaries many such words are indicated with a long narrow é, e.g. **véja** 'branch'; **vdóva** 'widow', but such pronunciation is now considered archaic.

(iii) ê and ô usually occur in the first syllable of disyllabic nouns with a mobile stress, e.g. **jêzik** 'language' – **jezíka** (gen. sing.); **ôtok** 'island' – **otóka** (gen. sing.).

(iv) The cardinal numerals 5, 6, 7, 9, 10 have é in the nominative but ê in their oblique cases. The numeral 8 has ó in the nominative but ô in its oblique cases, e.g. **pét** 'five' – gen./loc. **pêtih**, dat. **pêtim**, instr. **pêtimi**; **ósem** 'eight' – gen./loc. **ôsmih**, dat. **ôsmim**, instr. **ôsmimi**.

The ordinal forms of these numerals have ê and ô respectively, e.g. **pêti** 'fifth'; **ôsmi** 'eighth'.

(v) The suffix **-en** in the past participle passive becomes **-ên-** when it occurs before a vowel, e.g. **stopljèn** 'melted' (nom. sing. masc.); **stopljêna** (nom. sing. fem.).

(vi) Verbs in **-íti, -ím** with **o** in the preceding syllable (e.g. **nosíti – nósim** 'to carry – I carry') have **ô** in the second person sing. imperative, the masc. **-l** participle singular and the supine, i.e. **nôsi, nôsil, nôsit**.

(vii) Verbs in **-íti, -em; -áti, -em** with **e** in the preceding syllable (e.g. **kreníti – krénem** 'to set out – I set out'; **česáti – čéšem** 'to comb – I comb') have **ê** in the second pers. sing. imperative, the masc. **-l** participle singular and the supine, i.e. **krêni, krênil, krênit; čêši, čêsal, čêsat**.

(viii) Verbs in **-íti, -ím** with **o** or **e** in the preceding syllable (e.g. **delíti – delím** 'to divide – I divide'; **zvoníti – zvoním** 'to ring – I ring') have **ê**, **ô** in the second pers. sing. imperative, i.e. **dêli, zvôni**.

(ix) Most nouns with **ò** in the final syllable have **ô** in the oblique cases, e.g. **dvòr** 'courtyard' – **dvôra** (gen. sing.).

(x) The noun suffixes **-oba, -oča** and **-ota** have **ô**, e.g. **grenkôba** 'bitterness'; **čistôča** 'cleanliness'; **praznôta** 'emptiness'.

Note: Rare exceptions occur with **-óta**, e.g. **dobróta** 'kindness'.

1.4 THE TONEMIC SYSTEM

The tonemic system is typical of the dialects of Upper and Lower Carniola, the Carinthian dialects of Austria and Italy and the dialects of Venetian Slovenia. These dialects all have distinctive tone on long stressed vowels. Differences in tone are indicated in the tonemic system by superscript diacritics. The acute ´ indicates a long rising tone and the circumflex ˆ indicates a long falling tone. The distinction between the close and open **o, e** is indicated by a subscript dot beneath the close **ọ, ẹ**. In the absence of a long vowel stress falls on the final syllable. Short vowels, which have falling tones, are indicated by a double grave ``. The neutral vowel ə (schwa) written as an **e** carries a single grave ` if it has a rising tone. The phonetic details are very complex and disputed. Basically the circumflex is a high pitch accent with a rising falling contour, and the acute is a low pitch accent with a rising contour, which may be preceded by a slight fall. Unlike Serbo-Croat the Slovene tonemic system permits pitch distinctions in monosyllabic words. The following examples are given to illustrate the tonemic notation:

acc. sing.		instr. sing.
lípo	lime	**lîpo**
múlo	mule	**mûlo**
vệro	faith	**vêro**
péto	heel	**pêto**
lộko	meadow	**lộ̂ko**
nógo	leg	**nôgo**
vŕbo	willow	**vr̂bo**

nom. sing.		gen. sing.
mȉš	mouse	**míši**
fantè̏	lad	**fantéta**
brȁt	brother	**bráta**
kȕp	heap	**kúpa**
pè̏s (= pȁ̀s)	dog	**psȁ̀**
gròb	grave	**gróba**
mekè̏t	bleat	**mekéta**
mègla (= mȁ̀gla)	fog	**mègle**

1.5 STRESS

In Slovene most words have a stressed syllable. The only words without a stress of their own are proclitics (i.e. certain conjunctions and most prepositions) and enclitics (i.e. the short forms of the personal pronouns and the auxiliary verb 'to be' and certain particles). Proclitics and enclitics form a whole with either the following or the preceding word.

In Slovene the stress may fall on any syllable within a word. This stress may be fixed i.e. it remains on the same vowel in all forms of the word when it is declined or conjugated or it may be mobile, i.e. it changes place when the word is declined or conjugated. From an overall point of view fixed (i.e. non-mobile) stress is the norm in Slovene. Mobile stress is less common and now found in only a few nouns and adjectives and some verb forms. For details see (**2.23** and **6.48**).

Most words have only one stressed syllable. However, some words have two stresses. These are:

(a) Certain prefixed words which have two stresses: one stress is in the root and the secondary stress (which may be short) is on the prefix. Prefixes which may bear a secondary stress are **proti-, nad-, pod-, so-, pro-, med-, ne-**, e.g. **prótinapàd** 'counterattack': **nàdrealíst** 'surrealist'; **nèrjavèč** 'rust-proof'; **mèdnároden** 'international'; **próamêriški** 'pro-American'; **pòdodbòr** 'subcommittee'; **sòimenják** 'namesake'.

(b) Certain compounds which have two stresses. These are usually made from two nouns or a numeral plus an adjective, e.g. **živínozdravník** 'veterinary surgeon'; **dvódnéven** 'lasting two days'.

(c) The superlative forms of adjectives in which one stress occurs on the prefix **nàj-** and the other on the comparative form of the adjective, e.g. **nàjlépši** 'most beautiful'.

1.6 THE PRONUNCIATION OF VOWELS IN THE SPOKEN LANGUAGE

In the spoken language short stressed vowels and unstressed vowels are reduced or elided as they are in most dialects, especially the central dialects.

1.6.1 The pronunciation of short stressed vowels

In the modern spoken language the short stressed vowels **a**, **i**, **u** occurring within monosyllabic words tend to be pronounced as a schwa (i.e. a neutral vowel) e.g. **čàs** > **čə̀s** 'time'; **fànt** > **fə̀nt** 'boy'; **nìč** > **nə̀č** 'nothing'; **kùp** > **kə̀p** '**heap**'.

1.6.2 The pronunciation of short unstressed vowels

In the standard language unstressed vowels are pronounced clearly, but in the spoken language these vowels undergo extreme reduction and sometimes disappear completely.

Unstressed -i in word final position

Unstressed **-i** in word final position is lost in the following forms:

(a) infinitives, e.g. **délati** 'to work' > **délat**; **sodíti** 'to judge' > **sódit**; **rêči** 'to say' > **rêčt**

Note: If the consonant in the infinitive preceding the **-i** is **-č-** and not **-t-**, then **-t** is added by analogy to the **-č**.

(b) imperatives, e.g. **prôsi, prosíte** 'ask' > **prôs, prôste**; **vzêmi, vzemíte** 'take' > **vzêm, vzêmte**

(c) the masc. plural form of the **-l** participle, e.g.

		-l *part*	
délati	to work	**délali**	> **délal**
sodíti	to judge	**sodíli**	> **sódil** [or **sódəl**]
rêči	to say	**rêkli**	> **rêkl**

Exceptions are the **-l** participles of the verbs **bíti** 'to be' and **íti** 'to go', i.e. **bilí** [or **blí**] and **šlí**.

(d) the instrumental plural endings **-ami, -emi, -imi** (in nouns, pronouns and adjectives), e.g. **s témi lépimi stávbami** 'with these beautiful buildings' > **s tém lépim stávbam; nad tístimi abstráktnimi slíkami** 'above those abstract paintings' > **nad tístim abstráktnim slíkam.**

Note: The instrumental plural ending of masculine and neuter nouns **-i** is not lost, e.g. **s tákšnimi umázanimi čévlji** 'with such dirty shoes' > **s tákšnim umázanim čévlji.**

(e) the dative and locative singular of the personal pronouns, e.g. **méni** 'to me' > **mén; tébi** 'to you' > **téb.**

(f) the dative and locative singular of feminine nouns, e.g. **na mízi** 'on the table' > **na míz; pri Natáši** 'at Natasha's' > **pr Natáš; k híši** 'to the house' > **k híš.**

(g) the nominative sing. masc. of definite adjectives and pronouns, e.g. **angléški fílm** 'an English film' > **angléšk fílm; tísti mládi fànt** 'that young boy' > **tíst mlád fànt.**

(h) some adverbs, e.g. **sinóči** 'last night' > **snóč; jútri** 'tomorrow' > **jútr; dôsti** 'enough' > **dôst.**

(i) some prepositions, e.g. **skózi** 'through' > **skóz; zarádi** 'because' > **zarád; pri** 'at' > **pr.**

(j) the conjunction **àli** (> **àl**).

(k) the numeral **štíri** 'four' (> **štír**).

Unstressed -i- in non-final position

(a) Unstressed **-i-** in the penultimate syllable is lost in the following forms:

  (i) the present tense of second conjugation verbs, e.g.

  vídimo 'we see' > **vídmo; vídite** 'you see' > **vídte; míslimo** 'we think' > **míslmo**

  (ii) the feminine and neuter singular and the dual and plural forms of the **-l** participle of verbs in **-iti**, e.g.

  pozabíla 'she forgot' > **pozábla; pozabíli** 'they forgot' > **pozábli** [or **pozábəl**]; **čutíla** 'she felt' > **čútla**

  (iii) the suffix **-ica** (plur **-ice**), e.g.

  málica 'snack' > **málca; vílice** 'fork' > **vílce**

  (iv) infinitives in **-iti** where the penultimate **-i-** is lost as well as the final **-i**, e.g.

  govoríti 'to speak' > **govôrt; hodíti** 'to walk' > **hôdət; mísliti** 'to think' > **míslt**

(b)   Unstressed **-i-** in the initial syllable is lost in the following:

(i)   the prefix **pri-** in derived words, e.g.

pripeljáti 'to convey' > **prpêljat**; **prinêsti** 'to bring' > **prnêst**

(ii)   the adverb **sinóči** > **snóč(i)**

Unstressed *i-* at the beginning of a word

At the beginning of a word initial unstressed **i-** is lost in the following:

(a)   the verb **iméti** 'to have', e.g. **imám** 'I have' > **mám**; **imámo** 'we have' > **mámo**

(b)   words with the prefix **iz-**. This gives rise to alternative forms that are also admitted in the standard language, e.g. **izgaráti se** 'to wear oneself out' > **zgaráti se**; **izbezáti** 'to rake out' > **zbezáti**; **izdávna** 'long ago' > **zdávna**

Unstressed *-i-* in a final syllable

Unstressed **-i-** in the first person singular ending of the present tense of second conjugation verbs is reduced to ə, e.g. **prósim** 'I ask' > **prósəm**; **nósim** 'I carry' > **nósəm**.

Unstressed 'o'

(a)   Unstressed **-o** is lost in word final position in:

(i)   the nom./acc. singular of neuter nouns, adjectives and pronouns, e.g. **mléko** 'milk' > **mlék**; **nôvo mésto** 'new town' > **nôv [nôu̯] mést**; **tísto bélo písmo** 'that white letter' > **tíst bél [béu̯] písm**; **lépo pólje** 'beautiful field' > **lép pólje [póle]**

(ii)   some adverbs, e.g. **mŕzlo** 'cold' > **mŕzl**; **gotóvo** 'certainly' > **gotóv**

(b)   Unstressed **-o-** is lost in verbal nouns in **-ovánje**, e.g. **potovánje** 'travel' > **potvánje**; **stanovánje** 'flat' > **stanvájne**.

Note: Metathesis of **nj** > **jn**.

Unstressed *-o-* in a syllable preceding the stress

In the Ljubljana dialect unstressed **-o-** preceding the stress becomes **-u-**, e.g. **novéjši** 'newer' > **nuvéjš**; **otròk** 'child' > **utròk**; **govorí** '(he) says' > **guvurí**.

Unstressed 'e'

(a)   Unstressed **-e** is lost in adjectives and pronouns which premodify neuter nouns, e.g. **vróče mésto** 'a hot town' > **vróč mést**; **môje stanovánje** 'my flat' > **môj stanvájne**.

(b) Unstressed **-e-** is lost in the following:

(i) verbal nouns in **-evánje**, e.g. **zaničevánje** 'disdain' > **zaničvánje**; **poniževánje** 'humiliation' > **ponižvánje**

(ii) the gen. sing. of masc./neut. adjectives (i.e. **-ega**), e.g. **čŕnega** 'black' > **čŕnga**; **nôvega** 'new' > **nôu̯ga**

Note: When the ending **-ega** is preceded by a 'k' or 'g' the contracted ending > **-zga**, e.g. **drúgega** > **drúzga**; **velíkega** > **velízga**.

(iii) the word **člôvek** 'man' i.e. **člôu̯k**.

Final *-aj*

Final **-aj** > **-i** or **-ej** in the following:

(a) adverbs, e.g. **zméraj** 'always' > **zméri/zmérej**; **včéraj** 'yesterday' > **včéri/včérej**

(b) imperatives, e.g. **pomágaj** 'help' > **pomági/pomágej**; **čákaj** 'wait' > **čáki/čákej**

1.7 THE SLOVENE CONSONANT SYSTEM

Slovene has twenty-one distinctive consonantal phonemes and all but one are represented in the orthography by a different letter. The exception is **dž** which is represented by two letters. Several of these phonemes also have allophonic variants. These occur in pronunciation as positional variants of the phonemes, but do not occur as separate letters in the orthography. In terms of place of articulation, manner of articulation and voice the Slovene consonant system is illustrated by the following table. [Note that the allophones (i.e. the positional variants of phonemes) appear in square brackets.]

	labial	*labio-dental*	*dental*	*alveo-palatal*	*palatal*	*velar*
voiceless stops	p		t			k
voiced stops	b		d			g
voiceless fricatives		f	s	š		h
voiced fricatives		v	z	ž		[ɣ]
voiceless affricates			c	č		
voiced affricates			[dz]	dž		
nasals	m		n			[ŋ]

	labial	labio-dental	dental	alveo-palatal	palatal	velar
lateral			l			
roll			r			
glide					j	
approximants	[w] [ʌ] [u̯]					

1.7.1   Obstruents

The voiceless obstruents **p, t, f, k, s, š** have voiced counterparts which occur as separate letters in the orthography, i.e. **p-b, t-d, k-g, f-v, s-z, š-ž.**

The voiceless obstruents **h, c** have the voiced allophonic counterparts **ɣ, dz.** These occur in pronunciation as positional variants of **h, c** before voiced obstruents, e.g. **vŕh drevésa** '(at) the top of the tree' [pron. **vŕɣ drevésa**]; **stríc govorí** 'uncle says' [pron. **strídz govorí**]. **dž** has phonemic status in only a very limited number of loan words, e.g. **džúdo** 'judo'; **džém** 'jam'. For this reason it is often not given phonemic status in the Slovene consonant system. Normally in Slovene it is a voiced allophone, i.e. the positional variant of **č** before voiced obstruents, e.g. **odlóčba** 'rule, provision' [pron. **odlódžba**].

1.7.2   Sonorants

The sonorants **m, n, l, r, j** are all voiced.

n: The phoneme **n** has a nasal velar counterpart **ŋ** which is realised only before the phonemes **k, g, h**, e.g. **bánka** 'bank' [pron. **báŋka**].

r: The phoneme **r** is a dental roll and can function as either a consonant or a vowel, i.e. as a syllabic sonorant 'r' The syllabic sonorant **r** may appear initially before a consonant or between two consonants. Phonetically it is realised as **ə + r**, e.g. **smŕt** 'death' [pron. **smə̀rt**], **rjàv** 'brown' [pron. **ərjàu̯**].

1.7.3   The consonant v

Special attention must be paid to the pronunciation of the voiced labio-dental consonant 'v'. The voiced labio-dental consonant 'v' is pronounced as 'v' only before vowels or before a vocalic **r**, e.g. **vôda** 'water'; **lovíti** 'to catch'; **vàs** 'you'; **nôvi** 'new'; **vŕt** 'garden'.

In other positions **v** is realised as:

(a) diphthongal **ṷ**

(b) a voiced bilabial approximant **w** or a voiceless bilabial approximant **ʍ** [The voiced bilabial approximant occurs before voiced consonants or at the end of a word following a sonorant. The voiceless bilabial approximant occurs before voiceless obstruents.]

(c) the vowel **u**

The allophonic variants of *v*

(a) **v = ṷ**

(i) When it follows a vowel at the end of a word or when it occurs at the end of a syllable before a consonant **v** is pronounced as a diphthongal **ṷ**, e.g. **žív** 'alive' > **žíṷ**; **ôvca** 'sheep' > **ôṵca**; **povsód** 'everywhere' > **poṵsót**; **pràvzapràv** 'as a matter of fact' > **pràṵzapràṷ**; **cév** 'tube' > **céṷ**

Note: When the **-e-** preceding a final **-v** is a semi-vowel as in nouns like **búkev** 'beech', **cérkev** 'church', the ending **-ev** is pronounced either as **-ǝṷ** or **u**, e.g. **cérkev** > **cérkǝṷ/cérku**.

(ii) **v** is also realised as the diphthongal **ṷ** in syntagma where it occurs at the beginning of a word before a consonant and follows a word ending in a vowel, e.g. **bo vzéla** 'she will take' > **bo ṵzéla**; **bi vstáli** '(they) would have got up' > **bi ṵstáli**

(b) **v = w**

v is pronounced as a voiced bilabial approximant **w** in the following positions:

(i) At the beginning of a word, before a voiced obstruent or sonorant, e.g. **vzéti** 'to take' > **wzéti**; **vlák** 'train' > **wlák**; **vráta** 'door' > **wráta**; **vljúden** 'polite' > **wljúden**

(ii) When it occurs between obstruent/sonorant and obstruent/sonorant, e.g. **odvzéti** 'to take away' > **odwzéti**; **s krvjó** 'with blood' > **s krwjó**; **podvréči** 'to subjugate' > **podwréči**

(iii) At the end of a word following a sonorant, e.g. **čŕv** 'worm' > **čŕw**; **bárv** (gen. plur.) 'colour' > **bárw**

Note: In the spoken language or even slow speech **v** (**= w**) is often realised as **u**, e.g. **uzéti**, **oduzéti**, **báru**.

(c) **v = ʍ**

v is pronounced as a voiceless bilabial approximant in the following positions:

(i) At the beginning of a word, before voiceless obstruents, e.g. **vsák** 'every' > **ʍsák**; **vsè** 'all' > **ʍsè**; **vsebína** 'contents' > **ʍsebína**

(ii) When it occurs between a voiced obstruent and a voiceless obstruent, e.g. **predvsèm** 'above all' > **pretʍsèm**; **predvčérajšnjim** 'the day before yesterday' > **pretʍčérajšnjim**. [Note that here **-d-** devoices before **ʍ**.]

Note: In the spoken language or even slow speech **v** (= **ʍ**) is often realised as **u**, e.g. **usák, predusèm, usebína**.

(d) **v = u**

v is pronounced as **u** when it is a preposition, e.g.

v pívu ' in the beer' > **u pívu**; **v jámi** 'in the cave' > **u jámi**; **v lésu** 'in the forest' > **u lésu**; **v ígri** 'in the game' > **u ígri**; **v vôdi** 'in the water' > **u vôdi**

Note: The preposition **v** may also be pronounced as a voiced or voiceless bilabial approximant **w** or **ʍ**, e.g. **ʍ pívu, w ígri, w lésu**.

1.7.4 The consonant l

Special attention must also be paid to the pronunciation of the sonorant **l**.

(a) **l** is pronounced as **l**, when it occurs within a word before a vowel or **j**, e.g. **lés** 'wood'; **mlád** 'young'; **oblák** 'cloud'; **pólje** 'field'; **Slovénija**; **stôla** (gen. sing.) 'chair'; **béla** (nom. sing. fem.) 'white'.

(b) At the end of a word or at the end of a syllable before a consonant **-l(-)** is normally pronounced as **u̯**. This is moreover always so at the end of a word in the case of the masculine **-l** participle and adjectives and nouns in **e** (=ə) + **-l**, e.g. **bél** 'white' > **béu̯**; **brál** '(he) read' > **bráu̯**; **govóril** '(he) spoke' > **govóriu̯**; **stòl** 'chair' > **stòu̯**; **póln** 'full' > **póu̯n**; **dólg** 'long' > **dóu̯k**; **bólha** 'flea' > **bóu̯ha**; **sólza** 'tear' > **sóu̯za**; **jábolko** 'apple' > **jábou̯ko**; **živál** 'animal' > **živáu̯**; **zél** 'herb' > **zéu̯**; **jélša** 'alder' > **jéu̯ša**; **debélkast** > **debéu̯kast** 'thickish'.

There are, however, exceptions and inconsistencies with regard to the pronunciation of **-l** at the end of a word or at the end of a syllable before a consonant. These are the following:

(i) **-l(-)** is pronounced as **-l(-)** in final position in the genitive plural of feminine and neuter nouns in **-la, -lo** and in their suffixed derivatives, e.g.

darílo 'present', gen. plur. **daríl**, derived diminutive **darílce**
šóla 'school', gen. plur. **šól**, derived adjective **šólski** 'school'
skála 'cliff, rock', gen. plur. **skál**, derived adjective **skálnat** 'rocky'

(ii) -l(-) is pronounced as -l(-) before the noun instrumental plural ending **-mi**, e.g. **z živálmi** 'with the animals'; **s piščálmi** 'with the pipes'

(iii) -l(-) is pronounced as -l(-) in the following words: **stòlp** 'tower'; **film** 'film'; **skálp** 'scalp'; **napálm** 'napalm'; **spòl** 'sex'; **razkòl** 'split'; **pomòl** 'pier'; **glágol** 'verb'; **dôl** 'down'; **sôkol** 'hawk'; **tôpol** 'poplar'; **zakòl** 'slaughter'; **ôkel** 'tusk'; **svirél** 'pipe'; **pól** 'pole' [i.e. North, South]; **pôl** 'half' (used to denote a half hour)

Note 1: When **pól** means 'a half' in other than the time sense it is pronounced **póu̯**, e.g. **pól mésta** 'half the town' > **póu̯ mésta**. Similarly when used in compounds, **pól** is pronounced **póu̯**, even before vowels, e.g. **pólavtomátičen** 'semi-automatic' > **póu̯automátičen**; **pólodpŕt** 'half open' > **póu̯odpŕt**.

Note 2: In the noun **dél** 'share, part, portion' l is pronounced either as l or u̯.

(iv) -l(-) is pronounced as -l(-) in names, e.g. **Pável, Vílko, Kárel**

(v) -l(-) is pronounced as -l(-) in adjectives in **-lən/-ln-** (i.e. adjectives in **-aln-, -eln-, -iln-, -oln-, -uln-**) and nouns in **-lnost**.

Only a few adjectives in **-ilni, -elni** and two nouns in **-lnost** allow an alternative pronunciation in **-u̯ni, -u̯nost**, i.e. **velélni** 'imperative'; **želélni** 'optative'; **pepélni** 'ash'; **plevélni** 'weedy'; **zélni** 'herbal'; **kresílni** 'tinder'; **volílni** 'electoral'; **obílni** 'abundant'; **volílnost** 'voting right'; **obílnost** 'abundance'.

Note: The adjective **bólni** is always pronounced **bóu̯ni**.

(vi) -l(-) is more usually pronounced as -l(-) before the suffixes **-nik, -nica** but some nouns allow an alternative pronunciation in **-u̯nik, -u̯nica**, e.g. **gugálnik** 'rocking chair'; **pihálnik** 'blowpipe'; **klepálnik** 'anvil'; **pljuválnik** 'spittoon'; **velélnik** 'imperative'; **pepélnica** 'urn'; **solníca** 'salt cellar'; **kuhálnica** 'ladle'; **perílnik** 'washboard'; **popravljálnica** 'repair shop'; **nogálnik** 'pedal'; **zélnica** 'cabbage water'

Note: Only the pronunciation **-u̯n-** is allowed with the nouns **bolník** 'male patient'; **bolníca** 'female patient'; **vélnica** 'winnowing fan'.

(vii) When -l(-) appears before the suffixes **-stvo, -ski, -ka, -c** (the latter in the oblique cases of nouns in **-lec** [= lǝc]), it may sometimes be pronounced as -l(-) and sometimes as -u̯(-). In most cases as far as **-ka** and **-c(-)** are concerned an alternative pronunciation is allowed, but in some cases only one pronunciation is allowed. There are no hard and fast rules and so these pronunciations must be learnt individually. One basic hint is that in the case of nouns the pronunciation -u̯(-) is often found if the noun denotes a person and is derived from a verb.

Examples

-l(-) = -l(-)

kriminálca (gen. sing.) 'criminal'; **čŕpálka** 'pump'; **jadrálstvo** 'sailing'; **gasílski** 'fire'

-l(-) = -ṷ(-) or -l(-)

prevajálca (gen. sing.) 'translator'; **zmagoválka** 'winner' (f.); **krvodajálstvo** 'blood doning'; **igrálski** 'of play'

-l(-) = -ṷ(-)

spremljeválca (gen. sing.) 'companion'; **izdajálka** 'traitress'; **poslušálstvo** 'audience'; **ubijálski** 'homicidal'

(c)   When **-l** follows **r** in the masculine form of the **-l** participle it is pronounced as **w** or **u**, e.g. **odpŕl** '(he) opened' > **odpэ̀ru/odpэ̀rw**; **umŕl** '(he) died' > **umэ̀ru/umэ̀rw**.

(d)   When **-l** follows unstressed **e** or **i** in the masculine **-l** participle or when it occurs in final position in a noun or adjective following **e** (= э) then **-il** and **-el** are normally pronounced as **u**, e.g. **vídel** '(he) saw' > **vídu**; **nôsil** '(he) carried' > **nôsu**; **rékel** '(he) said' > **réku**; **vôzel** 'knot' > **vôzu**; **mŕzel** 'cold' > **mŕzu**.

Note: Also possible are the pronunciations **vídэṷ, nôsiṷ, rékэṷ, vôzэṷ, mŕzэṷ**.

1.7.5   The combinations lj, nj

The combinations **lj, nj** are digraphs. They have two phonetic realisations:

(a)   When they precede a vowel they represent **l + j, n + j**, e.g. **pólje** 'field'; **žêlja** 'wish'; **Ljubljána**

(b)   When they precede a consonant or occur at the end of a word they are pronounced as a simple **l** or **n**, e.g. **kònj** 'horse' > **kòn**; **kônjski** 'of a horse' > **kônski**; **pólj** 'field (gen. plur.)' > **pól**; **póljski** 'agrarian' > **pólski**

In the standard literary language this **lj** and **nj** may be slightly softened i.e. **l' n'**, but even in the literary language hard **l** and **n** are preferred in these positions.

Note 1: In the Ljubljana dialect and the spoken language **lj, nj** are pronounced as **l, n** even before vowels, e.g. **Ljubljána > Lublána**; **njegóv** 'his' > **negóṷ**; **knjíga** 'book' > **kníga**.

Note 2: In the Ljubljana dialect **nj** following a vowel is pronounced as **jn**, e.g. **stanovánje** 'flat' > **stanovájne**.

1.8 VOICED AND VOICELESS CONSONANTS

Voiced consonants are pronounced with vibration of the vocal cords and voiceless consonants without such vibration. In Slovene the following obstruents are phonemically paired for voicing:

Voiceless	Voiced
p	b
t	d
s	z
š	ž
k	g
f	v
č	dž
c	[dz]
h	[ɣ]

The labio-dental fricative **v** is the voiced equivalent of the labio-dental fricative **f**, but participates in voicing rules only to a limited extent. In Slovene grammar **v** is classified as a sonorant. (For the voiced allophones **ɣ**, **dz** see **1.7.1**.)

Note: the sonorants **l**, **m**, **n**, **r**, **j** are all voiced and are not phonemically paired for voicing.

1.8.1 The voicing and devoicing of obstruents

In Slovene voiced and voiceless obstruents are distinctively opposed before vowels, e.g.

pácek	dirty child	–	**bácek**	lambkin
tísk	print	–	**dísk**	discus
sád	fruit	–	**zád**	behind
šív	seam	–	**žív**	alive
konjáč	flayer	–	**gonjáč**	driver
fínski	Finnish	–	**vínski**	wine

In other positions, however, the obstruents participate in the following rules of voicing:

(a) Voiced obstruents devoice at the end of words (i.e. before a pause), e.g.

rób	slave	>	**róp**
mlád	young	>	**mlát**
vóz	cart	>	**vós**
láž	lie	>	**láš**
dólg	long	>	**dóu̯k**

This means that words like **rób** 'slave' and **róp** 'robbery' are pronounced the same, i.e. **róp**.

Note: Final -**v** does not devoice in this way (i.e. it does not become **f**). Final -**v** > **u̯** or **w** (see **1.7.3**).

(b) At the boundary of two words a final voiced obstruent is devoiced before the second word if the second word begins with a vowel or with a sonorant, e.g.

mlád učítelj	young teacher	>	**mlát učítelj**
sád je dóber	the fruit is good	>	**sát je dóber**
rób stréhe	the edge of the roof	>	**róp stréhe**
jéž ríje	the hedgehog is digging	>	**jéš ríje**

(c) Prepositions, together with the word they govern are treated as one word/unit.

(i) If the preposition ends in a voiced obstruent it does not devoice before the word it governs if the word begins with a vowel, a sonorant or a voiced obstruent, e.g.

pred ígro	before the game	**nad vôdo**	above the water
brez očéta	without father	**čez mésto**	through town

(ii) If the word governed by a preposition ending in a voiced obstruent begins with a voiceless obstruent then the final voiced obstruent of the preposition will devoice, e.g.

brez knjíge	without the book	>	**bres knjíge**
pred híšo	in front of the house	>	**pret híšo**
čez césto	across the road	>	**čes césto**

(d) If two obstruents occur next to each other in a word regressive assimilation takes place. The first obstruent will assimilate in voice to the second. Therefore (i) a voiced obstruent followed by a voiceless obstruent will become voiceless and (ii) a voiceless obstruent followed by a voiced obstruent will become voiced, e.g.

(i)	**sládko**	sweet	>	**slátko**
	têžki	heavy	>	**têški**
	razpòn	span	>	**raspòn**

(ii)	**kdó**	who	>	**gdó**
	glásba	music	>	**glázba**
	odlóčba	rule, order	>	**odlódžba**

(e) At the boundary of two words a final voiceless obstruent in the first word becomes voiced if the second word begins with a voiced obstruent, e.g.

časopís bêrem	I am reading a newspaper	>	**časopíz bêrem**
zdravník govorí	the doctor says	>	**zdrau̯níg govorí**
vŕh gôre	the top of the mountain	>	**vŕɣ gôre**
kíp bogínje	the statue of a goddess	>	**kíb bogínje**

This rule also applies to final **-f** which > **-v**, if the second word begins with a voiced obstruent, e.g. **šéf govorí** 'the boss says' > **šév govorí**.

Note: If the second word begins with a sonorant the final voiceless obstruent is not voiced, e.g. **pótnik mísli** 'the traveller thinks'; **stráh me je** 'I am afraid'.

1.8.2 The prepositions **s/z** 'from, with'

Before words beginning with a vowel, a voiced obstruent or a sonorant the preposition **z** 'with', 'from' is written and pronounced as **z**. Before words beginning with a voiceless obstruent it is written and pronounced as **s**, e.g. **s políce** 'from the shelf'; **z míze** 'from the table'; **z ávtom** 'with the car'; **s telétom** 'with the calf'; **z žógo** 'with the ball'.

1.8.3 Obstruents before sonorants

Although sonorants influence voice at word boundaries (see above), within a word both voiced and voiceless obstruents may occur before a sonorant, e.g. **práti** 'to wash' – **bráti** 'to read'; **sátje** 'honeycombs' – **sádje** 'fruit'; **svaríti** 'to warn' – **zvaríti** 'to weld'; **snésti** 'to eat up' – **znêsti** 'to lay'; **sméren** 'directional' – **zméren** 'moderate'.

1.8.4 Double consonants

Double consonants, both obstruents and sonorants, which occur at morpheme or word boundaries (including those caused by voice assimilation) tend in formal speech to be pronounced as one long consonant, e.g. **òn nóče** 'he doesn't want to' > **ònóče**; **sám mísli** 'he himself thinks' > **sámísli**; **s sêstro** 'with the sister' > **sêstro**; **oddáti** 'to give away' > **odáti**.

Note: **u̯** as a positional variant of **v** or **l** may also occur as a long sound at word boundaries, e.g. **njegóv vzdévek** 'his nickname' > **njegóu̯zdévek**; **on je glédal vzhòd lúne** 'he watched the moon rise' > **on je glédau̯zhòt lúne**.

In fast speech a double consonant is normally pronounced as a single consonant if this does not lead to ambiguity, e.g. **brez sína** 'without the son' > **bresína**.

If ambiguity is caused then a long consonant is pronounced, e.g. **potakníti** 'to plant' > **potakníti**; **podtakníti** 'to foist' > **potakníti**.

1.8.5 Pronunciation of obstruents at word or morpheme boundaries

(a) **-d, -t + c-, č-,** or **dž-**

When a stop **d** or **t** is followed by an affricate the rules of voicing/devoicing apply (e.g. **-d + c- > -t + c-**). However, in the spoken language the stop and the affricate may merge to form a long affricate, i.e.

> **-d + c-, -t + c- > -c̄-**
> **-d + č-, -t + č- > -c̄̌-**
> **-d + dž-, -t + dž- > -dž̄-**
> **odcepíti** 'to break off' > **očepíti/otcepíti**
> **od džúsa** 'from the juice' > **odžúsa/oddžúsa**

Note: In fast speech the resultant long affricate is shortened to a normal single affricate if such a pronunciation does not cause ambiguity.

(b) **-t, -d, -c, -č** or **-dž + s-, z-, š-, ž-**

When a stop **t** or **d** or an affricate are followed by a fricative the normal rules of voicing apply (e.g. **pod snégom** 'under the snow' > **pot snégom**). However, in the spoken language instead of two obstruents one long affricate may be pronounced, i.e.

> **-d, -t, -c + s- > c̄**
> **-d + z- > dz**
> **-d, -t + š- > c̄̌**
> **-d, -t + ž- > dž**
> **pod žágo** 'under the saw' > **podžágo**
> **stríc Sámo** 'Uncle Samo' > **stríčámo**

Note: In fast speech a single affricate may be pronounced.

(c) **-z, -s + š-**

When the fricatives **-z, -s** are followed by **š** a long **š** is pronounced, e.g. **iz šóle** 'out of school' > **išóle**

(d) When **-s** is followed by **č-**, the **-s > š**, e.g. **s čípko** 'with lace' > **ščípko**

1.9 MORPHOPHONEMIC ALTERNATIONS INHERITED FROM PROTO-SLAVONIC/PROTO-SLOVENE

Slovene has certain consonant alternations resulting from sound changes, which took place in the Proto-Slavonic language or the dialects of late Proto-Slavonic from which Slovene arose. These alternations were caused by processes known as palatalisation and jotation.

1.9.1   Palatalisation

Palatalisation was caused by front vowels and affected the preceding velar consonants **k, g, h** in two stages. These two stages are still reflected in Slovene. In stage one **k > č, g > ž, h > š, sk > šč** and in stage two **k > c, g > z**.

It is this historical palatalisation which explains the consonant alternations found in verbal inflection, noun declension and word formation, e.g. **okó** 'eye' – **očésa** 'eyes'; **nôga** 'leg' – **nožíca** 'little leg'; **uhó** 'ear' – **ušésa** 'ears'; **pékel** '(he) baked' – **pêče** '(he) bakes' – **pêci** 'bake!'; **strígel** '(he) cut' – **stríže** '(he) cuts' – **strízi** 'cut!'; **blèsk** 'glitter' – **bleščáti se** 'to glitter'; **otròk** 'child' – **otrôci** 'children'.

1.9.2   Jotation

Jotation was caused by the influence of **j** on preceding velars, labials and dentals and led to the following alternations in Slovene:

g + j > ž	**t + j > č**	**p + j > plj**	**r + j > rj**
k + j > č	**c + j > č**	**b + j > blj**	**n + j > nj**
h + j > š	**d + j > j**	**v + j > vlj**	**l + j > lj**
	s + j > š	**m + j > mlj**	**sl + j > šlj**
	z + j > ž		**st + j > šč**
			sk + j > šč
			zg + j > ž

The alternations resulting from these changes are found primarily in verbal inflection, the formation of comparative adjectives and word formation, e.g.

g/ž	**drág**	dear	:	**dráže**	dearer
k/č	**skakáti**	to jump	:	**skáčem**	I jump
h/š	**poslúh**	hearing	:	**poslúšati**	to listen
t/č	**metáti**	to throw	:	**méčem**	I throw
c/č	**stríc**	uncle	:	**stríčev**	uncle's
d/j	**rodíti**	to give birth	:	**rôjen**	born
s/š	**razglasíti**	to proclaim	:	**razglašèn**	proclaimed
z/ž	**rézati**	to cut	:	**réžem**	I cut
p/plj	**potopíti**	to immerse	:	**potopljèn**	sunken
b/blj	**zgubíti**	to lose	:	**zgubljèn**	lost
v/vlj	**prenovíti**	to renovate	:	**prenovljèn**	renovated
m/mlj	**mámiti**	to entice	:	**mamljív**	enticing
r/rj	**oráti**	to plough	:	**órjem**	I plough
l/lj	**zahvalíti**	to thank	:	**zaháljen**	thanked
n/nj	**zapleníti**	to seize	:	**zaplénjen**	seized
sl/šlj	**premísliti**	to think over, deliberate	:	**premíšljati**	to think over, deliberate

zg/ž	**rózga**	vine shoot	: **róžje**	cuttings from vine shoot
st/šč	**zapustíti**	to leave	: **zapúščati**	to leave
sk/šč	**iskáti**	to look for	: **íščem**	I am looking for

1.10   THE ALTERNATION o/e

In the Proto-Slavonic parent language the back vowel **o** was fronted to **e** after soft consonants. This change created a hard versus soft alternation which is described by the German term 'umlaut'. In Slovene **č, š, ž, c** and **j** are considered soft and as a result **e** replaces **o** after these consonants in certain cases in masculine and neuter noun declension, adjectival declension and pronominal declension and in certain derivative suffixes, e.g.

instr. sing. masc.:	**s fántom**	'with the boy' but **s prijáteljem** 'with a friend'
instr. sing. neuter:	**s sêdlom**	'with a saddle' but **s sŕcem** 'with a heart'
nom. sing. neuter:	**nôvo**	'new' but **vróče** 'hot'
infinitive:	**kupováti**	'to buy' but **izobraževáti** 'to educate'

2 NOUNS

There are two types of nouns in Slovene: proper nouns and common nouns.

Proper nouns refer to a particular person, place or institution by name, e.g. **Antón**; **Álpe** 'the Alps'; **Sáva** 'the river Sava'; **Ljubljána**; **Ánglija** 'England'; **Tríglav** 'Tríglav mountain'.

Common nouns are either concrete or abstract. A concrete noun refers to a person, thing, substance or mass, i.e. something we can touch or see, e.g. **ôče** 'father'; **vlák** 'train'; **délavec** 'worker'; **púnca** 'girl'; **gôra** 'mountain'; **réka** 'river'; **mésto** 'town'; **zlató** 'gold'; **ápno** 'lime'. An abstract noun is used to describe a quality, idea or experience, e.g. **lepôta** 'beauty'; **mladóst** 'youth'; **hrepenênje** 'longing, yearning'.

There is no equivalent in Slovene of the English articles 'a/an' and 'the'. Thus **híša** means either 'a house' or 'the house', the difference being resolved by context, word order or possibly an attributive adjective.

2.1 COMMON NOUNS

Common nouns may be divided into (a) count nouns and (b) uncount nouns.

(a) Count nouns can be singular, dual or plural, e.g. **pès** 'dog'; **psà** 'two dogs'; **psì** 'dogs'; **púnca** 'a girl'; **púnci** 'two girls'; **púnce** 'girls'.

(b) Uncount nouns refer to a general kind of thing rather than an individual item and so normally have only a singular form, e.g. **lepôta** 'beauty'; **resníca** 'truth'; **kisík** 'oxygen'. They may be either abstract, mass (matter or substance) or collective nouns, e.g.

abstract: **vôžnja** 'ride, drive'; **pretêklost** 'the past'; **ljubosúmnost** 'jealousy'; **vesêlje** 'happiness'.

mass (material or substance): **pések** 'sand'; **zlató** 'gold'; **mléko** 'milk'; **opéka** 'brick'; **zràk** 'air'; **jêklo** 'steel'.

collective: **perutnína** 'poultry'; **perílo** 'linen'; **žgánje** 'liquor, spirits'; **mladína** 'youth, young people'; **srnjád** 'roe deer'; **grmóvje** 'shrubbery'.

Uncount nouns are occasionally used in the plural and in such cases there is usually a partial or full change in the basic lexical meaning of the word. The plural of such nouns may denote the following:

(i) different types of something, e.g.

Tkaníne so razlíčne	The fabrics are different
Žgánja so túja in domáča	The spirits are foreign and home-made
Vsák člôvek imá dôbre in slábe lastnósti	Every man has good and bad attributes
Opêri soláto v dvéh vôdah	Wash the salad in two different lots of water

(ii) a specific concrete use of the noun, e.g. **Dvé kávi, prósim** 'Two cups of coffee, please'; **ljubljánske lepôte** 'the Ljubljana beauties (i.e the beautiful girls of Ljubljana)'.

The use of the dual or plural of a collective noun is rare but may occur, e.g. **dvé goróvji** 'two types of mountain chain'; **dvé ozvézdji** 'two constellations'.

Note: The construction **dvóje goróvij** is also possible but constructions using the cardinal numeral would be normal.

2.2 GENDER

(a) Slovene nouns belong to one of three genders: masculine (m.), feminine (f.) or neuter (n.), e.g. **krùh** (m.) 'bread', **réka** (f.) 'river', **mésto** (n.) 'town'.

(b) The grammatical gender of nouns is in most instances indicated by the ending of the noun. Adjectives, pronouns and the verbal predicate expressing gender (i.e. the -l participle or the past participle passive), normally agree in gender with the noun which they qualify.

2.2.1 Masculine nouns

Most nouns ending in a consonant are masculine, e.g. **stòl** 'chair'; **jêzik** 'language'; **čévelj** 'shoe'; **mèč** 'sword'; **hríb** 'hill'; **mésec** 'month'.

Exceptions are nouns in **-ost**, **-ev**, **-ezen**, **-ad** which are feminine and a few other nouns, e.g. **hitróst** 'speed'; **rešítev** 'rescue'; **ljubézen** 'love'; **perjád** 'poultry'; **nìt** 'thread'; **úš** 'louse'; **stvár** 'thing'; **lúč** 'light'; **bolést** 'grief'.

2.2.2 Feminine nouns

Most nouns ending in -a are feminine, e.g. **míza** 'table'; **césta** 'road'; **omára** 'cupboard'; **sêstra** 'sister'; **gláva** 'head'; **zêmlja** 'earth'.

Exceptions are:

(a) foreign loan words in **-á** which are masculine, e.g. **angažmá** 'engagement'; **abonmá** 'subscription'; **plasmá** 'placing'.

(b) masculine personal names in **-a**, e.g. **Lúka, Míha, Matíja**

(c) a small group of nouns ending in **-a** which naturally denote male persons: **vódja** 'leader, director'; **kolovódja** 'ringleader'; **računovódja** 'accountant'; **delovódja** 'foreman'; **strojevódja** 'engine driver'; **vlakovódja** 'train conductor'; **koléga** 'colleague'; **páša** 'pasha'; **slúga** 'servant'; **opróda** 'squire, shield bearer'; **zastavonóša** 'standard bearer'; **starešína** 'senior, doyen, chief'; **stárosta** 'elder, chief', **vójvoda** 'duke'.

These nouns decline like masculine or feminine nouns (see **2.11.3**), but adjectives and pronouns which qualify them and the verbal predicate expressing gender have masculine agreement, e.g. **Finánčni računovódja je prišèl** 'The financial director came'; **nášemu računovódji** 'to our accountant'; **náši nôvi kolégi** 'our new colleagues'.

(d) a small group of nouns in **-a** with a pejorative meaning, which may refer to male persons or to female persons. These nouns decline like feminine nouns. The agreement of pronouns and adjectives qualifying them is usually feminine as is the agreement of the verbal predicate if it expresses gender. The gender of the person referred to is determined by the context. However, masculine agreement of the qualifying adjective, pronoun and even the verbal predicate is also possible if the nouns refer to men. Nouns in this category include: **barába** 'blackguard, ruffian'; **čvéka** 'prattler'; **mévža** 'coward'; **neróda** 'clumsy person'; **pijandúra** 'drunkard'; **prismóda** 'stupid person'; **pokvéka** 'cripple'; **lenôba** 'lazybones'; **cméra** 'crybaby, sniveller'; **nadlóga** 'nuisance'.

Note: **barába, mévža, pijandúra** normally refer to men while the others refer to both men and women.

Examples

Òn je velíka mévža
He is a great big coward

Tá barába mi šè do dánes ní vŕnil denárja
This blackguard has still not repaid me that money

Tá cméra je rêkla, da bo tó storíla
That crybaby said that she would do it

(e) the noun **príča** 'witness' which may refer to a man or a woman. Agreement with this noun, however, is only feminine both in the case of a qualifying adjective or pronoun or in the verbal predicate, e.g.

bremenílna príča	witness for the prosecution
Príča je bilà podkúpljena	The witness was bribed
Príče so pripovedoválе, kàr so vídele	The witnesses gave an account of what they had seen

(f) the noun **siróta** 'orphan' which may refer to a man or a woman. Agreement with the qualifying adjective or pronoun is feminine, e.g. **Òn/ôna je vôjna siróta** 'He/she is a war orphan'.

The verbal predicate normally agrees with the gender of the person referred to, e.g.

Tá siróta mi je rékel, da . . .	This orphan (m.) told me that . . .
Tá siróta mi je rêkla, da . . .	This orphan (f.) told me that . . .

2.2.3 Neuter nouns

Most nouns ending in -o, -e are neuter, e.g. **mésto** 'town'; **pólje** 'field'; **mórje** 'sea'; **ôkno** 'window'; **teló** 'body'; **bogástvo** 'wealth'.

Exceptions are:

(a) foreign loan words in -o, -e which are masculine, e.g. **komité** 'committee'; **kíno** 'cinema'; **ávto** 'car'; **trikó** 'knitted wear'

(b) personal names in -o, -e which refer to male persons, e.g. **Márko, Tíne, Jánko, Jóže, Stáne**

(c) certain expressive or vulgar nouns in -e, -o denoting persons, e.g. **kasnè** 'sluggard'; **zmuznè** 'shirker'; **usranè** 'coward'; **trapè** 'stupid person'; **síne** 'son'; **fantè** 'lad'; **bímbo** 'blockhead'

(d) the noun **ôče** 'father' (see **2.10.2**)

2.2.4 Natural gender

Nouns that naturally indicate male persons or male animals are masculine, e.g. **člôvek** 'man'; **kováč** 'blacksmith'; **petêlin** 'cock'; **žrébec** 'stallion'; **ôče** 'father'.

Nouns that naturally indicate female persons or female animals are feminine, e.g. **žénska** 'woman'; **šivílja** 'seamstress'; **kobíla** 'mare'; **kokóš** 'hen'; **psíca** 'bitch'; **čaróvnica** 'witch'.

Two groups of neuter nouns in -e represent animate beings:

(a) the young of animals, e.g. **mačè** 'kitten'; **žrebè** 'foal, colt'; **prasè** 'piglet'; **têle** 'calf'; **deklè** 'young woman'; **píšče** 'chick'; **jágnje** 'lamb', **otročè** 'child'

(b) pejorative nouns used to describe people or animals, e.g. **človéče** 'a small thin man'; **kravšè** 'scraggy old cow'; **ženščè** 'puny old woman'; **revšè** 'poor fellow, wretch'; **zmenè** 'wretch, weakling'

Agreement with types (a) and (b) is neuter, both in the qualifying adjectives and pronouns and in the verbal predicate. Neither type has an animate accusative = genitive (see **2.3**) although colloquially pejorative nouns like **revšè** and **zmenè** may have.

Examples of usage

Da si vídel tísto zmenè/tístega zmenéta	If you had seen that wretch
Tísto revšè je biló . . .	That wretch was . . .
Ženščè je omagoválo pod breménom	The puny old woman staggered beneath the burden
Njíhovo mačè je dŕgnilo hŕbet ob njegóv gléženj	Their kitten rubbed its back against his ankle

2.2.5   Gender variation

A few nouns have more than one gender:

(a)   **pót** 'path, way'
In the singular this noun is either masculine or feminine although in the modern language the feminine form is preferred except in certain expressions, e.g. **blátna pót** 'muddy path'; **jávna pót** 'public path'; **Vsò pót sta molčála** 'They (d.) were silent the whole way', *but* **krížev pót** (m.) 'Way of the Cross'.
In the plural in addition to masculine and feminine forms there exists also a neuter plural form **póta** used expressively in a phrase like **nèdoumljíva póta usóde** 'the incomprehensible paths of fate'.

(b)   **sléd** 'trail, trace, track'
This noun was formerly either masculine or feminine. In the modern language it is normally feminine, e.g. **svéža sléd** 'fresh trail'; **krváva sléd** 'a bloody trail'; **tíste sledí** 'those tracks'.
The masculine form still appears, however, in phrases like **brez sledú izgíniti** 'to disappear without trace'.

(c)   **lòv** 'hunt, catch'
Formerly this noun was either feminine or masculine. In the modern language it is only masculine, e.g. **bogát lòv** 'a rich catch'; **Bíl je na lôvu** 'He was hunting'.

(d)   **okó** 'eye'
This noun is neuter in the singular and dual, but feminine in the plural: **škíliti na lévo okó** 'to squint with one's left eye'; **síve očí** 'blue eyes'; **Òn je slép na obé očési** 'He is blind in both eyes'.

2.2.6 Differentiation of gender through suffixes

(a) Suffixes are used to distinguish male and female representatives of various occupations, professions, organisations, nationalities, etc., e.g.

masculine	*feminine*	
učênec	**učênka**	pupil
profésor	**profésorica**	professor
Slovénec	**Slovénka**	a Slovene
natákar	**natákarica**	waiter, waitress
Francóz	**Francózinja**	Frenchman, Frenchwoman
Anglèž	**Angléžinja**	Englishman, Englishwoman
učítelj	**učíteljica**	teacher
študènt	**študêntka**	student

Occasionally, however, two different words are used to differentiate between the male and female, e.g. **šivílja** 'seamstress'; **krojáč** 'tailor'.

Masculine nouns denoting professions can be used to refer to women, although nowadays a feminine suffixed form is preferred, e.g. **Ánčka je téhnik/téhničarka** 'Ančka is a technician'.

The nouns **profésor/profésorica** *'professor' (m/f),* **dóktor/dóktorica** *'doctor' (m/f)*

The feminine form **profésorica** is used to address women professors. However, alongside this usage we also find **gospá profésor**, i.e 'Mrs Professor'.

If the title **profésorica/dóktorica** is used with a woman's surname, then the surname retains its masculine form, e.g. **profésorica Bóršnik**. If, however, the masculine forms **profésor** or **dóktor** are used to address a woman then the feminine form of the surname is used, e.g. **profésor Bóršnikova**.

If the masculine forms **profésor/dóktor** are used with the woman's Christian and surname then the masculine form of the surname is used, e.g. **dóktor Martína Bóršnik**.

In the spoken language the forms **profésor, dóktor** used with surnames are not declined although the masculine Christian and surnames do decline. In the case of feminine names, the Christian name alone declines if it is used with the surname. If the surname alone is used then it declines, e.g.

s profésor Bóršnikovo	with Professor Boršnik (fem.)
s profésor Martíno Bóršnik	with Professor Martina Boršnik (fem.)
s profésor Toporíšičem	with Professor Toporišič (masc.)

In the literary language the declension of **profésor, dóktor** is recommended when used with men and the declined feminine forms **profésorica** and **dóktorica** are recommended for women, e.g. **s profésorjem Toporíšičem; pri dóktorici Martíni Bóršnik**.

Note: Feminine Christian names and surnames
When you refer to a woman using her Christian name and surname then only the Christian name declines, but if you refer to her only by her family surname you add the suffix – -ov-/-ev- and decline the word like a possessive adjective, e.g. **Pogovárjali smo se o Bêrti Golób** 'We were talking about Berta Golob' but **Pogovárjali smo se o Golóbovi** 'We were talking about Golob'.

(b)   The male and female of animal species may be differentiated by the use of the two different words, e.g.

masculine		*feminine*	
bìk	bull	**kráva**	cow
petêlin	cock	**kokóš**	hen
žrébec	stallion	**kobíla**	mare

Normally, however, suffixes are used to differentiate the male form from the female form, e.g.

masculine		*feminine*	
lèv	lion	**levínja**	lioness
tíger	tiger	**tígrica**	tigress
pès	dog	**psíca**	bitch
lisják	dog fox	**lisíca**	vixen
máček	tom cat	**máčka**	she-cat
labód	swan, cob	**labodíca**	pen

When gender differences are not apparent or of no significance then one noun (either masculine or feminine) will denote both the male and female of the species, e.g. **sôva** 'owl'; **zébra** 'zebra'; **nój** 'ostrich'; **siníca** 'titmouse'; **ópica** 'monkey'.

Should one wish to distinguish gender in these cases then one uses the nouns **sámec** 'the male'; **samíca** 'the female' plus the genitive of the nouns, e.g. **samíca sôve** 'the female owl'; **sámec sôve** 'the male owl'.

Even if two forms differentiating male from female exist, (e.g. **vrábec** 'cock-sparrow'; **vrábčevka** 'hen sparrow'), **sámec** or **samíca** may be used with the normally used word, e.g. **samíca vrábca** 'the female sparrow'.

Another way of distinguishing between the genders is to use **sámec** or **samíca** with the classifying adjective from the name of the animal, e.g. **máčja samíca** 'the female cat'; **ópičji sámec** 'the male monkey'.

2.3 ANIMACY

(a) Masculine nouns are divided into two subtypes:

    (i)   those that denote animate beings (persons or animals), e.g. **zdravník** 'doctor'; **pès** 'dog'

    (ii) those that denote inanimate objects, e.g. **krùh** 'bread'; **telefón** 'telephone'; **stròj** 'machine'

This animacy feature is important in declension in that in the singular masculine animate nouns have an accusative case identical with the genitive singular, whereas inanimate nouns have an accusative case that is identical with the nominative singular, e.g.

Singular

N	**zdravník** 'doctor'	**krùh** 'bread'
G	**zdravník<u>a</u>**	**krúha**
A	**zdravník<u>a</u>**	**krùh**

Hence **vídim zdravníka** 'I see the doctor' but **vídim krùh** 'I see the bread'.

(b) In Slovene certain other nouns have the animacy feature (i.e. acc. sing. = gen. sing.) even though they represent inanimate objects. The following types of noun belong to this category:

    (i)   the names of cars: **fórd, ópel, fólksvágen, gólf, mercédes, rólsrójs, fíat, renó**

    (ii)   diseases named after animals: **ràk** 'cancer: crab'; **vólk** 'gall, chafing: wolf'

    (iii)   the names of certain instruments, devices named after animals: **petêlin** 'cocking mechanism: cock'; **francóz** 'spanner: Frenchman'; **skôbec** 'trap: sparrow hawk; ' **robót** 'robot'

    (iv)   creative works named after their author: **Rembrandt** 'a Rembrandt (painting)'; **Picasso** 'a Picasso (painting)'

    (v)   the names of chess pieces and playing cards: **kmèt** 'pawn'; **králj** 'king'; **ás** 'ace'; **pagát** 'Roman one (a card)'; **fànt** 'knave'

    (vi)   the names of wines: **vipávec, jeruzalémčan, bizéljčan**

    (vii) the names of mushrooms: **júrček, gobán, túrek, cigánček**

   (viii) the names of sport teams: **Partizán, Železničar**

    (ix) certain terms for money: **tisočák** 'a 1000 (tolar) note'; **stoták** 'a 100 (tolar) note'

(x) the names of dead persons or animals: **mŕtvec** 'corpse'; **pokójnik** 'the deceased'; **mrlìč** 'corpse'; **mrtvák** 'corpse'; **piščánec** 'chicken (i.e. food)'

(xi) a few isolated words: **zmáj** 'kite'; **konjíček** 'rocking horse'; **dúh** 'spirit'; **metúljček** 'bowtie: butterfly (swimming stroke)'

Note: Older grammars state that the names of planets belong to the animate category. However, in the modern language they are considered inanimate, e.g. **Vesóljska sónda letí na Satúrn** 'A Space probe is going to Saturn'.

Examples of usage

Otrôci spúščajo zmája	The boys are flying a kite
Milijonêr je kúpil Rembrandta	The millionaire bought a Rembrandt
Predsédnik imá rólsrójsa	The president has a Rolls Royce
Potégnil je za petelína	He pulled the trigger
Njén ôče imá ráka	Her father has cancer
Píli smo vipávca	We drank vipavec wine
Òn imá píkovega fánta	He has the jack of spades
Ràd jém piščánca	I like chicken
Posódi mi tisočáka	Lend me a thousand note
plávati metúljčka	to swim butterfly
Imá preróškega duhá	He has a prophetic gift
klicáti duhá	to raise a ghost
zavézati si metúljčka	to tie a bow tie

Note: **dúh** 'smell' does not behave like an animate noun, e.g. **Jéd imá zóprn dúh** 'The food has a nasty smell'.

(c) In children's speech or when addressing children, inanimate objects are often given animate accusative forms, e.g. **Nóska si obríši** 'Wipe your nose'; **Dàj mi poljúbčka** 'Give me a kiss'; **Postávi mlékca na mízo** 'Put the milk on the table'.

(d) If a word denoting an inanimate object is used to describe a person, it is then treated as an animate noun, e.g. **izrúvati štór** 'to uproot a tree stump' but **Poglèj tístega štóra** 'Look at that clumsy person'.

2.4 NUMBER

Three numbers are distinguished in Slovene: singular, dual (referring to two persons/things) and plural (referring to three or more persons/things), e.g.

masc.: **pótnik** 'traveller'; **pótnika** 'two travellers'; **pótniki** 'travellers' (three or more)

fem.: **híša** 'house'; **híši** 'two houses'; **híše** 'houses' *neuter:* **ôkno** 'window'; **ôkni** 'two windows'; **ôkna** 'windows'

Note: In declension the genitive and locative cases of the dual are identical with the genitive and locative cases of the plural.

2.5 PLURAL NOUNS

Whereas most nouns have three numbers, certain nouns are used only in the plural. Some of these nouns may denote an object, which is composed of two elements. They may be masculine, feminine or neuter nouns. The main nouns in this category are:

2.5.1 Masculine

alimênti 'alimony'; **agrúmi** 'citrus fruit'; **análi** 'annals'; **brókoli** 'broccoli'; **efékti** 'movable effects'; **fritáti** 'pancake noodles'; **gostosévci** 'the Pleiades (const.)'; **hemoroídi** 'haemorrhoids'; **memoári** 'memoirs'; **možgáni** 'brain'; **prástárši** 'ancestors; **saldakónti** 'current account book'; **stárši** 'parents'; **trópi** 'the tropics'

Note: **stárši** is sometimes used in its dual form **stárša**, and colloquially even occurs with a singular form, e.g. **Imám samó ênega stárša** 'I have only one parent'. Apart from the above mentioned nouns certain proper nouns such as the names of mountains, towns etc. only exist in a plural form, e.g. **Álpe, Karavánke, Jeseníce, Toplíce, Bŕda, Karpáti** 'the Carpathians'; **Hélsinki, Rádenci, Aténe** 'Athens'; **Benétke** 'Venice'; **Firénce** 'Florence'.

2.5.2 Feminine

bermúdke 'bermuda shorts'; **bikínke** 'bikini'; **bínkošti** 'Whitsun'; **búrkle** 'fire-tongs'; **címbale** 'cymbals'; **cítre** 'zither'; **devíze** 'foreign currency'; **dímije** 'wide trousers worn by Muslim women'; **finánce** 'finances, revenue'; **gáre** 'handcart'; **gárje** 'mange'; **gáte** 'pants'; **genitálije** 'genitalia'; **gósli** 'fiddle'; **gráblje** 'rake'; **grúdi** 'bosom'; **hláče** 'trousers'; **hláčke** 'shorts'; **hulahúpke** 'tights'; **íde** 'the Ides'; **'insígnije** 'insignia'; **jásli** 'hayrack'; **jáslice** 'crib'; **jútranjice** 'matins'; **katakómbe** 'catacombs'; **kávbojke** 'jeans'; **kléšče** 'pincers, tongs'; **kléščice** 'pincers'; **kolesárke** 'cycling shorts'; **kopálke** 'swimming trunks'; **kôze** 'smallpox'; **kvátre** (arch.) 'ember days' [nowadays only used in the phrase **vsáke kvátre** 'rarely']; **litaníje** 'litany; long winded story'; **muzikálije** 'sheet music'; **naturálije** 'kind (i.e. payment in goods or labour as opposed to money)'; **nečké** 'kneading trough'; **obrésti** 'interest (fin.)'; **órgle** 'church organ'; **órglice** 'mouth-organ'; **óšpice** 'measles'; **páre** 'death bed'; **pájkice** 'leggings'; **počítnice** 'holidays'; **pomíje** 'slops, swill'; **pŕsi** 'chest'; **púmparice** 'knickerbockers'; **rdéčke** 'chicken pox'; **róvte** 'remote (backward) area'; **sáje** 'soot'; **saní** 'sledge'; **sanitárije** 'washroom toilet'; **sánje** 'dream'; **smučí** 'skis'; **spódnjice** 'knickers'; **státve** 'loom'; **svísli** 'hayloft'; **škárje** 'scissors'; **toplíce** 'spa'; **trsténke** 'pan-pipes'; **večérnice** 'vespers'; **více** 'purgatory'; **víle** 'fork'; **vílice** 'fork'; **víslice** 'gallows'; **zórnice** 'matins'; **žábe** 'children's tights'; **žále** 'cemetery'

2.5.3 Neuter

aktíva 'assets'; **dáta** 'data'; **dŕva** 'firewood'; **dúrca** 'small door'; **erráta** 'errata'; **jétra** 'liver'; **méča** 'calf (of leg)'; **mokríla** 'urethra'; **nebésa** 'heaven, paradise'; **nédra** 'bosom'; **očála** 'spectacles'; **pasíva** 'liabilities (fin.)'; **pléča** 'back'; **pljúča** 'lungs'; **sečíla** 'urethra'; **skrípta** 'hectograph copies of lecture notes'; **tlà** 'ground, floor'; **ústa** 'mouth'; **vráta** 'door'

Note: In the modern language **skrípta** is often treated as a feminine singular noun and then has a plural form **skrípte**.

2.6 THE DUAL

(a) The dual denotes two persons or objects and may be expressed by the dual form of the noun used on its own or by the dual form used with the numeral 'two' (i.e. **dvá** m. **dvé** f./n.) or the pronoun 'both' (i.e. **obá** m., **obé** f./n.), e.g.

(Dvá) bráta sta v sôbi	The two brothers are in the room
(Dvé) sêstri sta bilì v trgovíni	The two sisters were in the shop
Poslúšala je, kakó se fánta prepírata	She heard the two boys quarrelling
Ôkni sta odpŕti	The two windows are open
Žénski govoríta slovénsko	The two women speak Slovene
Omára stojí med (obéma) ôknoma	The cupboard stands between the two windows
Z brátoma so stárši zeló zadovóljni	The parents are very pleased with the two brothers
Svínčnika sta nôva	The two pencils are new
Kjé bosta živéli sêstri?	Where will the two sisters live?
dvé úri hodá	two hours walk
Obá predlóga sta sprejemljíva	Both proposals are acceptable

Note: Although the dual is a firmly established category for all three genders in the modern standard language, this is not the case in the colloquial language. In the colloquial language whereas the masculine dual is used regularly, the feminine and neuter dual are not. The feminine dual is generally replaced by the feminine plural and any qualifying adjective and the verbal predicate will be in the plural. The neuter dual is replaced by a masculine dual form and any qualifying adjective will also be in the masculine. The verbal predicate, however, may be in either the masculine dual or neuter plural depending on the region the speaker is from. The following examples exemplify this and are taken from the colloquial speech of university educated Slovenes.

Dvé banáne so bilè šè dôbre, trí pa so bilè čísto gníle
Two bananas were still good, but three were completely rotten

Kóliko stánejo té dvé obléke?
How much do these two dresses cost?

V méstu sem sréčala dvé sošólke. A véš, da me níso pozdrávile
In town I met two of my school friends. And you know what, they didn't
say hello to me

Obá ôkna sta/so bilà odpŕta, pa je bilò šè védno zadušljívo
Both windows were open, but it was still stuffy

Dvá letála bosta iméla zamúdo
The two planes will be late

Dvá mésta sta/so popólnoma porúšena
The two towns are completely demolished

Vésni sem kupíla dvé knjíge. Zaníma me, če ji bójo všéč
I bought Vesna two books. I am interested if she will like them

Tísta dvá obmôrska mésta sta/so se nam zdéla pa rés zanimíva
These two coastal towns seemed very interesting to us

Káj, 1000 tólarjev si dál? Dvá píva pa žé nísta môgla bíti takó drága.
What, you paid 1000 tolars? But two beers could not be that expensive

(b) Some nouns are normally used in their plural form instead of the
expected dual form. These nouns include (i) body parts which occur in
pairs (ii) articles of clothing or instruments consisting of two elements
or parts (iii) biological pairs, e.g.

(i) **bêdra** 'thighs'; **goleníce** 'shins'; **komólci** 'elbows'; **koléna** 'knees';
kríla 'wings'; **lahtí** 'forearms'; **ledvíce** 'kidneys'; **líca** 'cheeks'; **líčnice**
'cheekbones'; **nôge** 'legs'; **nosníce** 'nostrils'; **obrví** 'eyebrows'; **očí**
'eyes'; **perúti** 'wings'; **perutníce** 'wings'; **ráme** 'shoulders'; **raména**
'shoulders'; **rôke** 'hands'; **sencà** 'temples'; **ušésa** 'ears'; **véke** 'eyelids';
zapéstja 'wrists'

(ii) **bérgle** 'crutches'; **copáte** 'slippers'; **čévlji** 'shoes'; **drsálke** 'skates';
hláčnice 'trouser legs'; **nakolénke** 'knee pads'; **nakomólčniki** 'elbow
pads'; **naúšniki** 'ear muffs'; **rokávi** 'sleeves'; **rokavíce** 'gloves'; **smučí**
'skis'; **smúčke** 'skis'; **škórnji** 'boots'; **uháni** 'earrings'

(iii) **stárši** 'parents'; **dvójčki** 'twins'

Examples of usage

skomígniti z raméni	to shrug one's shoulders
Nôge me bolíjo	My legs ache
Čévlji me žúlijo	My shoes pinch
Rokávi so preširôki	The sleeves are too long
Mój sôsed imá dvójčke	My neighbour has twins
Invalíd se je opŕl na bérgle	The invalid leant on his crutches
Ušésa mu štrlíjo	His ears stick out
Golób je zamáhnil s perutnícami in odlêtel	The pigeon flapped its wings and flew off
Prijél jo je za zapéstja in jo potégnil k sêbi	He seized her by the wrists and drew her towards him

The dual form of these nouns is only used when it is necessary to emphasise that both parts are affected or take part in the action. In these instances the numeral 'two' (**dvá** m., **dvé** f./n.) or the pronoun 'both' (**obá** m., **obé** f./n.) is normally used with the dual form, e.g.

Med vôjno je izgúbil obá stárša	He lost both parents during the war
Oslepél je na obé očési	He went blind in both eyes
Na smúčanju si je zlômil obé nôgi	He broke both legs skiing
Tù sta dvá čévlja	There are two shoes here
Prími stekleníco z obéma rokáma	Take the bottle with both hands

2.7 COLLECTIVE NOUNS

Collective nouns refer to a group of people or things. They are singular in declension and have singular agreement, e.g.

brálstvo 'readership'; **bŕstje** 'buds, sprouts'; **délavstvo** 'workers, workforce'; **divjád** 'game'; **govédo** 'cattle'; **grmóvje** 'shrubs, bushes'; **grózdje** 'grapes'; **hrastovína** 'oak wood'; **klásje** 'ears of corn'; **klientéla** 'clientele'; **ladjévje** 'fleet'; **lístje** 'leaves, foliage'; **meščánstvo** 'townspeople'; **perílo** 'linen'; **perjád** 'poultry'; **poslušálstvo** 'audience'; **skalóvje** 'rocks'; **vejévje** 'branches, boughs'; **zverjád** 'beasts of prey'

Examples of usage

Lístje je odpádlo	The leaves have fallen
Poslušálstvo je navdúšeno plôskalo	The audience clapped enthusiastically
Skríl se je v grmóvje	He hid in the bushes

2.8 CASE

Slovene nouns have six cases in the singular, dual and plural: nominative, genitive, dative, accusative, locative and instrumental. The genitive and locative cases in the dual are identical with the genitive and locative cases in the plural. The locative and instrumental cases are always governed by a preposition. The genitive, dative and accusative cases may be used with or without a preposition.

2.9 THE DECLENSION OF MASCULINE NOUNS

The basic declension of masculine nouns is as follows:

(a) *Inanimate:* **načŕt** 'plan'

		singular	*dual*	*plural*
N		načŕt	načŕta	načŕti
G		načŕta	načŕtov	načŕtov
D		načŕtu	načŕtoma	načŕtom
A		načŕt	načŕta	načŕte
L	pri	načŕtu	načŕtih	načŕtih
I	z	načŕtom	načŕtoma	načŕti

(b) *Animate:* **pótnik** 'traveller'

		singular	*dual*	*plural*
N		pótnik	pótnika	pótniki
G		pótnika	pótnikov	pótnikov
D		pótniku	pótnikoma	pótnikom
A		pótnika	pótnika	pótnike
L	pri	pótniku	pótnikih	pótnikih
I	s	pótnikom	pótnikoma	pótniki

If a masculine noun ends in **-c**, **-č**, **-š**, **-ž** or **-j** (e.g. **stríc** 'uncle'; **mèč** 'sword'; **prijátelj** 'friend') then the endings **-om**, **-oma**, **-om**, **-ov** of the instrumental singular, dative dual, dative plural and genitive plural are replaced by **-em**, **-ema**, **-em**, **-ev** respectively, e.g. **s strícem**, **mêčema**, **mêčem**, **prijáteljev**.

The same rule also applies if the noun ends in **-dž** but such examples are rare and confined to borrowed anglicisms such as **ímidž**, **brídž**, **kóledž**, e.g. **z brídžem**.

One should note, however, that in the colloquial language the endings with **-o-** are also sometimes used after these consonants, e.g. **z brúcom** 'with the fresher'.

Note: Foreign personal names, which retain their original spelling, but whose endings are pronouned **-c, -č, -š, -ž, -dž** or **-j** will also have the ending **-em** in the instrumental singular, e.g. **sestánek z Bushem/s Fitzroyem/z Lesageem** 'a meeting with Bush/Fitzroy/Lesage'.

2.9.1 The fleeting vowel -e-

The vowel **-e-** (= ə), which appears in the final syllable of many masculine nouns, is in most instances lost in the oblique cases. The nouns in which this **-e-** is lost are:

(a) Masculine nouns and personal names in **-ec, -ek** where **-e-** = ə, e.g.

Singular

N	**zájec** 'hare'	**gasílec** 'fireman'	**dédek** 'grandad'	**Čapek**
G	**zájca**	**gasílca**	**dédka**	**Čapka**
D	**zájcu**	**gasílcu**	**dédku**	**Čapku** etc.

Exceptions to this rule only occur if **-ec, -ek** are preceded by a group of two or more consonants. In these cases the nouns retain the **-e-** in the oblique cases, e.g.

Singular

N	**tékmec** 'rival'	**pomíslek** 'scruple'	**Lúštrek**
G	**tékmeca**	**pomísleka**	**Lúštreka**
D	**tékmecu**	**pomísleku**	**Lúštreku** etc.

(b) Masculine nouns in **-el, -em, -en, -er, -elj, -enj** where **-e-** = ə, e.g.

Singular

N	**smísel** 'sense'	**járem** 'yoke'	**ôven** 'ram'	**véter** 'wind'
G	**smísla**	**járma**	**ôvna**	**vétra**
D	**smíslu**	**jármu**	**ôvnu**	**vétru** etc.

N	**cúcelj** 'dummy'	**svéženj** 'bundle'
G	**cúclja**	**svéžnja**
D	**cúclju**	**svéžnju** etc.

This **e** ~ zero alternation in declension is productive and also occurs frequently in borrowed words or personal names ending in **-er, -el, -en** if **-e-** is pronounced as a schwa, e.g.

Singular

N	**méter** 'metre'	**báger** 'dredger'	**septêmber**	**ansámbel** 'ensemble'
G	**métra**	**bágra**	**septêmbra**	**ansámbla**
D	**métru**	**bágru**	**septêmbru**	**ansámblu**

N	**Hannover**	**Basel**	**Antwerpen**
G	**Hannovra**	**Basla**	**Antwerpna**
D	**Hannovru**	**Baslu**	**Antwerpnu** etc.

Note: Exceptions are Scandinavian names in **-sen** which normally retain the **-e-** in declension, e.g. **Andersen, Ibsen** gen. **Andersena, Ibsena**.

It should be noted that **-e-** is not lost in the suffixes **-itelj**, **-atelj**, because here **-e-** is a full vowel and not a schwa, e.g. **ravnátelj** 'headmaster', **redítelj** 'steward, monitor'. Similarly in native words or loan words in **-er**, where **-e-** is a full vowel, the **-e-** is retained throughout the declension, e.g. **večér** 'evening'; **frizêr** 'hairdresser'; **dispéčer** 'dispatcher' (see also **2.10**).

(c)   Three monosyllabic nouns where **-e-** = ə:

Singular

N	**pès** 'dog'	**sèl** 'messenger'	**sèn** 'dream'
G	**psà**	**slà**	**snà**
D	**psù**	**slù**	**snù** etc.

In other monosyllabic nouns where **-e-** = ə the **-e-** is retained in declension, because its loss would result in an initial consonant group strange to Slovene ears, e.g.

Singular

N	**kès** 'regret'	**bèt** 'stem'
G	**kèsa**	**bèta**
D	**kèsu**	**bètu** etc.

(d)   A few nouns in **-et**, **-eg** where **-e-** = ə, e.g. **mèzeg** 'mule'; **hŕbet** 'back'; **láket** 'forearm'; **válpet** 'steward'; **ócet** 'vinegar', e.g.

Singular

N	**mèzeg**
G	**mèzga**
D	**mèzgu** etc.

2.9.2   The fleeting vowels -o-, -a-, -i-

(a)   **-o-** is treated as a fleeting vowel in the Slovene noun **blágor** 'welfare', gen. **blágra**.

(b)   **-o-** and **-a-** are treated as fleeting vowels in Slavonic personal names in **-ok**, **-ac**, e.g. **Jákac**, gen. **Jákca**; **Dúdok**, gen. **Dúdka**.

(c)   **-a-** is treated as a fleeting vowel in the noun **dán** 'day' (see **2.11.2**). It is also treated as a fleeting vowel in the Croatian place name **Zádar**, gen. **Zádra**.

(d)   **-i-** is sometimes treated as a fleeting vowel in personal names in **-ic**, e.g. **Kastélic**, gen. **Kastélca**.

2.10 MODIFICATION OF THE STEM

In certain masculine nouns the stem is modified by the addition of the extensions -j-, -t-, -n-.

2.10.1 The extension -j-

(a) Most two or three syllable masculine nouns and personal names with the final groups -ar, -or, -ur, -ir or -er (except where e is a fleeting vowel, see 2.9.1) insert -j- between the stem and the oblique case endings. This means that these nouns have the endings -em, -ema, -em, -ev in the instr. sing., dat. dual, dat. plur. and gen. plur., e.g.

N	čevljár 'shoemaker'	sládkor 'sugar'	mehúr 'bladder'
G	čevljárja	sladkórja	mehúrja
D	čevljárju	sladkórju	mehúrju

N	krompír 'potato'	srakopêr 'shrike'	
G	krompírja	srakopêrja	
D	krompírju	srakopêrju etc.	

This category of noun includes hundreds of loan words with these final groups, e.g.

-ar: rádar; sónar; dólar; hángar; cirkulár
-or: ambasádor; matadór; meteór; spónzor; aligátor
-ur: trubadúr; púrpur; imprimátur; velúr; fémur
-ir: oficír; mušketír; bankír; eliksír; inženír
-er: teenager; bôjler; konvéjer; rócker; kompjúter

(b) A certain number of nouns with these final groups, however, do not add the extension -j-. There are approximately 180 such nouns. Many of them are loan words of a scientific or cultural nature and some are very obscure or archaic. In modern Slovene the most widely used of these nouns are the following:

-ar: udár 'blow'; prótiudár 'counterblow'; milodár 'alms'; navár 'welding'; velár 'velar'; požár 'fire'; síngular 'singular'; barbár 'barbarian'; mílibár 'millibar'; izobár 'isobar'; Madžár 'Hungarian'; Tatár 'Tatar'

-or: šôtor 'tent'; odbòr 'committee'; pòdodbòr 'sub-committee'; góvor 'speech' [and all prefixed derivatives numbering fourteen in all, e.g. dogóvor 'agreement'; ugóvor 'objection'; odgóvor 'answer']; prôstor 'space'; premòr 'pause'; folklór 'folklore'; tôvor 'cargo'; tábor 'camp'; odmòr 'rest'; napòr 'effort'; prenapòr 'over-exertion'; pomòr 'slaughter'; nabòr 'recruitment'; pribòr 'service, set, accessories';

jámbor 'mast'; razbòr 'analysis'; izbòr 'choice'; predòr 'tunnel'; podòr 'depression, rockfall'; prodòr 'break-through'; udòr 'landslip, landslide; vdòr 'invasion'; razdòr 'discord'; rókfor 'roquefort cheese'; cénterfór 'centre forward'; rodomòr 'genocide'; samomòr 'suicide'; bratomòr 'fratricide'; očetomòr 'patricide'; detomòr 'infanticide'; kraljemòr 'regicide'; umòr 'murder'; ponòr 'sink-hole'; zapòr 'imprisonment'; odpòr 'resistance'; pripòr 'detention'; stiropór 'polystyrene'; upòr 'rebellion'; razpòr 'rent, slit' izpòr 'lock-out'; zatòr 'suppression, extirpation'; zástor 'curtain'; utòr 'groove'; navòr 'lever'; prèddvòr 'forecourt'; kolodvór 'railway station'; pretôvor 'loading'; raztôvor 'unloading'; umotvòr 'work of art'; nestvòr 'monster'; izvòr 'origin'; práizvòr 'primeval source'; názor 'view'; rázor 'furrow'; nadzòr 'supervision'; pozòr 'attention'.

-ur: futúr 'future'; azúr 'azure colour'

-ir: obzír 'consideration'; prezír 'disdain'; ozír 'regard'; izvír 'source'; právír 'original source'; práizvír 'primeval source'; prepír 'quarrel'; satír 'satyr'; nemír 'riot'; ávtogír/ávtožír 'autogiro'; vsemír 'universe'; špetír 'quarrel'; empír 'empire style'; Alžír 'Algeria'

-er: primér 'example'; séver 'North'; bíser 'pearl'; večér 'evening'; prèdvečér 'eve'; zobodêr 'dentist'; romanciér 'novelist'; premiêr 'prime minister'; premér 'diameter'; polimêr 'polymer'; dežemér 'rain gauge'; vodomér 'water gauge'; vlagomér 'hygrometer'; tlakomér 'barometer'; jekomér 'echo sounder'; mlekomér 'lactometer'; toplomér 'thermometer'; svetlomér 'exposure meter'; globinomér 'depth gauge'; plinomér 'gas meter'; višinomér 'altimeter'; brzinomér 'speedometer'; vetromér 'wind gauge'; časomér 'chronometer'; potresomér 'seismograph'; taktomér 'metronome'; kotomér 'protractor'; ampêr 'ampere'; hárdvêr 'hardware'; sóftvêr 'software'; stožér 'hinge'

Note: If any of the above nouns is used as a surname, then -j- will be inserted in the oblique cases, e.g. Séver, gen. Séverja; Požár, gen. Požárja.

(c) A small number of nouns with the final groups -ar, -or, -ur, -ir and -er have alternative declensions, i.e. with or without the extension -j-. Nouns in this category include the following:

-ar: pêhar 'bread basket'; hektár 'hectare'; samovár 'samovar'

-or: flúor 'fluorine'; jávor 'maple'; lôvor 'laurel'; prápor 'flag'; koridór 'corridor'; termofór 'hot water bottle'; fósfor 'phosphorous'; lôgor 'camp'; dekór 'decor'; semafór 'traffic lights'; resór 'competence'

-ur: lemúr 'lemur'; avgúr 'augur'

-ir: **Kašmír** 'Kashmir'; **porfír** 'porphyry'; **suveník** 'souvenir'; **gejzír** 'geyser'; **okvír** 'picture frame; framework, scope'

-er: **interiêr** 'interior'; **eksteriêr** 'exterior'

In the spoken language the forms with **-j-** are more normally used except in a few instances where the forms without **-j-** are more common, e.g. **flúor, eksteriêr, interiêr.**

Note: The noun **okvír** has two meanings: 'picture frame' and 'framework, scope'. In the meaning 'picture frame' it is declined with the extension **-j-**, but in the figurative meaning 'framework' it is declined without **-j-**.

English and French surnames in **-eare, -iere** etc. where **-r** is the final pronounced consonant also have alternative forms with or without **-j-** but those with **-j-** are those recommended, e.g. **Shakespeare**, gen. **Shakespearja**.

(d) There are approximately forty-five monosyllabic nouns ending in **-r** in Slovene. Only three of these add the extension **-j-**. These are: **cár** 'tsar'; **fár** 'priest'; **júr** 'fool'; '1000 tolar note';

(e) Masculine nouns and personal names with a stressed ending in **-a, -o** or **-e** or with a stressed or unstressed ending in **-i, -u** add the extension **-j-** in the oblique cases before the case endings, e.g.

N	**komité** 'committee'	**metró** 'underground'	**emú** 'emu'
G	**komitéja**	**metrója**	**emúja**
D	**komitéju**	**metróju**	**emúju** etc.

N	**táksi** 'taxi'	**amandmá** 'amendment'	**krokí** 'sketch'
G	**táksija**	**amandmája**	**krokíja**
D	**táksiju**	**amandmáju**	**krokíju** etc.

N	**Néhru**	**Fránci**	**Zolá**
G	**Néhruja**	**Fráncija**	**Zolája**
D	**Néhruju**	**Fránciju**	**Zoláju** etc.

If, however, the foreign names end in these sounds but are written with a final unpronounced consonant, then the normal case endings are added e.g. **Diderot** (nom.) **Diderota** (acc./gen.). The oblique cases will, however, be pronounced as if there was a **-j-** extension, e.g. **Diderota** pron. **Didroja**.

Foreign proper names ending with these vowel sounds also behave in the same way, e.g.

N	**Rousseau**	**Poe**	**Disney**	**Swansea**
G	**Rousseauja**	**Poeja**	**Disneyja**	**Swanseaja** etc.

Note: Slavonic proper nouns in **-ki/ky** decline like adjectives (see **3.3**).

(f)   Masculine nouns in unstressed **-o**, **-e** adapt morphologically and in declension replace the **-o**, **-e** with the appropriate oblique case endings. They do not add the extension **-j-**, e.g.

N	**kíno**	**finále**	**váterpólo**	**kamikáze**
	'cinema'	'finale'	'waterpolo'	'kamikaze'
G	**kína**	**finála**	**váterpóla**	**kamikáza**
D	**kínu**	**finálu**	**váterpólu**	**kamikázu** etc.

Nouns in this category include:

(i)   Foreign loan words, e.g. **kónto** 'account'; **inkáso** 'takings'; **pianíno** 'piano'; **lumbágo** 'lumbago'; **móto** 'motto'; **rádio** 'radio'; **penále** 'penalty'; **konkláve** 'conclave'; **fíčko** 'Fiat car'; **stúdio** 'studio'; **dinámo** 'dynamo'; **Číle** 'Chile'; **sólo** 'solo'; **bolêro** 'bolero'; **inkógnito** 'incognito'

(ii)   Personal names in unstressed **-o**, **-e**, e.g. **Márko, Jánko, Bránko, Slávko**

(iii)   Certain expressive words in **-ko**, e.g. **debélko** 'fat man'; **čŕnko** 'black horse, black man'; **déčko** 'boy'; **rdéčko** 'chestnut horse'; **sréčko** 'lucky man'

(g)   Latin and Greek words in **-as**, **-es**, **-os**, **-us**, **-um** lose these endings in declension if they are preceded by a vowel. The extension **-j-** then follows the vowel before the oblique case endings, e.g.

N	**Menelaos**	**Sirmium**	**Livius**
G	**Menelaja**	**Sirmija**	**Livija** etc.

(h)   The noun **dež** 'rain' adds the extension **-j-** before its oblique case endings, e.g.

N	**dèž**
G	**dežjà**
D	**dežjù** etc.

2.10.2   The extension -t-

The following masculine nouns add the extension **-t-** in their oblique cases:

(a)   the nouns **ôče** 'father'; **médo** 'teddy bear'

(b)   expressive, pejorative and vulgar nouns ending in **-e** or **-o** referring to male persons, e.g. **bímbo** 'blockhead'; **fantè** 'lad'; **zmenè** 'wretch'; **síne** 'son'; **trapè** 'stupid person'; **robantè** 'grumbler'; **nihčè** 'nonentity'; **zaspanè** 'sleepy head'; **posranè** 'coward'; **umazanè** 'sloven'; **počasnè** 'laggard'; **zmuznè** 'shirker'. It should moreover be noted that these nouns have an accusative singular identical with the genitive, e.g.

N	ôče
G	očéta
D	očétu
A	očéta etc.

Note: In the spoken language masculine personal names in -o, -a and the expressive noun sínko 'son' often add the extension -t- in their oblique cases but these forms are considered non-literary, e.g. Márko, gen. Márkota; Míha, gen. Míhata; sínko, gen. sínkota.

2.10.3 The extension -n-

A limited number of masculine nouns in -elj (= əlj) mostly of German origin add the extension -n- in the oblique cases. Nouns in this category are: bútelj 'fool'; dátelj 'date'; nágelj 'carnation'; mándelj 'almond'; párkelj 'devil; hoof' and the personal name Fráncelj.

The noun párkelj adds -n- only in the meaning 'devil'. No -n- is added when it means 'hoof'. All the other nouns except nágelj and Fráncelj also allow forms without -n- but the forms with -n- are used in the spoken language, e.g.

N	nágelj	mándelj	or	mándelj
G	nágeljna	mándeljna		mándlja
D	nágeljnu	mándeljnu		mándlju etc.

2.11 CASE VARIANTS

(a) The genitive singular
The basic ending of the genitive singular masculine is -a. Certain mono-syllabic nouns, however, may have an alternative stressed ending in -ú. The following nouns belong to this group:

dár (arch.) 'gift'; lán 'flax'; mír 'peace'; móst 'bridge'; grád 'castle'; máh 'moss'; sád 'fruit'; pláz 'avalanche'; pót 'sweat'; stráh 'fear'; smrád 'stench'; tát 'thief'; stán 'status'; léd 'ice'; glás 'voice'; nós 'nose'; srám 'shame'; zíd 'wall'; ród 'stock'; méd 'honey'; lás 'hair'; pás 'belt'; glád 'hunger'; sín 'son'; jéz 'dam'; plód 'foetus'; vrát 'neck'; trák 'tape'

In the case of some nouns both forms -a/-ú are equally used (e.g. grád, zíd, jéz) while with others either the form in -ú is more common (e.g. glás, stráh, srám) or the form in -a (e.g. lán, plód, méd, ród).

Examples of usage

Hláče so iz lána/lanú	The trousers are made of linen
Ní izgubíla plóda	She did not lose the foetus
pomákniti pósteljo do zída	to push the bed against the wall

iz róda v ród	from generation to generation
Kóliko vŕst méda/medú imáte?	How many types of honey do you have?
Umŕl je brez sína	He died without a son
občútek sramú	a feeling of shame
Zmánjkalo mi je tráka/trakú	I ran out of tape
okrog vratú	around the neck
okrog pasú	around the waist
prijétna bárva glasú	a pleasant tone of voice
Srájco imá môkro od póta	His shirt is soaked with sweat
s tekóčega tráka	from the assembly line
trésti se od strahú	to tremble with fear

(b) Instrumental singular
The noun **rádio** has the alternative instrumental endings **z rádiom/rádiem**.

(c) The dual and plural
A large number of monosyllabic nouns (e.g. **glás** 'voice') add the infix
-óv- before the case endings in the dual and plural forms. In the gen.
dual/plur., however, the infix **-óv** is followed by a zero ending **-ø**, e.g.

		sing.	*dual*	*plural*
N		glás	glasóva	glasóvi
G		glasú	glasóv	glasóv
D		glásu	glasóvoma	glasóvom
A		glás	glasóva	glasóve
L	pri	glásu	glasóvih	glasóvih
I	z	glásom	glasóvoma	glasóvi

Note: The infix **-óv-** is not added to monosyllabic nouns in **-c, -č, -š, -ž, -j**.

The most common nouns which fall into this category are: **gòzd** 'forest';
dúh 'spirit'; **glás** 'voice'; **grád** 'castle'; **móst** 'bridge'; **nós** 'nose'; **dólg**
'debt'; **dóm** 'home'; **tòp** 'cannon'; **trám** 'beam'; **ród** 'race, stock'; **sín** 'son';
sláp 'waterfall'; **stráh** 'fear'; **svét** 'world'; **tók** 'current'; **vál** 'wave'; **vóz**
'cart'; **vrát** 'neck'; **bóg** 'god'; **zíd** 'wall'; **zvón** 'bell'; **žléb** 'groove'; **brég**
'bank'; **bród** 'ferry'; **cvét** 'flower'; **dróg** 'pole'; **pláz** 'avalanche'; **plód**
'fruit'; **rób** 'edge'; **róg** 'horn'; **tát** 'thief'; **dár** (arch.) 'gift'; **vólk** 'wolf'; **vŕt**
'garden'; **vŕh** 'summit'; **gròb** 'grave'; **réd** '(monastic) order'; **trák** 'tape';
gód 'name day'; **krés** 'bonfire'; **pás** 'belt'.

Note: The disyllabic noun **véter** 'wind' also falls into this category, i.e. **vetróvi** (nom. plur.).

Some of these monosyllabic nouns allow plural variants without the
infix **-óv-** (e.g. **trám, jéz, plót, róg**) but such forms are stylistically marked.
A notable feature of the modern language is a growing tendency to use
the dual forms of these nouns without the infix **-óv-**, but to retain it in
the plural forms, e.g.

Dvá vozníka nísta bilà privézana z várnostnima pásoma/pasóvoma
The two drivers were not using their seat belts

Préčkala sem obá mósta/mostóva
I walked across both bridges

(d) Nominative plural in -je

(i) Certain nouns denoting persons have an optional non-stressed nominative plural in -je, e.g. **gôstje/gôsti** 'guests'.

   Nouns belonging to this category are: **bràt** 'brother'; **fànt** 'boy'; **gospód** 'sir, Mr'; **gòst** 'guest'; **kmèt** 'peasant'; **sôsed** 'neighbour'; **škràt** 'dwarf; ' **študènt** 'student'; **déd** 'grandfather'; **golób** 'pigeon'; **svàt** 'wedding guest'; **škòf** 'bishop'; **gròf** 'count'; **zèt** 'son-in-law'; **ôče** 'father'; **práôče** 'ancestor'; **Hrvàt** 'Croat'.

   In the spoken language the plural in -i is usually preferred in these nouns.

   The forms in -je which in some of these nouns is now old fashioned (e.g. **zèt, gròf, golób**) is preferred if collectivity is indicated. It is also possible to find in newspapers examples like **reprezentántje** 'representatives', but such forms are not considered literary.

(ii) Three masculine nouns have a mandatory nominative plural in stressed -jé. They are **lás** 'hair'; **zób** 'tooth'; **móž** 'man'. These nouns also have the endings -ø, -ém, -é, -éh, -mí, -éma in the gen. plur./dual, dat./acc./loc./instr. plur. and dat./instr. dual. The nouns **móž** and **lás** also have a stressed genitive singular ending -á, -ú respectively, while **zób** allows an alternative genitive singular stress.

		sing.			dual	plural
N		zób	móž	lás	zóba	zobjé
G		zóbá	možá	lasú	zób	zób
D		zóbu	móžu	lásu	zobéma	zobém
A		zób	možá	lás	zóba	zobé
L	pri	zóbu	móžu	lásu	zobéh	zobéh
I	z	zóbom	móžem	lásom	zobéma	zobmí

(iii) The suppletive plural of the noun **člôvek** 'man' is **ljudjé**. In the singular **člôvek** declines regularly except for its stress (see **2.21**) but its dual and plural forms are:

		dual	plural
N		človéka	ljudjé
G		ljudí	ljudí
D		človékoma	ljudém
A		človéka	ljudí
L	pri	ljudéh	ljudéh
I	s	človékoma	ljudmí

(e) Genitive plural
The nouns **kònj** 'horse', **otròk** 'child' have the genitive plural forms **kónj**, **otrók**, **kònj** also has an alternative gen plur **kônjev**.

(f) Locative plural
The noun **gòst** 'guest' has a regular loc. plur. form **gôstih**. However, in newspapers and reports on sporting events one encounters the phrase **igráti v gostéh** 'to play away'.
   In archaeological texts the noun **kòl** 'pole, stake' is found with a loc. plur. form **koléh**, e.g. **stávba na koléh** 'a lake dwelling (i.e. built on stakes)'.

2.11.1 The noun **otròk** 'child'

The noun **otròk** 'child' declines regularly in the singular and dual. In the plural, however, its nominative and locative forms have **-c-** instead of **-k-** before the case endings, i.e.

N		**otrôci**
G		**otrók**
D		**otrôkom**
A		**otrôke**
L	pri	**otrócih**
I	z	**otróki**

2.11.2 The noun **dán** 'day'

This noun has the following alternative declensional forms:

		singular	*dual*	*plural*
N		**dán**	**dnéva/dní**	**dnévi**
G		**dnéva/dné**	**dnévov/dní**	**dní/dnévov**
D		**dnévu**	**dnévoma/dnéma**	**dnévom/dném**
A		**dán**	**dnéva/dní**	**dnéve/dní**
L	pri	**dnévu**	**dnévih/dnéh**	**dnévih/dnéh**
I	z	**dnévom/dném**	**dnévoma/dnéma**	**dnévi/dnémi**

The use of the different forms very much depends on context and in certain phrases only one form will be used. For example, only the gen. sing. form **dnéva** will be used in phrases like **v tóku dnéva** 'in the course of the day'; **proti kôncu dnéva** 'towards the end of the day'. The gen. sing. form **dné** is used in adverbial phrases such as **Lépega dné smo se odprávili v hríbe** 'One fine day we set off for the mountains'. In the accusative dual the form **dvá dní** 'two days' is normal e.g. **dvá dní je deževálo** 'It rained for two days'. If, however, one wished to stress the two days the form **dnéva** would be used, e.g. **Kàr dvá céla dnéva je deževálo** 'It rained for two whole days'. Similarly in the genitive dual we can find a phrase such as **Dvéh dní se zeló dôbro spómnim** 'I remember the two days very well', but if the two days are emphasised we will find the form **dnévov** used e.g. **Dvéh lépih dnévov se zeló dôbro spómnim** 'I remember the two beautiful days very well'.

Examples of the use of the oblique cases of **dán**

instr. sing.	**Z dném je pritísnil mràz** At daybreak there was a frost **Bolník je zaménjal nóč z dnévom** The patient confused night with day
gen. plur.	**Štirinájst dní počítnic na mórju mi je zadôsti** A fortnight's holiday at the seaside is enough for me **Dôbro se spómni tístih dólgih polétnih dnévov** He well remembers those long summer days
acc. plur.	**Za vsè svôje žíve dní si bom zapómnil** I will remember for all my life **Dnéve mladósti je prežível na dežêli** He spent the years of his youth in the country
instr. plur.	**pred trémi dnévi** three days ago
dat. plur.	**Odrêkla sem se tém trém dnévom na mórju in sem ráje délala** I gave up those three days at the seaside and preferred to work
loc. plur.	**Ob lépih dnévih grémo na sprehóde** On fine days we go for walks
nom. dual.	**Pretêkla sta dvá dnéva** Two days passed
dat. dual.	**Odrékel sem se dvéma dnévoma na mórju in ráje délal** I gave up two days at the seaside and preferred to work
loc. dual.	**V zádnjih dvéh dnévih/dnéh smo izgubíli dvá člána klúba** In the past two days we have lost two club members
instr. dual.	**Pred dvéma dnévoma/dnéma sem se vrníla** I returned two days ago

It should be noted that although variants are acknowledged for several cases, in some instances they are not really used, e.g. dat. plur. **dném**, instr. plur. **dnémi**.

2.11.3 Masculine nouns in -a which denote male persons (see 2.2.2)

These nouns decline in their oblique cases either like **načŕt** or like a feminine noun in **-a** (see **2.13**), e.g.

		singular		
N		**računovódja** 'accountant'	or	**računovódja**
G		**računovódja**		**računovódje**
D		**računovódju**		**računovódji**
A		**računovódja**		**računovódjo**
L	pri	**računovódju**		**računovódji**
I	z	**računovódjem**		**računovódjo** etc.

Whatever the declensional form agreement is always masculine in the case of adjectives or the **-l** participle. In actual practice one often finds a mixture of the two declensions with some words nearly always used in one specific form in the oblique cases. For example the word **koléga** 'colleague' is normally used with the masculine forms, e.g. dat. sing. **nášemu kolégu** 'to our colleague'; gen. plur. **od náših kolégov** 'from our colleagues'; instr. dual **z dvéma kolégoma** 'with two colleagues'. On the other hand older words like **vójvoda** 'duke', **slúga** 'servant', **opróda** 'squire' are more common with feminine declensional forms, e.g. **o téh opródah** 'about those squires'; **s slúgami** 'with the servants'; **nášemu vójvodi** 'to our duke'.

The group of nouns in **-vódja** (e.g. **strojevódja** 'engine driver'; **knjigovódja** 'accountant'; **vlakovódja** 'train conductor'; **delovódja** 'foreman'; **kolovódja** 'ringleader'; **poslovódja** 'manager'; **vódja** 'leader'; **žerjavovódja** 'crane driver') tend to favour masculine forms in some cases and feminine forms in others, e.g.

Feminine forms

| acc. sing. | **Imámo dôbrega računovódjo** | We have a good accountant |
| nom. plur. | **náši nôvi računovódje** | our new accountants |

Masculine forms

instr. sing.	**s tém računovódjem**	with this accountant
instr. dual.	**z dvéma računovódjema**	with two accountants
loc. plur. (d)	**o téh (dvéh) računovódjih**	about these (two) accountants
instr. plur.	**z računovódji**	with the accountants

Note: Masculine nouns in **-a** with a pejorative meaning, which refer to male persons, decline only like feminine nouns in **-a** (see **2.2.2**).

2.11.4 Abbreviations, the names of letters and musical notes

These are masculine and may or may not decline, e.g. **visôkega c** 'of high c'; **z málim d** 'with a small d'; **iskánje právih ET-jev** 'the search for real ETs'; **Á je**

rékel B-ju da C-ja ne bó na sestánek 'A told B that C would not be at the meeting'.

2.12 THE DECLENSION OF FEMININE NOUNS

Feminine nouns may be divided into two main types: (a) nouns in **-a**, (b) nouns ending in a consonant.

2.12.1 Feminine nouns in -a

These nouns decline as follows:

		sing.	dual	plur.
N		míza 'table'	mízi	míze
G		míze	míz	míz
D		mízi	mízama	mízam
A		mízo	mízi	míze
L	pri	mízi	mízah	mízah
I	z	mízo	mízama	mízami

Note: Feminine '*pluralia tantum*' (e.g. **počítnice** 'holidays') decline like the plural of **míza**.

The genitive dual/plural of feminine nouns

The genitive dual/plural of feminine nouns in **-a** is normally a zero ending. Nouns with a root that ends in two obstruents, two sonorants or a sonorant plus obstruent have the zero ending in these cases, e.g.

		gen. dual/plur.
dèska	board	dèsk
máčka	cat	máčk
gostílna	inn	gostíln
továrna	factory	továrn
bárva	colour	bárv
ôvca	sheep	ôvc
lájna	barrel organ	lájn

If, however, the root ends in an obstruent plus a sonorant or in an obstruent/ sonorant plus **-lj-** or **-nj-** then the neutral vowel **e** (i.e. schwa) is normally inserted between the two consonants in the genitive dual/plural, e.g.

		gen. dual/plur.
škátla	box	škátel
sêstra	sister	sêster

tékma	competition	**tékem**
kótva	anchor	**kótev**
mêtla	broom	**mêtel**
ópna	membrane	**ópen**
štórklja	stork	**štórkelj**
mrávlja	ant	**mrávelj**
zêmlja	earth	**zêmelj**
môšnja	purse	**môšenj**
môtnja	disturbance	**môtenj**

If a noun root ends in 'an obstruent plus -j-' or 'vowel plus -r- + -j-' then an -i- is inserted between the two consonants, e.g.

		gen. dual/plur.
škárje	scissors	**škárij**
zárja	dawn	**zárij**
ládja	ship	**ládij**

Feminine nouns in *-ia, -oa, -ea*

The few nouns in this category are of foreign origin. They decline regularly except that in the genitive dual/plural **-j** replaces final **-a**, e.g.

		gen pl
bóa	boa	**bój**
alínea	paragraph	**alínej**
láncia	lancia	**láncij**

(name of car pron. **lanča**)

Genitive plural in *-a*

A small number of feminine nouns in **-a** have an alternative gen. plural in stressed **-á** which is usually used in poetry, folklore or certain set phrases. The most common of these nowadays are: **žêna** 'woman'; **gôra** 'mountain'; **žêlja** 'wish'; **mêja** 'boundary'; e.g.

dán žená	Women's day
vrhóvi gorá	the mountain tops
zúnaj mejá Slovénije	beyond the frontiers of Slovenia
Zdráv člôvek imá stó željá, bolník	A healthy man has a hundred
pa lè êno	wishes, a sick man but one

The noun *beséda*

This noun has an alternative archaic gen. plur. in **-í** which is used in the expressive phrase **Kônec, mír besedí** 'That's enough, not another word'.

The noun **gospá** *'lady'*

This noun has its own special declension

		sing.	*dual*	*plural*
N		gospá	gospé	gospé
G		gospé	gospá	gospá
D		gospé	gospéma	gospém
A		gospó	gospé	gospé
L	pri	gospé	gospéh	gospéh
I	z	gospó	gospéma	gospémi

2.12.2 Feminine nouns ending in a consonant

Feminine nouns ending in a consonant may be divided into two types (a) nouns in **-ev** and (b) other feminine nouns ending in a consonant.

(a) Nouns in **-ev**

These nouns include a few unproductive nouns and a large number of productive verbal nouns, e.g. **pônev** 'pan'; **búkev** 'beech'; **cérkev** 'church'; **rešítev** 'rescue'; **spregátev** 'conjugation'.

These nouns differ from those in **-a** only in the nom./acc. singular and the instrumental singular, e.g.

		sing.	*dual*	*plural*
N		cérkev 'church'	cérkvi	cérkve
G		cérkve	cérkev	cérkev
D		cérkvi	cérkvama	cérkvam
A		cérkev	cérkvi	cérkve
L	pri	cérkvi	cérkvah	cérkvah
I	s	cérkvijo	cérkvama	cérkvami

(b) Other feminine nouns in a consonant

These nouns have two types of declension:

(i)

		sing.	*dual*	*plural*
N		malénkost 'trifle'	malénkosti	malénkosti
G		malénkosti	malénkosti	malénkosti
D		malénkosti	malénkost(i)ma	malénkostim
A		malénkost	malénkosti	malénkosti
L	pri	malénkosti	malénkostih	malénkostih
I	z	malénkostjo	malénkost(i)ma	malénkostmi

The alternative dat./instr. dual ending in **-ima** is always used instead of **-ma** following an obstruent + sonorant, e.g. **z dvéma míslima** 'with two thoughts', but **z obéma perútma** 'with both wings'.

(ii)		*sing.*	*dual*	*plural*
N		stvár 'thing'	stvarí	stvarí
G		stvarí	stvarí	stvarí
D		stvári	stvaréma	stvarém
A		stvár	stvarí	stvarí
L	pri	stvári	stvaréh	stvaréh
I	s	stvarjó	stvaréma	stvarmí

The two types differ only in the dat./loc. dual/plur. and the instr. dual.

Most disyllabic and trisyllabic feminine nouns in a consonant decline like **malénkost** (e.g. **pomlád** 'spring'; **bolést** 'grief'; **hitróst** 'speed'; **délavnost** 'activity'; **divjád** 'game') while most monosyllabic feminine nouns in a consonant decline like **stvár** (e.g. **dlán** 'palm'; **kóst** 'bone'; **pést** 'fist'; **skŕb** 'care, worry'; **nóč** 'night'; **bŕv** 'gang plank').

Monosyllabic nouns declining like **malénkost** are very few and include the following: **ból** 'pain'; **slúz** 'mucus'; **nìt** 'thread'; **smŕt** 'death; **mìš** 'mouse' and the *pluralia tantum* nouns **pŕsi** 'chest'; **grúdi** 'bosom'.

Disyllabic nouns declining like **stvár** are also very few and include: **oblást** 'authority'; **ravèn** 'level' (gen. sing. **ravní**); **raván** 'plain' (gen. sing. **ravní**); **láhet** 'forearm' (gen. sing. **lahtí**); **tésen** 'gorge' (gen. sing. **tesní**); **prásnóv** 'element'; **prèdjéd** 'hors d'oeuvre'; **pomóč** 'help'; **nemóč** 'weakness'; **primés** 'admixture'. The *pluralia tantum* noun **saní** 'sledge' and the feminine plural form **očí** 'eyes' also decline like the plural of **stvár**.

The noun **obŕt** 'trade' may decline like **malénkost** or **stvár**, e.g. **pri rôčnih obŕtih/obrtéh** 'in manual trades'.

The noun **krí** 'blood' in its oblique cases declines like **stvár** with -v- replacing the -i found in the nominative, i.e. nom. **krí**, gen. **krví**, dat. **kŕvi**, instr. **krvjó** etc.

Disyllabic and trisyllabic feminine nouns ending in 'e (= ə) + sonorant/ obstruent' lose this -e- in declension, e.g.

> **prikázen** 'ghost', gen. **prikázni**; **mísel** 'thought', gen. **mísli**; **láhet** 'forearm', gen. **lahtí**. The -e- is not lost if it = -é-, e.g. **zíbel** 'cradle', gen. **zíbeli**; **jesén** 'Autumn', gen. **jeséni**.

Feminine nouns in an 'obstruent + -e- (= ə) + sonorant' which decline like **malénkost** insert an -i- before the instrumental endings of all three numbers and before the dative dual ending, i.e. instead of -jo, -ma, -mi we find the endings -ijo, -ima, -imi, e.g. **pésem** 'song', instr. sing. **pésmijo**, instr./dat. dual **pésmima**, instr. plur. **pésmimi**.

The same rule applies to the *pluralia tantum* nouns **gósli** 'fiddle'; **svísli** 'hayloft'; **jásli** 'hayrack', i.e. instr. plur. **jáslimi** etc.

If a noun which declines like **stvár** ends in 'obstruent + -e- (= ə) + sonorant' it has an instr. sing. in -ijo, e.g. **tésen** 'gorge', instr. sing. **tésnijo**.

2.13 THE NOUNS **máti** 'MOTHER' AND **hčí** 'DAUGHTER'

These nouns both add the extension **-er-** in declension in their oblique case forms, e.g.

		sing.	dual	plural
N		máti	máteri	mátere
G		mátere	máter	máter
D		máteri	máterama	máteram
A		máter	máteri	mátere
L	pri	máteri	máterah	máterah
I	z	máterjo	máterama	máterami

2.14 INDECLINABLE FEMININE NOUNS

These nouns include the following: **mámi** 'mummy'; **púnči** 'girl'; **bábi** 'granny'; **míss** 'miss'; **spécies** 'species'; e.g.

z nášo mámi	with our mummy
Ní vídel míss svetá	He didn't see Miss World
Vídel sem lépo púnči	I saw a beautiful girl
določíti rastlínsko spécies	to determine a plant species

2.15 FEMININE CHRISTIAN AND SURNAMES

Christian names in **-a** normally decline, but those in a vowel other than **-a** or in a consonant do not decline. Feminine surnames ending in a consonant or **-a** do not normally decline e.g.

Vídim Métko Mežán in Ánko Ískra	I see Metka Mežan and Anka Iskra
Dál je knjígo Bêrti Golób	He gave the book to Berta Golob
Šlà sem v kíno s Kármen in z Béti	I went to the cinema with Karmen and Beti

2.16 THE DECLENSION OF NEUTER NOUNS

Neuter nouns in **-o**, **-e** decline as follows:

	sing.	dual	plural
N	mésto 'town'	mésti	mésta
G	mésta	mést	mést

D		méstu	méstoma	méstom
A		mésto	mésti	mésta
L	pri	méstu	méstih	méstih
I	z	méstom	méstoma	mésti

N		sónce 'sun'	sónci	sónca
G		sónca	sónc	sónc
D		sóncu	sóncema	sóncem
A		sónce	sónci	sónca
L	pri	sóncu	sóncih	sóncih
I	s	sóncem	sóncema	sónci

Pluralia tantum nouns in -a (e.g. **ústa** 'mouth'; **očála** 'spectacles') with the exception of **tlà** 'floor' and **dŕva** 'firewood' (see **2.18**) decline like the plural of **mésto**.

Note: The noun **sencè** 'temple' has in the colloquial language a loc. dual/plur. form **sencèh**, e.g. **V sencèh me zbáda** 'My temples throb'.

2.16.1   The genitive dual/plural of neuter nouns

If the root of a neuter noun ends in an obstruent + sonorant (except -**j**-) then an -**e**- (= ə) is inserted between the obstruent and the sonorant in the genitive dual/plural, e.g.

		gen. plural
stêgno	thigh	**stêgen**
sêdlo	saddle	**sêdel**
vêdro	bucket	**vêder**
déjstvo	fact	**déjstev**
gróblje	pile of stones, ruin	**gróbelj**
písmo	letter	**písem**

If a root ends in a consonant + -**j**- then an -**i**- is inserted between the consonant and the -**j**- in the genitive plural, e.g.

		gen. plural
mórje	sea	**mórij**
vesólje	universe	**vesólij**
osténje	walls	**osténij**
goróvje	mountain range	**goróvij**
bítje	being	**bítij**
poslópje	building	**poslópij**
okólje	environment	**okólij**
kópje	spear	**kópij**
obzórje	horizon	**obzórij**
nasélje	settlement	**nasélij**

Exceptions to this rule are (a) the nouns **povêlje** 'order'; **korênje** 'carrot' which have the genitive plural forms **povêlj, korénj** and (b) verbal nouns in **-nje**, e.g. **življênje** 'life' gen. plur. **življênj**.

2.17 MODIFICATION OF THE STEM

In certain neuter nouns the stem is modified by the addition of the extensions **-t-, -n-, -s-**, e.g.

(a) The extension **-t-**

Neuter nouns in **-e** denoting (i) the young of animals and (ii) neuter nouns in **-e** used as pejorative or expressive terms to describe sickly, small persons or animals add the extension **-t-** in their oblique cases, e.g.

		sing.	*dual*	*plural*
N		**têle** 'calf'	**teléti**	**teléta**
G		**teléta**	**telét**	**telét**
D		**telétu**	**telétoma**	**telétom**
A		**têle**	**teléti**	**teléta**
L	pri	**telétu**	**telétih**	**telétih**
I	s	**telétom**	**teléti**	**teléti**

Nouns in this category include: (i) **sčenè** 'puppy'; **žrebè** 'foal'; **svínče** 'piglet'; **jágnje** 'lamb'; **mačè** 'kitten'; **golóbče** 'little dove'; **cigánče** 'gypsy child'; **píšče** 'chick'; **déte** 'child'; **fantè** 'small boy'; **deklè** 'girl'; **punčè** 'small girl'; **otročè** 'child'; **jelénče** 'fawn'; (ii) **živínče** 'cattle; dumb ox'; **kljúse** (arch.) 'nag'; **revšè** 'wretch'; **ženščè** 'small, old woman'; **nihčè** 'non-entity; **zmenè** 'good for nothing'; **onè** 'what's his name'; **zaspanè** 'lazy-bones'; **človéče** 'a small, withered man'; **počasnè** 'laggard'; **drobnè** 'puny man'.

Note: The noun **plêče** 'shoulder (of meat)' also belongs to this category.

The nouns referring to the young of animals do not indicate animacy in the accusative singular, e.g.

zakláti jágnje   to slaughter a lamb
kupíti svínče za vzréjo   to buy a piglet for breeding purposes

However, those with an expressive or pejorative meaning sometimes do if they refer to a male person. This is because certain of these nouns may also be masculine (see **2.10.2**), e.g.

vréči zaspanéta iz póstelje   to throw the lazybones out of bed
Namésto njêga so posláli tó zmenè   Instead of him they sent that good
                                        for nothing

(b) The extension **-n-**
Ten neuter nouns in **-me** add the extension **-n-** in their oblique cases, e.g.

		sing.	*dual*	*plural*
N		plême 'tribe'	pleméni	pleména
G		pleména	plemén	plemén
D		pleménu	pleménoma	pleménom
A		plême	pleméni	pleména
L	pri	pleménu	pleménih	pleménih
I	s	pleménom	pleménoma	pleméni

The other nouns in this category are: **vrême** 'time'; **imé** 'name'; **slême** 'ridge'; **víme** 'udder'; **strême** 'stirrup'; **séme** 'seed'; **brême** 'burden'; **tême** 'crown (of head)'; **ráme** 'shoulder'.

The noun **ráme** is now considered archaic and is normally only used in the plural. The modern word for shoulder is **ráma**.

(c) The extension **-s-**
A small number of commonly used nouns in **-o** and one in **-e** add the extension **-s-** in their oblique cases. In nouns in **-o** the **-o- > -e-** before the **-s-**, e.g.

		sing.	*dual*	*plural*
N		teló 'body'	telési	telésa
G		telésa	telés	telés
D		telésu	telésoma	telésom
A		teló	telési	telésa
L	pri	telésu	telésih	telésih
I	s	telésom	telésoma	telési

The other nouns in the category are: **črevó** 'intestine'; **koló** 'bicycle'; **peró** 'feather'; **slovó** 'farewell'; **drevó** 'tree'; **ojé** 'shaft'.

The noun **črevó** declines normally with the extension **-s-** in the singular, but not in the plural, where **čréva** is used to indicate food or gut, e.g. **strúne iz črév** 'strings made of gut'. The collective noun **črevésje** is normally used as the plural of **črevó**.

The nouns **uhó** 'ear'; **okó** 'eye'; and **igó** 'yoke' also belong to this category but the velar consonant preceding **-o-** undergoes patalisation (see **1.9.1**) before **-es-**, e.g.

	singular		
N	uhó	okó	igó
G	ušésa	očésa	ižésa
D	ušésu	očésu	ižésu etc.

The normal plural of **okó** is **očí** (f.) (see **2.2.5**). The plural form **očésa** is used to mean 'the eyes of a potato' (**očésa na krompírju**) or 'corns on one's feet' (**kúrja očésa**).

Two other neuter nouns have the extension **-s-** but its use is limited. The noun **nebó** 'sky' has the extension **-s-** only in the plural with the meaning 'heavens' (i.e. **nebésa**). The noun **čúdo** 'miracle, wonder' has two plural forms; **čúda/čudésa**. The form **čudésa** is stylistically marked and would be used in such phrases as **sédem čudés svetá** 'the seven wonders of the world', whereas **čúda** would be used in phrases like **čúda sodôbne medicíne** 'the miracles of modern medicine'.

2.18   IRREGULAR NEUTER DECLENSIONS

The *pluralia tantum* nouns **tlà** 'floor' and **drva** 'firewood' have the following irregular declension:

		plural		
N		tlà		dŕva
G		tál		dŕv
D		tlóm		dŕvom
A		tlà		dŕva
L	pri	tléh		drvéh/dŕvih
I	s	tlémi	z	drvmí/dŕvi

The noun **dnò** 'bottom' declines in the singular and most of the plural like **mésto**.

In the gen. plur. and loc. plur., however, it has the forms **dnòv** and **dnéh**. It is not normally used in the dual form.

2.19   ADJECTIVES USED AS NOUNS

Adjectives used as nouns retain their adjectival declension and may be of any gender. They usually denote persons, but may also denote objects. In the case of the nominative singular masculine only the definite form of the adjective in **-i** is used. Most adjectives used as nouns result from the omission of the qualified noun, which is understood from the context, e.g.

Dežúrni (učítelj) je vstópil v rázred
The duty teacher entered the class

Obtóženi (člôvek) je priznál svôje dejánje
The accused admitted his crime

frizêr za môške (ljudí)
a men's hairdresser

Z désno (rôko) sem se prijél za ográjo, z lévo (rôko) sem dŕžal vréčo
With my right hand I caught hold of the fence, with my left I held the bag

S kôpnega je píhal véter
A wind blew from the shore

Umŕli (člôvek) ní narédil oporóke
The dead man did not make a will

Njegôva rájna (žêna) je bilà dôbra žénska
His late wife was a good woman

Síti (člôvek) láčnemu (človéku) ne verjáme
A sated man does not believe a hungry man

Masculine personal names in **-ski**, and place names in **-sko, -ško, -ska, ška** (e.g. **Gorénjsko** 'Upper Carniola', **Kŕško, Kitájska** 'China', **Nórveška** 'Norway') also decline like adjectives (see **3.10**). The masculine and neuter forms decline regularly, e.g. **Ne poznám Koséskega** 'I don't know Koseski'; **Domá sem iz Kŕškega** 'I come from Krško'.

Feminine place names, however, decline like feminine adjectives in the acc./gen./loc. sing. if they are used with the prepositions **v** (+ acc.), **iz** (+ gen.), **v** (+ loc.) but like neuter adjectives in the acc./gen./loc. sing. if they are used with the prepositions **na** (+ acc.), **z** (+ gen.), **na** (+ loc.), e.g.

Môja sêstra gré na Kitájsko/v Kitájsko
My sister is going to China

Prišlà je iz Gorénjske/z Gorénjskega
She came from Carniola

V Póljski/Na Póljskem je lepó
It is beautiful in Poland

2.20 USE OF CASES

The basic use of the cases is as follows:

(a) Nominative
The nominative is used as:

   (i)   The subject of the action or state, e.g. **Sêstra bêre** 'The sister is reading'; **Otrôci se igrájo** 'The children are playing'

   (ii) A complement after link verbs like **bíti** 'to be' and the verbs **postáti** 'to become'; **imenováti se** 'to be called'; **pisáti se** 'to be surnamed', e.g. **Kònj je živál** 'A horse is an animal'; **Postála sta prijátelja** 'They(d) became friends'; **Píšem se Novák** 'My name is Novak'.

   (iii) A noun in apposition to various generic terms such as 'book', 'film', 'cinema' etc., which may be in any of the cases, e.g. **Knjígo 'Tríje mušketírji' je napísal Dumas** 'Dumas wrote the book "The Three

Musketeers"'; **Fílm 'Títanik' so vrtéli v kínu 'Únion'** 'They showed the film "Titanic" at the "Union" cinema'; **Stanújem v hotélu Turíst** 'I am staying in the hotel "Tourist"'.

(iv) The vocative: **Natákar, jedílni líst, prósim** 'Waiter! May I have a menu please?'

(b) Genitive
The genitive is used to denote the following:

(i) The subject of the negated verb **bíti** 'to be' when it is used as a full meaning verb, e.g. **Očéta ní domá** 'Father is not at home'; **Jájc ní biló v hladílniku** 'There were no eggs in the fridge'

(ii) The direct object of a negated transitive verb, e.g.

Ne vídim híše	I cannot see the house
Náši sosédi nímajo avtomobíla	Our neighbours do not have a car
Nísem čákal ávtobusa	I did not wait for the bus
Níso povabíli tújih strokovnjákov na kongrés	They did not invite foreign experts to the congress
Tù ne prodájajo zelenjáve	They don't sell vegetables here
Ne bóm objávil svôjih spomínov	I will not publish my memoirs

(iii) The case governed by certain reflexive verbs, e.g.

Vnapréj se veselím počítnic	I am looking forward to the holidays
Navelíčala se je čévljev z visôkimi pêtami	She got fed up with high heeled shoes
Môja sêstra se bojí pájkov	My sister is afraid of spiders
Dodôbra smo se naužíli svéžega zráka	We thoroughly enjoyed the fresh air
učíti se mizárstva	to study joinery
Sramúje se svôje lahkovérnosti	He is ashamed of his gullibility
Z glávo se je dotíkal strôpa	His head touched the ceiling

(iv) The logical subject of the impersonal verbs **zmanjkováti** (perf. **zmánjkati**) 'to run out of'; **primanjkováti** 'to be short of, not have enough of', e.g.

Govórcu je zmanjkrválo beséd	Words failed the speaker
Sladkórja zmanjkúje	The sugar is running out
Za táko trdítev minístru primanjkúje dokázov	The minister does not have enough proof for such an assertion

Vôde primanjkúje	There is not enough water
Krúha je zmánjkalo	There was no bread to be had

(v) An object with a partitive meaning following transitive verbs, e.g.

Dàj mi krúha	Give me some bread
Otrôku je dála mléka	She gave some milk to the child
Máma je natočíla vôde v kopálno kàd	Mum poured some water into the bathtub

(vi) The measured noun after certain numerals, nouns and adverbs denoting a measure or amount, e.g. **skodélica káve** 'a cup of coffee'; **pét študêntov** 'five students'; **nékaj dní** 'a few days'; **pólna žlíca móke** 'a spoonful of flour'; **Kóliko známk?** 'How many stamps?'

(vii) Various relationships between one noun group and another, especially possession, authorship, connection, belonging:

Possession and authorship are normally indicated by a possessive adjective formed from the noun, e.g. **stríčev ávto** 'uncle's car'; **sosédova híša** 'the neighbour's house'; **Spielbergov film** 'Spielberg's film'.

If, however, the noun is qualified by an attributive adjective or a possessive pronoun, or if a christian name is used with a surname then a genitive construction is used. A genitive construction is also used if a possessive adjective cannot be formed from a noun, e.g. **híša môjega prijátelja** 'my friend's house'; **koló lépe púnce** 'the pretty girl's bike'; **film Stephena Spielberga** 'Stephen Spielberg's film'; **Móst vzdihljájev** 'The Bridge of Sighs'.

If authorship is not of one person in particular but very general, this may be indicated by the use of the simple genitive, e.g. **obtôžbe študêntov** 'the accusations of the students'; **upòr Albáncev** 'the Albanian uprising'.

Note: Such phrases as these may also be translated with classifying adjectives in **-ski/-ški**, e.g. **študêntske obtôžbe**; **albánski upòr**. The difference between the two is that the genitive construction emphasises 'the students', 'the Albanians', whereas the adjectival construction puts emphasis on 'the accusations', 'the uprising'.

Belonging and other relationships, e.g. part of, type of, subject or object of verbal noun are also indicated by the genitive, e.g.

člán sindikáta	member of a trade union
stréha avtomobíla	the roof of a car
plême Indijáncev	a tribe of Indians
típ avtomobíla	a type of car
vŕsta pšeníce	a variety of wheat

rezgetánje kónj	the neighing of horses
odstranjevánje odpádkov	the removal of waste
izkoríščanje atómske energíje	the use of atomic energy
poslédice popláv	the consequences of the floods
vónj cvetlíc	the smell of flowers
čút okúsa	the sense of taste

(viii) The case governed by certain adjectives, e.g.

Sìt sem čakánja	I am tired of waiting
Vájen sem mráza	I am used to the cold
Bíl je póln jéze	He was filled with rage
Bilà si je svésta nevárnosti	She was aware of the danger

(ix) An adverbial phrase of time or manner, e.g. **Vŕnil se bom apríla** 'I shall return in April'; **Umŕl je nágle smŕti** 'He died a sudden death'.

(x) A descriptive attribute qualified by an adjective following the verb **bíti** 'to be', e.g.

Móž je srédnje postáve	He is a man of medium build
Mídva sva ístih lét	We are the same age
Mój koléga je slábega zdrávja	My colleague is in poor health
Profésor je dánes dôbre vólje	The professor is in a good mood today

(xi) The case governed by certain prepositions (see Chapter 8 Prepositions).

(c) Dative

The dative case is used to denote the following:

(i) The indirect object of transitive verbs, i.e. the person for whom the action is performed, the recipient, the beneficiary, e.g.

Sínu je dála denár za kíno	She gave her son money for the cinema
Telefoníral sem sêstri	I telephoned my sister
Posláli bomo brzojávko tvôjemu brátu	We will send your brother a telegram
Koló sem posódil prijátelju	I lent the bike to a friend
Nêsi očétu časopís	Take your father the newspaper

(ii) The direct object of certain verbs and the verbal nouns derived from these verbs, e.g.

upírati se nasílju	to resist violence
upíranje nasílju	resistance to violence
Kajênje škodúje zdrávju	Smoking damages your health

za lás uíti nevárnosti	to escape danger by a hair's breadth
Hčí pomága máteri v kúhinji	The daughter helps her mother in the kitchen
pomóč nèrazvítim dežêlam	help for undeveloped countries
Čudíli so se njegóvemu neródnemu vedênju	They were surprised at his uncouth behaviour

(iii) The case governed by certain adjectives and by the predicative **kós** 'equal to', e.g.

Fànt je podóben očétu	The boy takes after his father
Té snoví so škodljíve zdrávju	These substances are detrimental to one's health
Òn je bíl zvést svôji obljúbi	He was true to his promise
Délavec ní kós téj nalógi	The workman is not equal to this task

(iv) The logical subject of certain impersonal constructions denoting a state of mind, feeling or attitude, e.g.

V ávtobusu je učêncu védno slabó	The pupil always feels ill in the bus
Têtki bo ljúbo, če jo boste obiskáli	Auntie will be pleased if you visit her
Med predstávo je študêntu postálo dólgčas	The student got bored during the performance
Májdi ní dôbro	Majda does not feel well
Učítelju je žàl fánta, ki je takó osámljen	The teacher feels sorry for the boy who is so lonely
Jánezu se spì	Janez is sleepy

(v) The logical subject of certain verbs used reflexively and impersonally, e.g.

Otrôku se je ponôči blêdlo	The child was delirious in the night
Knéžni se je sánjalo o vítezu	The princess dreamt about a knight
Jánezu se kólca	Janez has hiccups

(vi) The logical subject of the predicative constructions **bíti všéč** 'to like'; **bíti már** 'to dislike', e.g.

Modêrne slíke očétu níso všéč	Father does not like modern paintings
Ali je bilà váši sêstri všéč tá bárva?	Did your sister like this colour?
Tá slúžba je délavcu málo már	The workman does not like this job

(vii) The case governed by certain prepositions (see Chapter 8 Prepositions).

(d) Accusative
The accusative case denotes:

(i) The direct object of a transitive verb, e.g.

Snažílka je posprávila sôbo	The cleaning lady tidied the room
V nedéljo smo glédali tékmo	On Sunday we watched the match
Grém obískat znánca v bólnico	I am going to visit an acquaintance in hospital
Mídva imáva psà	We (d.) have a dog

Note: The verb **učíti** 'to teach' may take two direct objects in the accusative, e.g. **Púnco učím angléščino** 'I teach the girl English'.

(ii) The logical subject in certain impersonal constructions, e.g.

Učíteljico je biló stráh za otrôke	The teacher was afraid for the children
Vojáka je srám izrážati svôja čústva	The soldier is ashamed to express his feelings
Métko zébe	Metka is cold
Bolníka je grôza pred bolečínami	The patient is afraid of pains
Jóžeta je biló stráh	Jože was afraid

(iii) Adverbial phrases of time and duration, e.g.

Célo nóč se je premetávala po póstelji	All night long she tossed and turned in bed
Vsáko léto nas obíšče	He visits us every year
Vsò pót sta molčála	The two of them were silent for the whole journey

(iv) Cost, weight, measure, e.g.

Knjíga me je stála tísoč tólarjev	The book cost me a thousand tolars
Novorojênček je téhtal trí kilográme	The new-born child weighed three kilograms
Ôkno je širôko dvá čévlja	The window is two feet wide

(v) The case governed by certain prepositions (see Chapter 8 Prepositions).

(e) Locative and instrumental
These two cases are only used with prepositions (see Chapter 8 Prepositions).

2.21 THE STRESS OF NOUNS

(a) Masculine nouns
Masculine nouns are divided into the following types according to stress:

(i) Nouns with fixed stress
Most masculine nouns ending in a consonant and all those ending in a vowel have a fixed stress e.g. **délavec** 'worker'; **krompír** 'potato'; **trgóvec** 'merchant'; **kíno** 'cinema'; **delovódja** 'foreman'.

(ii) Nouns with a mobile stress
There are about seventy polysyllabic (usually disyllabic) nouns in which the stress is on the first syllable in the nominative and inanimate accusative singular (on the penultimate in trisyllabic nouns), but moves one syllable forward in the oblique cases, e.g. **bôžič** 'Christmas', gen. sing. **božíča**.

The most common nouns in this category are: **jêzik** 'language'; **jêsen** 'ashtree'; **člôvek** 'man'; **petêlin** 'cock'; **prêmog** 'coal'; **sôsed** 'neighbour'; **zákon** 'law'; **žêlod** 'acorn'; **prêdmet** 'object'; **slôves** 'reputation'; **šôtor** 'tent'; **tôvor** 'load'; **mêdved** 'bear'; **jêrmen** 'strap'; **kôžuh** 'fur coat'; **krêmen** 'flint'; **prêdlog** 'proposal'; **prêrok** 'profit'; **jêlen** 'stag'; **ôtok** 'island'; **prôstor** 'space'; **rázred** 'classroom'; **pêlin** 'wormwood'; **trébuh** 'belly'; **závod** 'institution'; **zárod** 'progeny'; **rázlog** 'reason'; **dúal** 'dual'; **rázor** 'furrow'; **tôpol** 'popular'; **prêstol** 'throne'; **pôtok** 'brook'; **cêsar** 'emperor'; **jêčmen** 'barley'; **strêmen** 'stirrup'; **kôstanj** 'chestnut'; **pôrok** 'guarantor'; **pôkoj** 'peace'; **ôreh** 'nut'; **pêhar** 'straw basket'; **plámen** 'flame'; **sôkol** 'falcon'; **náhod** 'cold'; **mêdmet** 'interjection'; **názor** 'opinion'; **zástor** 'curtain'.

(iii) Monosyllabic nouns with the infix -óv-
These nouns are stressed on the root in the singular, but on the infix -óv- in the dual and plural (see **2.11**), e.g. **rób** 'edge', gen. sing. **róba**, nom. pl. **robóvi**, nom. dual **robóva**.

(iv) The genitive singular ending -u used in some monosyllabic nouns is always stressed. In all other cases the stress remains on the root (unless the noun also takes the infix -óv- in the dual and plural (see above), e.g. **glád** 'hunger', gen. sing. **gladú**, dat. sing. **gládu**.

(v) In a few monosyllabic nouns the gen. sing. in -a is stressed. In all other cases the stress is on the root, e.g. **dólg** 'debt', gen. sing. **dolgá**, dat. sing. **dólgu**.
Other nouns in this category are **dúh** 'spirit'; **môž** 'man'; **snég** 'snow'; **svét** 'world'; **bóg** 'god'; **lés** 'wood'; **vóz** 'cart'.
The noun **hòd** 'walking' also has a stressed gen. sing. -á, when it is used to express quantity, e.g. **trí úre hodá** 'three hours walk'.

(vi) The nouns **lás** 'hair', **zób** 'tooth', **móž** 'man'
These nouns are stressed on the root in the singular (except the genitive) and the nom./acc. dual, but on the final syllable in the other cases of the dual and plural (see **2.11**).

(b) Feminine nouns
Most feminine nouns have a fixed stress, e.g. **lípa** 'lime tree', gen. sing. **lípe** etc. Exceptions are:

(i) A few disyllabic nouns in **-a** with **e** (= ə) in the first syllable, which have alternative stresses, e.g. **tèmà** 'darkness'; **mèglà** 'fog'; **stèzà** 'path'; **pèčkà** 'pip'.

Today in central Slovenia and Carniola there is a tendency for these nouns to be stressed on the first syllable, which is then pronounced as an open **ê**, e.g. **mêgla**.

(ii) Monosyllabic nouns which decline like **stvár** 'thing' (see **2.14**) are stressed on the root in the nom./acc./dat./loc. singular, but on the endings in all other cases.

(c) Neuter nouns
Most neuter nouns have a fixed stress, e.g. **mésto** 'town', gen. sing. **mésta**, dat. sing. **méstu** etc. Exceptions are:

(i) Neuter nouns in **-me** with the extension **-n-** in the oblique cases (see **2.19**). In these nouns the stress is on the root in the nom./acc. sing. and on the **-én-** in other cases. The only exceptions are **imé** 'name', which is stressed on the final **-é** in the nom./acc. sing. and **víme** 'udder' which is stressed on the root in all cases, e.g. gen. sing. **vímena**.

(ii) Most neuter nouns which add the extension **-t-** (see **2.17**) have a fixed stress throughout either on the root, e.g. **jágnje** 'lamb', gen. sing. **jágnjeta** or on the final **-e**, e.g. **ščenè** 'puppy', gen. sing. **ščenéta**. However, in the nouns **têle** 'calf' and **plêče** 'shoulder (of meat)' the stress moves from the root in the nom./acc. sing. to **-ét-** in all the oblique cases, e.g. gen. sing. **teléta**, **plečéta**.

(iii) A small number of neuter nouns in **-ó, -é** are stressed on the endings in the nom./acc./gen. sing., but on the root in all other cases, e.g.

	sing.	dual	plural
N	**srcé** 'heart'	**sŕci**	**sŕca**
G	**srcá**	**sŕc**	**sŕc**
D	**sŕcu**	**sŕcema**	**sŕcem**
A	**srcé**	**sŕci**	**sŕca**

L	pri	sŕcu	sŕcih	sŕcih
I	s	sŕcem	sŕcema	sŕci

Nouns in this category include: **blagó** 'goods'; **prosó** 'millet'; **nebó** 'sky'; **mesó** 'meat'; **zlató** 'gold'; **srebró** 'silver'; **testó** 'dough'; **senó** 'hay'.

3 ADJECTIVES

3.1 TYPES OF ADJECTIVE

In accordance with whether adjectives denote a quality, or relation or possession, they are divided into three types: qualitative adjectives, relational adjectives and possessive adjectives.

Qualitative adjectives form the majority of adjectives. They express the qualities possessed or exhibited by persons, things or abstract phenomena, e.g. **dóber** 'good', **slàb** 'bad', **sméšen** 'funny', **lép** 'beautiful', **gŕd** 'ugly', **stàr** 'old', **mlád** 'young', **bél** 'white', **glúh** 'deaf', **siròk** 'wide', **dêbel** 'fat' etc. Some adjectives express a quality in relation to another quality, e.g. **stàr** 'old' is only really understood by comparing the quality it expresses with the opposite quality expressed by the adjective **mlád** 'young'. In other words they do not express an absolute quality, but rather the speaker's comparative assessment of a given quality. This type of qualitative adjective occurs as one of a pair of antonyms and can express degrees of a quality, e.g. **lép** 'beautiful', **lépši** 'more beautiful', **nàjlépši** 'most beautiful'. Other qualitative adjectives express objectively observable facts and generally speaking cannot express degrees of a given quality (at least in their direct, non-figurative meanings), e.g. **bél** 'white', **šépav** 'lame', **mŕtev** 'dead', **nág** 'naked', **usáhel** 'withered'.

Relational adjectives express type, sort, class or numerical sequence, e.g. **lesén kríž** 'wooden cross'; **kémična spremémba** 'chemical change'; **prálni prášek** 'washing powder'; **angléški študènt** 'English student'; **dirkálni ávto** 'racing car'; **naslédnje léto** 'next year'; **sprédnja palúba** 'foredeck'.

Possessive adjectives denote that something or someone belongs to a given person, e.g.. **očétov klobúk** 'father's hat'; **têtin dežník** 'aunty's umbrella'; **stríčev ávto** 'uncle's car'; **učíteljeva družína** 'the teacher's family'; **učênčeva knjíga** 'the pupil's book'; **Maríjina tórba** 'Marija's bag'.

A special sub-class of possessive adjectives are generic possessives. Generic possessive adjectives denote that a given noun is characteristic of or relates to a class, i.e. possession is general and not special or specific, e.g. **môške hláče** 'men's trousers'; **ríbja koščíca** 'a fish bone'; **délavske híše** 'workers' houses'; **ptíčja klétka** 'a bird cage'.

3.2 USAGE

In Slovene adjectives may be used either attributively or predicatively. When used attributively they precede the noun, e.g. **mládi sín** 'the young son', **rdéče koló** 'the red bike'.

3.3 DECLENSION

Adjectives in Slovene, like nouns, distinguish gender, case and number, reflecting the gender, case and number of the noun they qualify. They decline as follows:

			m.	*f.*	*n.*
singular	N		nòv/nôvi 'new'	nôva	nôvo
	G		nôvega	nôve	nôvega
	D		nôvemu	nôvi	nôvemu
	A		nòv/nôvi, nôvega	nôvo	nôvo
	L	pri	nôvem	nôvi	nôvem
	I	z	nôvim	nôvo	nôvim
dual	N		nôva	nôvi	nôvi
	G		nôvih	nôvih	nôvih
	D		nôvima	nôvima	nôvima
	A		nôva	nôvi	nôvi
	L	pri	nôvih	nôvih	nôvih
	I	z	nôvima	nôvima	nôvima
plural	N		nôvi	nôve	nôva
	G		nôvih	nôvih	nôvih
	D		nôvim	nôvim	nôvim
	A		nôve	nôve	nôva
	L	pri	nôvih	nôvih	nôvih
	I	z	nôvimi	nôvimi	nôvimi

Note: Adjectives ending in **-c, -č, -ž, -š, -j** have **-e** instead of **-o** in the nom./acc. sing. neuter, e.g. **vróč** (m.), **vróča** (f.), **vróče** (n.) 'hot'; **túj** (m.), **túja** (f.), **túje** (n.) 'foreign'.

3.3.1 Fleeting vowels

Certain adjectives have in the final syllable in the nom. sing. masc. a fleeting vowel **e** (= ə) which disappears in all other cases. This fleeting **e** occurs between an obstruent/sonorant and a sonorant or between an obstruent/sonorant and **k**, e.g.

míren (m.)	**mírna** (f.)	**mírno** (n.)	peaceful
tôpel (m.)	**tôpla** (f.)	**tôplo** (n.)	warm

dóber (m.)	dôbra (f.)	dôbro (n.)	good
têžek (m.)	têžka (f.)	têžko (n.)	heavy

If, however, **e** in the final syllable is not a schwa then the **e** does not drop out in the other cases, e.g. **poštèn** (m.), **poštêna** (f.), **poštêno** (n.), 'honest' (as opposed to **póšten** (m.), **póštna** (f.), **póštno** (n.), 'postal').

A very few adjectives have a fleeting **a** in the final syllable. The only adjective, however, that always has a fleeting **a** is **bolán** (m.), **bólna** (f.), **bólno** (n.) 'sick'. Other adjectives in **-án, -ák, -ál** are merely alternative variants of those in **-en, -ek, -el**, e.g. **sládek/sladák** 'sweet', **hláden/hladán** 'cool', **svêtel/svetál** 'bright' etc. The forms with **a** are less usual or archaic, only three being used fairly regularly, i.e. **močán** 'strong', **težák** 'heavy', **želján** 'desirous of', e.g. **Òn je želján sláve** 'He seeks fame'.

3.3.2 The accusative singular masculine

In the accusative singular masculine the form of the adjective is either the same as that in the nominative singular or that in the genitive singular. The genitive form is used if the noun qualified is in the animate accusative/genitive (see **2.3**) while the nominative form is used if the noun qualified is in the inanimate accusative, e.g. **Péter imá nòv ávto** 'Peter has a new car' but **Péter imá nôvega prijátelja** 'Peter has a new friend'.

Examples of adjectival usage

> **nôva híša** 'a new house'; **sméšen dogódek** 'a funny incident'; **nôva stôla** 'two new chairs'; **dvé stári mízi** 'two old tables'; **z grômkim sméhom** 'with a loud laugh'; **mnógo slábih lastnósti** 'many bad qualities'; **Henry Ford je bíl sín írskega kméta** 'Henry Ford was the son of an Irish peasant'; **z vesóljskimi ládjami** 'with space ships'; **visôkima vojákoma** 'to the two tall soldiers'.

3.4 DEFINITE/INDEFINITE ADJECTIVES

In the nominative singular masculine adjectives distinguish between indefinite and definite forms. The definite form is used when the adjective refers to a known person or thing (i.e. English 'the') and the indefinite form is used when the adjective refers to an unknown person or thing (i.e. English 'a, an').

The definite form of the adjective is created by adding **-i** to the indefinite form, e.g. **mlád profésor** 'a young professor' but **mládi profésor** 'the young professor'.

In all cases other than the nom. sing. masc. there is no definite/indefinite distinction, e.g. **mláda púnca** 'a/the young girl'; **mládega profésorja** 'of a/the young professor'; **visôkemu vojáku** 'to a/the tall soldier'; **z lépo púnco** 'with a/the beautiful girl'.

Certain adjectives do not have an indefinite form in the nom. sing. masc., in which case the form in **-i** acts as either an indefinite or a definite adjective. Adjectives in this category are those in **-ski**, **-ški**, **-čki** and **-ji**, e.g. **slovénski** 'Slovene', **túrški** 'Turkish', **dívji** 'wild', **sínji** 'blue'. Therefore **sínji klobúk** may mean either 'a blue hat' or 'the blue hat' and **túrški časopís** may mean either 'a Turkish newspaper' or 'the Turkish newspaper'.

This category also includes the ordinal numbers (e.g. **pŕvi** 'first', **trétji** 'third') as well as comparatives and superlatives. A few other adjectives also have only nom. sing. masc. forms in **-i**. These are **právi** 'real, true', **désni** 'right', **lévi** 'left', **óbči** 'general', **rájni** 'deceased'.

Only two adjectives express the opposition definite–indefinite in all cases. These are the adjectives **májhen** (m.), **májhna** (f.), **májhno** (n.) 'small' (indefinite) and **vêlik** (m.), **velíka** (f.), **velíko** (n.) 'large' (indefinite). The definite form of **májhen** is the suppletive form – **máli** (m.), **mála** (f.), **málo** (n.) and the definite form of **vêlik** is created by a change in vowel quality and a stress shift, i.e **véliki** (m.), **vélika** (f.), **véliko** (n.), e.g.

Imá vêlik talènt	He has a great talent
Véliki slovénski pésnik Prešéren	The great Slovene poet Prešeren
májhen vŕt	a small garden
máli kazálec	the small hand (of a clock)

3.4.1 Obligatory use of the masculine definite form

(a) Obligatory use of the masculine definite form occurs if the adjective forms a whole with the noun it qualifies, i.e. it modifies the noun's meaning as in technical expressions, etc., e.g.

sádni vŕt	a/the orchard
but	
lép vŕt	a beautiful garden
pótni líst	a/the passport
jedílni líst	a/the menu
but	
číst líst	a clean sheet of paper
účni načŕt	a/the syllabus
but	
nòv načŕt	a new plan
šiválni stròj	a/the sewing machine
prálni stròj	a/the washing machine
but	
kompliciran stròj	a complicated machine

Véliki Mêdved	the Great Bear (the constellation)
béli mêdved	a/the polar bear
sívi mêdved	a/the grizzly bear
but	
môčen mêdved	a powerful bear

It should be noted that these fixed expressions with obligatory nom. sing. forms in **-i** may be made indefinite or definite by a preceding adjective, e.g. **nòv pótni líst** 'a new passport' but **nôvi pótni líst** 'the new passport'.

(b) Obligatory use of the masc. nom. sing. definite form occurs after possessive adjectives, possessive pronouns, demonstrative pronouns and the pronoun **vès** 'all', e.g.

očétov nôvi klobúk	father's new hat
tá prijétni vónj	this pleasant smell
njén nôvi učítelj	her new teacher
vès dólgi téden	all week long
vès prôsti čás	all spare time

(c) The nom. sing. masc. definite form of the adjective must be used if the adjective is used substantivally, e.g.

Kjé je dežúrni?	Where is the man on duty?
Obtóženi je priznál svój zločín	The accused man admitted his guilt
Blažè imá sív in rjàv plášč. Sívi je precéj ogúljen, rjávi je pa šè lép	Blaže has a grey coat and a brown coat. The grey one is rather shabby but the brown one is still in good condition

3.4.2 The indefinite form

The indefinite form has to be used in the predicate, e.g.

Fànt je mlád	The boy is young
Otrôk je bíl védno láčen	The child was always hungry
Zràk je bíl góst od cigarétnega díma	The air was thick with cigarette smoke

If an adjective has no separate indefinite form then the form in **-i** is used in the predicate, e.g. **Klobúk je sínji** 'The hat is blue'.

3.5 AGREEMENT OF THE PREDICATIVE ADJECTIVE

The predicative adjective agrees with a single subject in number and gender, e.g.

Híša je májhna	The house is small
Študênti so prizadévni	The students are ambitious
Dvé lopáti sta têžki	The two spades are heavy

If the subject consists of two separate nouns of the same gender then agreement should be as for the dual. If, however, one of the two nouns is masculine or if the two noun subjects are feminine and neuter then the predicative adjective is masculine dual, e.g.

Zdravník in bolník sta pléšasta	The doctor and patient are bald
Študêntka in njéna prijáteljica sta lépi	The student and her friend are beautiful
Peró in ravnílo sta nôvi	The pen and ruler are new
Klét in podstréšje sta hládna	The cellar and the attic are cold
Zdravník in bólničarka sta zdráva	The doctor and the nurse are healthy
Hrúška in jábolko sta gníla	The pear and apple are rotten

Note: Colloquially a subject consisting of two separate neuter nouns may also have masculine dual agreement in the predicative adjective, e.g. **Têle in jágnje sta bólna** 'The calf and the lamb are sick'.

If the subject is plural and consists of two or more nouns (in the singular, dual or plural) then the predicative adjective agrees in gender if the nouns are of the same gender. If, however, one of the nouns is masculine or if the nouns are a combination of neuter and feminine nouns then agreement is always masculine plural, e.g.

Njegóvo čêlo in líca so tetovírana	His forehead and cheeks are tattooed
Zdravník in bólničarke so prídni	The doctor and the nurses are hard working
Hrúške, jábolka in čéšnje so zréli	The pears, apples and cherries are ripe
Kljúčnica in dvé rêbri so zlómljeni	The collar-bone and two ribs are broken
Jétra in ledvíce so inficírani	The liver and kidneys are infected

Note: Colloquially the agreement of the predicative adjective may also be with the final noun if the subject consists of a combination of neuter and feminine nouns, e.g. **Hrúške, jábolka in čéšnje so zréle** 'The pears, apples and cherries are ripe'; **Ôvce in jágnjeta so zdráva** 'The sheep and lambs are healthy'.

3.6   COLLOQUIAL FORMS OF DEFINITE AND INDEFINITE ADJECTIVES

Colloquially the number **èn** 'one' is used with the adjective to express 'a, an' and the invariable article **ta** is used with the adjective to express 'the'. If **ta** is used with the nom. sing. masc of the adjective then this takes the indefinite form, e.g.

béli súknjič/ta bél súknjič
the white jacket

Mládi/ta mlád laboránt je pa rés dóber
The young laboratory assistant is really good

Kakó raznobárvni so šotóri! Katéri je vàš? Oránžni/Ta oránžen. Pa oránžna sta dvá, èn stàr in èn nòv. Nò, nôvi/ta nòv je nàš
The tents are so differently coloured! Which is yours? The orange one. But there are two orange tents, an old one and a new one. Well, the new one is ours

Oblékla je ta nôvo obléko
She put on the new dress

Pozími bo nôsil ta visôke čévlje
In winter he will wear the high boots

3.7   THE SO-CALLED 'ORPHAN' ACCUSATIVE

When the accusative of a masculine adjective is used in the direct object position without an accompanying noun and refers to a previously mentioned inanimate object, it is treated as animate and appears in the animate accusative genitive case. In English this accusative is often translated by 'one', e.g.

Môji sosédi imájo dvá ávta, ênega rdéčega in ênega zelênega
My neighbours have two cars – a red one and a green one

Podŕl je lástni svetóvni rekórd in postávil nôvega
He broke his own world record and set a new one

Na mízi sta dvá časopísa, ênega sem žé prebrál
There are two newspapers on the table, one of which I have already read

In the older language neuter adjectives were treated in the same way but in the modern language neuter adjectives now appear in the inanimate accusative form, e.g.

Kákšno pívo želíte, véliko ali málo?
What sort of beer do you want, a large one or a small one?

Colloquially, however, one may encounter examples such as the following:

Katéro koló želíte – rdéč(e)ga ali pláv(e)ga?
Which bike do you want – the red or the blue?

Note: The neuter adjective will automatically appear in the genitive case if the verb is negated, e.g. **Na izpítu sem dobíl tri vprašánja, a nobênega nísem razúmel** 'I got three questions at the exam and I couldn't understand one of them'.

3.8   POSSESSIVE ADJECTIVES

Possessive adjectives are formed from nouns by means of the suffixes **-ov/-ev**, **-in**. These adjectives are inherently definite and do not take **-i** in the nom. sing. masculine. The suffix **-ov/-ev** forms possessive adjectives from masculine and neuter nouns (**-ev** is used if the noun ends in **-c, -č, -š, -ž**, or **-j**) and the suffix **-in** forms possessive adjectives from feminine nouns, e.g. **očétov** 'father's', **stríčev** 'uncle's', **brátov** 'brother's', **trenêrjev** 'trainer's', **slônov** 'elephant's', **deklétov** 'girl's', **sêstrin** 'sister's', **têtin** 'aunty's'.

3.9   INDECLINABLE ADJECTIVES

A small number of adjectives in Slovene are not declined. They are mostly loanwords, and include the following: **róza** 'pink', **pocéni** 'cheap', **súper** 'super', **príma** 'first class', **dráp** 'light brown', **béž** 'beige', **fêr** 'fair', **séksi** 'sexy', **têšč** 'empty' (of stomach), **šík** 'chic', **žàl** 'bad'. The latter adjective is only used with the words **beséda** 'word' and **mísel** 'thought'.

Examples of usage

pocéni knjíga	a cheap book
fêr ígra	fair play
Žrebčárna imá príma kônje	The stud farm has first-class horses
šík obléka	chic clothes
s têšč želódci	with empty stomachs
séksi púnca	a sexy girl
róza blagó	pink material

na têšč želodec

3.10   SUBSTANTIVISED ADJECTIVES

In Slovene some adjectives function as nouns. They have arisen as a result of ellipsis, i.e. the omission of the noun qualified in the original expression, e.g. **môški** 'man' from **môški člôvek** 'male person', **rájna** 'deceased wife' from **rájna žéna**.

Substantivised adjectives may be classified as follows:

(a)   Those which designate persons, e.g. **môški** 'man' – **frizêr za môške** 'men's hairdresser'; **popótni** 'traveller' – **V tèmnem gózdu so popótnega napádli róparji** 'In the dark forest robbers attacked the traveller'; **dežúrna** 'duty nurse' – **Šèl sem k dežúrni**, 'I went to see the duty nurse' (see also **2.19**).

Note: The noun **žénska** 'woman' was originally the adjective in the phrase **žénska oséba** 'female person', but today it declines like a feminine noun in **-a**, e.g. **Razlíke med môškimi in** žénskami, 'The difference between men and women'; **Govorím o žénskah, ne o môških**, 'I am speaking about women, not about men'.

(b) Adjectives in **-ska, -ška** which designate countries (e.g. **Japónska** 'Japan', **Nórveška** 'Norway', **Kitájska** 'China', etc.) or regions in Slovenia (e.g. **Koróška** 'Carinthia', **Štájerska** 'Styria', **Primórska** 'The Littoral').

These place names decline like fem. adjectives except when used with the prepositions **na** + loc. and **s/z** + gen. indicating place where and motion from. In these instances these substantivised adjectives denoting place names decline like neuter adjectives. Strictly speaking they also decline like a neuter adjective after the preposition **na** + acc. indicating motion towards, but the neuter acc. sing. form of the adjective is anyway identical with the feminine acc. sing. form of the adjective. Where motion to or from, or location are involved the modern language favours the use of the prepositions **na** + acc., **iz** + gen. and **na** + loc. with these place names. The alternative use of the prepositions **v** + acc., **s/z** + gen. and **v** + loc. is possible but much rarer, e.g.

Gréva na Koróško/Kitájsko	We (d.) are going to Carinthia/China
Na Kitájskem je velíko ljudí	There are many people in China
Štájerska je hribovíta pokrájina	Styria is a hilly region
Prišlà je iz Gorénjske/z Gorénjskega	She came from Carniola
Kitájska zavída Japónski njén uspèh	China envies Japan its success
Zméraj govorí o Švédski	He is always talking about Sweden (see also **2.19**).

(c) Masculine surnames in **-ski**, e.g. **Koséski, Čajkóvski, Milčínski** and women's surnames in **-va**, e.g. **Málenškova, Černéjeva** which were originally possessive forms and derive from the original forms **Málenškova žêna, Černéjeva žêna**, i.e. 'Mr Malenšek's wife, Mr Černej's wife'.

Njén ôče pozná Koséskega	Her father knows Koseski
Govóril sem z Málenškovo	I was talking to Mrs Malenšek

(d) Street names in **-a** which arise as a result of the omission of the noun **úlica** 'street' (e.g. **Župančičeva, Kopítarjeva, Strítarjeva**).

Òn stanúje na Kopítarjevi 5	He lives at number 5 Kopitar Street
Grém v Župančičevo	I am going to Župančič Street

(e) The neuter forms **kôpno** 'mainland', **pláno** 'the open', e.g.

S kôpnega je píhal véter	A wind blew from the mainland
Spáli so na plánem	They slept in the open
Posádka je bilà na kôpnem várna	The crew was safe on shore

3.11 THE ADJECTIVE **ràd**

This adjective has only nominative forms for all genders and numbers. It is used in two ways: (a) with the verb **iméti** to mean 'to like, love'; (b) with other verbs to denote that the subject of the verb likes doing what the verb indicates. The adjective **ràd** always agrees with the subject in gender and number, e.g.

Òn imá ràd glásbo	He likes music
Môje sêstre imájo ráde glásbo	My sisters like music
Ônadva ráda délata	They (d.m.) like to work
Otrôci se rádi igrájo	The children like to play
Zeló ráda bi se poročíla	She would like to get married

3.12 CASES GOVERNED BY PREDICATIVE ADJECTIVES

Some adjectives when used in the predicate after a link verb may be followed by the oblique case of a noun or pronoun or by a prepositional phrase. The following is an illustrative list of adjectives governing various cases:

Genitive: **láčen** 'hungry for'; **póln** 'full of'; **sìt** 'sated with'; **vréden** 'worthy of'; **želján** 'desirous of'; **vájen** 'used to'; **krív** 'guilty of'; **deléžen** 'participating in'

Dative: **zvést** 'faithful, true to', **škodljív** 'harmful to', **podóben** 'similar to, like', **hvaléžen** 'grateful to', **nevoščljív** 'jealous of'

Prepositional phrases: **nòr na** + acc. 'mad about'; **jézen na** + acc. 'angry with'; **bolán od** + gen. 'sick with'; **pohlépen po** + loc. 'greedy for'; **bogàt z** + instr. 'rich in'

Examples of usage

Njén sín je láčen ljubézni
Her son is hungry for love

Stvár ní vrédna omémbe
The thing is not worthy of mention

Ostál je zvést svôjim načêlom
He remained faithful to his principles

Tobák je škodljív zdrávju
Tobacco is harmful to the health

Ali si tí krív nesréče?
Are you guilty of the accident?

Bíl mu je nevoščljív za uspèh
He was jealous of his success

Njegóv bràt je bolán od ljubosúmnosti
His brother is sick with envy

Vsè žénske so nôre nánj
All the women are wild about him

Zêmlja je bogáta z náfto
The land is rich in oil

3.13 THE NEGATIVE PREFIX nè-

The prefix **nè-** is added to adjectives to give them the opposite meaning and is equivalent to English in-, im-, un-, dis-, e.g. **(nè)deljív** '(in)divisible', **(nè)demokrátičen** '(un)democratic', **(nè)vljúden** '(im)polite', **(nè)spoštljív** '(dis)respectful'.

3.14 THE COMPARATIVE DEGREE

Most adjectives which denote the quality of something may form comparatives, which may be used either attributively or in the predicate as a complement after a link verb. In Slovene the comparative is formed either by means of the following derivational suffixes: **-ši** (m.), **-ša** (f.), **-še** (n.); **-ji** (m.), **-ja** (f.), **-je** (n.); **-ejši** (m.), **-ejša** (f.), **-ejše** (n.) or by analytical means using the comparative adverbial forms **bôlj** 'more' or **mànj** 'less' together with the positive form of the adjective.

3.15 COMPARATIVES FORMED BY DERIVATIONAL MEANS

(a) The suffix -ši, -ša, -še

   (i) This suffix is used to form the comparative of monosyllabic adjectives ending in **-d**, **-p**, **-b** preceded by a vowel or a vocalic **r**. In the case of adjectives ending in **-p** or **-b** the suffix is simply added to the masculine indefinite form. In the case of monosyllabic adjectives ending in **-d** this final **-d** changes to **-j** if it follows a vowel and the suffix **-ši** is then added to the **-j**. If the **-d** follows a vocalic **r** then the **-d** drops out and the suffix **-ši** is added to the **r**, e.g.

ljúb – ljúbši	dearer	**húd – hújši**	worse
lép – lépši	more beautiful	**ràd – rájši**	more glad
sláb – slábši	worse	**gŕd – gŕši**	uglier
mlád – mlájši	younger	**tŕd – tŕši**	harder

Note, however, the exception **bléd – bledéjši** 'paler'.

(ii) The suffix **-ši** is also used to form the comparative of the following adjectives in **-ok**, **-ek**. In these adjectives the suffixes **-ok**, **-ek** are dropped and consonant changes take place in the root (i.e. **n > nj**; **d/t > j**):

širòk – šírši	wider	**sládek – slájši**	sweeter
krátek – krájši	shorter	**tának – tánjši**	thinner

(iii) The suffix **-ši** is used in the suppletive comparative forms of the adjectives **dóber** 'good', **májhen** 'small' **dólg** 'long', i.e. **bóljši** 'better', **mánjši** 'smaller', **dáljši** 'longer'.

(iv) The adjectives **zál** 'pretty' and **zèl** 'evil' have the comparative forms **záljši** 'prettier', **zléjši** 'more evil'.

(b) The suffix **-ji**, **-ja**, **-je**

(i) The suffix **-ji** is used to form the comparatives of monosyllabic adjectives ending in a velar consonant: **-g**, **-k**, **-h**. These velar consonants change to **-ž**, **-č**, **-š** respectively before the suffix **-ji**, e.g.

drág – drážji	dearer
tíh – tíšji	quieter
blág – blážji	milder
stróg – stróžji	stricter
ják – jáčji	stronger (this adjective is now considered archaic and is normally replaced by **môčen**)

(ii) The suffix **-ji** is used to form the comparative of the following adjectives in **-ok**, **-ek**. These adjectives drop the suffixes **-ok**, **-ek** and subsequent consonant changes may occur in the root, e.g.

têžek – téžji	heavier	**láhek – lážji**	easier
blízek – blížji	nearer	**nízek – nížji**	lower
ózek – óžji	narrower	**visòk – víšji**	higher
globòk – glóblji	deeper		

(iii) The suffix **-ji** is also used in the suppletive comparative form of the adjective **vêlik** 'large', i.e. **véčji** 'larger'.

(c) The suffix **-ejši**, **-ejša**, **-ejše**
This suffix is used to form the comparative of:

(i) Monosyllabic adjectives ending in vowel plus consonant other than **-b**, **-p**, **-d**, e.g.

nòv – novéjši	newer
stàr – staréjši	older

krút – krútejši crueller
fín – finéjši finer

(ii) Monosyllabic adjectives ending in more than one consonant, e.g.

góst – gostéjši thicker   **póln – pólnejši** fuller
číst – čistéjši cleaner   **stŕm – stŕmejši** steeper
čvŕst – čvrstéjši firmer

(iii) Polysyllabic adjectives, e.g.

grênek – grenkéjši more bitter
krêpek – krepkéjši stronger
neváren – nevárnejši more dangerous
dêbel – debeléjši fatter
umljív – umljívejši more intelligible
tôpel – topléjši warmer
vesél – veseléjši happier
klávrn – klávrnejši more depressed
grôzen – grôznejši more dreadful

Note: If the adjective ends in a syllable containing the fleeting vowel **e** (= ə) then this **e** drops out before the suffix **-ejši**.

(iv) The indeclinable adjective **pocéni** 'cheap' has a declinable comparative form **cenéjši** 'cheaper'.

3.16 ANALYTICAL MEANS OF COMPARISON

Adjectives which form comparatives with the aid of the adverbs **bôlj** 'more', **mànj** 'less' are the following five types:

(a) Adjectives which do not have an indefinite form in the nom. sing. masculine, e.g. **dívji** 'wild' – **bôlj dívji** 'wilder', **mànj dívji** 'less wild'

(b) Adjectives derived from verbal participles, e.g.

umázan 'dirty' – **bôlj umázan** 'dirtier'
vróč 'hot' – **bôlj vróč** 'hotter'
uvél 'faded' – **bôlj uvél** 'more faded'
razvít 'developed' – **bôlj razvít** 'more developed', **mànj razvít** 'less developed'

(c) Adjectives derived with the suffixes **-ast**, **-at**, **-av**, e.g.

trávnat 'grassy' – **bôlj trávnat** 'more grassy'
múhast/múhav 'capricious' – **bôlj múhast/múhav** 'more capricious, temperamental'

(d)   Colour adjectives, e.g. **bél** 'white' – **bôlj bél** 'whiter'

(e)   Certain individual adjectives which include the following:

móker	wet	**sìt**	sated
súh	dry	**ráven**	level
túj	foreign	**jézen**	angry
zdràv	healthy	**krív**	guilty
lén	lazy	**žív**	alive

e.g. **bôlj zdráva živál** 'a healthier animal'; **mànj sìt** 'less sated'

Note: It should also be added that qualitative adjectives very frequently form their comparatives by analytical means in the colloquial language, e.g. **Úrška imá zanimívejšo knjígo/bôlj zanimívo knjígo** 'Urška has a more interesting book'.

3.17   CONSTRUCTIONS USING THE COMPARATIVE

When two nouns are compared English 'than' is rendered in Slovene either by **od** plus the genitive of the noun with which the comparison is made or by **kot** + the same case of the second noun as of the first, e.g.

Péter je mlájši od Tóneta
Peter is younger than Tone

Mójca je staréjša kot drúge učênke/od drúgih učênk
Mojca is older than the other schoolgirls

Njén obràz je bôlj bléd kot njegóv/od njegóvega
Her face is paler than his

Môški so mànj tŕmasti kot žénske/od žénsk
Men are less stubborn than women

Gláva je mànj poškodována kot rôka/od rôke
The head is less injured than the hand

Strokovnjáki za prebiválstvo napovedújejo déklicam za ósem lét dáljše življênje kot fántom
Demographers predict that girls will live eight years longer than boys

When two clauses are compared or the noun is qualified by a prepositional phrase, 'than' is translated by **kot**, **kàkor** or **ko**. However, **kàkor** is very rarely used nowadays and **ko** is used only in the spoken language, e.g.

Tomáž je bíl bôlj jézen, kot sem pričakovál
Tomaž was more angry than I expected

Na dežêli je zràk čistéjši kot/kàkor v méstih
The air in the country is cleaner than in the towns

Nóč srédi gózda je bôlj čŕna kot na plánem
Night in the forest is blacker than night in the open

3.18 PSEUDO-COMPARATIVES

In some instances comparative forms are not used in concrete comparison, but are used to indicate a large measure of the quality expressed, e.g. **staréjši člôvek** 'an elderly man'; **dáljši pogóvor** 'a lengthy conversation'; **véčje mésto** 'a large town'.

3.19 THE CONSTRUCTIONS 'MORE AND MORE ...', '....ER AND ....ER', 'EVEN MORE ...'/'LESS AND LESS ...', 'EVEN LESS ...'

These constructions may be translated by **bôlj in bôlj** and **mànj in mànj** + the positive degree of the adjective, e.g.

bôlj in bôlj bogàt   richer and richer/more and more rich
mànj in mànj prepríčan   less and less convinced

However more normally one would use the adverb **védno** + the comparative degree of the adjective, e.g.

V začétku šéstdesetih lét so fántje iz Liverpoola postájali védno slávnejši
At the beginning of the sixties the lads from Liverpool became more and more famous

Instead of **védno** one may also use **čedálje** (very literary) or **vse zmérom/zméraj** (colloquial), e.g.

Zmérom/zméraj/vse čedálje slávnejši so postájali
They became more and more famous

3.20 THE SUPERLATIVE

The superlative in Slovene is derived from the comparative form by means of the prefix **nàj-**, e.g. **nàjslábši** 'worst'; **nàjbogatéjši** 'richest'; **nàjvéčji** 'largest'.

In the case of comparatives formed by analytical means the prefix **nàj-** is added to the comparative adverbs **bôlj** and **mànj** (i.e. **nàjbolj, nàjmanj**), e.g. **nàjbolj zdràv** 'the healthiest'; **nàjmanj gúbast** 'the least creased'.

3.21 THE CONSTRUCTIONS 'THE MOST . . . OF (ALL)/ THE LEAST . . . OF (ALL)'

These constructions are translated by the superlative followed by **od** + gen./ **izmed** + gen./**med** + instr., e.g.

nàjpametnéjši med njími	the cleverest of them
nàjbóljši med učênci/izmed učêncev	the best of the pupils
nàjmanj korísten od vsèh	the least useful of all

3.22 THE CONSTRUCTION 'THE . . .EST POSSIBLE'

This construction is rendered by the adverb **čím** followed by the comparative, e.g. **Skrbéti za čím vêčji pridélek** 'To try and get the biggest harvest possible'.

3.23 THE PREFIX pre-

When the prefix **pre-** is used with the positive degree of an adjective it indicates either a high degree of the quality or an excessive degree of the quality, e.g. **predrág** 'too expensive'; **premlád** 'too young'; **prestàr** 'too old'; **prelép** 'too beautiful/very beautiful'; **preljubeznív** 'too kind/very kind'.

3.24 THE STRESS OF ADJECTIVES

Nearly all adjectives have a fixed stress. Only three adjectives in the modern language have a mobile stress where the stress in the nom. sing. masculine differs from the stress in the remaining cases. These adjectives are **dêbel** 'fat'; **vêlik** 'large'; **bolán** 'sick', e.g.

dêbel (m.)	**debéla** (f.)	**debélo** (n.)	**debélega** (gen.sing.m./n.) etc.
vêlik (m.)	**velíka** (f.)	**velíko** (n.)	**velíkega** (gen.sing.m./n.) etc.
bolán (m.)	**bólna** (f.)	**bólno** (n.)	**bólnega** (gen.sing.m./n.) etc.

3.25 THE STRESS OF THE COMPARATIVE

If a comparative is formed with the suffixes **-ši** or **-ji** the stress remains on the root, e.g. **slájši** 'sweater'; **glóblji** 'deeper'.

If a comparative is formed with the suffix **-ejši** then the stress remains the same as that of the positive degree of the adjective if this is polysyllabic, e.g. **plemenítejši** 'more noble'; **strahopétnejši** 'more cowardly'; **mamljívejši** 'more enticing'.

The only exceptions are **veseléjši** 'happier'; **bogatéjši** 'richer'; **debeléjši** 'fatter'; **pametnéjši** 'more intelligent'; **počasnéjši** 'slower'.

In the case of comparatives formed from monosyllabic roots (including monosyllabic roots appearing after the loss of e = ǝ in the final syllable) plus the suffix -**ejši** the stress may fall either on the root which is more common, e.g. **júžnejši** 'more southern'; **mírnejši** 'more peaceful'; **skŕbnejši** 'more careful' or it may fall on the suffix -**éjši**.

The comparatives which fall into this latter category are the following:

novéjši 'newer'; **svetléjši** 'lighter'; **gostéjši** 'thicker'; **gladkéjši** 'smoother'; **glasnéjši** 'louder'; **gorkéjši** 'warmer'; **hitréjši** 'quicker'; **hladnéjši** 'cooler'; **kasnéjši** 'later'; **krasnéjši** 'more beautiful, fairer'; **krepkéjši** 'stronger'; **krotkéjši** 'milder'; **mehkéjši** 'softer'; **miléjši** 'gentler, softer'; **močnéjši** 'more powerful'; **ostréjši** 'sharper'; **staréjši** 'older'; **svetéjši** 'holier'; **šibkéjši** 'weaker'; **temnéjši** 'darker'; **tesnéjši** 'tighter', **topléjši** 'warmer'; **zvestéjši** 'more faithful'; **bledéjši** 'paler'

It should be noted that a small number of comparatives allow alternative stresses. These are:

bístréjši 'more transparent'; **brídkéjši** 'more bitter'; **bŕhkéjši** 'prettier'; **hrábréjši** 'braver'; **jásnéjši** 'clearer'; **módréjši** 'wiser'; **mráčnéjši** 'gloomier'; **prôstéjši** 'freer'; **rédkéjši** 'rarer'; **résnéjši** 'more serious'; **strášnéjši** 'more terrible'; **mêdléjši** 'duller'; **gíbkéjši** 'more mobile'; **tŕdnéjši** 'firmer'; **sréčnéjši** 'happier'; **zrélêjši** 'riper'

In these cases the modern tendency would be to stress the suffix -**éjši**.

3.26 THE STRESS OF THE SUPERLATIVE

Superlatives have two stresses – one on the prefix **nàj-** and the other on the comparative form, e.g. **nàjčistéjši** 'cleanest'; **nàjlépši** 'most beautiful'.

4 PRONOUNS

Pronouns may be classified either as 'substantival pronouns' (i.e. they replace nouns) or as 'adjectival pronouns' (i.e. they behave like adjectives and agree in gender, case and number with the noun they qualify).

4.1 TYPES OF PRONOUNS

1. Personal pronouns
2. The reflexive pronoun
3. Possessive pronouns
4. Demonstrative pronouns
5. Interrogative pronouns
6. Relative pronouns
7. Indefinite pronouns
8. Negative pronouns
9. Pronouns of totality [distributive and summative pronouns]
10. Evaluative pronouns
11. Reciprocal pronouns
12. The emphatic pronoun

4.2 PERSONAL PRONOUNS

The personal pronouns are: **jàz** 'I'; **tí** 'you'; **òn** 'he'; **ôna** 'she'; **ôno** 'it'; **mí** 'we (m.)'; **mídva** 'we two (m.)'; **mé** 'we (f./n.)'; **médve** 'we two (f./n.)'; **ví** 'you (m.)'; **vídva** 'you two (m.)'; **vé** 'you (f./n.)'; **védve** 'you two (f./n.)'; **ôni/ône/ôna** 'they (m./f./n.)'; **ônadva** 'those two (m.)'; **ônidve** 'those two (f./n.)'.

In the singular the personal pronouns **jàz, tí** do not indicate gender distinction, whereas the third person singular does in the nominative case, i.e. **òn** (m.), **ôna** (f.), **ôno** (n.). In the oblique cases the third person sing. pronouns distinguish between masc./neuter on the one hand and feminine on the other. The first, second and third persons dual show gender distinction but only in the nominative case, where there is a distinction between masculine on the one hand and fem./neuter on the other, i.e. **mídva** (m.), **médve** (f./n.) 'we'; **vídva** (m.) **védve** (f./n.) 'you'; **ônadva** (m.), **ônidve** (f./n.) 'they'. In the plural all three persons show gender distinction in the nominative only. In the case of the first and second pronouns plural the distinction is between masculine on the one hand and fem./neuter on the other, i.e. **mí** (m.), **mé** (f./n.) 'we'; **ví** (m.), **vé** (f./n.) 'you'. The third person plural pronoun distinguishes all three genders, i.e. **ôni** (m.), **ône** (f.), **ôna** (n.), 'they'.

The personal pronouns also have special clitic (i.e. unstressed) forms for the first and second persons singular and the third persons singular, dual and plural in the genitive, dative and accusative. The first and second persons dual and plural also have clitic forms in the genitive, dative and accusative but these forms are identical with the full forms except that they are unstressed.

4.2.1 The declension of the personal pronouns

Note: Clitic forms appear in brackets

First person

		Singular 'I'	Dual 'we'	Plural 'we'
N		jàz	mídva (m.) médve (f./n.)	mí (m.) mé (f./n.)
G		mêne (me)	náju (naju)	nàs (nas)
D		mêni (mi)	náma (nama)	nàm (nam)
A		mêne (me)	náju (naju)	nàs (nas)
L	pri	mêni	náju	nàs
I	z	menój/máno	náma	námi

Second person

		Singular 'you'	Dual 'you'	Plural 'you'
N		tí	vídva (m.) védve (f./n.)	ví (m.) vé (f./n.)
G		têbe (te)	váju (vaju)	vàs (vas)
D		têbi (ti)	váma (vama)	vàm (vam)
A		têbe (te)	váju (vaju)	vàs (vas)
L	pri	têbi	váju	vàs
I	s	tebój/tábo z	váma	vámi

Third person singular

		Masculine 'he'	Feminine 'she'	Neuter 'it'
N		òn	ôna	ôno
G		njêga (ga)	njé (je)	njêga (ga)
D		njêmu (mu)	njéj (ji)	njêmu (mu)
A		njêga (ga/-nj)	njó (jo)	njêga (ga/-nj)
L	pri	njêm	njéj	njêm
I	z	njím	njó	njím

Third persons: dual and plural

	Dual 'they'	Plural 'they'
N	ônadva (m.) ônidve (f./n.)	ôni (m.) ône (f.) ôna (n.)
G	njíju (ju)	njìh (jih)
D	njíma (jima)	njìm (jim)

A		**njíju (ju/-nju)**	**njìh (jih/-nje)**
L	pri	**njíju**	**njìh**
I	z	**njíma**	**njími**

Variants

(a) The instrumental of the first and second persons singular appears in two forms. The forms **menój, tebój** are very literary, while **máno, tábo** are normal and colloquial.

(b) In the spoken language we find several alternative forms. In the nominative dual we find the following alternative fem./neut. forms for all three persons: **mídve, vídve, ônedve**. In the locative dual of all three persons we also find the alternative forms **náma, váma, njíma** which are identical with the dat./instr. forms. The accusative plural form **jih** may replace the accusative dual **ju** and the locative plural form **njìh** may replace the locative dual form **njíju.**

4.2.2 Usage of the personal pronouns

In both the written and spoken language the nominative forms of the personal pronouns, functioning as the subjects of verbs, are normally omitted unless they are required for emphasis or unless their omission would cause confusion. In the genitive, dative and accusative the clitic forms of the personal pronouns are the forms normally used, with the full forms only being used for emphasis. However, only the full forms may be used in the genitive and dative cases if they follow prepositions. In the accusative both full and clitic forms may be used after a preposition although the clitic forms are those normally used (see **4.2.3**). The instrumental and locative forms of the personal pronouns are always stressed and are always governed by a preposition.

Note: The position of clitic forms is governed by certain rules and where clitics occur successively they follow the order 'dative, accusative, genitive' (see **12.4**).

Examples of usage

(a) *Nominative omitted*
  Posódil mi je svój dežník
  He lent me his umbrella

  Ráda imá kávo brez sladkórja
  She likes coffee without sugar

  Káj bêrete?
  What are you reading?

Njegóvo sêstro imámo rádi
We like his sister

Ne véjo, kjé je njén bràt
They do not know where her brother is

Včásih se skúpaj péljeta z ávtobusom
Sometimes they (d.) travel together by bus

Zbíram známke
I collect stamps

Ste za àli próti omejêni hitrósti na ávtocésti?
Are you for or against a speed limit on the motorway?

Čákava nánj
We (d.) are waiting for him.

(b) *Clitic forms*
Ali jo poznáš?
Do you know her?

Pogléj ga
Look at him

Obískal ju je Márko
Marko visited them (d.)

Kdáj nas boš obískal?
When will you visit us?

Tónček ji je dál šôpek vŕtnic
Tonček gave her a bunch of flowers

Počákam te pri izhódu
I will wait for you by the exit

Náju so povabíli na zabávo
They invited us (d.) to a party

Zdravník mi je dál néko mazílo
The doctor gave me some ointment

(c) *Forms with prepositions*
Ali je Ánka pri váju?
Is Anka with you (d.)?

Grém lahkó z vámi?
May I go with you?

Dobíl sem knjígo od njêga
I got the book from him

Romána vsák dán príde k mêni
Romana comes to visit me every day

Včéraj sem bíl pri njéj
Yesterday I was at her place

Pójdi z máno na sladoléd
Come with me for an ice-cream

V dolíni je biló jézero. V njêm so se kópali ljudjé
In the valley was a lake. People were bathing in it

(d) *Full forms used for emphasis*
Pomágaj mêni, ne pa njêmu
Help me, not him

Ne sprašúj védno mêne
Do not always ask me

Njó sem poklícal, ne têbe
I called her not you

Če povém têbi, móram še njêmu
If I tell you then I must tell him

Métka se je vrníla na univêrzo, jàz pa sem odhitéla domóv
Metka returned to the University and I hurried home

Njíju od nekód poznám
I know those two from somewhere

Kdó je bíl v kúhinji? Jàz
Who was in the kitchen? I was

4.2.3 Bound clitics

If the accusative clitic forms in the first and second persons singular and in the third person singular, dual and plural are governed by a monosyllabic preposition, then they are written together as one word. The stress then falls on the preposition, e.g. **záme** 'for me'; **prédte** 'in front of you'; **skózte** 'through you', etc. There are special bound clitic forms for the third persons although the fem. sing. form is the same as the full form of the pronoun: **-nj** (m./n.), **-njo** (f.), **-nju** (d.), **-nje** (pl.), e.g. **Odšèl je pónj/pónjo/pónju/pónje** 'He went to fetch him/it(m./n.)/her/them(d.)/them(plur.).'

The masculine and neuter form **-nj** is always preceded by **e** (= ə) if the monosyllabic preposition governing it ends in a consonant, e.g. **prédenj** 'in front of him/it'; **nádenj** 'above him/it'; **skózenj** 'through it'.

Note: A disyllabic preposition does not take **-nj**. It has to take the full form **njêga**, e.g. **zóper njêga** 'against him'.

When the preposition **v** 'into' precedes a bound clitic it takes the form **va-**, e.g. **váme** 'into me'; **váte** 'into you'.

Examples of usage

Skôraj sem pozabíla nánj/náte
I almost forgot about him/you

Ávto je pridrvél po césti in máčka je skočíla prédenj
A car came speeding along the road and a cat ran out in front of it

Vŕgla je kámen váme
She threw a stone at me

Zaúpaj vánju
Rely on them (d.)

Prídi zvečér póme
Come for me this evening

Móst je váren. Čézenj vózijo tovornjáki
The bridge is safe. Lorries drive across it

Note: The use of the full accusative form after a preposition is much rarer and only for emphasis, e.g. **Ôna ne zaúpa v njêga** 'She does not trust him'.

4.3 THE REFLEXIVE PRONOUN: sêbe 'SELF, SELVES'

This pronoun has no nominative case and only a singular form:

N		–
G		**sêbe (se)**
D		**sêbi (si)**
A		**sêbe (se)**
L	pri	**sêbi**
I	s	**sebój/sábo**

The reflexive pronoun distinguishes neither gender nor number and refers back to the subject of the sentence. The same form is used for all persons. It is used as the object of a verb when the person affected by the action is the same as the person carrying out the action. As in the case of the personal pronouns there are full forms and clitic forms in the gen./dat./acc. The long forms are only used for emphasis. The accusative clitic form is written together with any preposition governing it and the preposition then bears the stress, e.g. **pódse** 'beneath oneself', **váse** 'into oneself', **prédse** 'in front of oneself' etc. In the genitive and dative only full forms are used with prepositions.

Examples of usage

Posadíla sva otrôka na stòl médse
We (d.) sat the child on the chair between us

Knjígo vzêmi s sábo
Take the book with you

Andràž si je kúpil kraváto
Andraž bought himself a tie

poglédati okóli sêbe
to look around oneself

Nájprej postrézi sêbi
Help yourself first

Vládek se šè ní oblékel
Vladek has not got dressed yet

Tíne nóče govoríti o sêbi
Tine won't speak about himself

The emphatic pronoun **sám** (see **4.13**) is often used with the reflexive pronoun **sêbe** to stress that something happens of its own accord, e.g.

Vráta so se odpŕla sáma od sêbe   The door opened by itself.

The emphatic pronoun **sám** is also used with **sêbe** to emphasise the person to whom it refers. In a non-prepositional construction it usually agrees with **sêbe** in case but need not do so. In a prepositional construction it must agree with **sêbe** in case, e.g.

S tákim ravnánjem škódi sámemu sêbi
With such behaviour he discredits himself

Alkohólik ní vèč gospodár sámega sêbe
An alcoholic is no longer master of himself

Hváli sámega/sám sêbe
He blows his own trumpet

zaúpanje v sámega sêbe
self confidence

4.4 POSSESSIVE PRONOUNS

The basic possessive pronouns are: **mój** 'my', **tvój** 'your', **njegóv** 'his/its', **njén** 'her', **nàš** 'our (pl.)', **nájin** 'our (d.)', **vàš** 'your (plur.)', **vájin** 'your (d.)', **njíhov** 'their (plur.)', **njún** 'their (d.)'. They all decline like adjectives and agree with the noun they qualify in gender, number and case, e.g. **njén sín** 'her son'; **môja úra** 'my watch'; **vájine knjíge** 'your (d.) books'; **v njíhovi sôbi** 'in their room'.

Examples of usage

Vídeli smo njegóvo žêno
We saw his wife

Ali je vájin ávto nòv?
Is your (d.) car new?

Tó je njéna tórbica
This is her bag

Nájinih perés níso nášli
They did not find our (d.) pens

Govoríli smo o njíhovih načŕtih
We were talking about their plans

Poslúšajte nàš nasvèt
Listen to our advice

Ne máram njúnega prijátelja
I do not like their (d.) friend

Strínja se z môjimi predlógi
He agrees with my proposals

4.4.1   The reflexive possessive pronoun: **svój** 'one's own'

This pronoun declines like an adjective and agrees with the noun it qualifies in gender, case and number. It always refers back to the subject of the sentence.

Examples of usage

Pobóžal sem svôjega psà
I stroked my dog

Vésna mi je predstávila svôje stárše
Vesna introduced me to her parents

Obléci svôjo nôvo obléko
Put on your new dress

V svôjih článkih tŕdite nasprótno
In your articles you assert the opposite

Svôjim gôstom smo razkazáli híšo
We showed our guests the house

Prepíral se je s svôjimi soródniki
He quarrelled with his relatives

When there is a third person subject care must be made to distinguish between **svój** and the possessive pronouns **njegóv** 'his/its', **njén** 'her', **njíhov** 'their (pl.)', **njún** 'their (d.)'.

For example the English sentence 'The boy grabbed his bag and ran away' can be translated in two ways in Slovene, i.e.

(a) **Otròk je zgrábil njegóvo tórbo in stékel**

or

(b) **Otròk je zgrábil svôjo tórbo in stékel**

In sentence (a) **njegóvo** means that the bag did not belong to the boy but to someone else. In sentence (b) **svôjo** means his own bag, i.e. it did belong to the boy.

The English sentence 'Metka and Adriana were telling me about their parents' can be rendered three ways in Slovene, i.e.

(a) **Métka in Adriána sta mi pripovedováli o svôjih stárših**
(b) **Métka in Adriána sta mi pripovedováli o njúnih stárših**
(c) **Métka in Adriána sta mi pripovedováli o njíhovih stárših**

In sentence (a) **svôjih** means their own parents, in sentence (b) **njúnih** means the parents of two other people and in sentence (c) **njíhovih** means the parents of more than two other people.

When ownership is obvious from the context it is possible to dispense with **svój**, e.g.

Požúgala je s pestjó	She shook her fist
Zmájal je z glávo	He shook his head
Pès je máhal z répom	The dog wagged its tail

It should also be noted that **svój** is used in many set expressions, e.g.

vsák po svôje	each in his own way
délati na svôjo rôko	to do of one's own accord
vzéti stvarí v svôje rôke	to take matters into one's own hands
íti svôjo pót	to go one's own way.

Colloquially **svój** is also used to denote approximation, e.g.

Jáma je globôka svôjih trídeset métrov	The case is about thirty metres deep
Ní vèč mlád, imá svôjih pétdeset	He is no longer young, he is about fifty

In clauses which have a first or second plural subject **svój** may be replaced by the posssessive pronouns **nàš** 'our', **vàš** 'your', where the ownership implied is universal or common and not particular. For example in newspapers one can encounter examples such as the following:

Od náših smúčarjev smo létos pričakováli vèč, kot so doségli
We (i.e. the nation) expected more from our skiers this year than they achieved

Od váših špórtnikov pričakújete velíko uspéhov
You (i.e. the public) expect great successes from your sportsmen

4.4.2 Other possessive pronouns

(a) **nikógaršen/nikógaršnji** 'of no man'
This is a relatively new pronoun and is derived from the genitive of the negative pronoun **nihčè/níkdo** 'no-one' with the suffix **-šen** or **-šnji**. It declines like an adjective with a fleeting **e** (= ə) in the final syllable, e.g.

Pès ní nikógaršnji	The dog is no-one's
nikógaršnje ozémlje	no man's land
Tá gòzd je nikógaršen	This forest belongs to no-one

(b) **vsákogaršnji** 'of every man'
This is also a relatively new pronoun and is derived from the genitive of the pronoun **vsákdo** 'everyone' with the suffix **-šnji**, e.g.

Tá gòzd je vsákogaršnja zêmlja   This forest belongs to everyone

Note: Instead of **nikógaršnji** and **vsákogaršnji** one may use the preposition **od** with the genitive forms **nikógar** and **vsákogar**, e.g.

Tá pès ní od nikógar	This dog is no-one's
Tá gòzd je od vsákogar	This forest belongs to everyone

(c) **màrsičigáv** 'of many a person'
This pronoun declines like an adjective, e.g.

Màrsičigáv kònj se je pásel v tísti dételji
Many a person's horse has grazed in that clover

(d) **čígar** 'whose, of whom'
This pronoun is indeclinable and only indicates possession by an individual masculine person, e.g.

Fànt, čígar ôče je trenêr, je postávil nòv rekórd v téku na stó métrov
The boy, whose father is a trainer, set a new record in the 100 metres

Môški, čígar híša je zgoréla, je mój stríc
The man whose house burnt down is my uncle

Mój stríc, o čígar smŕti ste mórali zvédeti, je žível v Parízu
My uncle, whose death you must have heard about, lived in Paris

Note 1: When 'whose' refers to possession by things or persons other than an individual masculine person, the genitive of the relative pronoun **katéri** 'who, which' is used. This mostly
precedes the item possessed unless this latter is governed by a preposition, e.g.

Kmétje, katérih híše vídite, so náši nàjblížji sosédje
The peasants, whose houses you can see, are our nearest neighbours

Ljúdstvo, v iménu katérega nastópate
The people in whose name you are appearing

Predpísi, na podlági katérih se dolóča dohodnína
The rules on the basis of which income tax is determined (see also **4.7**)

Note 2: **čígar** and the genitive of **katéri** may be used with the particle **kóli** in the meaning
'whosever', i.e. arbitrary possession, e.g. **Čígar kóli** (m.)/**katére kóli** (f.) **sín je, príden je**
'Whosever (m./f.) son he is, he is hardworking'.

Possession may also be indicated by the construction **od** + the genitive of a
pronoun or simply by the genitive of a pronoun. The constructions which fall
into this category are: **od kógarkóli** 'whosever'; **od nekóga** 'someone's'; **od
kóga** 'anyone's'; **od drúgega/od drúgih** 'someone else's'.

Examples of usage

Od kógarkóli je tá knjíga, káže, da je nemáren, ker je knjíga poškodována
Whosever book this is shows that he is negligent because it is damaged

Na kógarkóli pomóč se zanáša, úpam, da ne bó razočáran
On whosever help he is relying I hope that he will not be disappointed

Od nekóga tá híša vèndar móra bíti
This house must be someone's

Ko bi bilà knjíga od kóga, ne bi ležála na smetéh
If the book was anyone's it would not be lying on the rubbish heap

Tá počítniška híša je od drúgih, ne očétova
This holiday home is someone else's, not father's

4.5 DEMONSTRATIVE PRONOUNS

In Slovene the demonstrative pronouns are: **tá** 'this'; **tísti** 'that'; **óni** 'that'; **oné**
'that one, what's his name'; **ták(šen)** 'such a, of such a kind'; **tólikšen** 'of such
a size'.

(a) **tá** 'this'

This pronoun refers to something close at hand. It agrees in gender,
number and case with the noun it qualifies and declines as follows:

		m.	f.	n.
Sing.	N	**tá**	**tá**	**tó**
	G	**téga**	**té**	**téga**
	D	**tému**	**téj (tèj, tì)**	**tému**

	A		tá/téga	tó	tó
	L	pri	tém	téj (tèj, tì)	tém
	I	s	tém	tó	tém
Dual	N		tá	tí (té)	tí (té)
	G		téh	téh	téh
	D		téma	téma	téma
	A		tá	tí (té)	tí (té)
	L	pri	téh	téh	téh
	I	s	téma	téma	téma
Plural	N		tí	té	tá
	G		téh	téh	téh
	D		tém	tém	tém
	A		té	té	tá
	L	pri	téh	téh	téh
	I	s	témi	témi	témi

Note 1: The masc. acc. singular has two forms **tá/téga**, the latter being used for an animate accusative.

Note 2: In the dat./loc. sing. feminine and in the nom./acc. dual feminine and neuter we find alternative forms. The nom./acc. dual form **té** can be used as an alternative to **tí** if the number **dvé** is also used, i.e. **tí dvé/té dvé**.

Examples of usage

Odídite skózi tá vráta tù, tísta tàm so zaklénjena
Leave by this door, that door is shut

Kám naj dénem tó tórbo?
Where should I put this bag?

Pojdíte po téj póti, óna drúga je prestŕma
Go along this path, the other one is too steep

S témi prijátelji smo igráli nogomèt
With these friends we played football

Téga človéka ne poznám
I do not know this man

V tém trenútku zamenjáva ní primérna
At this moment an exchange is not convenient

Note: **tá** can function as a noun, e.g.

> **Ogléj si té fánte. Tá na lévi je znán košárkar**
> Take a good look at these lads. The one on the left is a well-known basketball player

(b) **tísti** 'that'

This pronoun indicates something further away and declines and behaves like an adjective. It can also function as a noun.

Examples of usage

Ali boš oblékla tísto jópico?
Are you going to put that cardigan on?

Tísto drevó je čéšnja
That tree is a cherry tree

Vás leží za tístim gózdom
The village lies beyond that forest

Hráno bom nêsla tístima délavcema
I will take the food to those two workmen

Pospeševáli bodo razvòj tístih dejávnosti, ki so življênjsko pomémbne
They will promote the development of those activities, which are of vital importance

Pogléj, tísti tàm je nàš známec
Look, that man there is an acquaintance of ours

(c) **óni** 'that'

This pronoun indicates something further away than **tísti**. It declines and behaves like an adjective. Like **tá** and **tísti** it can also function as a noun. In the modern language it is often replaced by **tísti**.

Examples of usage

Med ónim hríbom in césto têče réka
A river runs between that mountain and the road

Ónega gospóda sem sréčal na sestánku na univêrzi
I met that man over there at a meeting at the University

Med počítnicami smo stanováli pri ónih/tístih ljudéh
During the holidays we stayed with those people

Govóril je o tém in ónem
He spoke about this and that

Note: Very often **tá, tísti** and **óni** are used together in the same sentence to differentiate people or objects at different distances from the speaker, e.g.

> **Téga človéka poznám osébno, tístega na vídez, ónega pa splòh nè**
> This man I know in person, that one by sight and that one (over there) I do not know at all

(d) **oné** 'what's his name'

This pronoun is normally indeclinable but may have an alternative instr./loc. form **oném**. It has a contemptuous, scornful meaning and indicates someone/something that one is unable to name or does not wish to name, e.g.

Tísti oné je bíl spét pri mêni
That what's his name was at my place again

Sàj véš, káj je rékel oné
I'm sure you know what what's his name said

Kdó je prišèl? Oné, tísti bedák
Who came? What's his name, that idiot

Pri oné sem bíl, kakó mu je žé imé?
I was at what's his name's place, what is his name?

Ali si rés bíl pri oném, pri pádarju?
Were you really at what's his name's, that quack?

(e) **ták/tákšen** 'such a, of such a kind'

These pronouns decline like adjectives. The **e** in the final syllable of **tákšen** is a fleeting e (= ə). **Ták** is the neutral form, while **tákšen** is the colloquial and more emotional form.

Examples of usage

Táka bárva vam ne pristája
Such a colour does not suit you

Táko vrême je primérno za sprêhod
Weather of this kind is suitable for walking

V tákem razpoložênju vas šè nikóli nísem vídel
I have never seen you in such a mood

Tákih beséd nísem pričakovàl od njé
I did not expect to hear such words from her

Želím si tákšnega psà, kot ga imá Ána
I want a dog such as the one Ana has

V tákšnem trenútku ne mórem ostáti míren
I cannot stay calm at such a moment as this

Imá tákšne očí kot bràt
She has eyes just like her brother

(f) **tólikšen** 'of such a size'

This pronoun declines like an adjective with a fleeting **e** in the final syllable. Its use is rare and it is normally replaced by **takó vêlik**, e.g.

Plǎčaj tólikšen/takó vêlik znések, kot je potrébno
Pay such an amount as is necessary

Híša je bilà tólikšna/takó velíka, da so iméli vsì dovòlj prostóra
The house was of such a size that everyone had enough space

Nísem si míslil, da je Jóže tólikšen/takó vêlik
I did not think that Jože was so big

4.5.1 The particle '-le'

The demonstrative pronouns **tá, tísti, óni, ták(šen)** are used with particle **-le** for emphasis. The particle is added to the pronoun in which case they are written together as one word. These forms are common in the spoken language, e.g.

Tále jópica mi je bôlj všéč
I prefer this jacket

Tákele stvarí se dánes dogájajo po vsèm svétu
Such things happen today throughout the whole world

Stópimo v sénco pod tístole smréko
Let us go into the shade beneath that pinetree

The particle **le-** may also precede the demonstrative pronoun in which case it is separated from the pronoun by a hyphen. These forms have the meaning 'the latter' and refer back to the last noun of the previous sentence, e.g.

Nekatéri rodóvi so se razvíli v poljedélce, drúgi v pastírje. Le-tí níso poználi stálne naselítve
Some tribes evolved into agriculturalists, others into herdsmen. The latter had no permanent settlements

4.6 INTERROGATIVE PRONOUNS

These pronouns are used to introduce a question and inquire about persons, objects, qualities etc. not completely familiar to the speaker. They include the following: **kdó** 'who', **káj** 'what', **katéri** 'which', **kákšen** 'what sort of', **čigáv** 'whose', **kólikšen** 'how large'.

(a) **kdó** 'who' and **káj** 'what'
These pronouns have only singular forms and decline as follows

N	kdó	káj
G	kóga	čésa
D	kómu	čému

A		kóga	káj
L	pri	kóm	čém
I	s	kóm	čím

Examples of usage

Kdó je pozvónil?
Who rang?

S kóm gréš na zabávo?
Who are you going to the party with?

Česa se bojíš?
What are you afraid of?

S čím boš plačála?
What will you pay with?

Káj íščete?
What are you looking for?

H kómu pójdeš popóldne?
Who are you going to see in the afternoon?

Note: If when one uses 'who' one is asking only about a person of one sex, then the interrogative pronoun **katéri** 'which one' is used, e.g. **Katéra (od vàs) je pozvoníla?** 'Who rang?' ' (i.e. which woman); **Katéri (od vàs) je pozvónil?** 'Who rang?' (i.e. which man).

If when using **kdó** or **káj** one has in mind several persons or objects (i.e. what persons, which things?) then the pronoun **vsè** 'all' follows **kdó**, **káj**, e.g.

Kdó vsè je bíl domá? Ôče, máti, bràt in sêstra
Who was at home? Father, mother, brother and sister

Káj vsè je biló na vŕtu? Klópca in tríje stôli
What was in the garden? A bench and three chairs

Note: In the colloquial language the form **kogá** is very commonly used instead of **káj**, e.g. **Kogá si mu povédala, da je takó dôbre vólje** What did you tell him, that he is in such a good mood?

(b) **katéri** 'which, what'
This pronoun declines like an adjective agreeing in gender, case and number with the noun it qualifies.

Examples of usage

Katéro obléko imáš ráje?
Which dress do you prefer?

V katérih dežêlah si bíl?
In which countries have you been?

Katére pásme je tvój múc?
What breed is your cat?

Katérim šálam se nàjráje sméješ?
What jokes do you prefer to laugh at?

Katéro števílko čévljev imáte?
What size shoes do you take?

Pri katéri híši si se ustávil?
Which house did you stay in?

Note: **katéri** is used with **od** + gen. or **med** + instr. in the meaning 'which of', e.g.

> **Katéri/Katéra med vámi je to stóril/storíla?**
> Which one of you (men/women) did this?

> **Katére med vámi so tó storíle?**
> Which of you (women) did this?

> **Katéri od vàs so se udeležíli sestánka**
> Which of you took part in the meeting?

(c)   **kákšen** 'what (kind of, sort of)'
This pronoun declines and behaves like an adjective with a fleeting **e** in the final syllable. It is frequently used with the appropriate noun in the gen. case to ask about the size, colour, type or other characteristic of an object.

Examples of usage

Kákšno je vrême dánes?
What is the weather like today?

Kákšne bárve je plášč?
What colour is the coat?

Povéj, kákšen je nôvi učítelj?
Tell me, what is the new teacher like?

Kákšne novíce nam prinášaš?
What news do you bring us?

Kákšne velikósti je tá jákna?
What size is this jumper?

Kákšne vŕste blagó je to?
What sort of material is this?

Kákšnega kalíbra je tá tóp?
What bore is this gun?

Note: The pronoun **kákšen** has an alternative form **kák**. This, however, is archaic and disappearing from usage.

(d) **čigáv** 'whose'

This pronoun declines like an adjective agreeing with the noun it qualifies in case, gender and number, e.g.

Čigáv je tá zvézek?
Whose notebook is this?

Čigávo knjígo bêreš?
Whose book are you reading?

O čigávih dvéh otrócih govoríš?
Whose two children are you talking about?

(e) **kólikšen** 'how big, how large'

This pronoun declines like an adjective with fleeting **e** in the final syllable. It is however, nowadays, normally replaced by **kakó vêlik**, e.g.

Kólikšna/Kakó velíka je bilà ríba?
How big was the fish?

Kólikšen/Kakó vêlik bó dobíček?
How large will the profit be?

4.7 RELATIVE PRONOUNS

Relative pronouns are those which introduce a relative clause, which gives more information about someone or something mentioned in the main clause. They include the following: **kdór** '(the person) who'; **kàr** '(the thing) which'; **katéri/ki** 'who, which'; **kákršen** 'such as, the like of which'; **kólikršen** 'of such a size, of the same size'.

(a) **kdór** '(the person) who' and **kàr** '(the thing) which'

These are the substantival pronouns and decline as follows:

N		**kdór**	**kàr**
G		**kógar**	**čésar**
D		**kómur**	**čémur**
A		**kógar**	**kàr**
L	**pri**	**kómer**	**čémer**
I	**s**	**kómer**	**čímer**

Examples of usage

Kdór dáje krí, je krvodajálec
A person who gives blood is a blood donor

Kdór se zádnji sméje, se nàjslájše sméje
He who laughs last, laughs longest

Kógar se bojíš, téga ne ljúbiš
A person who you fear, you do not love

Narêdi, kàr hóčeš
Do what you want

Kàr ste mi vzéli, takój vrníte
Return immediately what you took from me

Kómur je naráva dála talènt, tá ga je dólžen razvíjati
A person to whom nature has given talent is obliged to develop it

Česar ne želíš sêbi, túdi drúgim ne požéli
Do not wish on others what you do not wish for yourself

Tó je edíno, s čímer se ne strínjam
This is the only thing with which I disagree

Note: **kdór** may be replaced by **člôvek, ki** or **tísti, ki** 'a man who', e.g. **člôvek/tísti, ki dáje krí, je krvodajálec**.

(b) **katéri/ki** 'who, which'
The pronoun **katéri** declines like an adjective and is used to introduce relative clauses with animate and inanimate antecedents. The pronoun **ki** is also used in the same way, but is undeclinable. In the oblique cases **ki** must be used with the appropriate clitic form of the personal pronouns, the number and gender of which will agree with the antecedent noun referred to in the main clause, i.e. **ki mu** 'to whom' (dat. m./n.); **ki ji** 'to whom (dat. f.); **ki jim** 'to whom (dat. plur.)' etc.

katéri
The difference in use between the two forms is that **katéri** is used specifically in the following ways:

(i)   It is always used with prepositions.

(ii) It is used to avoid ambiguity, which can arise in some instances.

(iii) Its genitive form is used to denote possession 'whose, of whom, of which'.

Examples of usage

(i) *With prepositions*
Tó je vprašánje, na katéro je težkó odgovoríti
This is a question which it is difficult to answer

Césta, po katéri smo hodíli, je bilà strma
The path along which we were walking was steep

Pisála mi je gospá, pri katéri sem stanovála v čásu štúdija
The lady with whom I stayed during my studies wrote to me

Prijátelj, o katérem sem vam pripovedovàl, me bo dánes obískal
The friend who I was telling you about will visit me today

(ii) *To avoid ambiguity*

The Slovene sentence **Tó je môški, ki mu je dál knjígo** has two possible meanings: (i) 'This is the man to whom he gave the book' or (ii) 'This is the man who gave the book to him'. In order to avoid the ambiguity if meaning (i) is intended, the masc. dat. singular of **katéri** is used, i.e. **Tó je môški, katéremu je dál knjígo.**

(iii) *Possession*

Iz papírja izréži pravokótnik, katérega robóva mérita 5 cm in 8 cm
Cut out of the paper a rectangle, whose sides measure 5cm by 8cm

Púnca, katére denárnico si ukrádel, je policístova sêstra
The girl whose purse you stole is the policeman's sister

V planínah so ledeníki, katérih belína se odráža na nébu
In the mountains there are glaciers whose whiteness is reflected in the sky

ki

This relative pronoun is used to represent 'who, which' in the nom. gen. dat. and acc. cases. It is indeclinable and stands alone in the nominative case, but in the oblique cases must be used with the clitic form of a personal pronoun, the gender and number of which agree with the noun in the main clause to which it refers, e.g.

Knjíga, ki je na mízi, je darílo
The book, which is on the table, is a present

Réšil je otrôka, ki se je utápljal
He rescued a child who was drowning

Prodáli smo híšo, ki smo jo zgradíli
We have sold the house which we built

Zaprávil je denár, ki ga je zaslúžil
He has spent the money which he earned

Fílmi, ki so jih vídeli, so iméli angléške pòdnapíse
The films, which they saw, had English subtitles

Tó sta púnci, ki smo ju iskáli v hotélu
They are the two girls, who we looked for in the hotel

Učênci, ki ste jim dáli knjíge, so naredíli izpít
The pupils to whom you gave the books have passed the exam

Govoríš o stvaréh, ki jih ne poznáš
You are talking about things which you know nothing about

(c) **kákršen** 'such as, the like of which'
This pronoun declines like an adjective with a fleeting **e** in the final syllable, e.g.

Pokázal se je tákšnega, kákršen je v resníci
He showed himself in his true colours (i.e. such as he is in truth)

Dobíla je tákšnega možá, kákršnega si je želéla
She got just such a husband as she wanted

Tó so nôva določíla, kákršnih ne nájdemo v pŕvem osnútku
These are new provisions the like of which we do not find in the original draft

Utŕgala je róžo, kákršna ne ráste pri njìh domá
She plucked a flower the like of which did not grow at home

(d) **kólikršen** 'of such a size'
This pronoun declines like an adjective. It is now archaic and only used in proverbs etc., e.g. **Kólikršen délež bó tvój, tólikšen bó tudi mój** 'Whatever size your share will be, mine will be just as much'.

4.7.1 The particle -kóli '-ever'

The relative pronouns **katéri, kákršen, kdór** and **kàr** can be combined with the generalising particle **-kóli**. They then indicate optional or arbitrary choice.

(a) **katérikóli** 'any whatever, whichever'

Na sprêhod gréš lahkó v katérikóli obléki
You can go for a walk in any clothes whatever

Katérakóli stránka príde na oblást, móra sprejéti nòv proračún
Whichever party comes to power it must adopt a new budget

Utŕgaj si róžo, katérokóli hóčeš
Pick a flower, whichever you want

(b) **kákršenkóli** 'of any kind whatever'

Njegóv film prikazúje življênje brez kákršnegakóli olepšávanja
His film depicts life without any kind of embellishment whatever

Kákršnekóli so poslédice, zdàj se zdíjo nèpomémbne
Whatever the consequences are, they seem insignificant now

Ali imá tó kákršnokóli zvézo z máno?
Has this anything whatever to do with me?

(c) **kdórkóli** 'anyone whosoever, anyone at all'

Tó písmo lahkó bêre kdórkóli
Anyone at all can read this letter

Kdórkóli tó tŕdi, láže
Whosoever asserts this is lying

(d) **kàrkóli** 'anything whatsoever, whichsoever'

Naj se zgodí kàrkóli, na vsè sem priprávljen
Let anything whatsoever happen, I am ready for everything

Fevdálni gospód nikóli ní mógel priznáti, da imá kàrkóli skúpnega s kmétom
A feudal lord could never admit that he had anything whatsoever in common with a peasant

4.8 INDEFINITE PRONOUNS

Indefinite pronouns are used to refer to people or things when one does not know exactly who or what they are or when one does not wish to identify who or what they are. They include the following: **kdó** 'anyone, someone'; **kàj** 'anything, something'; **katéri** 'any(one), some(one)'; **nekdó** 'someone, somebody'; **nékaj** 'something'; **nekatéri** 'some, certain'; **néki** 'a certain, some'; **nekàk(šen)** 'some sort of/of some sort'; **kàk(šen)** 'any sort of, some (sort) . . . or other'.

(a) **kdó** 'anyone, someone'
This pronoun declines like the interrogative pronoun **kdó** and refers to someone indefinite or one of an unspecified number still to be decided or chosen, e.g.

Naj stópi kdó po zdravníka
(Let) someone go for a doctor

Naj gré kdó odprét vráta
(Let) someone go and open the door

Ali me je kdó iskál?
Has anyone been looking for me?

Bó še kdó kàj pojédel?
Is anyone going to eat any more?

Če je kdó pred vráti, ga povábi nóter
If there is anyone at the door ask them to come in

Ali se boš še s kóm pogovóril o tem problému?
Will you speak to anyone else about this problem?

Ali boš še kóga povábil?
Will you invite anyone else?

(b) **kàj** 'something, anything'
This pronoun declines like the interrogative pronoun **káj** and refers to an arbitrary thing or to one of an unspecified number of things still to be selected or decided, e.g.

Če se bo kàj spremenílo, mi sporôči
If anything changes let me know

Če se čésa bojíš, me poklíči
If you are afraid of anything call me

Nímaš se za kàj jezíti
There is nothing for you to get angry about

The hypothetical nature of **kdó** and **kàj** accounts for their usage in conditional and imperative constructions. It should be noted that both **kdó** and **kàj** are often used as indefinite pronouns in conjunction with the evaluative pronoun **drúg** 'other' in which case they have the meaning 'someone else, something else', e.g.

očístiti z mílom ali s čím drúgim
to clean with soap or something else

Naj ga zaménja kdó drúg
Let someone else deputise for him

(c) **katéri** 'any(one), some(one)'
This pronoun declines like an adjective. It does not imply a particular person or thing, but someone or something indefinite that is one of a type or series. It is often used with a noun, e.g.

Včásih katéri zamudí
Sometimes someone is late [Note: one would normally use **kdó** here]

Če bi katéremu délavcu na ódru spodŕsnilo, bi bíló húdó
If any worker slipped on the scaffolding it would be serious

(d) **nekdó** 'someone, somebody'
This pronoun declines like the interrogative pronoun **kdó**. It denotes one particular person, who is unknown to or unnamed by the speaker, e.g.

Nekdó te je klícal po telefónu
Someone telephoned you

Nekómu sem posódil šílček, pa sem pozábil kómu
I lent the pencil sharpener to someone, but I have forgotten who

(e) **nékaj** 'something'
This pronoun declines like the interrogative pronoun **káj**. It denotes one particular object or thing, details of which are unknown to the speaker or which the speaker does not wish to identify, e.g.

Nékaj imá v žêpu
He has something in his pocket

Nečésa sem se domíslil
Something occurred to me

Nékaj ga móti pri délu
Something is troubling him at work

Udáril ga je z nečím tŕdim
He struck him with something hard

(f) **nekatéri** 'some, certain'
This pronoun declines like an adjective. It indicates an indefinite number of persons or things of a certain type. It is selective rather than quantitative like the indefinite adverb **nekóliko** 'some, a few' (see **5.17**), e.g.

Nekatéri vozníki vózijo prehítro
Some/certain drivers drive too fast

Spoznál sem se z nekatérimi článi klúba
I met some members of the club

Med udeléženci so nekatéra znána iména
Among the participants are certain well-known names

The contrast between the quantitative **nekóliko** and the selective **nekatéri** can be seen in the following sentence:

V náši skupíni je nekóliko tújih študêntov. Nekatéri (od njíh) so dôbri lingvísti
In our group there are some foreign students. Some of them are good linguists

(g) **néki** 'a certain, some'
This pronoun declines like an adjective and agrees with the noun it qualifies. It denotes an unknown person or thing, or a person or thing which the speaker does not wish to name, e.g.

Prišèl je néki mlád môški
Some young man came

Sréčal sem néko žénsko
I met some woman

Néko letálo je bíló sestreljêno
Some plane was shot down

Bíl sem pri nékem znáncu na kosílu
I was at some/a certain friend's house for lunch

na néki načín
in some way

V nékem smíslu je tá trdítev pravílna
In a certain sense this statement is true

In the colloquial spoken language **néki** is often replaced by the numeral **èn** 'one', e.g.

Govoríti móram s tábo o néki/êni stvári, ki me múči
I must talk to you about some/a certain matter that is worrying me

Tù je néki/èn fànt z ránjeno rôko
There is some boy here with an injured hand

(h) **nekàk(šen)** 'some sort of, of some sort'
This pronoun exists in two forms both of which decline like adjectives. They do not imply particular persons or things, but someone or something indefinite or one of an unspecified number still to be decided or selected. The form **nekàk** is neutral, while **nekàkšen** is more emotive and colloquial, e.g.

Nekàka pomóžna padála so potrébna
Some sort of auxiliary parachutes are necessary

Rísal je v pések nekàkšne líke
He was drawing figures of some sort in the sand

Obšlà me je nekàkšna čúdna slútnja
I was seized by some sort of strange presentiment

Prôstor je bíl nekàkšno dvoríšče
The site was some sort of backyard

(i) **kàk(šen)** 'any sort of, some(sort) . . . or other'
This pronoun exists in two forms and both decline like an adjective. They do not qualify a particular person or thing but refer to someone or something arbitrarily indefinite. The form **kàk** is now considered old fashioned and **kàkšen** is the form normally used in speech and writing, e.g.

Verjétno se je zgodíla kàka nesréča
Probably some sort of accident has happened

Ali načŕt predvidéva kàkšna nôva nasélja?
Does the plan envisage any sort of new settlements?

Zméraj imá kàkšne težáve
He always has some difficulties or other

Obláči se kàkor kàkšna princésa
She dresses like some sort of princess

Note: **kàk(šen)** is also used to express approximate quantity in the meaning 'about, some', e.g. **Prídem kàko úro poznéje** 'I'll come about an hour later'; **Kàkih/Kàkšnih pétdeset lét je žível v Amêriki** 'He lived in America for some fifty years'.

4.8.1   Indefinite pronouns formed with **màrsi-, mnógo-** 'many' and **málo-, rédko-** 'few, hardly any'

Pronouns formed in this way decline either substantivally or adjectivally in accordance with the pattern of the pronoun used with these prefixes. **Màrsi-** and **mnógo-** have the same meaning but **mnógo-** is very literary and rarely used.

Currently the following forms of these pronouns are used:

(a)   **màrsikdó** 'many a person, many persons'

Màrsikdó se s tábo ne bó strínjal	Many a person will not agree with you
O màrsikóm bi se dálo rêči ísto	One could say the same about many a person

(b)   **màrsikàj, mnógokàj** 'many a thing, many things'
Of these two forms **màrsikàj** is the form normally used. The form **mnógokàj** is very literary.

Zdàj se je màrsikàj spremenílo	Now many things have changed
V tujíni se je màrsičésa naúčil	He learnt many a thing when he was abroad

(c)   **màrsikatéri, màrsikàk, màrsikàkšen** 'many a . . .'
These pronouns are identical in meaning and always qualify a noun. The form **màrsikàk** is very literary and normally replaced by **màrsikatéri** in the modern language.

Prebedéla je màrsikatéro nóč pri bolníku
She spent many a sleepless night at the patient's bedside

Màrsikàko/màrsikatéro nóč je prejokála
She spent many a night weeping

Naprável je žé màrsikàkšno neúmnost
He has already committed many a stupid act

(d)   **málokdó, rédkokdó** 'hardly anyone, very few people'

Málokdó se ga šè spómni
Hardly anyone still remembers him

Tá pót je málokómu znána
This path is known to very few people

Rédkokdó pozná tó rastlíno
Very few people know this plant

(e) **málokàj** 'hardly anything, very few things'

V tém kráju se je v desêtih létih málokàj spremenílo
In this place hardly anything has changed in ten years

(f) **málokatéri, rédkokatéri** 'very few'
These pronouns always qualify a noun, e.g.

V málokatéri knjígi je opís takó žív
In very few books is the description so lively

Rédkokatéra mésta imájo tóliko lépih zgrádb
Very few towns have so many beautiful buildings

4.9 NEGATIVE PRONOUNS

Negative pronouns denote the general non-existence of persons or things. The negative pronouns are: **nihčè/níkdo** 'nobody, no-one'; **nobêden/nobèn** 'nobody, no-one, no . . .'; **nìč** 'nothing'; **nikákršen** 'no . . ., no sort of'. They are always used with the negative particle **ne**.

(a) **nihčè/níkdo** 'nobody, no-one'
This pronoun declines as follows:

N		**nihčè/níkdo**
G		**nikógar**
D		**nikómur**
A		**nikógar**
L	pri	**nikómer**
I	z	**nikómer**

Níkdo is a very literary form and is no longer used in speech. **Nihčè** is the preferred form in both speech and writing. It is used in negative sentences with negated verbs. It takes masculine singular agreement in the **-l** participle, e.g.

Nihčè ní prišèl
Nobody came

Prevárani nikómur ne verjáme
A man who has been deceived believes no-one

Nikógar ni bíló na sestánku
There was no-one at the meeting

O tém fílmu nísem šè z nikómer govóril
I still haven't talked to anyone about this film

(b) **nobêden/nobèn** 'nobody, no-one, no . . .'
This pronoun declines like **êden/èn** 'one', i.e. like an adjective. The form
nobêden is only used substantivally in the nom. sing. masc. with the
meaning 'nobody' although in speech it is often replaced by **nobèn**. In the
meaning 'no . . ., not one . . .' only the form **nobèn** is used, e.g.

Nobêden ga ne pozná
Nobody knows him

Nobêna ga ne mára
Not one woman likes him

Nobèn člôvek ní nèzmotljív
No man is infallible

Nobênega dvóma ní
There is no doubt

Níma nobênih skrbí
He has no worries

The basic difference between **nihčè** 'nobody' and **nobêden/nobèn** is that **nihčè**
is the opposite of **vsákdo** 'everyone' and refers to an unlimited number of
persons, whereas **nobêden/nobèn** tends to relate to a limited number of
persons or things already mentioned. For this reason **nihčè** tends to be found
in generalised statements, e.g.

Nihčè na tém svétu mu ne móre vèč pomágati
No-one in this world can help him any more

Nihčè ne móre slúžiti dvéma gospodárjema hkráti
Nobody can serve two masters at one and the same time

but

**V razrédu je biló trídeset učêncev, pa nobêden/nobèn ní znál odgovoríti na
vprašánje**
In the class there were thirty pupils and not one (nobody) could answer
the question

**V ênem sámem popoldnévu sta si oglédala kàr trí fílme, vèndar jima ní
nobêden/nobèn prevèč ugájal**
In one afternoon the two of them watched three films although not one
of them pleased them very much

Similarly, in answer to a question one would use **nihčè** in response to **kdó** and
nobêden/nobèn in response to **katéri (od vàs)**, e.g.

Kdó je bíl na sestánku? Nihčè   Who was at the meeting. No-one
Kóga poznáš? Nikógar ne poznám   Who do you know? Nobody

but

Katéri od vàs je bíl na sestánku?	Which of you was at the meeting?
Nobêden	No-one
Katérega poznáš? Nobênega ne	Which one (who) do you know?
poznám	I know no-one

nobêden/nobèn is frequently used with **od** + genitive to mean 'not one of . . .', e.g.

Nobêden od zavéznikov se ní strínjal	Not one of the allies agreed with
s Fráncijo	France
Nobêna od náju ne bó prišlà	Not one of us (f.d.) will come

(c) **nìč** 'nothing'
This pronoun declines as follows:

N		**nìč**
G		**ničésar**
D		**ničémur**
A		**nìč**
L	pri	**ničémer**
I	z	**ničímer**

nìč is used in negative sentences with negated verbs, e.g.

V trgovíni ní kúpil ničésar
He bought nothing in the shop

Tù ní ráslo nìč
Nothing grew here

Z ničímer me ne bóš prepríčal, da imáš pràv
There is nothing you can say that will convince me that you are right

O ničémer se nísva uspéla zmeníti
Neither of us could agree on anything

Ničésar nísem nášel
I found nothing

Tù ní ničésar
There is nothing here

It should be noted that the accusative form **nìč** is very often used instead of the genitive form **ničésar** after negated verbs, e.g.

Nìč nísem nášel
I found nothing

V trgovíni ní nìč kúpil
He bought nothing in the shop

Nìč ní pústil v sôbi
He left nothing in the room

nìč ne márati
to care for nothing

When **nìč** is used with an adjective in the genitive case then it is usually not declined, e.g.

Nìč nôvega mi nísi povédal
You have told me nothing new

Njegóv nastòp ní obétal nìč dôbrega
His approach augured nothing good

Nìč lážjega ní kot tó
There is nothing easier than this

Dánes nísem popíl nìč tôplega
I have drunk nothing warm today

It does, however, decline if it is used with an adjective in the other oblique cases, e.g.

Ne ukvárja se z ničímer nôvim
He is not engaged in anything new

Òn ne zná govoríti o ničémer drúgem kot o sêbi
He can talk about nothing else but himself

(d) **nikákršen** 'no, not of any kind'
This is a very literary form and declines like an adjective. In the modern language it has the same meaning as **nobèn** 'no . . . ', e.g.

Nikákršnih/nobênih novíc nímam, ne dôbrih ne slábih
I have no news either good or bad

Nikákršnih/nobênih šál ne pozná
He knows no jokes

Strictly speaking **nikákršen** should be used in response to a question containing **kákšen** 'what sort of' and **nobèn** in response to **katéri** (see **4.9b**), e.g.

Katére potíce hóčete? Nobênih   Which cakes do you want? None

but

Kákšne potíce hóčete? Nikákršnih   What sort of cakes do you want? None (of any sort)

4.10 PRONOUNS OF TOTALITY: DISTRIBUTIVE AND SUMMATIVE PRONOUNS

These are pronouns which are used to express the total number of persons or things involved. Distributive pronouns refer to each individual of a class (e.g. **vsák** 'each, every'), whereas summative pronouns refer to the class collectively (e.g. **vès** 'all', **obá** 'both').

4.10.1 Distributive pronouns

These include the following: **vsákdo** 'everyone, everybody'; **vsák** 'each, every'; **sléherni** 'each, every'.

(a) **vsákdo** 'everyone, everybody'
This pronoun declines like the relative pronoun **kdór** (see **4.7**). It means every individual in a group without exception, e.g.

Vsákdo imá pravíco do počítka
Everybody has a right to take a rest

Profésor se ne strínja z vsákomer
The professor does not agree with everybody

Vsákdo od njìh je dobíl božíčno darílo
Each of them received a Christmas present

Nàš razrédnik se zaníma za vsákogar izmed nàs
Our teacher is interested in everyone of us

(b) **vsák** 'every, each'
This pronoun declines like an adjective and emphasises each individual person or thing in a group or class, e.g.

Trenêr spoštúje vsákega človéka v móštvu
The coach respects every man in the team

Pri vsákem gíbu je čutíla húde bolečíne
With every movement she felt severe twinges of pain

Vsáko jútro telovádi
He does exercises every morning

Pràv vsák člôvek móra opráviti svôjo dolžnóst
Each and every man must do his duty

vsák drúgi téden
every other week

vsák may be used in the dual or the plural with cardinal numerals. In the plural it is also used with *pluralia tantum* nouns, e.g.

vsáka dvá dnéva
every two days

vsákih pét dní
every five days

Vsákih pét korákov se je ustávil
He stopped every five paces

Vsáke vílice na mízi imájo trí zobé
Every fork on the table has three prongs

Z vsákima naslédnjima odgóvoroma bóste dobíli 10 tóčk
With each of the following two answers you will get 10 points

Note too the phrase **vsáke tóliko čása** 'every now and then'.

Note: **vsák** may also be used instead of **vsákdo**, e.g. **Tó se lahkó priméri vsákemu** 'This can happen to anyone'; **vsákemu svôje** 'to each his own'; **Vsák od vàs imá pràv** 'Each of you is right'.

(c) **sléherni** 'every, each, every single, each and every'
This pronoun declines like an adjective. It is a very literary stressed form and is normally replaced by **vsák**, e.g.

poudárjati odgovórnost sléhernega člána
to emphasise the responsibility of each and every member

Sléherni dán jo sréčam
I meet her every single day

sléherni may also be used with **vsák** for emphasis, e.g.

Na tó naj bo priprávljen vsák sléherni občàn
Let each and every citizen be prepared for this

Sprémljala je vsáko in sléherno besédo govórnika
She listened to the speaker's each and every word

Both **sléherni** and **vsák** may be used to replace **kákršenkóli** (see **4.9**), e.g.

Izgubíla je vsáko/sléherno úpanje na rešítev
She lost any hope whatsoever that she had of being rescued

4.10.2 Summative pronouns

These include: **vès** 'all, the whole/entire'; **obá/obé** 'both'; **obój** 'both sorts of'; **vsákršen** 'all sorts of, of all sorts'.

(a) **vès** 'all, the whole/entire'
This pronoun refers to persons or things in totality. It declines as follows:

			Masc.	Fem.	Neuter.
Sing.	N		vès	vsà	vsè
	G		vsèga	vsè	vsèga
	D		vsèmu	vsèj	vsèmu
	A		vès/vsèga	vsò	vsè
	L	pri	vsèm	vsèj	vsèm
	I	z	vsèm	vsò	vsèm
Dual	N		vsà	vsì	vsì
	G		vsèh	vsèh	vsèh
	D		vsèma	vsèma	vsèma
	A		vsà	vsì	vsì
	L	pri	vsèh	vsèh	vsèh
	I	z	vsèma	vsèma	vsèma
Plural	N		vsì	vsè	vsà
	G		vsèh	vsèh	vsèh
	D		vsèm	vsèm	vsèm
	A		vsè	vsè	vsà
	L	pri	vsèh	vsèh	vsèh
	I	z	vsèmi	vsèmi	vsèmi

Examples of usage

Hrána je všéč vsèm gôstom
All the guests like the food

Vsèh desét je zbolélo
All ten fell ill

Bilà je dôbra z vsèmi bolníki
She was good with all the patients

Med vsò vôžnjo je spál
He slept throughout the entire journey

Vsà družína je na dopústu
The whole family is on holiday

vès may also be used to indicate the complete or total degree of some property or state, e.g.

bíti vès bléd   to be completely pale

Od vónja je vsà omámljena   She is completely intoxicated by the
                                 smell

Note: **vès** also has the meaning 'the very' as in the phrase **Od vsèga začétka sem tó slútil** 'From the very beginning I had a hunch about this'.

The pronoun **vès** should be distinguished from the adjective **cél** 'whole, intact'. The adjective **cél** indicates that something has not been divided into parts or means the whole of a given quantity or measure, e.g.

Pojédel je célega piščánca
He ate a whole chicken

Na polícah so ležáli céli in razrézani hlébci
On the shelves lay whole and cut loaves

Koláč je šè cél, níso ga šè pokúsili
The cake is still whole, they have not tried it yet

Pavarotti je óperni pévec, znàn po célem svétu
Pavarotti is an opera singer known throughout the whole world

In time phrases, however, one may use either **vès** or **cél**, e.g. **Vès/cél dán smo se igráli** 'We played all day/for the whole day'.

Similarly when a noun represents a personified group it may take either **vès** or **cél**, e.g. **Vès/cél rázred se mi je zasmejál** 'All the class/the whole class laughed at me'.

(b) **obá**(m.)/**obé**(f./n); **obádva**(m.)/**obédve**(f./n.) 'both'
This pronoun may be substantival and stand alone or is used with the dual. It declines and behaves like the numeral **dvá/dvé** 'two' (see **5.3.3**). In the alternative forms **obádva/obédve** both parts decline, e.g. **obéh dvéh** (gen.) **obéma dvéma** (dat./instr.) etc.

Examples of usage

Tó sta bràt in sêstra, obá sta zaposlêna v hotélu 'Slòn'
They are brother and sister, both work in the Hotel 'Slon'

Náma je obéma težkó
It is difficult for both of us

Predstávniki obéh držáv
The representatives of both countries

Obé réki se izlívata v Čŕno mórje
Both rivers flow into the Black Sea

Z obéma rokáma je zgrábil za véjo
He grabbed the branch with both hands

Vsák dán prídeta obédve k nàm
Both of them (f.) come to see us every day

(c) **obój** 'both sorts of'
This pronoun declines like an adjective and behaves like a collective or differential numeral (see **5.5** and **5.6**), e.g.

mladína obójega spôla	young people of both sexes
Obóji čévlji ga tiščíjo	Both pairs of shoes pinch him
Otròk je raztŕgal obóje hláčk	The boy ripped both pairs of trousers

(d) **vsákršen** 'all sorts of, of all sorts'
This pronoun declines like an adjective and denotes arbitrary totality,
e.g.

Vsákršne šále pozná	He knows all sorts of jokes
Vsákršnih stvarí je biló na podstréšju	There were all sorts of things in the attic

The pronoun **vsákršen** may be replaced by the adjective **vsakovŕsten** 'all
sorts of', e.g. **vsakovŕstne nevárnosti** 'all sorts of dangers'.

4.11 EVALUATIVE PRONOUNS

These pronouns denote a comparison or contrast and include the following:
ísti 'same'; **enák** 'identical'; **drúg** 'other, another'; **drugáčen** 'another,
different'.

(a) **ísti** 'same'
This pronoun declines like an adjective. It means identical, unvarying,
allowing no exception, e.g.

Poslóvneža stanújeta v ístem hotélu
The two businessmen are staying in the same hotel

Vsák dán odhája od dóma ob ístem čásu
Everyday he leaves home at the same time

Rojêna sta ístega léta
They were born in the same year

Zákon je za vsè ísti
The law is the same for everyone

Sva íste stárosti
We are the same age

Šè ísti dán je izpólnil obljúbo
The very same day he fulfilled his promise

ísti is used with the cardinal numeral **èn** 'one' in the construction **èn in ísti**
'the same old, the very same'. This construction expresses the unchanged
nature of or repetition of something, e.g.

Vsáko léto hódi v èn in ísti kràj na počítnice
Every year he goes to the same old place for his holidays

(b) **enák** 'identical, equal'

This pronoun declines like an adjective and indicates that the persons or things one is talking about do not differ in their properties or characteristics, e.g.

dvé enáki števílki	two equal numbers
Dvójčici sta čísto enáki	The twin girls are identical
Vsì smo v enákem položáju	We are all in the same situation
bòj med enákima nasprótnikoma	an equal fight
Sêstri imáta obléki enáke bárve	The two sisters have dresses of the same colour
Pred zakónom so vsì enáki	Everyone is equal before the law

Note: **enák** is in some of these senses colloquially often replaced by **ísti**, e.g. **Vsì smo v ístem položáju**

enák also has the meaning 'to be the equal of, a match for, on a par with' or 'equal in value or power to', e.g.

Ní mu enákega	He has no equal
nájti sêbi enákega	to meet one's match
Ní ti enáka	She is no match for you
Léva strán enáčbe je enáka désni	The left side of the equation is equal to the right side

(c) **drúg** 'other, another'

This pronoun declines like an adjective. It means (a) not the same as one or some persons or things already mentioned (b) further, additional (c) the alternative of two persons or things, e.g.

šóle in drúgi vzgójni zavódi	schools and other educational establishments
Ôna ní kàkor drúge žénske	She is not like other women
Drúge izbíre ní	There is no other choice
Prídi ráje drúg dán	It is better to come another day
Odprí drúgo okó	Open your other eye
Šè nékaj drúgih primérov	Just a few other examples

drúg may also be used substantivally, e.g.

Tá mi ní všéč, prósim drúgega	I do not like this one, give me another
Bólni naj ostánejo domá, drúgi pa naj gredó na délo	Let those who are ill stay at home and let the others go to work

(d) **drugáčen** 'another, different'

This pronoun declines like an adjective with fleeting **e** in the final syllable. It means that someone or something is different in their properties or characteristics from someone or something mentioned or implied, e.g.

Pričakovàl sem drugáčen odgóvor	I expected another/a different answer
Jóže je drugáčen od očéta	Jože is different from his father
Tó blagó je drugáčno kot tísto v izlóžbi	This material is different from that on display

4.12   THE RECIPROCAL CONSTRUCTION **drúg drúgega/ drúgemu**, ETC. 'EACH OTHER, ONE ANOTHER'

This construction indicates that persons or things do the same thing, feel the same way or have the same relationship. The first part of the construction appears only in the nominative singular masculine, feminine or neuter depending on the gender of the subject of the verb. The second part is the same gender and in the appropriate singular case governed by the verb. If the verb governs a preposition then this appears between the two elements, e.g.

Sovrážita drúg drúgega	They hate one another
Púnci zaúpata drúga drúgi	The two girls confide in each other
Umírajo drúg za drúgim	They are dying one after another
Tréba je drúg drúgemu pomágati	It is necessary to help one another
Jezíli sta se drúga na drúgo	The two of them (f.) got angry with each other
Ôvce se dŕgnejo drúga ob drúgo	The sheep are rubbing against each other
Môški se ne strínjajo drúg z drúgim	The men do not agree with one another

Note: It is possible to replace **drúg drúgega** etc. with **èn/êden drúgega** etc., e.g. **Sovrážita èn drúgega**; **Púnci zaúpata êna drúgi**.

4.13   THE EMPHATIC PRONOUN **sám** '-SELF'

This pronoun declines like an adjective and agrees with the noun or pronoun it qualifies. It is used as follows:

(a)   It emphasises that someone does something without the participation of others, e.g.

Vsè délo je mórala opráviti sáma	She had to do all the work herself
Sám bom govóril z njó	I will speak to her myself
Túdi ví sámi ste málo krívi	You yourselves are somewhat guilty
Pomágali so nàm, čepràv tudi sámi nímajo dovòlj	They helped us even though they themselves do not have enough
Otròk žé sám hódi	The child can already walk by himself

(b) It is used with prepositional constructions containing the reflexive pronoun **sêbe** to emphasise that something happens of its own accord without external influence, e.g.

Lasjé se mu sámi od sêbe kódrajo	His hair curls by itself (i.e. of its own accord)
Tó se razúme sámo po sêbi	That goes without saying
Okóliščine sáme po sêbi níso ugódne	The conditions by themselves are not favourable

(c) It is used to add emphasis to the reflexive pronoun **sêbe** (see **4.3**), e.g.

Hváli sámega/sám sêbe	He praises himself
obvládati sámega sêbe	to control oneself
zaúpanje v sámega sêbe	self confidence
S tákim ravnánjem škódi sámemu sêbi	With such behaviour he discredits himself
zmága nad sámim sebój	a victory over oneself

(d) It is used with the possessive pronoun **svój** with the meaning 'one's own (person)', e.g.

Sem sám svój in ravnám, kàkor hóčem
I am my own man and I do what I want

Poročíla se je in postála sáma svôja gospodaríca
She got married and became her own mistress

(e) It is used to mean 'alone, on one's own' (i.e. without others present), e.g.

Sám talènt šè ní dovòlj, móral se bo túdi učíti
Talent alone is still not enough, he will also have to study

Poudárili so, da sáme kázni ne bódo rešíle téga probléma
They emphasised that punishments alone would not solve this problem

(f) When used with the numeral **èn** 'one' it means 'just one', e.g.

V êni sámi nôči je izgúbil vsè
In just one night he lost everything

Preostál jim je èn sám izhòd
They had just one resort left

(g) **sám** has the meaning 'the very . . .' in certain phrases, e.g.

žé od sámega začétka
right from the very beginning

prodréti v sámo bístvo probléma
to get to the very core of the problem

5 NUMERALS

In Slovene we find the following types of numeral:

1. Cardinal numerals
2. Ordinal numerals
3. Collective numerals
4. Differential numerals
5. Multiplicative numerals
6. Adverbial numerals

5.1 GENDER

The three genders are differentiated in the cardinal numeral 'one', i.e. **êden/èn** (m.), **êna** (f.), **êno** (n.) and the ordinal, multiplicative and differential numerals. The cardinal numerals two, three, four, however, only distinguish gender in the nominative case, where they differentiate masculine on the one hand from feminine/neuter on the other, i.e. **dvá** (m.), **dvé** 'two'(f./n.); **tríje** (m.), **trí** (f./n.) 'three'; **štírje** (m.), **štíri** (f./n.) 'four', e.g. **dvá študênta** 'two students', **dvé knjígi** 'two books', **dvé mésti** 'two towns'.

The other cardinal numerals do not distinguish gender, e.g. **pét študêntov/ knjíg/mést** 'five students/books/towns' etc. Similarly the collective numerals do not distinguish gender.

5.2 LIST OF CARDINAL AND ORDINAL NUMERALS

The cardinal and ordinal numerals up to four thousand million are:

	Cardinals	*Ordinals*
1	**êden/èn/êna/-o**	**pŕvi/-a/-o**
2	**dvá/dvé**	**drúgi/-a/-o**
3	**tríje/trí**	**trétji/-a/-e**
4	**štírje/štíri**	**četŕti/-a/-o**
5	**pét**	**pêti**
6	**šést**	**šêsti**
7	**sédem**	**sêdmi**
8	**ósem**	**ôsmi**
9	**devét**	**devêti**

10	desét	desêti
11	enájst	enájsti
12	dvánajst	dvánajsti
13	trínajst	trínajsti
14	štírinajst	štírinajsti
15	pétnajst	pétnajsti
16	šéstnajst	šéstnajsti
17	sédemnajst	sédemnajsti
18	ósemnajst	ósemnajsti
19	devétnajst	devétnajsti
20	dvájset	dvájseti
21	ênaindvájset	ênaindvájseti
22	dváindvájset	dváindvájseti
23	tríindvájset	tríindvájseti
24	štíriindvájset	štíriindvájseti
25	pétindvájset	pétindvájseti
30	trídeset	trídeseti
40	štírideset	štírideseti
50	pétdeset	pétdeseti
60	šéstdeset	šéstdeseti
70	sédemdeset	sédemdeseti
80	ósemdeset	ósemdeseti
90	devétdeset	devétdeseti
100	stó	stôti
101	stó êden/èn/êna/-o	stopŕvi
200	dvésto	dvéstoti
300	trísto	trístoti
400	štíristo	štíristoti
500	pétsto	pétstoti
600	šéststo	šéststoti
700	sédemsto	sédemstoti
800	ósemsto	ósemstoti
900	devétsto	devétstoti
1000	tísoč	tísoči
2000	dvá tísoč	dvátísoči
100000	stó tísoč	stótísoči
1000000	milijón	milijónti
2000000	dvá milijóna	dvámilijónti
1000000000	milijárda	milijárdni
4000000000	štíri milijárde	štírimilijárdni

Note: The cardinal and ordinal numerals from twelve to nineteen may have an alternative stress on **-nájst(-)**.

The compound numerals between 21 and 99, as in German, have their elements reversed as compared with the Arabic numeral order used in English, i.e. 21 is 'one and twenty', 32 is 'two and thirty' etc. In the above table only 21 to 25 are illustrated, but 26–29, 31–39, 41–49 etc. behave in the same way.

Note: These numerals have two stresses.

Hundreds, thousands and millions occur initially, e.g. **stó êden** '101', **stó dváindvájset** '122', **tísoč pétsto tríintrídeset** '1,533' etc.

5.3   CARDINAL NUMERALS

5.3.1   The numeral 'one': **êden/èn** (m.), **êna** (f.), **êno** (n.)

This numeral declines as follows:

		m.	*f.*	*n.*
N		êden/èn	êna	êno
G		ênega	êne	ênega
D		ênemu	êni	ênemu
A		èn/ênega	êno	êno
L	pri	ênem	êni	ênem
I	z	ênim	êno	ênim

Whether used on its own or as the final part of a compound numeral (e.g. **stó êden** '101', **tísoč êden** '1,001') the numeral 'one' agrees in gender and number with the noun it qualifies. It takes a verbal predicate in the singular which also agrees in gender and number if it is an **-l** participle.

Note: This agreement does not apply in compound numerals where 'one' is the first element, e.g. **ênaindvájset** '21'.

In the nominative singular masculine there are two forms: **êden/èn**. The form **êden** is used substantivally and the form **èn** adjectivally.

Examples of usage

Samó êna študêntka je znála angléško	Only one girl student knew English
Samó êden zná angléško	Only one (person) knows English
Êden izmed strážnikov ga je opázil	One of the guards noticed him
Imáta ênega otrôka	They have one child
Êno žêljo šè imám	I have one more wish
èn moški in êna žénska	one man and one woman
Bíl je zmagoválec z ósemsto ênim glásom	He was the victor with 801 votes
Univêrza imá stó ênega profésorja	The university has 101 professors

Po êni stráni sem s tém zadovóljen,	On the one hand I am satisfied
po drúgi pa ne	with this, on the other I am not
z êno knjígo	with one book

The numeral **êden/èn** also has a plural adjectival form which is used with nouns that only occur in the plural (see **2.5**), e.g.

Êna vráta so šè odpŕta
One door is still open

Imá samó êne gráblje, a dvóje vílic
He has only one rake but two forks

The plural of **èn** is also used in the sense 'a pair' if the *pluralia tantum* noun is something which normally occurs in two or consists of two parts, e.g.

Prišèl je samó z ênimi škárjami
He came with only one pair of scissors

Imá samó êne čévlje
He has only one pair of shoes

Êni čévlji so na mízi, êni pod mízo
One pair of shoes is on the table, the other pair is under the table

In counting the feminine form **êna** is used to express 'one' and is then undeclined, e.g.

êna, dvá, trí, štíri	one, two, three, four
Êna in êna je dvé	One and one are two
Tékma se je končála s trí proti êna	The match ended 3–1
Péter je izenáčil stánje na êna	Peter equalised the score to bring it
proti êna	to one all

5.3.2   The adjective **edíni** 'one (and only)'

This is used in expressions of the following type:

Edíni sín mu je umŕl
His only son died

Tó je šè edína móžnost, da bi prepréčila nesréčo
This is the only way to prevent an accident

5.3.3   The numeral 'two': **dvá** (m.), **dvé** (f./n.)

The numeral 'two' declines like the demonstrative pronoun **tá** 'this'. It has only a dual form with a masculine versus feminine/neuter opposition in the nom. and acc. cases:

		m.		*f./n.*
N		dvá		dvé
G			dvéh	
D			dvéma	
A		dvá		dvé
L	pri		dvéh	
I	z		dvéma	

The numeral 'two' whether used on its own or as the final part of a compound numeral (e.g. **stó dvá** '102') agrees in gender and case with the dual forms of the nouns, adjectives and pronouns it qualifies. It takes a dual verbal predicate, which agrees with it in gender if it is an **-l** participle.

Note: This agreement does not apply if 'two' is the first element of a compound numeral, e.g. **dváinpétdeset** '52'.

The number 'two' may also be used substantivally. In counting, the masculine form is used in the spoken language.

Examples of usage

Dvá nôva študênta imáta lépo stanovánje
The two new students have a lovely flat

pred dvéma létoma
two years ago (colloquially: **pred dvémi léti**)

román v dvéh délih
a novel in two parts

dvé drevési
two trees

z dvéma kolégoma
with two colleagues

Trísto dvá vojáka sta umŕla v vôjni
302 soldiers died in the war

Dvésto dvé letáli sta bilí sestreljêni
202 planes were shot down

dvé nôvi knjígi
two new books

Ní naju stráh, sàj sva dvá
We are not afraid, there are two of us

Êden je odšèl, dvá pa sta počakála
One left and two waited

V trgovíni níso iméli niti dvéh enákih pláščev
In the shop they did not even have two of the same coats

5.3.4 The pronouns **obá** (m.), **obé** (f./n.) 'both'

These decline and behave in exactly the same way as **dvá/dvé** (see **4.10.2** and **5.3.3**)

5.3.5 The numerals 'three' and 'four': **tríje** (m.)/**trí** (f./n.); **štírje** (m.)/**štíri** (f./n.)

These numerals show the opposition masculine versus feminine/neuter only in the nominative case.

		m.		*f./n.*
N		tríje		trí
G			tréh	
D			trém	
A		trí		trí
L	pri		tréh	
I	s		trémi	

		m.		*f./n.*
N		štírje		štíri
G			štírih	
D			štírim	
A		štíri		štíri
L	pri		štírih	
I	s		štírimi	

'Three' and 'four' function in the same way as the plural of adjectives and agree in gender and case with the noun they qualify. The verbal predicate is plural and agrees in gender if it is an **-l** participle. Compound numerals ending in 'three' or 'four' (e.g. 304, 503) follow the same rules. Note, however, that these rules do not apply where 'three' or 'four' are the first element in a compound numeral, e.g. **tríindvájset** '23'. The numerals 'three' and 'four' may also be used substantivally. In counting the fem./neut. forms are used.

Examples of usage

Obvláda trí svetóvne jezíke
He speaks three world languages

stó štírje hlébci
104 loaves

Od desêtih bonbónov so ostáli samó štírje
Out of ten sweets only four remained

Štíri reaktívna letála so bilà sestreljêna
Four jets were shot down

Trí čŕne máčke so se igrále na vŕtu
Three black cats were playing in the garden

mát v tréh potézah
checkmate in three moves

Bilà je zmagoválka s stó štírimi tóčkami
She was the winner with 104 points

s trémi udárci
with three blows

5.3.6   The numerals 5–999

These numerals (excluding those compound numerals ending in one, two, three or four) do not distinguish gender. They decline like the plural of adjectives in their genitive, dative, locative and instrumental cases. Note that in the case of **stó** '100' a **-t-** is added before the adjectival endings.

		five	*one hundred*
N		**pét**	**stó**
G		**pêtih**	**stôtih**
D		**pêtim**	**stôtim**
A		**pét**	**stó**
L	pri	**pêtih**	**stôtih**
I	s	**pêtimi**	**stôtimi**

When used in the nom./acc. case these numerals take the genitive plural of the nouns, adjectives and pronouns which they qualify. The verbal predicate is always in the third person singular and if there is an **-l** participle in the predicate it takes the neuter form **-lo**. When used in the gen., dat., loc. and instr. cases the numerals up to 'one hundred' agree in case with the nouns, adjectives and pronouns which they qualify. In the numerals over 'one hundred' (e.g. 178, 200, 347, etc.) the hundred element is not declined but the rest of the numeral is. All these numerals may be used substantivally.

Examples of usage

Dvájset délavcev déla v továrni
Twenty workers are employed in the factory

Pred vráti je stálo pét vojákov
The five soldiers stood in front of the door

V sôbi je biló enájst lépih slík
In the room were eleven beautiful pictures

trísto šéstintrídeset tólarjev
336 tolars

s petnájstimi móžmi
with fifteen men

s stó sédemintrídeset(imi) vojáki
with 137 soldiers

plačáti v dvanájstih obrókih
to pay in twelve instalments

pri trídesetih stopínjah pod níčlo
at thirty degrees below zero

Z osemnájstimi léti dobíš volílno pravíco
At eighteen you get the right to vote

Med stôtimi/trísto kandidáti je bíl izbrán lè êden
From one hundred/three hundred candidates only one was chosen

v zádnjih pétsto létih
in the last 500 years

Od enájstih so žívi šè tríje
Out of eleven three are still alive

Ansámbel 'Beatles' je bíl populáren v šéstdesetih létih
The 'Beatles' pop group was popular in the sixties

Note: In the modern spoken language the higher numerals (other than 6–19 and the simple multiples of 10) are often not declined, e.g.

izmed stó ljudí
out of 100 people

z dvésto pétindvájset študênti
with 225 students

v zádnjih stó tríinštírideset létih
in the last 143 years

5.3.7 Stotína 'one hundred'

This is a special noun normally used in the plural to denote 'hundreds of', e.g.

Potováli smo stotíne kilométrov	We travelled hundreds of kilometres
Plačála sem stotíne fúntov za tó slíko	I paid hundreds of pounds for this picture

The phrase **na stotíne** + gen. is used in the meaning 'by the hundred', e.g. **Posékali so na stotíne drevés** 'They chopped down trees by the hundred'.

5.3.8   The numeral **tísoč** 'one thousand'

This numeral is normally indeclinable, but may be declined as a masculine noun in the plural when it means 'thousands'. When used in the nominative or accusative it takes the genitive case of the noun, adjective or pronoun it qualifies. When used in the gen., dat., loc. and instr. cases the noun which it qualifies will be in the corresponding case. When **tísoč** is part of a compound numeral (e.g. 4000, 1303, 2044, etc.) it does not decline. The verbal predicate is always in the third person singular and if an -l participle is involved it takes the neuter form **-lo**. If the plural form **tísoči** 'thousands' is used then the verbal predicate is in the third person plural and the -l participle is masculine plural.

Examples of usage

štéti do tísoč
to count to one thousand

Tísoč gôstov je biló na svátbi
A thousand guests were at the wedding

Rdéči kríž je pomágal tísoč begúncem
The Red Cross helped one thousand refugees

Rdéči kríž je pomágal tísočim begúncem
The Red Cross helped thousands of refugees

Govorímo o šést tísoč dólarjih
We are speaking about six thousand dollars

Továrna s tísoč délavci
A factory with a thousand workers

Knjíga je izšlà v pét tísoč izvódih
The book was published in 5000 copies

V Áfriki so tísoči umírali od gladú
In Africa thousands were dying of hunger

soródniki tísočih begúncev
the relatives of thousands of refugees

Od trí tísoč trísto ênega možá sta ostála žíva lè tísoč dvá
Out of 3301 men only 1002 remained alive

Med skôraj štíri tísoč državljáni je dvájset procêntov bólnih
Out of almost 4000 citizens twenty per cent are sick

na tísoče + *genitive*

This phrase means 'by the thousand, thousands of'. It takes a verbal predicate in the third person singular and the **-l** participle takes the neuter singular form **-lo**, e.g. **Na protéstnem zborovánju se je zbrálo na tísoče ljudí** 'Thousands of people gathered at the protest meeting'.

5.3.9   The numeral **milijón** 'one million'

This numeral does not normally decline in the singular unless preceded by a fraction (e.g. 'half a million'). When used in the nom. or acc. case it takes the gen. plur. of the noun, adjective or pronoun which it qualifies. When used in the gen., dat., loc. and instr. it takes the corresponding case of the noun etc. which it qualifies.

Examples of usage

štéti do milijón(a)
to count to a million

dežêla z milijón prebiválci
a country with a million inhabitants

Posojílo znáša milijón dólarjev
The loan amounts to one million dollars

Injékcije so dáli milijón otrôkom
They gave the injections to one million children

Knjížnica imá pól milijóna knjíg
The library has half a million books

Škóda gré v milijóne
The damage runs to millions

Compounds of 'a million'

When preceded by another numeral (e.g. 'two million', 'five million') both parts decline (**milijón** like a masc. noun) and the noun, adjective or pronoun which the numeral qualifies appears in the genitive plural in all cases, e.g.

Briljántna ogŕlica stáne pét milijónov tólarjev
The diamond necklace costs five million tolars

mésto s šêstimi milijóni prebiválcev
a town with six million inhabitants

Govoríla sta o šêstih milijónih dólarjev
They (d.) were talking about six million dollars

The phrase **na milijóne** + genitive

This phrase means 'millions of'. It takes a verbal predicate in the third person singular and the -l participle appears in the neuter singular form, e.g.

Na milijóne lét je potrébnih, da nastáne iz ogljíka diamánt
It takes millions of years for a diamond to be created from carbon

5.3.10 The numeral **milijárda** 'one thousand million'

This numeral declines like a feminine noun and takes the genitive plural, e.g. **milijárda fránkov** 'a thousand million francs'; **z milijárdo dólarjev** 'with a thousand million dollars'.

When preceded by another numeral both parts of the compound decline, e.g. **s pêtimi milijárdami fránkov** 'with five thousand million francs'.

na milijárde + genitive

This phrase means 'thousands of millions'. The verbal predicate is in the third person singular and the -l participle is in the neut. sing. form -lo, e.g. **V vesólju je na milijárde zvézd** 'There are thousands of millions of stars in the universe'.

5.4 ORDINAL NUMERALS

Apart from **pŕvi** 'first' and **drúgi** 'second' these numerals are derived from the cardinal numerals. In compounds such as 104th, 236th etc. only the final component has the form of an ordinal, e.g. **stóčetŕta strán** 'the one hundred and fourth page'; **dvéstošéstintrídeseti dán** 'the two hundred and thirty sixth day'.

Ordinal numerals decline like adjectives and agree in gender, number and case with the nouns they qualify, e.g.

šéstnajsto stolétje
the sixteenth century

Ánja sedí v pêti klópi pri ôknu
Anja sits in the fifth seat by the window

Pomlád se začnè ênaindvájsetega márca
Spring begins on the twenty first of March

V astronomíji račúnajo z bilijónskimi števílkami
In astronomy they calculate in billions

One should note the difference between the forms **milijónti** 'millionth' and **milijónski** 'consisting of a million', e.g.

milijónti obiskoválec razstáve	the millionth visitor to the exhibition
milijónsko mésto	a town with a million inhabitants
pridobíti si milijónsko premožênje	to acquire a fortune of one million

5.5   COLLECTIVE NUMERALS

The collective numerals are: **dvóje** 'two', **tróje** 'three', **četvéro** 'four', **petéro** 'five', **šestéro** 'six', **sedméro** 'seven', **osméro** 'eight', **devetéro** 'nine', **desetéro** 'ten'. If required for a higher number they are formed from the basic cardinal numeral with the suffix **-éro**, e.g. **dvajsetéro** 'twenty'.

Note: The indeclinable numeral **obóje** 'both' also belongs to this group.

The collective numerals above 'three' are, in fact, hardly ever used nowadays and in general even the lower collectives are used less frequently. They are only used in the nominative and accusative case and take the genitive plural. In the oblique cases they are replaced by the cardinal numerals.
   Collective numerals are used in the following ways:

(a)   They are used with nouns which exist only in a plural form. The verbal predicate is in the third person singular and the **-l** participle if used appears in the neuter sing. form **-lo**, e.g.

dvóje úst	two mouths
tróje očál	three pairs of spectacles
tróje hláč	three pairs of trousers
Na mízi je dvóje vílic	There are two forks on the table
Dvóje vrát je biló odpŕtih	Two doors were open
híša s trémi vráti	a house with three doors
Govorím o tréh škárjah, ki	I am speaking about the three pairs of
so jih ukrádli	scissors which were stolen

In the colloquial language the collective numerals are replaced by cardinal numerals even in the nominative and accusative cases, e.g.

trí gráblje	three rakes
Trí vráta so bilà odpŕta	Three doors were open
Na mízi so trí vílice	There are three forks on the table

(b) The collective numeral **dvóje** 'two' is used with nouns that exist in pairs to emphasise that fact, e.g. **Člôvek imá dvóje ušés in dvóje očí** 'Man has two eyes and two ears'.

(c) Collective numerals are used with words like **čévelj** 'shoe', **rokavíca** 'glove', which are conceived as existing in a pair. The use of the collective numeral implies 'so many pairs of', e.g. **dvóje čévljev** 'two pairs of shoes' (but normally **dvá pára čévljev** is preferred).

(d) Very often the collective numerals **dvóje**, **tróje** replace the cardinal numerals **dvá/dvé**, **trí** used with nouns like **novíca** 'piece of news', **dél** 'piece', **réč**, **stvár** 'thing', **primér** 'example'. In these cases they may be declined like a singular neuter adjective, e.g:

Dvóje (= dvé novíci) ti imám povédati
I have two things to tell you

Posóda ji je pádla iz rók in se razletéla na tróje (= na trí déle)
The dish fell out of her hand and broke into three pieces

O dvójem (= o dvéh primérih) se govorí
One is speaking about two examples

Obljubíla mi je dvóje (= dvé rečí)
She promised me two things

raztŕgati na dvóje
to tear in two

Tróje je mogóče: ali so ga ujéli ali je ušèl ali se je kjé skríl
Three things are possible; either they took him or he ran away or he hid somewhere

Čúdim se dvójemu, njegóvi nepremíšljenosti in uspéhu
I'm amazed at two things, his thoughtlessness and his success

Bežím pred dvójim, odgovórnostjo in dolžnóstjo
I avoid two things – responsibility and duty

(e) The collective numerals are also used to represent the number of persons involved in an activity in phrases such as: **vesláti v dvóje** 'to row as a pair'; **večérjati v tróje** 'to dine as a threesome'; **v dvóje jáhati na kônju** 'to ride double'; **V dvóje gré láže** 'It is easier with two people'.

5.6 DIFFERENTIAL NUMERALS

The differential numerals are: **dvój** 'two ', **trój** 'three', **četvér** 'four', **petér** 'five', **šestér** 'six', **sedmér** 'seven', **osmér** 'eight', **devetér** 'nine', **desetér** 'ten'. These numerals, which are often confused with the collective numerals, decline like adjectives, i.e. **dvój** (m.), **dvója** (f.), **dvóje** (n.) etc. They agree with the noun they qualify and are used to denote a qualitative differentiation in the counted items, i.e. 'different types/sorts of'. Differential numerals do not exist above 'ten' except for **stotér** 'one hundred', **tisočér** 'one thousand'.

Examples of usage

Imámo tróje délavce: vozníke, zidárje in tesárje
We have three types of worker; drivers, builders and carpenters

Postrégli so mi z dvójim mêsom, govédino in telétino
They served me with two sorts of meat – beef and veal

seznám stotérih/tisočérih rastlín
a list of a hundred/thousand types of plants

In the modern language these numerals are very literary and are normally replaced by the cardinal numerals used with the noun **vŕsta** 'type' or a similar noun, e.g.

štíri vŕste vína
four types of wine

trí vŕste očál: za blízu, za dáleč in sónčna
three sorts of spectacles – for short sight, for long sight and sunglasses

Pri nàs vsáko léto kúhamo trí vŕste marmeláde
Every year we make three sorts of jam

5.7 MULTIPLICATIVE NUMERALS

These numerals denote the multiple occurrence or existence of a counted item. They are formed in two ways:

(a) From the collective numerals 2–4 with the aid of the suffix **-en**, i.e. **dvójen** 'double', **trójen** 'triple, threefold', **četvéren** 'fourfold'.

Note: By analogy with the collectives **dvójen, trójen** we also find **enójen** 'single'.

(b) From the cardinal numerals with the suffix **-kraten**, e.g. **dvákraten** 'double, twofold', **tríkraten** 'triple, threefold', **pétkraten** 'fivefold' etc.

In both cases these numerals decline like adjectives and agree with the noun they qualify. The **e** of the suffix **-en** is a fleeting **e**.

Examples of usage

Igrálka imá dvójno brádo
The actress has a double chin

ôkno z dvójnimi šípami
a double-glazed window

enójno knjigovódstvo
single entry book keeping

V klásičnih drámah je izpeljána trójna enôtnost
In classical dramas the three unities are observed

Mój stríc imá dvójno življênje
My uncle leads a double life

dvákratni stróški
twofold expenses

Pláčal sem dvójno céno
I paid double the price

Zêmlja je dála létos štírikraten sád
The earth produced a fourfold fruit this year

trójni sálto
a triple somersault

trójni zmagoválec
a triple winner

Dvójni vôzel tŕdneje držî kot enójni
A double knot is stronger than a single knot

5.8 FRACTIONS

Fractions denote parts of whole numbers. With the exception of **pól/polovíca** 'half', fractions up to 'one thousand' are formed from their corresponding ordinal numerals with the suffix **-ína**, e.g. **tretjína** 'one third', **osmína** 'one eighth', **stotína** 'one hundredth, **tisočína** 'one thousandth' etc. The fractions from **milijón** and **milijárda** are **milijonína/milijonínka** and **milijardínka**.

Fractions may also be formed from ordinal numerals with the suffix **-ínka**. These forms are used as time measurements or indicate musical terms, e.g. **osmínka** 'quaver'; **tisočínka sekúnde** 'a thousandth of a second'.

The fractions decline like fem. nouns in **-a** and take the genitive of the noun they qualify. If the fraction is the subject of a clause the verbal predicate will be in the third person singular and the **-l** participle will be in the feminine singular. If the fraction subject, however, is preceded by another numeral then the verbal predicate will be governed by the first number, i.e. if the fraction is preceded by **dvé** then the agreement will be feminine dual, if preceded by **trí/ štíri** the agreement will be feminine plural, if by **pét**, **šést** etc. the verbal predicate will be third person singular neuter.

Examples of usage

Prebrál je pŕvo četrtíno knjíge
He read the first quarter of the book

Dvé petíni prebiválstva sta stári pod dvájset lét
Two fifths of the population are under twenty

Dobíl je desetíno dobíčka
He received a tenth of the profit

Ob potrésu je bilà porúšena tretjína híš
In the earthquake a third of the houses were destroyed

Ob potrésu so bilè porúšene trí četrtíne híš
In the earthquake three quarters of the houses were destroyed

Ob potrésu je biló porúšenih pét šestín híš
In the earthquake five sixths of the houses were destroyed

Za êno desetínko sekúnde je bíl hitréjši
He was one tenth of a second faster

5.8.1 A 'Half': **pól**; **napól**; **polovíca**

pól

The form **pól** is indeclinable and refers to measure, time or a whole. It takes the genitive of the noun it qualifies and the verbal predicate is in the third person singular. If there is an **-l** participle this takes the neuter sing. form **-lo**. If there is an adjective in the predicate it agrees with the genitive of the noun qualified.

Examples of usage

pól kilográma mesá	a half kilogram of meat
pól lítra vína	a half litre of wine
Pól jábolka je gnílega	Half the apple is rotten
Pretêklo je pól úre	A half an hour went by
Pól obráza ji zakríva rúta	A scarf covers half her face
kupíti za pól céne	to buy at half price
Do vasí je úro in pól hodá	It is a half hour's walk to the village

If **pól** is preceded by a pronoun or adjective or by a preposition + pronoun or adjective, the pronoun or adjective will agree with the noun qualified by **pól**, e.g.

vsáke pól úre	every half hour
v slábe pól úre	in less than half an hour
Prišèl je pred dôbrega pól léta	He arrived more than half a year ago

Note: One also finds colloquially **pred dôbre pól léta**.

pól may also be used to express an approximate half measure or degree, e.g.

Pól vasí se je zbrálo pred šólo	Half the village gathered in front of the school
Tó ní vrédno pól tóliko, kot si pláčal	This is not worth half what you paid for it
Ob potrésu je biló porúšenih pól híš	Half the houses were destroyed in the earthquake
Híša je pól leséna, pól zídana	The house is half wooden, half brick
Pól v spánju je upíhnila svéčo	Half asleep she blew out the candle

pôl is used to denote the half hour in time phrases, e.g. **Je pôl ôsmih** 'It is half past seven'.

pól is also used in certain colloquial phrases such as: **Ti bom žé dál hudíča in pól** 'I'll show you/I'll get my revenge'; **Òn je lópov in pól** 'He is an utter rogue'.

napól/na pól

This form means either (a) on a fifty-fifty basis, or (b) approximately half. In this latter sense it normally precedes an adjective.

Examples of usage

(a) **razdelíti si stróške napól s kóm**	to share the expenses fifty-fifty with someone
(b) **napól prázen vóz**	a half empty train
napól izpráznjen kozárec	a half empty glass
Bíl je napól mžtev od strahú	He was half dead with fright
Vŕnil se je napól ŕív	He came back half dead
Samó napól me poslúšaš	You are only half listening to me
govoríti napól za šálo	to say half jokingly
na pól kàj napráviti	to do things by half

polovíca

This word declines like a feminine noun and takes the genitive of the noun it qualifies. It denotes either (a) half of an equally divided object or (b) an approximate half of a measure or quantity or (c) a degree.

Examples of usage

(a) **plačáti polovíco stróškov**	to pay half the expenses
(b) **Polovíca ljudí téga ne vé**	Half the people do not know that
(c) **Za polovíco mlájša je od njêga**	She is half as old as he is
Stróški so bilí za polovíco véčji,	The expenses were half as much
kot so predvidévali	again than they had anticipated

Note too that **polovíca** is used instead of **pól** if it is qualified by a number or an adjective, e.g.

pobárvana polovíca zidú	the painted half of the wall
léva in désna polovíca obráza	the left and right sides of the face
obé polovíci jábolka	both halves of the apple
Tó je môja bóljša polovíca	This is my better half (i.e. wife)

5.8.2 A 'quarter': **četrtína**; **četŕt**

In the sense of a fraction **četrtína** is the noun normally used. The form **četŕt** has two meanings:

(a) It means 'quarter' in the sense 'district or quarter' of a town in which case it declines like a feminine noun in a consonant, e.g. **v délavski četŕti mésta** 'in the workers' quarter of the town'.

(b) It means 'quarter' in time phrases or in measurement in which case it does not decline, e.g.

trí četŕt na sédem	a quarter to seven
Ávtobus odpélje vsáke četŕt úre	A bus leaves every quarter of an hour
Naróčil je četŕt vína, spíl ga je	He ordered a quarter bottle of wine,
lè četrtíno	but drank only a quarter of it

5.8.3 The adjectival forms of fractions

From 'three' upwards these are formed from the ordinary fractions by replacing final **-a** with the adjectival suffix **-ski**, e.g. **tretjína – tretjínski** 'a third'.

Examples of usage

tretjínski/osmínski délež	a third/an eighth share
desetínsko števílo	a decimal number

The adjectival form for 'half' is **polovíčni**, e.g. **polovíčna resníca** 'a half truth'; **polovíčna hitróst** 'half speed'.

5.9 NUMERALS IN -ka

These numerals are formed from the collective/differential numerals in the case of 'two' and 'three' and from the cardinal numerals in the case of 'one' and the numerals 'four' and above, e.g. **ênka/enójka** 'one', **dvójka** 'two', **trójka** 'three', **štírka** 'four', **pétka** 'five', **šéstka** 'six', etc. These numerals decline like feminine nouns and are used colloquially to represent the cardinal numeral or to indicate an object bearing the number in question, e.g. a bus, a mark in school, a playing card. The following examples exemplify current usage.

Na téj prógi vózi ênka/devétka/ enájstka	The number one/nine/eleven (bus) goes along this route
Dobíl je ênko/trójko/pétko	He got a (mark of) one/three/five
píkova dvójka	the two of spades
kríževa trójka	the three of clubs
károva šéstka	the six of diamonds
vréči desétko	to throw away a ten

We also find the numerals **četvórka** 'four', **petérka** 'five', **šestérka** 'six' formed from the collective numerals with the suffix **-ka**. These plus **dvójka** and **trójka** may be used to indicate a group of people, e.g.

združeváti se v dvójke in trójke	to make friends in groups of twos and threes
plesáti četvórko	to dance a quadrille
Gledálci so búčno spodbújali domáčo petérko/šestérko	The spectators noisily urged on the home team (of five/six players)

5.10 NUMERALS IN -ica

These numerals are formed either from the collective numerals (e.g. **dvojíca** 'two', **trojíca** 'three', **četvérica** 'four', **petérica** 'five', **enajstérica** 'eleven' etc.) or from the cardinal numerals 'four to twenty' (i.e. **eníca** 'one', **štiríca** 'four', **petíca** 'five', **sedmíca** 'seven' etc.). They decline like feminine nouns.

(a) The numerals in **-ica** derived from collective numerals denote groups of people, e.g.

obísk švédske kraljévske dvojíce
the visit of the Swedish royal couple

znána igrálska četvérica
a well-known quartet

Postáli so nèrazdružljíva trojíca
They became an inseparable trio

Za pŕvo mésto se potegúje šést enajstéric
Six teams [i.e. football teams of eleven players] are in contention for first place

Sestánek minístrov šestérice evrópskih držáv
A meeting of the ministers of the six European states

(b) Numerals in **-ica** derived from cardinal numerals like those in **-ka** mean the number in question, a mark in school, a bus or a playing card, e.g.

prečŕtati petíco
to cross out the five

károva desetíca
the ten of diamonds

peljáti se z dvanajstíco
to travel on the number twelve bus

Nóče se vselíti v sôbo s trinajstíco na vrátih
He will not move into a room with number thirteen on the door

Dobíl je štiríco
He got a [mark of] four

5.11 NUMERALS IN -ec

These numerals include 'two' and those from 'four to twelve'. They are derived from the collective numerals and decline like masculine nouns. They have restricted meanings related to the sport of rowing or to poetry, e.g. **dvójec** 'a double scull'; **četvérec** 'a four-seater sculler'; **šestérec** 'hexameter'; **osmérec** 'octosyllabic verse; a rowing eight'; **dvanajstérec** 'an Alexandrine line'.

5.12 NUMERALS IN -ak

These are very few and have specific meanings. They decline like masculine nouns, e.g. **stoták** 'a hundred tolar note'; **tisočák** 'a thousand tolar note' or 'a thousand metre high mountain'; **šesterák** 'a deer [with three sprouts on each antler]'.

5.13 NUMERALS IN -ček

These represent numbers of children at birth and are used in the plural or dual in the case of twins, e.g.

Rodíla je trójčke/četvérčke	She gave birth to triplets/quadruplets
Dvójčka sta si takó podóbna, da ju ljudjé lè s težávo lóčijo	The twins are so alike that people find it difficult to distinguish between them

5.14 NUMERALS IN ARITHMETIC

Addition, division, multiplication and subtraction are expressed in the following ways:

trí in štíri je sédem	$3 + 4 = 7$
devét deljêno z dvá/dvé je pét	$10 \div 2 = 5$
dvákrat štíri je ósem	$2 \times 4 = 8$
desét mínus šést je štíri	$10 - 6 = 4$

5.14.1 Verbs indicating multiplication

Verbs indicating multiplication by a number are derived from collective numerals with the prefix **po-** and the verbal suffix **-iti**, e.g. **podvojíti** 'to double'; **potrojíti** 'to triple'; **početvériti** 'to quadruple'; **popetériti** 'to increase fivefold' etc. Note too **postotériti** 'to increase one hundredfold'.

5.14.2 nil, nought, zero: **nìč, níčla**

nìč is indeclinable, e.g. **Tékma se je končála s trí proti nìč** 'The match ended three nil'; **nìč célih pétindvájset** '0.25'.

The adjective from **nìč** is **níčti**, e.g. **níčta končníca** 'a zero ending (in linguistics)'.

níčla declines like a feminine noun and means 'zero', e.g. **Dánes je temperatúra okóli níčle** 'Today the temperature is around zero'; **desét stopínj nad níčlo** 'ten degrees above zero'; **števílo s trémi níčlami na kôncu** 'a number with three zeros at the end'.

5.15 NUMERALS IN COMPOUND ADJECTIVES AND NOUNS

The numeral components of compound adjectives and nouns may have a link vowel **-o-**. The numeral 'one' takes the form **eno-**, the numerals 'two to four' take the forms **dvo-/dve-**, **tro-/tri-**, **četvero-/štiri-**. The numerals 'five to ten' take the form **petero-**, **šestero-** etc. Above 'ten' the simple cardinal is used.

Examples of usage

ênožénstvo 'monogamy'; **dvóbárven** 'two coloured'; **dvóbòj** 'duel'; **dvóglásnik** 'diphthong'; **dvójezíčen** 'bilingual'; **dvóléten** 'lasting two years'; **dvéléten** 'two years old'; **dvéúren** 'lasting two hours'; **trókoló** 'tricycle'; **trikótnik** 'triangle'; **tróskòk** 'triple jump'; **trikóten** 'triangular'; **četveronóžec/štírinóžec** 'quadruped'; **štírikolésen** 'four wheeled'; **peterobòj** 'pentathlon'; **petnájstlítrski** '15 litre'; **pétdesetkílski** '50 kilogram'; **stolétje** 'century'; **tísočlétno obdóbje** 'a thousand year period'

5.16 DISTRIBUTION

Numerically equal distribution is expressed by the adverb **po** + the cardinal or collective numeral in whichever case the sentence requires, e.g.

Dál sem otrôkom po dvé knjígi/po pét bonbónov/po tísoč tólarjev
I gave the children two books each/five sweets each/a thousand tolars each

Jájca so bilà na tŕgu po êno márko
The eggs cost one mark each at the market

Fánta imáta po dvóje hláč
The boys (d.) have two pairs of trousers each

V klópi sedíjo po tríje učênci
The pupils sit three to a bench

Obsójena sta bilà na po desét lét
They (d.) were sentenced to ten years each

Vsáka skupína imá po ênega vodníka
Each group has one leader

Vzgójil je nágeljne s po dvéma cvétoma
He grew carnations with two flowers on each one

Razdeljêni so bilì v skupíne po pét
They were divided into groups of five

Phrases such as 'in ones/in twos/in threes' are expressed by **(êden) po êden/po dvá (in dvá)/po tríje** etc., e.g.

Korákali so po dvá in dvá	They were marching in twos
stópati v vŕsti (êden) po êden	to walk in single file
Prósim, prihájajte v pisárno po tríje	Come to the office in threes please

5.17 ADVERBIAL NUMERALS

(a) Adverbs of frequency
These are derived by adding the suffix **-krat** to the cardinal numeral, e.g. **ênkrat na dán** 'once a day'; **Òn je dvákrat staréjši od sína** 'He is twice as old as his son'; **Poskúsil je tríkrat, potém pa odnéhal** 'He tried three times and then gave up'.

(b) Adverbs of time
These are derived by adding the suffix **-ič** to the ordinal numeral, e.g. **pŕvič** 'for the first time'; **drúgič** 'for the second time'; **trétjič** 'for the third time'.

Examples of usage

drúgič se oženíti	to marry for a second time
Pétkrat je zmágal, šêstič pa izgúbil	He won five times, but on the sixth occasion he lost

(c) Indefinite adverbs expressing amount, measure
These include such words as: **vèč** 'several'; **nékaj** 'some, a little'; **mnógo** 'many'; **dôsti** 'enough, a lot of'; **nàjveč** 'most'; **nàjmanj** 'least, fewest'; **málo** 'few, a little'; **velíko** 'many, much'; **nekóliko** 'a few, some, a little'; **precéj** 'many, much, a great deal of'; **kóliko** 'how many, how much'; **tóliko** 'so many, so much'.

These indefinite adverbial numerals are indeclinable and take the genitive case when they are used in the nominative or accusative. In the oblique cases the noun they qualify appears in the appropriate oblique case form if it is a count noun, but if it is a non-count noun then it always occurs in the genitive case even in the oblique cases.

Examples of usage

(i) *With count nouns*
V dôsti primérih je Jánko ugánil právo rešítev
In a lot of examples Janko guessed the right answer

vèč prijáteljev
several friends

Tóča je v vèč krájih okléstila vinógrade
The hail damaged the vineyards in several regions

Vsákih nékaj korákov se je ozŕla
Every few steps she looked back

Pred nékaj dnévi sem ga sréčal
I met him a few days ago

Mnógo ljudém sem tó povédal
I told this to many people

z velíko napákami
with many mistakes

z málo izjémami
with few exceptions

V nàjveč primérih tí bolníki ozdravíjo
In most cases these patients recover

Kóliko napákam bi se izôgnil, če bi bíl pazljívejši
How many mistakes would he have avoided if he had paid more attention

Tó sem narédil z nekóliko pomočníki
I did that with a few helpers

Pri tóliko ovírah je hítro délo nèmogóče
Given so many obstacles it is impossible to do the job quickly

Note: Colloquially some of these adverbial numerals are declined like adjectives and one encounters forms such as **v vêčih primérih** 'in several examples'; **z dôstimi ljudmí** 'with a lot of people'.

(ii) *With non-count nouns*

    málo krúha 'a little bread'; **z velíko trúda** 'with great effort'; **s precéj pogúma** 'with a great deal of courage'; **zíma z nàjmanj snegá** 'the winter with the least snow'; **Prodám híšo z nékaj zêmlje** 'I am selling a house with some land'.

Note: Colloquially one can find the non-count noun in the appropriate oblique case especially in the case of **málo, tóliko, nékaj, nekóliko**, e.g. **z málo trúdom** 'with little effort'.

6 VERBS

In dictionaries Slovene verbs are given in their infinitive form, which ends in
-ti or **-či**, e.g. **zídati** 'to build', **têči** 'to run'.

6.1 VERBAL MORPHOLOGY

The basic grammatical categories of the Slovene verb are aspect, person,
number, gender, tense, mood and voice.

The Slovene verb distinguishes finite and non-finite verb forms. The finite
forms which indicate person (first, second, third) and number (singular, dual
and plural) are the present tense and the imperative which are expressed
synthetically and the future, past and pluperfect tenses, which are expressed
analytically with the auxiliary verb **bíti** 'to be'. Non-finite verb forms, which
cannot be inflected for person, are the participles, the verbal adverbs (gerunds), the present and past conditional moods, the infinitive, the supine and
the verbal noun. The present and past active participles and the past participle passive decline like adjectives. The so-called resultative **-l** participle is
also adjectival and is used to form the future, past and pluperfect tenses and
the present and past conditional. In the analytical constructions, however, the
-l participle is used only in the nominative case.

6.2 ASPECT

Aspect is an inherent category of the Slovene verb and qualifies a verbal
action, process or state with regard to its completion (perfective aspect) or
non-completion (imperfective aspect). The opposition between the two
aspects is expressed in the form of correlated pairs of verbs (perfective and
imperfective) which are differentiated formally either by prefixation or suffixation or even by suppletion, although suppletive aspectual pairings are very
rare, e.g.

Imperfective verb	*Perfective verb*	
čístiti	**počístiti**	to clean
kúhati	**skúhati**	to cook
líkati	**zlíkati**	to iron
pomívati	**pomíti**	to wash

kupováti	kupíti	to buy
délati	naredíti	to do
jemáti	vzéti	to take

The fundamental distinction between the aspects is that the use of the perfective form of the verb indicates the completed action of the verb or its foreseen or expected completion (its delimitation in time) whereas the use of the imperfective form of the verb does not explicitly characterise the action or state this way but focuses on its progress, duration, frequency or repetition (its extension over time in one way or another). The perfective form of the verb is therefore used to denote completion of an action, a limited action, the result of an action, the beginning or end of an action, instantaneous, sudden or momentary action, excess of action or a sudden change of state. The imperfective form of the verb on the other hand denotes action in progress, continuous action, duration of action, frequency of action, habitual or repeated action, lengthy action, state or gradual change.

From both aspects of a verb one can form the present, future, past, and pluperfect tenses, the -l participle, the imperative, the present and past conditional, the supine and the verbal noun. The present verbal adverb (gerund) and the present participle active are formed only from imperfective verbs, while the past verbal adverb (gerund) is formed only from perfective verbs. The past participle passive is formed normally only from perfective verbs, but may occasionally be formed from imperfective verbs (see **6.36**).

Examples of aspect

(a) *Duration (imperfective verbs)*

Vsà družína je délala: medtém ko je Míha čístil stanovánje, je Zdénka líkala perílo, Jóže pa je pomíval posódo

All the family were doing something: while Miha was cleaning the flat, Zdenka was ironing the clothes and Jože was washing the dishes

Máti kúha kosílo v kúhinji

Mother is cooking lunch in the kitchen

(b) *Result/completion (perfective verbs)*

Ko so vsè naredíli: ko je Míha počístil stanovánje, ko je Zdénka zlíkala perílo in Jóže pomìl posódo, so odšlí na sprêhod

When they had done everything, when Miha had cleaned the flat, when Zdenka had ironed the clothes and when Jože had washed the dishes, they went for a walk

Včéraj je ôče skúhal kosílo

Father cooked lunch yesterday

(c) *Repetition/frequency (imperfective verbs)*
Krompír kupújem védno pri ísti kmetíci
I always buy potatoes from the same peasant woman

Ôče jêmlje tá zdravíla žé večlét
Father has been taking these medicines for many years

(d) *Completion (perfective verbs)*
Dánes sem kupíla kílo krompírja
Today I bought a kilogram of potatoes

Vzél sem aspirín, ker me je boléla gláva
I took an aspirin, because my head was aching

6.2.1 Restrictions of aspectual usage

Only an imperfective infinitive may be used after so-called phasal verbs, i.e. verbs which express beginning or ending, even though phasal verbs themselves may be perfective or imperfective.

Examples

Začél je govoríti	He began to speak
Začéla se je obláčiti v čŕno	She began to wear black
Prenéhal je kadíti	He stopped smoking
Zídati so končáli šè pred mrákom	They stopped building before dusk
Ràd bi néhal kadíti	I would like to stop smoking
Začénja se mračíti	It is beginning to get dark

6.2.2 Biaspectual verbs

Although the majority of Slovene verbs exist in correlated aspectual pairs, a certain number of verbs in Slovene have only one form, which serves to express both the perfective and imperfective aspects. These verbs are to all intents and purposes biaspectual and include the following common verbs: **rodíti** 'to give birth to'; **tékniti** 'to be to one's taste'; **darováti** 'to give, donate'; **voščíti** 'to wish, bid'; **ubógati** 'to obey'; **imenováti** 'to name'; **bírmati** 'to confirm' (i.e administer religious rite); **krstíti** 'to christen'; **tvégati** 'to risk, venture'; **blagoslovíti** 'to bless'; **stáviti** 'to bet'; **čestítati** 'to congratulate'; **vídeti** 'to see'; **ločíti** 'to separate'; **žrtvováti** 'to sacrifice'; **kaznováti** 'to punish'; **práviti** 'to say, tell'.

Verbs with the derivative suffix **-írati** formed from loan words are also biaspectual. About 1,200 verbs in the modern language belong to this group, e.g. **protestírati, deklamírati, idealizírati, telefonírati, fotograf-**

írati, eksplodírati, diskreditírati, likvidírati, formulírati, signalizírati, deformírati.

In the case of biaspectual verbs it is the concrete context that reveals which aspect is in use, e.g.

Môja sêstra je rodíla (pf.) **zdrávega otrôka**	My sister gave birth to a healthy baby
but **uredíti prôstor, v katérem mátere rodíjo** (imp.)	to tidy up the area where mothers give birth
V vsèm ga ubóga (imp.)	He obeys him in everything
but **Ubógal je** (pf.) **očéta in naredil tó**	He obeyed his father and did this
S prijátelji je stávil (pf.), **da bódo zmágali**	He bet his friends that they would win
but **Če mi ne verjámeš, pa stáviva** (imp.)	If you do not believe me, let us have a bet
'Dober dán vóščim,' (imp.) **je rékel**	'I bid you good day,' he said
but **Vóščil mi je** (pf.) **sréčno nôvo léto**	He wished me a Happy New Year
Telefoníral sem (pf.) **ob šêstih**	I rang at six
but **Vès dán sem telefoníral** (imp.)	I have been ringing all day

Only very rarely are verbs in **-irati** given a prefix to create an aspectual pair, e.g.

Imperfective	*Perfective*	
študírati	**preštudírati**	to study
bombardírati	**zbombardírati**	to bombard
komponírati	**skomponírati**	to compose

Even more rare are verbs in **-írati** which are used only in a prefixed perfective form, e.g. **zabarikadírati** 'to barricade'. Since this verb has no imperfective counterpart one would have to use a construction like **postávljati** or **délati barikáde** 'to make barricades' in order to express the imperfective aspect, e.g.

Demonstránti so zabarikadírali césto	The demonstrators barricaded the street
but **Na úlicah so demonstránti postávljali barikáde**	The demonstrators were barricading the streets

6.2.3 Simple (non prefixed) verbs

The vast majority of simple verbs are imperfective, e.g. **spáti** 'to sleep'; **bleščáti se** 'to shine'; **bóžati** 'to caress'; **drážiti** 'to tease'; **glédati** 'to look, watch'; **gníti** 'to rot'; **tkáti** 'to weave'; **trésti** 'to shake'; **švígati** 'to shoot along, out'; **máhati** 'to wave'; **zéhati** 'to yawn'; **díhati** 'to breathe'; **rováriti** 'to plot'; **kíhati** 'to sneeze'; **têči** 'to run'; **dréti** 'to flay', etc.

A limited number of simple verbs are, however, perfective. The most common of these are: **plačáti** 'to pay; **končáti** 'to finish'; **póčiti** 'to burst'; **néhati** 'to stop, cease'; **zmágati** 'to conquer'; **sréčati** 'to meet'; **kupíti** 'to buy'; **lotíti se** 'to start, commence, undertake'; **jáviti** 'to inform'; **píčiti** 'to sting'; **pustíti** 'to allow, permit'; **raníti** 'to wound'; **rešíti** 'to save, solve'; **veléti** 'to command'; **skočíti** 'to leap'; **pokoríti** 'to subdue'; **sprémiti** 'to accompany'; **stopíti** 'to step'; **storíti** 'to do'; **tŕčiti** 'to collide (with)'; **tréščiti** 'to crash, strike'; **dejáti** 'to put; say'; **pásti** 'to fall'; **sésti** 'to sit down'; **léči** 'to lie down'; **séči** 'to reach for'; **rêči** 'to say'; **vréči** 'to throw'; **jéti** (arch.) 'to begin, start'; **dáti** 'to give'; **skópiti** 'to castrate'; **posodíti** 'to lend'; **ménjati** 'to change'; **zíniti** 'to utter'.

6.2.4 Verbs in -niti

(a) Simple semelfactive verbs with the suffix **-niti**, which denote instantaneous actions are perfective, e.g. **kríkniti** 'to cry out'; **súniti** 'to thrust, strike'; **máhniti** 'to give a wave'; **kíhniti** 'to sneeze'; **dahníti** 'to draw a breath'; **zéhniti** 'to yawn'; **svístniti** 'to whistle'.

(b) On the other hand simple verbs in **-niti** which denote processes are imperfective, e.g. **gásniti** 'to fade, die out'; **gíniti** 'to pine for, languish'; **sáhniti** 'to wither, dry up'; **toníti** 'to sink, founder'; **dŕgniti** 'to rub, chafe'.

6.3 TRANSITIVITY

6.3.1 Transitive verbs

Transitive verbs describe actions which must, in addition to the subject, involve someone or something else. They are followed by a direct object in the accusative case, e.g.

Andréj píše písmo	Andrej is writing a letter
Ána je kupíla knjígo	Ana bought a book

If, however, the transitive verb is negated the accusative case is replaced by the genitive case, e.g.

Bêrem knjígo	I am reading the book
but **Ne bêrem knjíge**	I am not reading the book
Razuméli smo vprašánja	We understood the questions
but **Nísmo razuméli vprašánj**	We didn't understand the questions

The genitive is also used as the direct object of the infinitive of a transitive verb if the infinitive occurs after a negated modal verb, e.g. **môči** 'to be able', **sméti** 'to be allowed', etc., e.g.

Tákih kredítov ne bóm mógel odplačeváti	I will not be able to pay off such loans
Poškodováne rôke ne sméte premíkati	You must not move the injured hand

If, however, the infinitive of a transitive verb occurs after verbs other than modal verbs, then the direct object may be in the accusative or the genitive, e.g.

Ne bojím se povédati resníco/resníce	I am not afraid to tell the truth

Should, however, the direct object precede the verbal predicate the genitive is the case more frequently used, e.g. **Resníce se ne bojím povédati**.

6.3.2 Intransitive verbs

These are verbs describing an action that does not involve anyone or anything other than the subject, e.g.

Andréj je zbéžal	Andrej ran away
Bréda je zaspáno zazéhala	Breda yawned sleepily

Simple verbs of motion and verbs of state are always intransitive, e.g.

Káča léze	A snake crawls
Ôče spí	Father is sleeping

However, when prefixed they may become transitive, e.g.

Káča je prelézla césto	The snake crawled across the road
Na vláku je prespál vsè postáje do Ljubljáne	On the train he slept through all the stations as far as Ljubljana

With certain verbs transitivity is expressed by the suffix **-iti**, while their counterpart in **-eti** expresses intransitivity, e.g.

Nebó je hítro potemnélo	The sky darkened quickly
but **Lák je potemníl narávno bárvo lesá**	The varnish darkened the natural colour of the wood

Some verbs may be either transitive or intransitive depending on the context, e.g.

Vêra dôbro slíši	Vera hears well
Vêra je slíšala koráke	Vera heard footsteps

Note too that transitive verbs become intransitive when they become reflexive verbs (see **6.4**), e.g.

Začéli so pogájanja s sovrážnikom	They began negotiations with the enemy

Pogájanja s sovrážnikom so se začéla	Negotiations with the enemy began

6.3.3 Verbs governing cases other than the accusative

It should be noted that a certain number of verbs in Slovene govern an object in the dative or genitive case or are followed by a prepositional construction. These verbs may be reflexive (see **6.4**), e.g.

škodováti + dat.	to harm
zahvalíti se + dat.	to thank
kljubováti + dat.	to defy
spómniti se + gen.	to remember
kesáti se + gen.	to repent, regret
dotakníti se + gen.	to touch
pozabíti na + acc.	to forget

6.4 REFLEXIVE VERBS

Reflexive verbs are those used with the accusative clitic form of the reflexive pronoun, i.e. **se**. They may be verbs which can only be used with **se**, many of which reflect the physical or psychological state of the subject, e.g. **báti se** 'to be afraid'; **zdéti se** 'to seem'; **počutíti se** 'to feel'; **posréčiti se** 'to succeed'; **smejáti se** 'to laugh'; **sramováti se** 'to be ashamed'; **navelíčati se** 'to weary of', **čudíti se** 'to wonder at'; **kesáti se** 'to regret'; **kújati se** 'to sulk'; **dotakníti se** 'to touch', or they may be non-reflexive verbs made reflexive verbs by the use of the morpheme **se**, e.g.

utopíti	to drown (something)	**utopíti se**	to drown
strníti	to join together, unite (something)	**strnítise**	to unite, join together
zgubíti	to lose (something)	**zgubíti se**	to get lost
razvedríti	to cheer up (someone)	**razvedríti se**	to cheer up
obléči	to put on (something)	**obléči se**	to get dressed
umíti	to wash (something)	**umíti se**	to wash (oneself)
preplašíti	to frighten (someone)	**preplašíti se**	to be frightened

It should be noted that although a verb and its reflexive form usually correspond in meaning, there are cases where the reflexive verb has in reality become a separate verb with a lexical meaning distinct from that of the non-reflexive verb, e.g.

dajáti	to give	**dajáti se**	to quarrel, fight
napráviti	to do	**napráviti se**	to pretend
klátiti	to knock down	**klátiti se**	to roam

Reflexive verbs have the following functions:

(a) The reflexive morpheme **se** changes an active sentence into a passive one where the subject is not indicated, e.g. **Arhitékt zída híšo** 'The architect is building a house'; **Híša se zída** 'A house is being built'. (See also **6.10.**)

(b) The reflexive morpheme **se** functions as a direct object and indicates that the verbal action is directed at an object identical with the subject, i.e. 'self', e.g. **Máti je oblékla otrôka** 'The mother dressed the child'; **Otròk se je oblékel** 'The child got dressed' (i.e. dressed himself).

(c) The reflexive morpheme **se** changes transitive verbs into intransitive verbs, e.g. **držáti besédo** 'to keep one's word'; **držáti se diéte** 'to keep/ adhere to a diet'; **prepríčati nasprótnika** 'to convince an opponent'; **Prepríčal sem se na lástne očí** 'I saw it with my own eyes'.

(d) Together with certain verbal prefixes (**na-, raz-, za-**) **se** emphasises the excessive nature of the verbal action, e.g. **najésti se** 'to eat one's fill, be satiated'; **nahodíti se** 'to tire oneself out by walking'; **razgovoríti se** 'to expatiate'; **zaklepetáti se** 'to chatter too long'.

(e) The morpheme **se** denotes a reciprocal reflexive meaning 'each other, one another', e.g. **Nikóli se ne prepírata** 'They (d.) never quarrel (i.e. with one another)'; **Držávnika sta se pŕvič sréčala v Lóndonu** 'The two statesmen first met (each other) in London'.

(f) The morpheme **se** is used with a few verbs in the third person singular form to convey impersonal constructions.

   (i) With a general undetermined subject, e.g.

Ne vé se šè, kjé je bíl cénter potrésa	It is not yet known where the epicentre of the earthquake was
O njêm se je govorílo, da je hudôben člôvek	It was said that he is a wicked man
O tém se dánes velíko píše	Much is written today about this
Tàm se dôbro jé	One eats well there

   (ii) To express that the action takes place involuntarily with the logical subject expressed by the dative case, e.g.

Spét se mi kólca	I've got hiccups again
Zéha se mi	I am yawning

   (iii) To express general impersonal constructions of the type:

Daní se	Day is breaking
Svíta se	It is dawning
Zúnaj se meglí	It is getting foggy outside

6.4.1   The dative enclitic **si**

The dative enclitic of the reflexive pronoun **sebe**, i.e. **si** may be used with a limited number of verbs instead of **se**, e.g. **odpočíti se/si** 'to rest'; **premísliti se/si** 'to change one's mind'; **opomôči se/si** 'to recover'; **úpati se/si** 'to dare'; **oddahníti se/si** 'to recover one's breath'; **dŕzniti se/si** 'to dare'; **prizadévati se/si** 'to endeavour'.

A few verbs, however, are used only with **si**, e.g. **zapómniti si** 'to bear in mind, remember'; **mísliti si** 'to imagine, conceive'; **zamísliti si** 'to imagine'; (but c.f. **zamísliti se** 'to be absorbed in thoughts').

Note: **si** may also indicate that the action is performed by the subject for himself/herself, e.g.

Ôče si je privóščil butéljko šampánjca	Father treated himself to a bottle of champagne
Andràž si je kúpil knjígo	Andràž bought himself a book

6.5   PERSON

Slovene expresses three persons in finite verbal forms: first person, second person and third person. Each person occurs in the singular, dual and plural. Person is expressed in the present tense primarily in inflections and secondarily, usually for emphasis, by personal pronouns. Syncretism occurs in Slovene in the second and third persons dual, e.g. **Délata v továrni** means 'You (d.)/They (d.) work in a factory'; **Délala sta v továrni** means 'You (d.)/They (d.) worked in a factory'; **Bosta délala v továrni** means 'You (d.)/They (d.) will work in a factory'.

In the third persons verbs are normally used with a noun subject, e.g. **Sín déla** 'The son is working; **Sinóva délata** 'The sons (d.) are working; **Sinóvi délajo** 'The sons are working'. If, however, the subject of a verb is a personal pronoun it is normally omitted in all persons unless required for emphasis or to avoid ambiguity, e.g.

Ali poznáš Jóžeta? Govorí zeló hítro.	Do you know Jože? He speaks very quickly
Smo v sredíšču mésta	We are in the centre of town
Ne vém številke váše sôbe	I do not know the number of your room
Ali imáš kàj drobíža? Potrebújeva ga za ávtobus?	Do you have any change? We (d.) need it for the bus

but

(a) *emphasis, contrast*	
Jàz bom narekovál, tí boš pa pisála	I shall dictate and you will write
Tí mêne ne bóš učíl! Òn je bíl tàm, tí pa nè	You cannot teach me anything. He was there, you were not

(b) *to avoid ambiguity*

Hénri in Vêra se učíta slovénsko. Òn se   Henri and Vera are studying
 učí prídno   Slovene. He studies diligently

Note: A personal pronoun will also be used if it forms part of the subject in conjunction with another name, e.g. **Tí in Péter slabó govoríta némško** 'You and Peter speak German badly'.

6.5.1 Impersonal forms

Some verbs are used impersonally and have only third person singular forms, e.g. **deževáti** 'to rain'. In these cases no concrete grammatical subject is present, e.g. **dežúje** 'it is raining'; **sneží** 'it is snowing'. When such verbs are used in compound tenses or moods it is the neuter form of the **-l** participle that is used, e.g. **deževálo je** 'it was raining'.

Sometimes the third person plural of a verb is used without a pronoun to make general statements of the type: **govoríjo, da**; **právijo, da** 'they say that' where 'they' is understood to mean the authorities, people in general, other third parties.

6.6 NUMBER

Slovene express three numbers in finite verbal forms: singular (one participant), dual (two participants), plural (more than two participants), e.g. present tense:

Singular:	**sedím, sedíš, sedí**	I, you, he/she/it sits
Dual:	**sedíva, sedíta, sedíta**	We two, you two, they two sit
Plural:	**sedímo, sedíte, sedíjo**	We, you, they (i.e. more than two) sit

Similarly, in compound tenses, e.g. **sedéla sva** 'We (d.m.) were sitting'; **sedél sem** 'I was sitting'; **sedéli sva** 'We (d.f.) were sitting'; **sedéli smo** 'We (plur.m.) were sitting'; **sedéle so** 'They (plur.f.) were sitting', etc.

Ambiguity as to number arises only from the honorific use of the second person plural instead of the second person singular to address one person. This polite, formal use, in which the pronoun (if used) and the **-l** participle are always masculine, even when addressing a woman, is known as **víkanje**, i.e. the use of **ví** instead of **tí** which is known as **tíkanje**, e.g

Kám gréste, gospód/gospodíčna?   Where are you going Sir/Miss?
Kdáj ste prišlì, gospód/gospodíčna?   When did you arrive Sir/Miss?

Víkanje is used in formal situations and to address someone whom you meet for the first time. It is also used to address colleagues of senior rank or authority. **Tíkanje** is used to address parents, friends, relatives or children.

In colloquial speech one also widely encounters so-called **polovíčno víkanje** 'half vikanje'. This means that in a compound tense form with the **-l** participle, the participle distinguishes the gender of the person addressed in the singular, but the verb 'to be' occurs in the second person plural form, e.g.

Káj ste zgubíla, gospodíčna?	What have you lost, Miss?
Tóne, boste píl sók?	Tone, will you have a juice?
Adriána, ali boste prišlà na sestánek?	Adriana, will you come to the meeting?

6.7 GENDER

Gender qualifies a person or object in terms of masculine, feminine or neuter categories. In compound tenses and conditional moods the gender opposition is expressed by the -l participle. In the passive it is also expressed by the past participle passive. These participles are adjectival but are used only in the nominative case, e.g.

sín je píl vôdo	the son was drinking water
sêstra je píla . . .	the sister " " "
žrebè je pílo . . .	the foal " " "
sinóva sta píla . . .	the sons (d.) were drinking
sêstri sta píli . . .	the sisters (d.) " "
žrebéti sta píli . . .	the foals (d.) " "
sinóvi so píli . . .	the sons (plur.) " "
sêstre so píle . . .	the sisters (plur.)" "
žrebéta so píla . . .	the foals (plur.) " "
sín je bíl ránjen	the son was wounded
sinóva sta bilà ránjena	the sons (d.) were wounded
sinóvi so bilí ránjeni	the sons (plur.)" "
sêstra je bilà ránjena	the sister was wounded

6.8 TENSE

Slovene has four tenses: present, future, perfect and pluperfect. The latter is very rarely used in the modern language, where it is replaced by the perfect. The present tense is expressed as a one-word verb form as is the future tense of the verb **bíti** 'to be', e.g. **délam** 'I work/I am working'; **ste** 'you are'; **imájo** 'they have'; **bómo** 'we will be'.

Note: The English distinction between simple and continuous forms of the present tense, i.e. 'I work/I am working' are not paralleled in Slovene, where both are rendered by the one simple form.

All the other tenses are compound forms that combine the simple forms of the verb **bíti** 'to be' with the -l participle, which only has nominative forms distinguishing gender and number, e.g. **sem délal** 'I worked', **bova délala** 'we (d.m.) will work'.

This three member tense system is then further refined by the category of aspect.

6.9 MOOD

There are four moods expressed in Slovene: indicative, imperative, conditional and optative. The indicative includes the declarative mood which makes positive or negative statements and the interrogative which elicits information in the form of a question. All four tenses of the verb are used indicatively.

The imperative is used in certain constructions to express an order or request. It has simple forms for the second persons (sing./dual/plur.) and the first persons plural and dual.

The conditional is used in certain constructions to express actions which the speaker perceives as merely being possible, actions which are not real at the time of the utterance in which they are expressed. The present conditional is formed with the invariable word **bi** and the -l participle. The past conditional is formed with the invariable word **bi**, the -l participle of the verb **bíti** 'to be' and the -l participle of the main verb. It should be noted, however, that the past conditional is a very literary form that is rarely used. In the colloquial language it is never used and is replaced by the present conditional.

The optative mood is not recognised as distinct in modern Slovene grammars. It complements the imperative and expresses a wish, desire, exhortation, appeal, which the speaker makes to himself/herself or to a third person or persons. The optative is used to render English phrases with the meaning 'Let . . . ', 'May . . . ', ' . . . should' which are translated by the word **naj** plus the present tense of the verb or by **naj** plus the future of the verb **bíti** 'to be' or by **naj** plus the conditional (see **6.30**), e.g.

Pa naj bó po tvôjem	Let it be as you desire
Káj naj naredímo?	What should we do?
Vrág naj ga vzáme	May the devil take him
Polítiki naj bi uresničeváli žêlje ljúdstva	Politicians should carry out the wishes of the people

6.10 VOICE

Slovene distinguishes between active and passive voice. In the active voice the subject is the person or thing performing the action, e.g. **Učítelj je pohválil učênko** 'The teacher praised the pupil'. In the passive voice the subject is the person or thing at which the action of the verb is directed, e.g. **Učênka je bilà pohváljena od učítelja** 'The pupil was praised by the teacher'. In the passive construction the natural object i.e. 'the pupil' becomes the grammatical subject. The agent is expressed by **od** plus the genitive of the noun or may be omitted, i.e. **Učênka je bilà pohváljena**. This passive may only be formed from transitive verbs which take a direct object in the accusative.

Slovene expresses the passive meaning in the following two ways:

(a)   The passive is expressed with the present, perfect, future, conditional or infinitive of the verb **bíti** 'to be' and the past participle passive of the main verb in **-n** or **-t**. In these cases the tense and aspect will remain the same as in the active voice, e.g.

Alèš je bíl okrégan od očéta	Aleš was scolded by his father
Stanovánje je číščeno vsák téden	The flat is cleaned every week
Domáča nalóga bo hítro napísana	The homework will be done quickly
Híša bi bilà hitréje sezídana, ko bi (bilí) iméli dovòlj opéke	The house would have been built more quickly if they had had enough bricks
Tó móra bíti storjêno šè dánes	This has to be done today

Passive constructions of this type may always be converted into active constructions, e.g.

Ôče je okrégal Alêša	The father scolded Aleš
Stanovánje čístijo vsák téden	They clean the flat every week

One should note, however, that when a past active construction is transformed into a construction involving the present tense of the verb 'to be' and a past participle passive, this construction expresses a state and not the passive voice, e.g.

Vráta so odpŕli	They opened the door
– **Vráta so odpŕta**	The door is open
Sôbo so pomêtli	They swept the room
– **Sôba je pometêna**	The room has been swept

The same applies if the present tense of an active verb is transformed into a construction involving the present tense of the verb 'to be' and the past participle passive, e.g.

Ográje obdájajo vrtóve	Fences surround the gardens
– **Vrtóvi so obdáni z ográjami**	The gardens are surrounded by fences

(b)   The passive is expressed by the use of the reflexive morpheme **se** with the active form of a transitive verb. In these cases the subject is not indicated, e.g.

Híša se zída	The house is being built

Knjíga se tíska	The book is being printed (i.e. is at press)
Tarót se ígra s kártami	Tarot is played with cards
Kárte se razdelíjo igrálcem	The cards are dealt to the players

6.11 CONJUGATION

Each Slovene verb, whether perfective of imperfective has two stems; an infinitive stem and a present stem.

From the infinitive stem are formed the infinitive, the supine, the -l participle, the past participle passive and the past gerund (the latter only from perfective verbs). From the present stem are formed the present tense, the imperative, the present gerund and the present participle active (the latter two only from imperfective verbs).

6.12 THE INFINITIVE

Most infinitives in Slovene end in **-ti**, e.g. **délati** 'to do', **mísliti** 'to think', **krásti** 'to steal', **têpsti** 'to beat' while a smaller number end in **-či**, e.g. **léči** 'to lie down', **pêči** 'to bake'. In the infinitives in **-či** the final **-či** derives from original forms in **-kti, -gti**, i.e. __*legti, *pekti__.

6.12.1 The use of the infinitive

The infinitive is normally used as the complement of verbs and verb phrases. These include modal verbs and constructions (see **6.39**), phasal verbs (see **6.2.1**) and certain other verbs or verb phrases which express perception, feeling, e.g.

Mórali so délati, če so hotéli živéti	They had to work if they wanted to live
Začéla je hodíti v šólo	She began to go to school
Namerávajo gradíti híšo	They intend to build a house
Tó je tréba storíti	This must be done
Ne mórem ga vídeti	I cannot see him
Izpláča se védeti	It is worth knowing
Bála se je zaplávati	She was afraid to start swimming
Ali zná bráti?	Does he know how to read?
Dála se je ogoljufáti	She let herself be cheated

After verbs of perception the infinitive can replace a subordinate clause containing the conjunction **kakó**, e.g.

Skózi ôkno je vídel prihájati vojáke	Through the window he saw the
(= kakó vojáki prihájajo)	soldiers approaching
Slíšala sem te govoríti	I heard you talking

The infinitive may also sometimes be used instead of a noun or occasionally as an imperative, e.g.

Naročíli so jésti (= jéd) in píti	They ordered food and drink for a
(= pijáčo) za cél téden	whole week
Kadíti (= kajênje) je prepovédano	Smoking is forbidden
Tího bíti (= Tího bódi)	Be quiet

Note 1: In the spoken language one often meets the construction **za** + infinitive, e.g. **Nímam nìč za brát(i)** 'I have nothing to read'. In the literary language other constructions are preferred, e.g. **Nímam kàj bráti**.

Note 2: In the spoken language the final **-i** of infinitives is often dropped, i.e. **délat** 'to work'; **dvígnit** 'to lift'; **pêč** 'to bake' (see also **1.6.2**).

6.12.2   The infinitive stem

In the case of verbs in **-ti** the infinitive stem is derived by removing the final **-ti**, e.g. **déla-ti**, **mísli-ti**. In the case of verbs in **-sti**, the infinitive stem is also formed by removing the final **-ti** if the **-s-** preceding the **-ti** is part of the original root, e.g. **trés-ti** 'to shake'. In many cases, however the **-s-** preceding the **-ti** derives from an original **-d-**, **-t-** or **-z-**, which is still retained in the present tense of the verb, e.g. **krásti** 'to steal' – **krádem** 'I steal'; **plêsti** 'to weave' – **plêtem** 'I weave'; **mólsti** 'to milk' – **mólzem** 'I milk'. In these verbs the infinitive stem is formed by removing the **-sti** and reintroducing the original consonant, i.e. **krad-**, **plet-**, **molz-**. In verbs ending in **-psti**, **-bsti**, e.g. **têpsti** 'to beat', **dólbsti** 'to chisel', the infinitive stem is formed by removing the **-sti**, i.e. **tep-**, **dolb-**.

The infinitive stems of verbs in **-či** are derived by removing **-či** and reintroducing the original **k** or **g**, i.e. **pêči** – **pek-**; **léči** – **leg-**.

6.13   THE PRESENT STEM

The present stem is derived by removing the personal endings of the present tense, e.g.

délati	to do	:	**déla-m**	I do
mísliti	to think	:	**mísli-m**	I think
pêči	to bake	:	**pêče-m**	I bake

In some verbs the infinitive and present stems may coincide, e.g.

Infinitive stem	*Present stem*
déla-ti	**déla-m**
mísli-ti	**mísli-m**

More often than not, however, the infinitive and present stems will differ, e.g.

Infinitive stem		Present stem	
pisá-ti	to write	**píše-m**	I write
držá-ti	to hold	**drží-m**	I hold
kupová-ti	to buy	**kupúje-m**	I buy
stríči/strig-	to cut	**stríže-m**	I cut

6.14 THE PRESENT TENSE

Each Slovene verb inflects in the present tense in accordance with one of five conjugations. The first four conjugations are thematic, i.e. a thematic vowel (-a-, -i-, -je- or -e-) precedes the personal endings. The fifth conjugation includes a limited number of so-called athematic verbs in which the personal endings are added directly to the root of the verb without the presence of an athematic vowel.

The personal endings of the four thematic conjugations are:

	Singular	Dual	Plural
First person	**-m**	**-va**	**-mo**
Second person	**-š**	**-ta**	**-te**
Third person	**-ø**	**-ta**	**-jo (-é/-ó)**

The endings express person and number but not gender. Gender is expressed by the personal pronouns or by the noun subject. The personal pronouns are not normally used (see **4.2.2**) but are given below with the paradigm for the first conjugation verb **délati** for illustrative purposes. In the examples for the other thematic and athematic conjugations only the verb paradigm is given.

6.15 THE THEMATIC CONJUGATIONS

The **-a-** conjugation, i.e. the first conjugation:

délati 'to do'

Sing.	1.	**jàz**	**délam**	I do
	2.	**tí**	**délaš**	you do
	3.	**òn/ôna/ôno**	**déla**	he/she/it does
Dual	1.	**mídva/médve**	**délava**	we (m./f.) do
	2.	**vídva/védve**	**délata**	you (m./f.) do
	3.	**ônadva/ônidve**	**délata**	they (m./f./n.) do
Plur.	1.	**mí/mé**	**délamo**	we (m./f.) do
	2.	**ví/vé**	**délate**	you (m./f.) do
	3.	**ôni/ône/ôna**	**délajo**	they (m./f./n.) do

The **-i-**, **-je-** and **-e-** conjugations, i.e. the second, third and fourth conjugations:

		mísliti	**kupováti**	**razuméti**
		'to think'	'to buy'	'to understand'
		-i-	-je-	-e-
Sing.	1.	**míslim**	**kupújem**	**razúmem**
	2.	**mísliš**	**kupúješ**	**razúmeš**
	3.	**mísli**	**kupúje**	**razúme**
Dual	1.	**mísliva**	**kupújeva**	**razúmeva**
	2.	**míslita**	**kupújeta**	**razúmeta**
	3.	**míslita**	**kupújeta**	**razúmeta**
Plur	1.	**míslimo**	**kupújemo**	**razúmemo**
	2.	**míslite**	**kupújete**	**razúmete**
	3.	**míslijo**	**kupújejo**	**razúmejo**

Variants

The stressed variants in **-ó/-é** found in the third plural are very literary forms and are restricted stylistically in their use. The variant **-ó** may replace the ending **-ejo** of verbs of the **-e-** conjugation and the variant **-é** may replace the ending **-ijo** of the **-i-** conjugation, e.g.

nêsejo/nesó	they carry
rástejo/rastó	they grow
začnéjo/začnó	they begin
pôjejo/pojó	they sing
stojíjo/stojé	they stand
sušíjo se/sušé se	they become dry

In the spoken language the variants in **-ó**, **-é** are never used.

The verbs **pêči** 'to bake', **rêči** 'to say' have the variants **pekó**, **rekó** alongside the normal forms **pêčejo**, **rêčejo** but these forms are now considered archaic.

6.16 THE ATHEMATIC CONJUGATION

The present tense endings of the athematic conjugation differ from those of the thematic conjugations only in the second and third persons dual, the second person plural and in some cases in the third person plural.

	Sing.	*Dual*	*Plural*
First person	**-m**	**-va**	**-mo**
Second person	**-š**	**-sta**	**-ste**
Third person	**-ø**	**-sta**	**-do/jo**

The athematic verbs in Slovene are: **dáti** 'to give'; **íti** 'to go'; **jésti** 'to eat'; **védeti** 'to know'; and **bíti** 'to be'. Prefixed derivatives of **dáti**, **jésti** and **védeti** are also athematic, as is the verb **povédati** 'to tell' and its prefixed derivatives. The prefixed forms of the irregular verb **íti** are, however, not athematic but belong to the **-e-** conjugation, e.g. **príti** 'to come' – **prídem** 'I come'.

The athematic verbs

		dáti	íti	jésti	védeti	povédati
Sing.	1.	dám	grém	jém	vém	povém
	2.	dáš	gréš	jéš	véš	povéš
	3.	dá	gré	jé	vé	pové
Dual	1.	dáva	gréva	jéva	véva	povéva
	2.	dásta	grésta	jésta	vésta	povésta
	3.	dásta	grésta	jésta	vésta	povésta
Plur	1.	dámo	grémo	jémo	vémo	povémo
	2.	dáste	gréste	jéste	véste	povéste
	3.	dájo	gredó/gréjo	jedó/jéjo	vedó/véjo	povéjo

In the third person plural forms the alternative endings in **-dó/-jo** are used equally frequently in writing, but in speech the forms in **-jo** are preferred. In the prefixed derivatives from **jésti** and **védeti** only the ending **-jo** is used. The alternative form **dadó** is also found but is used only stylistically.

It should also be noted that the prefixed derivatives from the verb **dáti** also allow a variant in **-ate** in the second person plural, e.g. **dodáste/dodáte** 'you add', **predáste/predáte** 'you hand over'.

*The verb **bíti** 'to be'*
This verb has an irregular present tense:

	Sing.	Dual	Plur.
First person	sem	sva	smo
Second person	si	sta	ste
Third person	je	sta	so

Its future form also conjugates like an athematic verb:

	Sing.	Dual	Plur.
First person	bóm	bóva	bómo
Second person	bóš	bósta	bóste
Third person	bó	bósta	bódo/bójo

The third person plural **bódo** is more common in the literary language, while the form **bójo** is used in the colloquial language.

Note: Prefixed derivatives from the verb **bíti** 'to be' conjugate like thematic verbs in **-i-** or **-je-**, e.g. **dobíti** 'to get' – **dobím** 'I get'; **prebíti** 'to spend (time)' – **prebíjem** 'I spend'. Forms like **dobóm**, **prebóm** are now archaic.

6.17   NEGATION OF THE PRESENT TENSE

The present tense forms of verbs are negated with the negative particle **ne**, e.g.
ne grém 'I am not going/I do not go'; **ne bêremo** 'We are not reading/we do not
read', etc.

Three verbs, however, have special negative forms in their present tense: **bíti**
'to be'; **iméti** 'to have'; **hotéti** 'to want'.

Sing	1.	**nísem** 'I am not'	**nímam** 'I do not have'		**nóčem** 'I do not want'	
	2.	**nísi** 'you are not'	**nímaš**	etc.	**nóčeš**	etc.
	3.	**ní** etc.	**níma**		**nóče**	
Dual	1.	**nísva**	**nímava**		**nóčeva**	
	2.	**nísta**	**nímata**		**nóčeta**	
	3.	**nísta**	**nímata**		**nóčeta**	
Plur.	1.	**nísmo**	**nímamo**		**nóčemo**	
	2.	**níste**	**nímate**		**nóčete**	
	3.	**níso**	**nímajo**		**nóčejo**	

Examples

Nísem študènt	I am not a student
Nímate vzróka za jézo	You do not have a reason to be angry
Otròk se nóče učíti	The child does not want to study

6.18   FIRST CONJUGATION VERBS IN -a-

The vast majority of verbs in **-ati** conjugate like **délati**, e.g. **mórati** 'to have to';
plávati 'to swim'; **znáti** 'to know'; **glédati** 'to look'; **kúhati** 'to cook'; **vprašáti**
'to ask'; **plačáti** 'to pay'.

There are, however, a certain number of exceptions:

(a)   All verbs in **-ováti/-eváti**. These belong to the third conjugation in **-je-**
(see **6.20**). Note, however, that verbs in **-évati**, e.g. **odštévati** 'to subtract'
are first conjugation verbs.

(b)   The following verbs in **-jati** and their prefixed forms which belong to the
third conjugation in **-je-**: **majáti** 'to shake'; **dajáti** 'to give'; **smejáti se** 'to
laugh'; **sejáti** 'to sow'. To this group also belongs the verb **dejáti** 'to say:
to put', but this verb is nowadays used only in the past tense.

(c)   Certain old unproductive verbs in **-čati**, **-žati**, **-šati** and their prefixed
forms, which belong to the second conjugation in **-i-**. The most common
verbs in this category are: **ležáti** 'to lie down'; **klečáti** 'to kneel'; **frčáti** 'to
fly'; **dišáti** 'to scent'; **režáti se** 'to smirk'; **drčáti** 'to slide'; **molčáti** 'to be

silent'; **smrčáti** 'to snore'; **kričáti** 'to shout'; **vršáti** 'to rush'; **prežáti** 'to lie in wait'; **držáti** 'to hold'; **ječáti** 'to groan'; **slíšati** 'to hear'; **bežáti** 'to flee'; **brenčáti** 'to buzz'; **tiščáti** 'to squeeze'; **mižáti** 'to have one's eyes closed'; **bleščáti se** 'to glitter'; **cvrčáti** 'to chirp'; **vreščáti** 'to shriek'.

(d) Verbs in **-ati** which undergo consonant changes in the present tense and their prefixed forms. These belong to the fourth conjugation in **-e-**, e.g.

Infinitive		*First person present tense*
pásati	to suit	**pášem**
súkati	to twist	**súčem**
kresáti	to strike sparks	**kréšem**
česáti	to comb	**čéšem**
metáti	to throw	**méčem**
iskáti	to seek	**íščem**
rézati	to cut	**réžem**
mázati	to grease	**mážem**
brísati	to wipe	**bríšem**
rísati	to draw	**ríšem**
plesáti	to dance	**pléšem**
skakáti	to jump	**skáčem**
klícati	to call	**klíčem**
lízati	to lick	**lížem**
lagáti	to tell lies	**lážem**
pisáti	to write	**píšem**
klesáti	to carve	**kléšem**
vézati	to bind	**véžem**
tesáti	to hew	**téšem**

(e) The verbs **spáti** 'to sleep'; **státi** 'to stand'; **báti se** 'to be afraid' and their prefixed forms, which belong to the second conjugation in **-i-** and have the present tense forms: **spím; stojím; bojím se**.

(f) The following verbs and their prefixed forms: **zváti** 'to call'; **gnáti** 'to drive'; **práti** 'to wash'; **bráti** 'to read'; **státi** 'to cost'; **žgáti** 'to burn'; **tkáti** 'to weave'; **peljáti** 'to lead, drive'; **kopáti** 'to dig'; **stláti** 'to strew'; **posláti** 'to send'; **klepáti** 'to sharpen, hammer'; **oráti** 'to plough'; **kláti** 'to slaughter'; **pláti** 'to winnow'; **sráti** 'to defecate'; **scáti** 'to urinate'. These verbs conjugate as follows: **zóvem; žênem; pêrem; bêrem; stánem; žgèm; tkèm; péljem; kópljem; stéljem; póšljem; klépljem; órjem; kóljem; póljem; sérjem; ščíjem** (see **6.20** and **6.21**).

To this group also belongs the verb **jemáti** 'to take' which conjugates **jêmljem, jêmlješ**, etc. Its prefixed forms, however, normally behave like first conjugation verbs in **-a-**. Certain of its prefixed forms, however, do allow stylistic variants, which conjugate like the basic verb, e.g.

objémati	to embrace	–	**objémam/objémljem**
pojémati	to wane, decline	–	**pojémam/pojémljem**

but only

zajémati	to ladle out	–	**zajémam**
prejémati	to receive	–	**prejémam**

(g) The verbs **dáti** 'to give' and **povédati** 'to tell' and their prefixed forms which are athematic verbs.

6.18.1 Verbs in **-ati** with alternative conjugations

Certain verbs which usually belong to the first conjugation in **-a-**, may have alternative conjugations. These include the following:

(a) Verbs in **-otáti/-etáti** and their prefixed forms. In these verbs the **-a-** conjugation type is the more usual. The alternative forms conjugate like fourth conjugation verbs in **-e-** with the final **-t-** of the root replaced by **-č-**, e.g.

ropotáti	to rattle, rumble	–	**ropotám/ropóčem**
hohotáti se	to roar with laughter	–	**hohotám se/hohóčem se**
drgetáti	to shudder	–	**drgetám/drgéčem**
trepetáti	to tremble	–	**trepetám/trepéčem**

(b) Some verbs in **-uvati** and their prefixed forms, although nowadays the first conjugation forms in **-a-** are preferred. The alternative forms conjugate **-ujem, -uješ**, etc, e.g.

kljúvati	to peck	–	**kljúvam/kljújem**
bljúvati	to vomit	–	**bljúvam/bljújem**
rúvati	to root out	–	**rúvam/rújem**

(c) The following verbs in **-ati**, and their prefixed forms, where the **-ati** is preceded by a labial consonant (**b, p, m**). The alternative forms conjugate **-ljem, -lješ**, etc. instead of **-am, -aš**, etc, e.g.

kápati	to drip	–	**kápam/kápljem**
škrípati	to grate	–	**škrípam/škrípljem**
sípati	to strew	–	**sípam/sípljem**
drémati	to slumber	–	**drémam/drémljem**
gíbati	to move	–	**gíbam/gíbljem**
zíbati	to swing	–	**zíbam/zíbljem**
zóbati	to peck	–	**zóbam/zóbljem**

6.19 SECOND CONJUGATION VERBS IN -i-

The following verbs belong to the second conjugation and conjugate like **mísliti**.

(a) The vast majority of verbs in **-iti**, e.g. **govoríti** 'to speak'; **hodíti** 'to go'; **polníti** 'to fill'; **zmotíti** 'to disturb'; **ceníti** 'to value', etc.

There are three types of exception. These are:

(i) All verbs in **-niti**, where **n** is part of the suffix and not part of the root. These verbs belong to the fourth conjugation in **-e-**, e.g.

ugásniti	to extinguish	–	**ugásnem**
sahníti (arch.)	to disappear	–	**sáhnem**
véniti	to wither	–	**vénem**
vzdígniti	to lift		**vzdígnem**
hlípniti	to gasp	–	**hlípnem**

(ii) The following, mainly monosyllabic, verbs and their prefixed forms: **bíti** 'to beat'; **píti** 'to drink'; **ríti** 'to dig'; **víti** 'to wind'; **líti** 'to pour'; **gníti** 'to rot'; **šíti** (arch.) 'to sew'; **počíti (se)** 'to rest'. These verbs all belong to the third conjugation in **-je-**, and conjugate as follows: **bíjem; píjem; ríjem; víjem; líjem; gníjem; šíjem; počíjem (se)**.

(iii) The verb **bíti** 'to be' which is an athematic verb. Note, however, that its prefixed forms may decline like second or third conjugation verbs (see **6.16**).

(b) Most verbs in **-eti** and their prefixed forms, e.g.

hrométi	to fall lame	–	**hromím**
bledéti	to turn pale	–	**bledím**
sedéti	to sit	–	**sedím**
goréti	to burn	–	**gorím**
trpéti	to suffer	–	**trpím**
hrepenéti	to yearn for	–	**hrepením**
tléti	to glow	–	**tlím**
živéti	to live	–	**živím**
vídeti	to see	–	**vídim**

Exceptions are:

(i) the verb **uméti** 'to know how' and the verb **hotéti** 'to want' and their prefixed forms, which conjugate like fourth conjugation verbs, i.e. **úmem; hóčem**.

(ii) The verb **védeti** and its prefixed forms, which are athematic verbs.

(iii) The following monosyllabic verbs and their prefixed forms which belong either to the third or the fourth conjugation (see **6.20** and **6.21**): **gréti** 'to warm'; **véti** 'to blow; **štéti** 'to count'; **mléti** 'to grind'; **péti** 'to sing'; **žéti** 'to reap'; **žéti** 'to squeeze'; **vréti** 'to boil'; **dréti** 'to flay'; **kléti** 'to curse'; **žréti** 'to devour'; **déti** 'to say, put'; **tréti** 'to crush'; **péti se** 'to climb'; **spréti** 'to set at variance'; **cvréti** 'to fry'; **zréti** 'to look at'; **mréti** 'to die'; **méti** 'to rub'; **sméti** 'to dare'.

(c) Certain old unproductive verbs in **-čati, -žati, -šati**, e.g **ležáti** 'to lie' – **ležím** (see **6.18**).

(d) The verbs **spáti** 'to sleep', **státi** 'to stand', **báti se** 'to be afraid' (see **6.18**).

6.20 THIRD CONJUGATION VERBS IN -je-

Verbs that belong to this conjugation are:

(a) All verbs in **-ováti/-eváti**, which conjugate like **kupováti**, i.e. the infinitive suffix **-ova-/-eva-** is replaced by **-uje-**, e.g.

kováti	to forge	–	**kújem**
daróvati	to donate	–	**darújem**
vpraševáti	to ask	–	**vprašújem**

(b) The verb **počíti se** 'to rest' and its prefixed forms and the following monosyllabic verbs in **-iti** and their prefixed forms: **bíti** 'to beat'; **píti** 'to drink'; **líti** 'to pour'; **ríti** 'to dig'; **víti** 'to wind'; **gníti** 'to rot'; **šíti** (arch.) 'to sew'. These verbs conjugate as follows: **počíjem se; bíjem; píjem**; etc. (see **6.19**).

(c) The verbs **majáti** 'to shake'; **sejáti** 'to sew'; **smejáti se** 'to laugh'; **dejáti** 'to say, put' and their prefixed forms. These verbs conjugate as follows: **májem; séjem; sméjem se; déjem**. The verb **dajáti** 'to give' also conjugates this way, i.e. **dájem** but not its prefixed forms which are first conjugation verbs, e.g. **prodájati** 'to sell' – **prodájam**.

(d) The verbs **péti** 'to sing'; **štéti** 'to count'; **véti** 'to blow'; **gréti** 'to warm' and their prefixed forms. These verbs conjugate as follows: **pôjem, štéjem, véjem, gréjem**.

(e) The verbs **rúti** 'to uproot'; **čúti** 'to hear'; **dúti** (arch.) 'to blow'; **súti** (arch.) 'to strew' and their prefixed forms and the verbs **obúti** 'to put on (shoes)' and **sezúti** 'to take off (shoes)'. These verbs conjugate as follows: **rújem; čújem; dújem; sújem; obújem; sezújem**.

(f) The following verbs in **-ati** and their prefixed forms where the **-je-** follows the consonant preceding **-ati**, sometimes with other changes in the root as well: **stláti** 'to strew'; **posláti** 'to send'; **oráti** 'to plough'; **kláti** 'to slaughter'; **pláti** 'to winnow'; **sráti** 'to defecate'; **klepáti** 'to hammer'; **kopáti** 'to dig'. These verbs conjugate as follows: **stéljem; póšljem; órjem; kóljem; póljem; sérjem; klépljem; kópljem.**

(g) The vulgar verb **scáti** 'to urinate' which conjugates **ščíjem, ščíješ,** etc. This verb also has an alternative conjugation **ščím, ščíš,** etc.

(h) Some verbs in **-uvati** and their prefixed forms, which normally conjugate like first conjugation verbs, e.g. **kljúvati** 'to peck' – **kljújem** (see **6.18.1**).

(i) The verb **mléti** 'to grind' and its prefixed forms: **méljem, zméljem, preméljem.**

(j) Certain verbs in **-ati** where the **-ati** is preceded by a labial consonant (see **6.18.1**). These verbs conjugate either like first conjugation verbs in **-a-** or like third conjugation verbs in **-je-**. In the latter case the **-je-** follows the labial consonant and **-l-**, e.g. **zíbati** 'to swing' – **zíbljem.**

6.21 FOURTH CONJUGATION VERBS IN -e-

The following verbs conjugate like **razuméti**:

(a) All verbs with an infinitive in **-či**. Their present tense forms have either **-č-** or **-ž-** (as a result of palatalisation) depending on whether the original final consonant of the root was **-k-** or **-g-**, e.g.

pêči (< *pekti)	to bake	–	**pêčem**
stríči (< *strigti)	to cut	–	**strížem**
vléči (< *vlekti)	to drag	–	**vléčem**
vpréči (< *vpregti)	to harness	–	**vpréžem**

Note: The verb **môči** 'to be able' and its prefixed forms have replaced original -ž- with -r-, i.e. **môči** – **môrem;** opomôči se 'to recover' – **opomôrem se.**

(b) All verbs in **-sti**, (for the formation of the present stems of these verbs see **6.12.2**), e.g.

grísti	to bite	–	**grízem**
trésti	to shake	–	**trésem**
rásti	to grow	–	**rástem**
bôsti	to sting	–	**bôdem**
skúbsti	to pluck	–	**skúbem**
sésti	to sit down	–	**sédem**

(c) The following monosyllabic verbs in **-eti** and their prefixed forms:

žéti	to squeeze	–	**žmèm/žámem**
vréti	to boil	–	**vrèm**
dréti	to flay	–	**dêrem/drèm**

kléti	to curse	–	kólnem
žréti	to devour	–	žrèm
déti	to put	–	dénem
tréti	to crush	–	trèm/tárem
péti se	to climb	–	pnèm se
spéti (arch.)	to hurry	–	spèm
spréti	to set at variance	–	sprèm
cvréti	to fry	–	cvrèm
zréti	to look at	–	zrèm
mréti	to die	–	mrèm
méti	to rub	–	mánem
sméti	to dare	–	smém

Note: The verb **mréti** and its prefixed forms may also conjugate like verbs of the third conjugation, i.e. **mŕjem, mŕješ** etc.

(d)   The verb **verjéti** 'to believe' and the verb **jéti** (arch.) 'to begin' and its prefixed forms, which form their present tense in **-mem/-amem**, e.g.

verjéti		–	verjámem
jéti		–	jámem
otéti	to save	–	otmèm
objéti	to embrace	–	objámem
vzéti	to take	–	vzámem
snéti	to take down	–	snámem
prejéti	to receive	–	préjmem

(e)   Verbs in **-četi, -preti**, e.g.

začéti	to begin	–	začnèm
zapréti	to close	–	zaprèm
načéti	to eat into	–	načnèm
odpréti	to open	–	odprèm

(f)   All verbs in **-niti** where **-n-** is part of the suffix (see **6.19**).

(g)   The verbs **plúti** 'to sail' and **rjúti** 'to roar' and their prefixed forms which have the present tense forms **plôvem, rjôvem**. These verbs may also conjugate like third conjugation verbs but this is rare, e.g. **plújem, rjújem**.

(h)   Verbs in **-ati** and their prefixed forms, where the consonant preceding **-ati** undergoes a change in the present tense, e.g. **česáti** 'to comb' – **čéšem** (see **6.18**).

(i)   Verbs in **-otáti/-etáti** and their prefixed forms, e.g. **ropotáti** 'to rumble' – **ropóčem** (see **6.18.1**).

(j)   The verb **hotéti** 'to want', its prefixed form and its negated present tense (see **6.17**), e.g. **hóčem, nóčem, zahóčem se** (arch.) 'I long for'.

(k) The following verbs and their prefixed forms: **zváti**; **gnáti**; **práti**; **bráti**; **státi**; **žgáti**; **tkáti** (see **6.18**).

(l) Prefixed forms of the verb **íti** 'to go' which in its simple form is athematic, e.g.

obíti	to go round	–	**obídem**
príti	to come	–	**prídem**
nájti	to find	–	**nájdem**
odíti	to go away	–	**odídem**

6.22 THE USE OF THE PRESENT TENSE FORMS OF PERFECTIVE VERBS

The English simple present and present continuous are normally expressed by the present tense of the imperfective verb, e.g. **délam** 'I work/am working'; **bêre** 'he reads/is reading' etc. There are, however, exceptions to this rule, when the present tense form of the perfective verb is used instead. This occurs in the following instances.

(a) *Verba dicendi* (i.e verbs expressing declaration or decision)
     The perfective forms of these verbs are used to express the present if the speaker is the first person, e.g.

Povém ti, pázi se, káj govoríš	I tell you, be careful what you say
Obljúbim, da bom prišèl	I promise I shall come
Naj se odkríto spovém, da . . .	Let me confess frankly that . . .
Vsè je rés, priséžem	Everything is true, I swear
Vsè preklíčem	I take it all back
Rêčem vam, dôbro premíslite	I say to you, think it over

(b) The present tense of perfective verbs is used after the expressions:
     Počákaj, da 'Wait until'; **Gléj, da** 'Make sure, try to', e.g.

Počákaj, da prídem nazáj	Wait until I come back
Počákaj, da odklénem vráta	Wait until I open the door
Gléj, da ne pozábiš	Make sure you don't forget
Gléj, da potŕkaš	Make sure you knock

(c) The present tense form of the perfective verb may be used to express future intention. In such instances the future is clear from the context, e.g.

Zvečér prídem k têbi	I'll come to see you this evening
Če zadénem na loteríji, ti dám polovíco	If I win on the lottery I'll give you half
Vŕnem se čez desét minút	I'll return in ten minutes

Ko prídem domóv, se preobléčem   When I get home I'll get changed
Jàz pa medtém skúham večérjo   In the meantime I'll cook dinner

(d) The present tense forms of perfective verbs may be used with a past meaning. This is the so-called historic present and brings the action more graphically before the mind's eye of the reader or listener. It is a narrative or descriptive device used mainly in literature, e.g.

Skupína planíncev je počási lézla navkréber. Nenádoma Jákobu zdŕsne, fantìč zamáhne z rokámi, zavpíje in žé se kotalí po strmíni proti skáli. Šè sréča, da se je uspél zaustáviti z nogámi, sicèr bi se ne biló dôbro končálo.
The group of mountaineers was climbing slowly upwards. Suddenly Jacob *slipped*. The boy *flung up* his hands, *cried out* and began to roll down the slope towards the cliff. Luckily he managed to stop himself with his feet, otherwise the incident would have ended badly

Sprehájala sem se po gózdu. Nenádoma *zaglédam* véverico
I was walking in the wood. Suddenly *I caught sight of* a squirrel

(e) The present tense forms of perfective verbs may be used to express repeated completed actions with certain temporal adverbs like **védno/ zméraj** 'always' or in temporal clauses containing the pronoun **vsák** 'every', e.g.

Vsák dán vstánem ob sêdmih   I get up at seven every day
Vsák dán obíšče mámo   He visits his mum every day
Príde védno v neprávem trenútku   He always comes at the wrong time

Note, however, that the use of both aspects is possible in phrases like:

Ob pétkih obíščem/obiskújem mámo   On Fridays I visit mum
Védno ga znóva vznemíri/vznemírja   She always upsets him again
Védno dobíš/dobívaš velíko písem   You always get a lot of letters
Zméraj ga pustím/púščam pri míru   I always let him alone

The difference between the two aspects is that when one uses the present tense of the perfective verb this is often qualified in some way (but not always), e.g.

Zméraj ga pustím pri míru, kàdar je   I always let him alone, when
  slábe vólje   he is moody
Védno ga vznemíri s pripovedovánjem   She is always upsetting him
  o svôjih problémih   with her talk of her problems

In the sentence **Zméraj dobíš/dobívaš velíko písem** the use of the perfective verb is neutral, while the use of the imperfective verb implies some sort of feeling on the part of the speaker (e.g. envy).

(f) The present tense of perfective verbs is used in proverbs, sayings, instructions, rules, laws and statements, which are empirical truths, e.g.

Če odbòr ugotoví, da je rokopís nèčitljív, ga zavŕne	If the board finds that a manuscript is illegible, it rejects it
Vrána vráni ne izkljúje očí	There is honour among thieves (lit. A crow does not peck out another crow's eyes)
Po zími príde pomlád	After winter comes spring
Lahkó pripélješ kônja k vôdi, ne móreš pa ga prisíliti, da píje	You can lead a horse to water, but you can't make him drink

(g) Modal usage

The present tense of perfective verbs may be used when a wish, command, intention, willingness, or possibility are expressed, e.g.

Kdó preskóči pôtok?	Who can leap across the stream?
Da mi izgíneš	Get out of my sight
Ali strèš ôreh s pŕsti?	Can you break open a nut with your fingers?
Kakó dáleč skóčiš na smučéh?	How far can you jump on skis?
Zakáj ne odgovoríte?	Why don't you answer?

(h) The present tense of perfective verbs is also used in stage directions in plays, e.g.

Vráta tího zaškrípljejo in se odpró	The door creaks softly and opens
Odpnè telóvnik, potégne lístnico in naštéje denár	He unbuttons his waistcoat, takes out his wallet and counts out the money

6.23 THE COMPOUND TENSES AND MOODS: THE -l PARTICIPLE

All compound tenses and moods are formed with the so-called -l participle, which expresses gender and number. It has the same endings as adjectives and is used only in the nominative case. The -l participle is formed from the infinitive stem with the aid of the suffix -l, e.g. déla-ti 'to work'.

	masc.	fem.	neuter
Sing.	délal	délala	délalo
Dual	délala	délali	délali
Plur.	délali	délale	délala

The identity of the person is provided by the auxiliary verb used with the -l participle in the future, perfect and pluperfect tenses and by the personal pronoun or the context in the conditional mood, e.g.

sva délala	we (d.m.) were working
bo délal	he will work

médve bi délali	we (d.f.) would work
si bilà délala	you (f.s.) had worked

Note: In the masculine plural form -li, the final -i is often lost in the spoken language. The final -l
is then pronounced as -l not ṷ.

6.23.1 Agreement of the -I participle

The -l participle agrees with a single subject in person and number in all
tenses and moods, e.g.

Dvé púnci sta jokáli	The two girls were crying
Njéna bráta bosta prišlà	Her two brothers will come
Študénti so odšlì	The students have left
Njegóva sêstra se je bilà premíslila	His sister had changed her mind
Délovne míze so bilè v laboratóriju	The work tables were in the laboratory

Where, however, there is more than one subject usage varies. If the subject
consists of two conjoined singular nouns or pronouns the following rules
apply:

Note: Examples are illustrated by the perfect tense.

(a) Agreement is masculine dual unless both nouns/pronouns are feminine,
e.g.

kònj in kráva		the horse and cow	
stréha in ôkno		the roof and window	
drevó in gnézdo	**sta bilà . . .**	the tree and nest	were . . .
tí (m.) **in Sabína**		you (m.) and Sabina	
tí (f.) **in Jóže**		you (f.) and Jože	

(b) Agreement is feminine dual if both nouns/pronouns are feminine, e.g.

sêstra in têta		the sister and aunt	
tí (f.) **in têta**	**sta bilí . . .**	you and auntie	were . . .

Note: If the two conjoined nouns are thought of as a whole and are of different genders then
agreement will be with the nearest subject, e.g. **Žálost in hrepenênje je biló razlíto po njénem
nagúbanem lícu** 'Sadness and longing were etched on her wrinkled face'.

Similarly where the total number of subjects of any gender and number is
three or more the following rules normally apply:

(a) Agreement is masculine plural unless all the subjects are feminine, e.g.

kônji, kráve in teléta		the horses, cows and calves	
ôkno, drevó in gnézdo		the window, tree and nest	
òn, Jóže in Métka	**so bili . . .**	he, Jože and Metka	were . . .
kráva in dvé teléti		the cow and two calves	
perésa in knjíge		the pens and books	

(b) If all the nouns/pronouns are feminine then the agreement is feminine plural, e.g.

sêstra, nečákinja in têta		the sister, niece and aunt	
obé sêstri in njúna máti	so bilè ...	both sisters and the mother	were ...
têta in nečákinje		the aunt and nieces	

It should also be noted that if the -l participle precedes a feminine or neuter plural subject, which is conjoined with another plural subject, it is possible for the -l participle to agree in gender with the feminine or neuter plural subject, e.g.

Mímo ôkna so brzéle njíve in trávniki	Fields and meadows flashed past the window
Podražíla so se perésa in svínčniki	Pens and pencils became more expensive

Moreover, if there is no masculine plural subject it is also possible for the -l participle to agree with the second plural subject preceding it, e.g. **Kráve in teléta so se pásla** 'The cows and calves were grazing'.

6.23.2 Formation of the -l participle

(a) In verbs ending in **-ati, -iti, -eti, -uti** the -l participle is formed by removing the **-ti** and adding **-l, -la, -lo** etc., e.g.

govoríti	to say	:	**govóril, govoríla, govorílo**
vzéti	to take	:	**vzél, vzéla, vzélo**
kupováti	to buy	:	**kupovàl, kupovála, kuproválo**
plúti	to sail	:	**plúl, plúla, plúlo**

(b) In verbs ending in **-sti**, where the **-s-** has arisen from an original **-t-, -d-, -z-**, the **-sti** is removed and the original consonant reintroduced (see **6.12.2**). To these forms the fleeting vowel **e** (schwa) + **l** are added. The fleeting vowel only appears in the masc. sing. form. In all other forms it is lost, e.g.

krásti	to steal	:	**krádel, krádla, krádlo**
plêsti	to weave	:	**plêtel, plêtla, plêtlo**
lésti	to crawl	:	**lézel, lézla, lézlo**
jésti	to eat	:	**jédel, jédla, jédlo**

In verbs ending in **-sti** where the **-s-** is part of the root the **-ti** is removed and the fleeting vowel **e** + **l** are added. Again this fleeting vowel only appears in the masculine form of the -l participle, e.g.

trésti	to shake	:	**trésel, trésla, tréslo**

Note: The verb **rásti** 'to grow' has two alternative forms in the masc. -l participle: **rástel/rásel**, **rásla, ráslo** etc.

In verbs ending in **-bsti, -psti** the **-sti** is removed and the fleeting vowel **e + l** is added to the **-b-** or **-p-**. Again the fleeting vowel only appears in the masc. sing. form e.g.

têpsti	to beat	:	**tépel, têpla, têplo**
grêbsti	to rake	:	**grébel, grêbla, grêblo**

(c)   In verbs ending in **-či** the **-či** is removed and the original **-k-** or **-g-** reintroduced (see **6.12** and **6.12.2**). The fleeting vowel **e + l** is added to the **-k-** or **-g-**. Again this fleeting vowel only appears in the masc. sing. form, e.g.

môči	to be able	:	**mógel, môgla, môglo**
rêči	to say	:	**rékel, rêkla, rêklo**

In verbs ending in **-reti** where **-reti** is preceded by a consonant the **-l** participle is formed by removing **-eti** and adding **-l** directly to the **-r-**, e.g.

cvréti	to fry	:	**cvŕl, cvŕla, cvŕlo**
tréti	to crush	:	**tŕl, tŕla, tŕlo**

Two exceptions are the verbs **gréti** 'to heat' and **vréti** 'to boil' and their prefixed forms which have the **-l** participle forms **grél, vrél, pogrél, zavrél**. The verb **vréti** 'to boil' and its prefixed forms should not be confused with the verbs **zavréti** 'to brake', **odvréti** 'to ease the brake', which have the regular **-l** participle forms **zavŕl, odvŕl**.

(d)   The verb **íti** 'to go' and its prefixed forms have a suppletive form in the **-l** participle:

íti		:	**šèl, šlà, šlò**
odíti	to go away	:	**odšèl, odšlà, odšlò**
nájti	to find	:	**nášel, nášla, nášlo**
zaíti	to lose one's way	:	**zašèl, zašlà, zašlò**

Note: **nájti** also has the colloquial -l participle form **nájdel, nájdla, nájdlo**.

6.23.3   Adjectival use of the -l participle

The -l participle of a stative verb may also be used attributively and it then has a full adjectival declension. This usage, however, is rare, e.g.

uvéla rastlína	a withered plant
odrásli ljudjé	grown-ups
vréla vôda	boiling water
Z otêklo rôko ne móreš délati	You can't work with a swollen hand
Preperéle zavése smo odnêsli na smetíšče	We took the mouldy curtains to the rubbish tip

6.24 THE PERFECT TENSE

This tense is formed from the present tense of the verb **bíti** 'to be' and the **-l** participle of verbs of either aspect. It translates the English simple past, present perfect, past continuous and even the past perfect continuous, e.g. 'I read, I have read, I was reading, I had been reading' and even 'I used to read/I would read' when used to describe repeated actions in the past. The following paradigm illustrates the verb **bráti** 'to read'.

		masc.	*fem.*	*neuter*
Sing.	1. **sem**			
	2. **si**	**brál**	**brála**	**brálo**
	3. **je**			
Dual	1. **sva**			
	2. **sta**	**brála**	**bráli**	**bráli**
	3. **sta**			
Plur.	1. **smo**			
	2. **ste**	**bráli**	**brále**	**brála**
	3. **so**			

The negated perfect tense is formed by using the negated present tense of the verb **bíti** plus the **-l** participle (i.e **nísem brál** etc., see **6.17**).

Examples of usage

Ali si bilà v sôbi?	Were you (f.) in the room?
Nekóč sem žível v Lóndonu	I used to live in London
V nedéljo smo glédali tékmo	We watched a match on Sunday
Púnce so kupíle sladoléd	The girls bought an ice-cream
Sréčali sva zdravníka v méstu	We (d.f.) met the doctor in town
Péter je bíl v knjížnici	Peter was in the library
Nísem jédel večérje	I did not eat any dinner
Ôna ní nášla písma	She did not find the letter
Nísva vídela psà	We (d.m.) have not seen the dog
Stára rána se je odpŕla	The old sore has reopened

6.25 THE FUTURE TENSE

The future tense is formed from the unstressed simple future of the verb **bíti** 'to be' (i.e **bom**, **boš** etc., see **6.16**) and the **-l** participle of verbs of either aspect. The following paradigm illustrates the future of the verb **rêči** 'to say':

		masc.	*fem.*	*neuter*
Sing.	1. **bom**			
	2. **boš**	**rékel**	**rêkla**	**rêklo**
	3. **bo**			
Dual	1. **bova**			
	2. **bosta**	**rêkla**	**rêkli**	**rêkli**
	3. **bosta**			
Plur.	1. **bomo**			
	2. **boste**	**rêkli**	**rêkle**	**rêkla**
	3. **bodo**			

The negative future is formed by using the negative particle **ne** before stressed **bóm, bóš** etc.

Examples of usage

Popóldne bomo šlí v kíno	This afternoon we will go to the cinema
Ôče in jàz ga bova čakála	Father and I will wait for him
Kám ga boste peljáli?	Where will you take him?
Jútri bo prišèl mój stríc iz Ánglije	My uncle from England will come tomorrow
Učítelj ne bó šèl na izlèt	The teacher will not go on the outing
Ne bó rabíla žáge	She will not use the saw
Ne bósta čakála sêstre	They (d.m.) will not wait for their sister

6.26   THE PLUPERFECT TENSE

The pluperfect is formed from the perfect tense of the verb **bíti** 'to be' (e.g. **sem bíl**) and the **-l** participle of the main verb, e.g. **dáti** 'to give': **sem bíl dál, si bíl dál, je bilà dála, smo bilí dáli** etc. 'I, you, she, we had given' etc.

This tense is mainly formed from perfective verbs. It is a very literary form and is stylistically very restricted in its use. It is no longer used in the spoken language where it is replaced by the perfect tense often with **žé** added.

Examples of usage

Ko se je bíl vŕnil domóv, je vpŕášal očéta	When he (had) returned home he asked his father
Ko se je Jánez zvečér vŕnil domóv, so bilí že večérjali	When Janez returned home in the evening they had already eaten dinner

| **Káj si ji bíl obljúbil, da te je čakála tóliko čása** | What did you promise/had you promised her that she waited for you so long? |

6.27 THE PRESENT CONDITIONAL

The present conditional is formed with the invariable particle **bi** and the -**l** participle of the verb. Since **bi** is used for all persons and the -**l** participle denotes only gender and number, the person is established either by the use of the personal pronoun or by the context. The following paradigm illustrates the verb **íti** 'to go':

				masc.	*fem.*	*neuter*
Sing.	1.	**jàz**	**bi**			
	2.	**tí**	**bi**	**šèl**	**šlà**	**šló**
	3.	**òn/ôna/ôno**	**bi**			
Dual	1.	**mídva** (m.)/**médve** (f./n.)	**bi**			
	2.	**vídva** (m.)/**védve** (f./n.)	**bi**	**šlà**	**šlì**	**šlì**
	3.	**ônadva** (m.)/**ônidve** (f./n.)	**bi**			
Plur.	1.	**mí** (m.)/**mé** (f./n.)	**bi**			
	2.	**ví** (m.)/**vé** (f./n.)	**bi**	**šlì**	**šlè**	**šlà**
	3.	**ôni/ône/ôna**	**bi**			

The conditional is negated with the particle **ne** which precedes **bi**, e.g. **òn nê bi šèl**, **ôna nê bi šlà** etc. 'he, she would not go'.

Conditional sentences describe a hypothetical situation and very often consist of two parts: the condition and the result. If this is the case the conditional appears in both parts of the sentence. The result clause may precede or follow the condition. The condition 'if' is introduced by the conjunction **če**. In the literary language the conjunction **ko** may also be used, but this is now considered archaic.

Examples of usage

Če bi biló vrême lépo, bi šlì otrôci v živálski vŕt
If the weather was fine the children would go to the zoo

Če bi imél čàs, bi šèl na kávo
If I had time I would go for a coffee

V kólikem čásu bi prepêljal ávto iz krája A v 180 km oddáljeni kràj B, če bi vôzil s povpréčno hitróstjo 120 km na úro?
How long would it take a car to travel from A to B, a distance of 180 kilometres, if it travelled at an average speed of 120 kilometres an hour?

The basic uses of the conditional in Slovene are:

(a)   To give the condition for the realisation of the statement in the main clause, e.g.

Če bi málo pomíslila, bi drugáče govoríla	If she thought about it a little, she would say otherwise
Če bi prinésel knjígo, bi jo brál	If he brought the book, I would read it

(b)   To indicate a willingness or desire to complete an action, e.g.

Sók bi píl	I could do with a drink of juice
Ràd bi ti pomágal	I would like to help you
Mój sín bi ràd šèl s tebój	My son would like to go with you

(c)   To urge or stimulate someone to do something or make a request, e.g.

Pa bi tí pomágal, Jánez?	Janez, would you help?
Bi šlì z menój?	Would you go with me?
Bi mi dál ôgenj?	Would you give me a light?
Bi mi posódil knjígo?	Would you lend me a book?

(d)   To express duty, advisability, strong possibility, e.g.

Móral bi telefonírati	I ought to telephone
Mórala bi ti pokazáti písmo	I should have shown you the letter
Vsè skúpaj bi znêslo 1000 tólarjev	Altogether that should come to 1000 tolars
Po tém sporazúmu naj bi velesíle zmánjšale oborožítev	According to this agreement the Great Powers should reduce the number of weapons

(e)   Following the verb **báti se** 'to be afraid' the negative conditional may replace the future, e.g.

Bojím se, da bo prišèl/da nê bi prišèl	I am afraid that he will come

Sometimes the conditional clause is omitted and only the result expressed. In these instances the emphasis is 'this is what I would do if I had my way', e.g. **Jàz bi prepovédal prodájo nôžev** 'I would ban the sale of knives'.

Omission of the verb

In conversation the verb may be omitted and only **bi** used if it is clear to what one is referring, e.g.

Ali bi še kàj drúgega?	Would you *like* something else?
Ali bi čáj ali kávo?	Would you like a tea or a coffee (*to drink*)?

The use of **skôraj** *'almost'*

When used with the adverb **skôraj** the conditional indicates that an action very nearly took place, e.g.

Skôraj bi zgréšil	I almost missed
Skôraj bi ti pozábil povédati	I almost forgot to tell you
Skôraj je nê bi vèč spoznál, takó se je spremeníla	He would almost not have recognised her any more, she had changed so much

6.28 THE PAST CONDITIONAL

The past conditional is formed with the conditional of the verb **bíti** 'to be' and the **-l** participle of the main verb as illustrated by the following paradigm for the verb **príti** 'to come'.

			masc.	*fem.*	*neuter*
Sing.	1.				
	2.	**bi**	**bil prišèl**	**bila prišlà**	**bilo prišlò**
	3.				
Dual	1.				
	2.	**bi**	**bila prišlà**	**bili prišlì**	**bili prišlì**
	3.				
Plur.	1.				
	2.	**bi**	**bili prišlì**	**bile prišlè**	**bila prišlà**
	3.				

The past conditional is used to denote a supposed or desired, but unrealised, act in the past, e.g.

Že zdávnaj bi bil móral tó storíti, pa ní bilo čása	He should have done that a long time ago, but there was no time
Ò bi bil umŕl, če nê bi biló mêne	He would have died if it had not been for me
Prišèl bi bil k mêni, pa bi ti prišíla gúmb	If you had come to me, I would have sewn your button on

In the modern Slovene language the past conditional is considered a literary form. It is not normally used in the spoken language where it is replaced by the present conditional. It is, however, still used where ambiguity might arise, e.g.

Če bi imél knjígo, bi ti jo posódil	If I had the book, I would lend it to you

but **Če bi bil imél knjígo,**   If I had had the book, I would
     bi ti jo posódil   have lent it to you

6.29 THE IMPERATIVE

The imperative expresses a command, order, request, direction, prohibition or warning. The simple forms of the imperative are the second persons sing./ dual/plur. and the first persons dual/plur. The first person forms usually imply an appeal, wish or exhortation.

The imperative forms are based on the present stem of the verb. There are two possible suffixes -**j**- or -**i**- to which the following personal endings are added:

Sing.	2.	-ø
Dual	1.	-va
	2.	-ta
Plur.	1.	-mo
	2.	-te

Verbs with a present tense in -**am** drop the final -**m** and add the suffix -**j**- to which the personal endings are added. Verbs with a present tense in -**ujem**, -**ijem**, -**ojem**, -**ejem** drop the final -**em** and add the personal endings to the -**j**. All other verbs in -**em**, i.e. verbs in consonant + -**jem** (e.g. **kópljem**) and verbs in consonant (other than **j**) plus -**em** (e.g **začnèm**) drop the final -**em** and add the suffix -**i**- to which the personal endings are then added. Verbs in -**im** simply drop the final -**m** and add the personal endings.

Examples

		délati (délam) 'to do'	**kupováti (kupújem)** 'to buy'
Sing.	2.	**délaj**	**kupúj**
Dual	1.	**délajva**	**kupújva**
	2.	**délajta**	**kupújta**
Plur.	1.	**délajmo**	**kupújmo**
	2.	**délajte**	**kupújte**

		mísliti (míslim) 'to think'	**peljáti (péljem)** 'to drive'	**začéti (začnèm)** 'to begin'
Sing.	2.	**mísli**	**pêlji**	**začnì**
Dual	1.	**mísliva**	**peljíva**	**začníva**
	2.	**míslita**	**peljíta**	**začníta**
Plur.	1.	**míslimo**	**peljímo**	**začnímo**
	2.	**míslite**	**peljíte**	**začníte**

Verbs in **-či** which have present tenses in **-čem**, **-žem** replace **č**, **ž** with **c**, **z**, respectively, e.g.

		Imperative
stréči (stréžem)	to serve	: **strézi, strézite**
rêči (rêčem)	to say	: **rêci, recíte**

6.29.1 Irregular imperatives

(a) Athematic verbs

With the exception of **dáti** 'to give' (and its prefixed forms) the athematic verbs and their prefixed forms have the following irregular imperatives:

		Imperative
védeti (vém)	to know	: **védi, védite**
povédati (povém)	to tell	: **povéj, povéjte**
jésti (jém)	to eat	: **jéj, jéjte**
bíti (sem)	to be	: **bódi, bodíte**
íti (grém)	to go	: **pójdi, pojdíte**

(b) The following verbs and their prefixed forms

		Imperative
báti se (bojím se)	to be afraid	: **bój se, bójte se**
glédati (glédam)	to look	: **gléj, gléjte**
státi (stojím)	to stand	: **stój, stójte**
iméti (imám)	to have	: **iméj, imejte**
majáti (májem)	to shake	: **májaj, májajte**

(c) Prefixed forms of the now archaic simple verb **jéti** 'to begin', e.g.

		Imperative
zajéti (zajámem)	to capture	: **zajêmi, zajemíte**
objéti (objámem)	to embrace	: **objêmi, objemíte**

6.29.2 The use of the imperative: aspect

In positive commands, orders, requests, warnings etc. the verb is usually perfective, but may be imperfective in general statements, e.g.

Odpríte zvézke	Open your notebooks
Sléci si plášč	Take off your coat
Pójdi vèn in si očísti čévlje	Go outside and clean your shoes
Lè vôzi 100 km na úro, te bo žé rádar odkríl	Merely drive at 100 km an hour, and the radar will catch you out
Objêmi mámo in se poslóvi	Give mummy a hug and say goodbye
Počákajta málo	Wait (d.) a minute
Vstaníta	Get up (d.)
Skríjmo se, učítelj prihája	Let us hide, the teacher is coming

In negative commands, orders, requests, warnings etc. the verb is normally in the imperfective form, e.g.

Ne klepetájte	Do not chatter
Ne hodíte po trávi	Do not walk on the grass
Popóldne ne gléj televízije	Do not watch TV in the afternoon
Ne sláči si plášča, je hladnó	Do not take your coat off, it's cold
Ne zavíjaj na lévo	Do not turn left

The negated imperative may be reinforced by the adverb **nikár** 'on no account', e.g.

Nikár ne dráži psà	Do not tease the dog
O tém nikár nikómur ne právi	Do not tell this to anyone

It should be noted that more and more in both the spoken and written language, the negated perfective verb is used if one wishes to draw attention to the unwanted consequences if the advice given is not heeded, e.g.

Ne odprì vrát za nobêno céno	Do not open the door on any account
Ne vŕni se spét prepôzno	Do not return too late again
Jútri pa ne pozábi príti na sestánek	Do not forget to come to the meeting tomorrow

Occasionally the imperative of the verb **dáti** 'to give' is used with the imperative of the autosemantic verb to express the imperative, e.g. **Dàj, vstáni** 'Get up'; **Dàj no, pomágaj mi** 'Help me'.

Note: An alternative form of **dàj/te** is **dèj/te**, e.g. **Dèj, sédi** 'Sit down'.

Colloquially the imperative of **dáti** is used with the infinitive to denote the imperative, e.g. **Dàj vzét** (= **vzêmi**) 'Take it'.

In public notices the infinitive is used with the neuter past participle passive of the verb **prepovédati** 'to forbid' to express prohibition, e.g.

Nagíbati se skózi ôkno je prepovédano	Do not lean out of the window
Kadíti prepovédano	Smoking prohibited

6.29.3 The imperative in reported speech

In Slovene the imperative is retained in reported speech following the conjunction **da** only if the person being addressed, who is to perform the action, is the second person singular, dual or plural, e.g.

Òn ti/vama/vam je naróčil, da prídi/prídita/prídite	He ordered you (sing./d./plur.) to come

This construction may, however, be replaced by '**da** + the conditional' or even by '**da** + the present tense of **mórati** 'must' + the infinitive', e.g.

Òn ti je naróčil, da bi prišèl/prišlà   He ordered you (m./f. sing.) to come
or Òn ti je naróčil, da móraš príti

If, on the other hand, the person being addressed, who is to perform the action, is the first or third person (sing./d./plur.), then the imperative is replaced in reported speech by the construction '(da) naj + the present tense', e.g.

Òn mi/nama/nam je naróčil, (da) naj   He ordered me/us (d.)/us to come
  prídem/prídeva/prídemo
Òn mu/ji/jima/jim je naróčil, (da) naj   He ordered him/**her**/them (d.)/
  príde/príde/prídeta/prídejo   them to come

This construction may, however, be replaced by '**da naj** + the conditional' or even by '**da** + the present tense of **mórati** 'must' + the infinitive' e.g.

Òn mi je naróčil da naj bi prišèl
or Òn mi je naróčil, da móram príti

6.30   THE OPTATIVE

The optative complements the imperative and expresses a wish, desire, necessity, mild command, exhortation or regret on the part of the speaker. It may also indicate hesitation in a question or statement on the part of the speaker with the expectation of advice from the person(s) addressed. The optative is used to render English phrases with the meanings 'let', 'may', 'should'. It is formed with the particle **naj** and either (a) the first or third persons of the present tense, or (b) the future of the verb **bíti** 'to be', or (c) the third persons of the conditional.

Examples of usage

Vsè naj ostáne, kàkor je	Let everything remain as it is
Naj strokovnjáki rêčejo, kàr hóčejo	Let the experts say what they want
Dobítnik nagráde naj póšlje svój naslòv	Let/will the prize winner send his address
Pa naj bó po tvôjem	Let it be as you wish
Ní védel, ali naj se jóka ali sméje	He did not know whether he should laugh or cry
Predvsèm naj oménim pisáteljevo doslédnost	Above all I should mention the author's consistency
Naj ti povém, kakó se je tó zgodílo	Let me tell you how it happened
Naj se zgodí, kàr hóče	Come what may
Káj naj naredímo?	What should we do?
Kakó naj vém, káj nameráva	How should I know what he intends?

Tó je potrébno, če naj se izógnemo poslédicam	This is necessary if we are to avoid the consequences
Polítiki naj bi uresničeváli žêlje ljúdstva	Politicians should carry out the wishes of the people

Note: In prayers one can also find the archaic third person singular imperative forms of two verbs used in the sense 'may', i.e. **Pa bódi po tvôjem/Zgódi se tvôja vólja** 'May thy will be done'.

6.31   GERUNDS (VERBAL ADVERBS)

Gerunds are indeclinable forms of the verb, which may replace adverbial clauses of time, manner, cause, condition, etc.

Slovene has two gerunds: a present gerund and a past gerund. The English equivalent of the Slovene present gerund is the present participle in '-ing', e.g. 'Waiting (= While waiting) for the bus, he read his newspaper'. This English participle form in -ing should not be confused with English verbal nouns in '-ing', e.g. 'Waiting for the bus is tedious'. The English equivalent of the Slovene past gerund is 'having done something', e.g. 'Having waited (= When he had waited) for the bus for a half hour, he decided it wasn't coming.' The Slovene gerunds are used mainly in the written literary language where the present gerund is more frequently used than the past gerund, which is almost never used. Moreover many verbs lack gerunds. In the spoken language adverbial clauses or coordinate clauses are used instead of gerunds.

6.32   THE PRESENT GERUND

The present gerund denotes an action that is simultaneous with the action of the main verb. It is formed from the present tense stem of imperfective verbs with the suffixes **-č**, **-áje** or **-é**.

(a)   The suffix **-č**

    (i)   Verbs of the first conjugation in **-am** and athematic verbs form the present gerund by adding **-č** to the third person plural of the present tense, e.g. **prebirajóč** 'reading'; **zardevajóč** 'blushing'; **gredóč** 'going'; **vedóč** 'knowing'; **gledajóč** 'watching'; **mrmrajóč** 'muttering'; **mahajóč** 'waving'; **opotekajóč se** 'staggering'.

If a verb has two possible conjugations, then the present gerund is formed from the first conjugation form, e.g. **škripajóč** 'grating', **zibajóč** 'rocking', **trepetajóč** 'trembling'.

(ii)   Verbs of the second conjugation in **-im** drop the **-im** and add **-èč**, e.g. **vabèč** 'inviting'; **mislèč** 'thinking': **stojèč** 'standing'; **sedèč** 'sitting': **govorèč** 'speaking': **držèč** 'holding'; **bojèč se** 'fearing'.

(iii)   Verbs of the third and fourth conjugations in **-jem**, **-em** drop **-em** and add **-óč** (except in roots ending in **-b-**, **-p-**, **-v-**), e.g. **smejóč se** 'laughing'; **iščóč** 'seeking'; **pričakujóč** 'expecting'; **razkazujóč** 'showing'; **pišóč** 'writing'; **režóč** 'cutting'; **pojóč** 'singing'.

If the verb root ends in **-b-**, **-p-**, **-v-** then **-èč** is added instead, e.g. **plovèč** 'sailing'; **sopèč** 'panting'; **grebèč** 'scraping'.

Verbs with an infinitive in **-či** and a present tense in **-čem** or **-žem** drop **-em** and add **-óč** but at the same time replace **č**, **ž** with the original velar (see **6.12.2**), e.g. **tekóč** 'running', **vlekóč** 'dragging', **strigóč** 'cutting'.

Note too the present gerund form from the perfective verb **rêči**: **rekóč** 'saying'. This is usually used in the phrase **takó rekóč** 'so to say/as it were'.

Irregular forms of the present gerund in **-č**:
The verbs **majáti**, **dajáti**, **hotéti** have the irregular present gerunds **majajóč** 'shaking', **dajajóč** 'giving'; **hotèč** 'wanting'.

(b)   The suffix **-áje**
Present gerunds in **-áje** are derived from the infinitive stem of verbs in **-ati** without regard to their conjugation. The **-ati** is dropped and **-áje** added to the root. These forms are now considered archaic and are avoided in favour of forms in **-č**. They are never used in conversation, e.g. **trepetáje** 'trembling'; **vzdihováje** 'sighing'; **godrnjáje** 'grumbling', **grgráje** 'gargling'; **kazáje** 'pointing'; **skakáje** 'jumping'.

(c)   The suffix **-é**
Present gerunds in **-é** are limited in number. They are formed from the present tense of second conjugation verbs in **-im** by removing **-im** and adding **-é**, e.g. **molčé** 'silently'; **sedé** 'sitting'; **klečé** 'kneeling'; **ležé** 'lying'; **stojé** 'standing'; **ječé** 'groaning'; **mižé** 'closing one's eyes'; **kričé** 'crying'; **strmé** 'gazing'.

The verbs **smejáti se**, **íti**, **védeti** and **hotéti** also have present gerund forms in **-é**: **smejé se** 'laughing', **gredé** 'going', **(nè)vedé** '(un)knowingly', **(nè)hoté** '(un)intentionally'.

The present gerund forms in **-é** are nowadays used as adverbs of manner, e.g. **Molčé so šli domóv** 'They walked home in silence'.

Examples of usage

Prenašajóč opéko na gradbíšču, se je poškodovàl
Carrying bricks at the building site he injured himself

Pišóč s črnílom, sem si zamázal pŕste
Writing with ink I stained my fingers

Obnavljajóč cérkev, so odkríli zanimíve fréske
Renovating the church they found interesting frescos

Bíl je takó utrújen, da je stojé zaspál
He was so tired that he fell asleep (while) standing

Živál je rjovèč bežála
The beast fled roaring

Glasnó smejóč se, ga je poslúšala
Laughing loudly she listened to him

Kakó boste pojédli séndvič, stojé ali sedé?
How will you eat the sandwich, standing or sitting?

Jézno godrnjáje je odšèl
Grumbling angrily he left

Plezáje na drevó, si je déček stŕgal hláče
Climbing up the tree, the boy tore his trousers

6.33 THE PAST GERUND

The past gerund describes an action which is completed prior to the action of the main verb. It is used only with a limited number of perfective verbs and is now found only in the archaic literary language and even then very rarely. It is formed from the infinitive stem of verbs in **-ti** by removing **-ti** and adding **-vši**.

Note: Prefixed perfective forms of the verb **íti** 'to go' have a past gerund in **-šédši**, e.g. **prišédši** 'having arrived'.

Examples of usage

Začutívši napétost med gôsti, sta móž in žêna poskúšala zaménjati témo pogóvora
Sensing (Having sensed) the tension between the guests, the husband and wife tried to change the conversation

Odštévši denár na mízo, je kúpec vstàl in odšèl
Counting (Having counted) out the money on to the table, the customer stood up and left

Pozabívši na bolečíne, se je prijázno nasméhnila
Forgetting (Having forgotten) her pains, she smiled amiably

Prišédši v mésto, je poískal prijátelja
Arriving (Having arrived) in the town he sought out his friend

Note: In English this past gerund is usually translated with a present gerund.

6.34 THE PRESENT PARTICIPLE ACTIVE

The present participle active replaces relative clauses with the meaning 'who/which/that is . . . ing' introduced by the pronouns **ki** or **katéri**. It denotes an action that is simultaneous with the action in the main verb. It declines like an adjective and agrees in gender, case and number with the noun it qualifies. The present participle active is formed from the present stem of imperfective verbs in exactly the same way as gerunds in -**č** (see **6.32**). Adjectival endings are then added to the -**č**, e.g. **nesóč, nesóča, nesóče** (m./f./n.) 'carrying'; **gorèč, goréča, goréče** 'burning'; **jokajóč, jokajóča, jokajóče** 'sobbing'.

Examples of usage

Prebudílo me je pétje ptíčev, spreletavajóčih se po drévju
I was awoken by the song of birds flying to and fro among the trees

Občudovàl je vŕtnice, razširjajóče prijéten vónj
He admired the roses giving off the pleasant smell

Because of their adjectival usage many present participles active have come to function as simple attributive adjectives, e.g. **skeléča rána** 'a smarting wound'; **vojskujóča se národa** 'the two warring nations'; **angléško govoréči ljudjé** 'English speaking people'; **plapolajóča zastáva** 'a fluttering flag'; **smejóče očí** 'laughing eyes'.

In newspapers one can even occasionally find such participles used in the predicate, e.g. **Céne smúčarskih vozóvnic ne bódo posébej razveseljujóče** (= **razveseljíve**) 'The price of ski lift tickets will not be especially pleasing'.

6.35 THE PAST PARTICIPLE ACTIVE

This participle is adjectival in form and totally archaic, being never used in the modern literary language. It was formed like the past gerund in -(**v**)**ši** and declined like an adjective e.g. **vstopívši, -vša, -vše** etc. 'who had entered'.

Note: Prefixed perfective forms of the verb **íti** 'to go' had a past participle active in -**šédši**.

The following example is provided simply for illustrative purposes: **Prišédše**

gôste so vsì glasnó pozdrávili 'Everyone loudly greeted the guests who had arrived'.

6.36 THE PAST PARTICIPLE PASSIVE

The past participle passive is formed from transitive perfective verbs and declines like an adjective. It also follows the rules of adjectival agreement in the predicate (see **3.5**). Its main use is in the passive voice (see **6.10**) but it may also be used to replace a relative clause denoting an action completed prior to the action in the main verb or it may be used as an attributive adjective. This participle may occasionally also be formed from transitive imperfective verbs in which case it usually denotes a state.

6.36.1 Formation of the past participle passive

The past participle passive is normally formed from the infinitive stem but may sometimes be formed from the present stem. It is formed with the suffixes **-n**, **-en**, **-t** to which the adjectival endings are then added.

(a) The suffix **-n**

All verbs in **-ati**, **-ovati/-evati** form the past participle passive by dropping **-ti** and adding **-n**, e.g.

premágati:	**premágan** (m.)	**premágana** (f.)	**premágano** (n.)	defeated
poškodováti:	**poškodován**	**poškodována**	**poškodováno**	damaged
navézati:	**navézan**	**navézana**	**navézano**	tied
zažgáti:	**zažgán**	**zažgána**	**zažgáno**	set on fire

(b) The suffix **-en**

(i) Second conjugation verbs with an infinitive in **-iti** drop **-iti** and add **-en**. The consonant preceding the **-en** is then normally replaced by another consonant in accordance with jotation changes (see **1.9.2**). There is no change however, if the consonant is **-č-**, **-š-** or **-ž-**, e.g.

	Infinitive		*Past part. passive*	
d – j	**uredíti**	–	**urejèn**	tidied, settled
t – č	**presenétiti**	–	**presenéčen**	surprised
z – ž	**uvozíti**	–	**uvóžen**	imported
s – š	**ponosíti**	–	**ponóšen**	worn out
st – šč	**oprostíti**	–	**oprošččèn**	forgiven
l – lj	**pohvalíti**	–	**pohváljen**	praised
sl – šlj	**zamísliti**	–	**zamíšljen**	conceived

n – nj	spremeníti	– spremenjèn	changed
r – rj	upériti	– upérjen	directed
b – blj	izrabíti	– izrábljen	used
p – plj	okrepíti	– okrepljèn	strengthened
m – mlj	zlomíti	– zlómljen	broken
v – vlj	pozdráviti	– pozdrávljen	greeted

No change:

izkljúčiti	– izkljúčen	excluded
zložíti	– zložèn	folded
posušíti	– posušèn	dried

A few verbs in **-iti** do not undergo the jotation changes expected. These are verbs in obstruent + **-riti** and a few others given below:

odobríti	– odobrèn	approved
poostríti	– poostrèn	sharpened
ohrabríti	– ohrabrèn	encouraged
posrebríti	– posrebrèn	silver plated, silvered
začudíti	– začúden	astonished
obljúditi	– obljúden	populated
zanétiti	– zanetèn	kindled
zalotíti	– zalóten	caught
občutíti	– občúten	felt, perceived
zaposlíti	– zaposlèn	employed
nagrmáditi	– nagrmáden	piled up

(ii) Second conjugation verbs in **-eti** drop **-eti** and add **-en**, e.g.

vídeti	– víden	seen
zaželéti	– zaželèn	wished for

(iii) Fourth conjugation verbs in **-niti** with a present stem in **-em** drop the **-iti** and add **-en**. The preceding **-n-** becomes **-nj-**, e.g.

vzdígniti	– vzdígnjen	raised
okrniti	– okrnjen	truncated
ugasníti	– ugásnjen	extinguished

(iv) All fourth conjugation verbs in **-či, -sti, -psti, -bsti**, with a present stem in **-em** drop the **-em** and add **-en**, e.g.

postríči	– postrížen	cut
spêči	– spečèn	baked
izvréči	– izvržen	ejected
ukrásti	– ukráden	stolen

zabôsti	– **zabodèn**	stabbed
zaplêsti	– **zapletèn**	entangled
pomólsti	– **pomólzen**	milked
pretêpsti	– **pretepèn**	beaten
izdólbsti	– **izdólben**	hollowed out

(v) The fourth conjugation verb **hotéti** and prefixed forms of the athematic verb **jésti** have the past participle passive forms **hotèn** 'desired' and **-jéden**, e.g. **izjéden** 'eroded'.

(c)   The suffix **-t**

The following verbs form their past participle passive with **-t** by dropping the final **-i** of the infinitive.

(i)   Prefixed forms of monosyllabic third conjugation verbs in **-iti**, **-uti**, **-eti**, e.g.

pokríti	– **pokrít**	covered
ubíti	– **ubít**	killed
obúti	– **obút**	shoed, with footware on
naštéti	– **naštét**	counted
ogréti	– **ogrét**	warmed
premléti	– **premlét**	ground up

(ii)   Prefixed forms of monosyllabic fourth conjugation verbs in **-eti** and verbs in **-četi**, e.g

prekléti	– **preklét**	cursed
začéti	– **začét**	begun
ožéti	– **ožét**	squeezed
spéti	– **spét**	tied together
zadéti	– **zadét**	struck
prejéti	– **prejét**	received

Prefixed forms of the fourth conjugation verbs **cvréti** 'to fry', **tréti** 'to crush', **zréti** 'to look', **žréti** 'to devour', **dréti** 'to flay' and verbs in **-vréti**, **-préti** form their past participle passive by dropping the final **-eti** and adding **-t**, e.g.

ocvréti	– **ocvŕt**	fried
zatréti	– **zatŕt**	suppressed
prezréti	– **prezŕt**	overlooked
prefŕéti	– **prežŕt**	gnawed
zavréti	– **zavŕt**	braked, held in check
odpréti	– **odpŕt**	opened
podréti	– **podŕt**	razed

6.36.2 The use of the past participle passive

(a) Passive voice

Stávka je bilà napovédana za srédo	A strike was declared for Wednesday
Nôvo vreménsko poročílo je biló objávljeno po televizíji	A new weather forecast was broadcast on TV
Amêrika je bilà odkríta léta 1492	America was discovered in 1492
Zastáva Rdéčega kríža je bilà dvígnjena na dróg pred táborom	The flag of the Red Cross was raised on the pole in front of the camp
Pét ljudí je biló ubítih	Five people were killed

The agreement in the last example should be noted. If the subject is a number which takes the genitive plural and the auxiliary verb is in the neuter singular then the past participle passive agrees with the noun in the genitive plural.

(b) Replacing a relative clause

Písma, spéta s spónkami, so bilà na mízi	The letters tied with paper clips were on the table
Fílm, odobrèn od cénzorja, ní priméren za otrôke	The film passed by the censor is not suitable for children

(c) Used as an attributive adjective

ukráden avtomobíl	a stolen car
pokríta tŕžnica	a covered bazaar
ponóšena obléka	worn-out clothes
skrbnó zlíkani robóvi na hláčah	the carefully ironed creases of the trousers
dôbro oprávljeno délo	a well-done job
Pomólzene kráve so odgnáli na pášo	They drove the milked cows to pasture

(d) Used as a noun

Obtóženi je priznál svój zločín	The accused admitted his crime
Móramo pomágati ránjenemu	We must help the injured man

(e) Used impersonally

Kadíti prepovédano	Smoking is forbidden
Nìč konkrétnega ní povédano o tém, kakó bomo naredíli nalógo	Nothing concrete has been said about how we will carry out the task

(f) Used with the present tense of the verb 'to be' to express a state

Súknjič je prevèč ponóšen	The jacket is much too shabby
Vsè híše so zídane iz opéke	All the houses are built of brick
Hláče níso zlíkane	The trousers are not ironed
Pípa za plín je zapŕta	The gas pipe is shut off

6.37 THE SUPINE

The supine is used instead of the infinitive after verbs with meanings involving some kind of motion. It is formed by dropping the final -i of the infinitive, e.g. **prodàt** 'to sell'; **pêč** 'to bake'; **spát** 'to sleep'; **obléč se** 'to get dressed'.

In colloquial Slovene the formal distinction between the infinitive and the supine is often neutralised, especially in the Ljubljana dialect, where the final -i of the infinitive is not pronounced. Ocasionally, however, even in these instances a distinction is maintained because the accent of the shortened infinitive differs from that of the supine, e.g.

Hóčem spáti/spàt	I want to sleep
but **Grém spát**	I am going to sleep/to bed

Examples of usage

Nàjprej pa se grém obléč	First of all I am going to go and dress
Hitéla je naznánit novíco	She hurried to announce the news
Stékel je poglédat, če je trgovína šè odpŕta	He ran to see if the shop was still open
Prídi mi povédat, kdó je zmágal	Come and tell me who won
Jútri želím íti obískat têto	Tomorrow I want to go and visit auntie

6.38 THE VERBAL NOUN

(a) The verbal noun in Slovene is usually the equivalent of the English verbal noun in -ing. It is formed by adding the suffix -je to the past participle passive form of the verb in -n or -t and declines like a neuter noun. It was noted earlier that past participle passives are normally formed only from perfective verbs (see 6.36). However, verbal nouns are most often formed from the past participle passive forms of imperfective verbs. Moreover, verbal nouns may also be formed from intransitive verbs, reflexive verbs and impersonal verbs, e.g. **ponávljanje** 'repetition'; **razdeljevánje** 'distribution'; **pridobívanje** 'acquisition'; **bránje** 'reading'; **zvonjênje** 'chiming'; **trpljênje** 'suffering'; **grmênje** 'thunder(ing)'; **spánje** 'sleep'; **pogájanje** 'negotiation'; **kesánje** 'regret'; **grétje** 'warming'; **razbúrjenje** 'agitation'; **razdráženje** 'incensing, rousing'; **pétje** 'singing'; **odpŕtje** 'opening'; **zavŕtje** 'braking'.

There are only a few exceptions where the verbal noun is not formed regularly from the past participle passive. These are verbal nouns from the following fourth conjugation verbs (see **6.36.1**): **žréti** 'to devour', **zréti** 'to look at'; **cvréti** 'to fry', **tréti** 'to crush' i.e. **žrétje; zrênje; cvrênje** (note also, however, **cvŕtje** 'fried food'); **trênje**. The verb **vréti** 'to boil' has the verbal noun **vrétje**.

(b) Nowadays in Slovene many verbal nouns are also created with the suffixes: **-tev, -ba, -nja, -va, -a, -ja**, e.g: **zložítev** 'folding'; **razdelítev** 'division'; **iznájdba** 'invention'; **spremémba** 'change'; **prétnja** 'threat'; **vôžnja** 'ride, drive'; **zamenjáva** 'exchange'; **preiskáva** 'search'; **péka** 'baking'; **presója** 'judgement'.

It should be noted that sometimes verbs have two verbal nouns, e.g. **lóčenje/ločítev** 'separation'; **kajênje/kája** 'smoking'; **tesnjênje/tesnítev** 'sealing'; **gradítev/grádnja** 'building, construction'; **pečênje/péka** 'baking'; **košênje/kôšnja** 'mowing'.

(c) Verbal nouns may also be formed by so-called deaffixation, i.e. the root of the verb forms the noun, e.g. **preglèd** 'examination'; **pretísk** 'surcharge'; **prevòz** 'transport'; **uvòz** 'import'; **uvòd** 'introduction'; **prevòd** 'translation', **ték** 'running'.

Examples of usage

Tó je izvŕstna vólna za pletênje smúčarskega pulóverja	This is excellent wool for knitting a ski pullover
opustíti kajênje	to give up smoking
Márko se žé dólgo ukvárja z zbíranjem známk	Marko has been involved with stamp collecting for a long time
Iznájdba ôgnja je bilà za človéka zeló pomémbna	The discovery of fire was very significant for man
Utrjevánje je pomémben člén učênja	Consolidation is an important tenet of learning

Note: In the modern language verbal nouns are often used with the verbs denoting 'to begin' or 'to end'. In these cases it is often better to use the infinitive, e.g. **Začnì z bránjem/Začnì bráti** 'Begin reading'; **Takój prenéhaj s čečkánjem/Takój prenéhaj čečkáti** 'Stop doodling'.

6.39 MODAL VERBS

Modal verbs are auxiliary verbs used with a main verb to indicate a particular attitude to what is being said. They are used to express ability, possibility, permission, necessity, volition, etc., i.e. English 'can, could, may, might, must, want', etc. In Slovene these are expressed by the following verbs or constructions.

(a) **mórati** + infinitive 'to have to, to be obliged to, ought to'
It should be noted that the infinitive often precedes the present tense of **mórati** at the beginning of a sentence if no personal pronoun is used.

Počívati mórate in píti velíko tekočíne	You must rest and drink a lot of liquid
Ali bom móral ostáti v bolníšnici?	Will I have to stay in hospital?
Ob štírih móraš bíti túkaj	You must be here at four
Tó bi tí móral védeti	You ought to have known this
Íti móram	I must go
Jàz móram íti v slúžbo, tí pa ne sméš	I must go to work, but you are not allowed to

(b) **tréba** + verb 'to be' + infinitive (+ dative) 'to be necessary, to have to'

Tréba je/je biló/bó obiskáti zdravníka	It is/was/will be necessary to visit the doctor
Têmelje stávbe je tréba okrepíti	It is necessary to strengthen the building's foundations//The building's foundations have to be strengthened
Zákon je tréba spremeníti	The law has to be changed
Véčkrat ga je tréba opómniti	He has to be reminded repeatedly
Níste šè na vŕsti, tréba bó málo počákati	It is not your turn yet, you will have to wait a little
Če bó tréba, ga bodo operírali	If it is necessary they will operate on him
Ne bó ti tréba ostáti v bolníšnici	You will not have to stay in hospital
Ní se ti tréba báti za njéno zdrávje	You needn't worry about her health
Ní ti tréba skrbéti	You need not trouble

Note: '**tréba** + dative, genitive' means 'to need', e.g. **Tó zímo mu ní tréba nôvih čévljev** 'He does not need new shoes this winter'; **Če ti je tréba prijátelja, ne pozábi náme** 'If you need a friend, don't forget me'.

(c) **lahkó** 'to be able, can'
This adverb is used with the main verb in all tenses and moods to express 'can, could, might'. It is only used when the verb is positive, e.g.

A lahkó prídete ob šéstih?	Can you come at six?
A bi lahkó prišèl kasnéje?	Could you come later?
Dánes grém lahkó v kinó, ker imám čàs	I can go to the cinema today, because I have time

Pól úre šè lahkó ostánem, če želíte	I can stay for another hour, if you want
Továrna bo lahkó délala z vsò zmogljívostjo	The factory will be able to work at full capacity
Lahkó bi se zgodílo, da bom potrebovàl tvôjo pomóč	It could well be that I will need your help
Lahkó, da je zbôlel	He could be ill
Lahkó, da je pozabíla	She might have/could have forgotten

Note: **lahkó** may also be used elliptically on its own to express permission or agreement, e.g. **Ali smém telefonírati? Lahkó** 'May I telephone? Of course'.

In interrogative sentences **lahkó** may express a request for permission, e.g.

V kíno bi šèl, máma, a lahkó?	I would like to go to the cinema, Mum, may I?

(d) **utegníti** + infinitive 'may, might'

Tó ti utégne korístiti	This may help you
Tó bi ti utegnílo korístiti	This might help you
Utégnil bi šè zamudíti vlák	You might still miss the train
Táko govorjênje utégne iméti húde poslédice	Such talk may have dire consequences
Tó utégne pràv príti	It may come in useful

(e) **ne môči** + infinitive 'to be unable'
This construction is used in negative statements and is the opposite of **lahkó**.

Jásna ní môgla péti, ker jo je bolélo gŕlo	Jasna could not sing, because her throat was sore
Dánes ne mórem íti v kíno, ker nímam čása	I cannot go to the cinema today, because I do not have time
Téga ne móremo razuméti	We cannot understand this
Tákih kredítov ne bom mógel odplačeváti	I will not be able to pay off such loans

(f) **sméti** + infinitive 'be allowed to, may' (i.e. permission, authorization)

A smém vstopíti?	May I come in?
Ko bóš stàr 18 lét, boš smél vozíti ávto	When you are 18 you will be allowed/may drive a car
Sméš kupíti sladoléd?	Are you allowed to buy icecream?
Káj pa si slíšal, če smém vprašáti?	What did you hear, if I may ask?
Zdravník mu je obljúbil, da bo smél čez nékaj dní domóv	The doctor promised him that he would be allowed to go home within a few days

(g) **ne sméti** + infinitive 'to not be allowed' (i.e. prohibition)

Ôna ne smé iz híše	She is not allowed to/may not leave the house
Ní se smél igráti s sosédovimi otróki	He was not allowed to play with the neighbour's children
Túkaj ne sméte parkírati	You are not allowed to park here
Kot otròk nísem smél hodíti v dísko	As a child I was not allowed to go to the disco

(h) **hotéti** + infinitive 'to want'

Hóčem védeti, kdó je tó narédil	I want to know who did this
Hotéla sem te poklícati, pa telefón ní délal	I wanted to call you, but the phone was out of order
Spét bi hôtel bíti sréčen	I would like to be happy again

(i) **ne hotéti** + infinitive 'to not want'

Péter nóče príti na zabávo	Peter does not want to come to the party
Nísmo vas hotéli motíti	We didn't want to disturb you

(j) **želéti** + infinitive 'to desire, want'

Kátka si želí postáti zdravníca	Katka wants to become a doctor
Káj želíš dobíti za rôjstni dán	What do you want to get for your birthday?

(k) **ne želéti** + infinitive 'to not desire'

Ne bi želéla zamudíti vlák	I don't want to miss the train
Šéf ne želí govoríti s tájnico	The boss does not want to talk to the secretary

6.40 VERBS USED WITH AN ENCLITIC PERSONAL PRONOUN

A special feature of a few Slovene verbs is the use of the third person accusative enclitic form of a personal pronoun with the verb, which is then used in a transferred meaning, e.g. **sékati jo** 'to go'; **lomíti ga, pokrónati ga, posráti ga** 'to act stupidly'; **pobráti jo** 'to run away'; **odnêsti jo** 'to stay alive'; **izkupíti jo/jih** 'to catch it, be wounded, hurt'; **zvozíti jo** 'to pull through (illness), come through'; **zavozíti jo** 'to make a mistake'; **ubráti jo** 'to go'; **popíhati jo** 'to run away'; **primáhati jo** 'to arrive'; **nalésti se ga** 'to get drunk'

Examples of usage

Kám jo pa sékaš?	Where are you going?
Móral jo je pobráti iz mésta	He had to flee the town
Zdravníki úpajo, da jo bo zvôzil	The doctors hope that he will pull through
Hčérka jo je popíhala z neznáncem	The daughter ran away with a stranger
Vsì so pádli, samó òn jo je odnésel	Everyone perished, only he remained alive

6.41 ASPECTUAL DERIVATION

The most common means used to derive aspectual pairs are prefixation and suffixation. Suppletion is also used but is very rare.

6.42 THE DERIVATION OF PERFECTIVE VERBS (PREFIXATION)

Perfective verbs are formed from simple (unprefixed) imperfective verbs by means of prefixes, most of which also function as prepositions and share with them their basic meanings (see **8.3**).

Slovene uses the following verbal prefixes: **do-**; **iz-**; **z-/s-/se-**; **na-**; **nad-**; **o-/ob-**; **od-**; **po-**; **pre-**; **pred-**; **pri-**; **pro-**; **raz-**; **u-**; **v-**; **vz-**; **za-**.

A prefix may merely perfectivise a simple imperfective verb, e.g. **pisáti** (imp.) 'to write' – **napisáti** (pf.) 'to write'; **braníti** (imp.) 'to defend' – **ubraníti** (pf.) 'to defend'. In these cases the addition of a prefix does not lead to the emergence of any new lexical meaning. It should be noted, however, that simple (unprefixed) imperfective verbs only rarely have an exact perfective lexical counterpart formed by means of a prefix. In most cases the addition of a prefix will usually modify the lexical meaning of the verb in a variety of ways, e.g. **trésti** (imp.) 'to shake' – **iztrésti** (pf.) 'to shake out'; **pisáti** (imp.) 'to write' – **opisáti** (pf.) 'to describe, depict'. In these cases a new imperfective verb with the same lexical meaning is then normally formed from the prefixed perfective verb by means of suffixation, e.g. **iztrésti** (pf.) 'to shake out' – **iztrésati** (imp.) 'to shake out'; **opisáti** (pf.) 'to describe' – **opisováti** (impf.) 'to describe' (see **6.44**).

One should also note that a new imperfective counterpart to a prefixed verb is occasionally formed even when the addition of the prefix does not lead to the emergence of any new lexical meaning of the original simple imperfective verb, e.g. **krivíti** (imp.)'to bend, curve' – **ukrivíti** (pf.) 'to bend, curve' – **ukrívljati** (imp.) 'to bend, curve'; **gubíti** (imp.) 'to lose' – **(i)zgubíti** (pf.) 'to lose' – **(i)zgúbljati** (imp.) 'to lose'. It should also be noted that a new imperfective is not always formed from a prefixed simple verb, even when the prefixed perfective is marginally different in meaning from that of the simple verb, e.g. **krivíti** (imp.) 'to bend' – **nakrivíti** (pf.) 'to bend a little'.

The function of a prefix is primarily semantic and from one simple imperfective verb several perfective forms may be created each with a different meaning. From these perfective forms, imperfective counterparts are then normally (but not always) created by suffixation, e.g.

Simple imperfective	Prefixed perfective	Imperfective	
čŕtati 'to draw line, rule'	**načŕtati**	**načrtávati**	to design, make a plan
	očŕtati	**očrtávati**	to outline, sketch
	podčŕtati	**podčrtávati**	to underline
	prečŕtati	**prečrtávati**	to cross out
	včŕtati		to engrave
	začŕtati	**začrtávati**	to design, trace out

New perfective verbs can also be formed from simple perfective verbs (see **6.2.3**) by means of prefixation, e.g. **dáti** (pf.) 'to give' - **prodáti** (imp.) 'to sell'. In these cases the prefix does modify the lexical meaning of the verb and the new prefixed verb will have its prefixed imperfective counterpart (i.e **prodájati** (imp.) 'to sell') which is normally the prefixed form of the imperfective counterpart of the simple perfective verb (i.e **dajáti**).

As in the case of simple imperfective verbs, various prefixes may be used to create new perfectives with various meanings from a simple perfective verb, e.g.

Simple perfective	Prefixed perfective	Imperfective	
dáti to give	**dodáti**	**dodájati**	to add
	obdáti	**obdájati**	to encircle
	podáti	**podájati**	to hand, pass
	izdáti	**izdájati**	to betray

6.43   THE BASIC MEANINGS OF THE VERBAL PREFIXES

Essentially each prefix has its own basic lexical meaning, while some prefixes have more than one meaning. In Slovene the basic meanings conveyed by the prefixes are as follows.

Note: Only the perfective form of the prefixed verb is given here, although most prefixed perfectives will have an imperfective counterpart formed by suffixation. However, some of the meanings (**Aktionsarten**) predictably do not form an imperfective (see **6.45**).

do-

(a) Completion of the action

zídati (imp.)	to build	**dozídati** (pf.)	to finish building
péti (imp.)	to sing	**dopéti** (pf.)	to finish singing
služíti (imp.)	to serve	**doslužíti** (pf.)	to finish serving

(b) Performing the action up to a fixed point in space or time

plávati (imp.)	to swim	**doplávati** (pf.)	to swim to, as far as
têči (imp.)	to run	**dotêči** (pf.)	to catch up with, reach by running
rásti (imp.)	to grow	**dorásti** (pf.)	to grow up
goréti (imp.)	to burn	**dogoréti** (pf.)	to burn down

(c) Addition to the action

líti (imp.)	to pour	**dolíti** (pf.)	to add by pouring
dáti (imp.)	to give	**dodáti** (pf.)	to append, add, affix
polníti (imp.)	to fill	**dopolníti** (pf.)	to supplement
gnojíti (imp.)	to fertilise	**dognojíti** (pf.)	to add fertiliser to

iz-

(a) Perfectivisation of the simple verb (no change in lexical meaning)

račúnati (imp.)	**izračúnati** (pf.)	to calculate
mériti (imp.)	**izmériti** (pf.)	to measure
sušíti (imp.)	**izsušíti** (pf.)	to dry

(b) Movement away from, out of

têči (imp.)	to run	**iztêči** (pf.)	to run out, leak
sesáti (imp.)	to suck	**izsesáti** (pf.)	to suck out
líti (imp.)	to pour	**izlíti** (pf.)	to pour out
íti (imp.)	to go	**izíti** (pf.)	to come out, be published

(c) Achievement of desired aim of the action

beráčiti (imp.)	to beg	**izberáčiti** (pf.)	to obtain by begging
sledíti (imp.)	to follow	**izsledíti** (pf.)	to detect, track down
prosíti (imp.)	to ask	**izprosíti** (pf.)	to obtain by entreaty, get by asking

z-/s-/se-

(a) Perfectivisation of the simple verb (no change in lexical meaning)

budíti (imp.)	**zbudíti** (pf.)	to wake
óžiti (imp.)	**zóžiti** (pf.)	to narrow
plašíti (imp.)	**splašíti** (pf.)	to frighten
sekljáti (imp.)	**sesekljáti** (pf.)	to mince
gréti (imp.)	**segréti** (pf.)	to warm, heat

(b) Movement away from, aside or downwards

lésti (imp.)	to climb	**zlésti** (pf.)	to climb down
têči (imp.)	to run	**stêči** (pf.)	to run away
peljáti (imp.)	to lead	**speljáti** (pf.)	to lead away
bíti (imp.)	to beat, strike	**zbíti** (pf.)	to knock off

(c) Movement upwards

lésti (imp.)	to climb	**zlésti** (pf.)	to climb up
rásti (imp.)	to grow	**zrásti** (pf.)	to grow up
plézati (imp.)	to climb	**splézati** (pf.)	to climb up

(d) Amalgamation, combination, unification

bíti (imp.)	to beat, strike	**zbíti** (pf.)	to nail, join together
varíti (imp.)	to weld	**zvaríti** (pf.)	to weld together
rásti (imp.)	to grow	**zrásti se** (pf.)	to grow together
plêsti (imp.)	to weave	**splêsti se** (pf.)	to become interwoven
grabíti (imp.)	to rake	**zgrabíti** (pf.)	to rake together

na-

(a) Perfectivisation of the simple verb (no change in lexical meaning)

pisáti (imp.)	**napisáti** (pf.)	to write
rísati (imp.)	**narísati** (pf.)	to draw
močíti (imp.)	**namočíti** (pf.)	to wet, moisten
gúbati (imp.)	**nagúbati** (pf.)	to fold, wrinkle
magnétiti (imp.)	**namagnétiti** (pf.)	to magnetise

(b) Movement onto or into

líti (imp.)	to pour	**nalíti** (pf.)	to pour in
lepíti (imp.)	to stick, paste	**nalepíti** (pf.)	to stick on, paste on
letéti (imp.)	to fly	**naletéti** (pf.)	to come across, meet, hit on
bôsti (imp.)	to sting, prick	**nabôsti** (pf.)	to impale, pierce, spear

tláčiti (imp.) to press, squeeze **natláčiti** (pf.) to stuff, squeeze into

(c) Beginning and partial completion of the action

glôdati (imp.)	to gnaw	**naglôdati** (pf.)	to gnaw at, nibble at
rézati (imp.)	to cut	**narézati** (pf.)	to begin to cut, slice up
krivíti (imp.)	to bend	**nakríviti** (pf.)	to bend a little
gníti (imp.)	to rot	**nagníti** (pf.)	to begin to rot, become a little rotten
grísti (imp.)	to nibble	**nagrísti** (pf.)	to bite into, nibble at

(d) The obtaining of a sufficient quantity (of something) as a result of the action

cepíti (imp.)	to chop	**nacepíti** (pf.)	to chop a sufficient quantity of
kosíti (imp.)	to mow	**nakosíti** (pf.)	to mow a sufficient quantity of
lúpiti (imp.)	to peel	**nalúpiti** (pf.)	to peel a sufficient quantity of
pêči (imp.)	to bake	**napêči** (pf.)	to bake a sufficient quantity of
lovíti (imp.)	to hunt, chase	**nalovíti** (pf.)	to catch a sufficient quantity of

(e) Completion of the action to an excessive degree (reflexive verbs)

igráti (imp.)	to play	**naigráti se** (pf.)	to play to one's heart's content, to get tired of playing
jésti (imp.)	to eat	**najésti se** (pf.)	to eat one's fill, be satiated
hodíti (imp.)	to go	**nahodíti se** (pf.)	to tire oneself out by walking
píti (imp.)	to drink	**napíti se** (pf.)	to get drunk, drink one's fill

nad-

(a) To surpass, out do

kríliti (imp.)	to flutter, flap one's wings	**nadkríliti** (pf.)	to surpass, outflank
igráti (imp.)	to play	**nadigráti** (pf.)	to overcome, beat
vládati (imp.)	to govern, rule	**nadvládati** (pf.)	to overpower, overcome, get better of
živéti (imp.)	to live	**nadživéti** (pf.)	to outlive

(b) Addition on top of something

gradíti (imp.)	to build, construct	**nadgradíti** (pf.)	to build onto, add superstructure to something
zídati (imp.)	to build	**nadzídati** (pf.)	to add superstructure to something

o-, ob-

(a) Movement around or past (something)

brízgati (imp.)	to splash	**obrízgati** (pf.)	to bespatter
čŕtati (imp.)	to draw	**očŕtati** (pf.)	to outline
jáhati (imp.)	to ride	**objáhati** (pf.)	to ride round
letéti (imp.)	to fly	**obletéti** (pf.)	to fly round
íti (imp.)	to go	**obíti** (pf.)	to go round, evade, bypass
plézati (imp.)	to climb	**obplézati** (pf.)	to climb round, avoid

(b) Perfectivisation of the action (no change in lexical meaning)

bríti (imp.)	**obríti** (pf.)	to shave
hladíti (imp.)	**ohladíti** (pf.)	to cool, chill
čutíti (imp.)	**občutíti** (pf.)	to feel
čístiti (imp.)	**očístiti** (pf.)	to clean

(c) To remain in the state indicated by the simple verb

ležáti (imp.)	to lie	**obležáti** (pf.)	to remain lying
viséti (imp.)	to hang	**obviséti** (pf.)	to remain hanging
sedéti (imp.)	to sit	**obsedéti** (pf.)	to remain seated

od-

(a) Movement away or separation (from something)

stopíti (pf.)	to step	**odstopíti** (pf.)	to resign, withdraw, retire
íti (imp.)	to go	**odíti** (pf.)	to go away
letéti (imp.)	to fly	**odletéti** (pf.)	to fly away
plúti (imp.)	to sail	**odplúti** (pf.)	to sail away
nêsti (imp.)	to carry	**odnêsti** (pf.)	to carry off
žágati (imp.)	to saw	**odžágati** (pf.)	to saw off
píhati (imp.)	to blow, puff	**odpíhati** (pf.)	to blow away
rézati (imp.)	to cut	**odrézati** (pf.)	to cut off

(b) Total completion of the action

večérjati (imp.)	to dine	**odvečérjati** (pf.)	to finish one's dinner
péti (imp.)	to sing	**odpéti** (pf.)	to sing to the end
igráti (imp.)	to play	**odigráti** (pf.)	to play to the end
cvetéti (imp.)	to blossom	**odcvetéti** (pf.)	to finish flowering

(c) Nullification, annulment of the action

lepíti (imp.)	to stick, glue	**odlepíti** (pf.)	to unstick, unglue
pečátiti (imp.)	to seal	**odpečátiti** (pf.)	to unseal
mótati (imp.)	to wind	**odmótati** (pf.)	to unwind
svetováti (imp.)	to advise	**odsvetováti** (pf.)	to dissuade
vézati (imp.)	to tie	**odvézati** (pf.)	to untie

(d) Response

govoríti (imp.)	to speak	**odgovoríti** (pf.)	to reply
pisáti (imp.)	to write	**odpisáti** (pf.)	to reply in writing
zváti (imp.) (arch.)	to call	**odzváti se** (pf.)	to respond

po-

(a) Perfectivisation of the action or state (no change in lexical meaning)

bárvati (imp.)	**pobárvati** (pf.)	to paint
jésti (imp.)	**pojésti** (pf.)	to eat
hvalíti (imp.)	**pohvalíti** (pf.)	to praise
ščétkati (imp.)	**poščétkati** (pf.)	to brush
bledéti (imp.)	**pobledéti** (pf.)	to turn pale

(b) Limited duration of the action or state

gúgati (imp.)	to rock	**pogúgati** (pf.)	to rock for a while
molčáti (imp.)	to be silent	**pomolčáti** (pf.)	to be silent for a while
kramljáti (imp.)	to chat	**pokramljáti** (pf.)	to chat for a while
čehljáti (imp.)	to scratch	**počehljáti** (pf.)	to scratch for a while
spáti (imp.)	to sleep	**pospáti** (pf.)	to sleep for a while
filozofírati (imp.)	to philosophise	**pofilozofírati** (pf.)	to speculate for a while

(c) Application of the action to several objects successively

gubíti (imp.)	to lose	**pogubíti** (pf.)	to lose one after another
lomíti (imp.)	to break	**polomíti** (pf.)	to break one after another
cepíti (imp.)	to innoculate	**pocepíti** (pf.)	to innoculate one after another
kláti (imp.)	to slaughter	**pokláti** (pf.)	to slaughter one after another

pod-

Action below or beneath

čŕtati (imp.)	to rule, draw lines	**podčŕtati** (pf.)	to underline
pisáti (imp.)	to write	**podpisáti** (pf.)	to sign
kopáti (imp.)	to dig	**podkopáti** (pf.)	to undermine
céniti (imp.)	to value	**podcéniti** (pf.)	to underestimate
zídati (imp.)	to build	**podzídati** (pf.)	to underpin, support
kováti (imp.)	to forge	**podkováti** (pf.)	to shoe (a horse)
kupíti (imp.	to buy	**podkupíti** (pf.)	to bribe

pre-

(a) Perfectivisation of the action (no change in lexical meaning)

debatírati (imp.)	**predebatírati** (pf.)	to debate
diskutírati (imp.)	**prediskutírati** (pf.)	to discuss
levíti se (imp.)	**prelevíti se** (pf.)	to slough, cast one's skin
zráčiti (imp.)	**prezráčiti** (pf.)	to ventilate

(b) Movement across or through

žágati (imp.)	to saw	**prežágati** (pf.)	to saw through
grísti (imp.)	to bite	**pregrísti** (pf.)	to bite through
vesláti (imp.)	to row	**prevesláti** (pf.)	to row across
peljáti (imp.)	to lead, convey	**prepeljáti** (pf.)	to carry, convey across
letéti (imp.)	to fly	**preletéti** (pf.)	to fly across
čŕtati (imp.)	to rule, draw lines	**prečŕtati** (pf.)	to cross out, through, cancel

(c) Repetition or reworking of the action

bárvati (imp.)	to paint	**prebárvati** (pf.)	to repaint
oblikováti (imp.)	to form, shape	**preoblikováti** (pf.)	to remodel
formulírati (imp.)	to formulate	**preformulírati** (pf.)	to reformulate

grupírati (imp.)	to group, arrange	**pregrupírati** (pf.)	to regroup, rearrange
kováti (imp.)	to forge	**prekováti** (pf.)	to reshoe (a horse)
téhtati (imp.)	to weigh	**pretéhtati** (pf.)	to reweigh

(d) Excess of action

rásti (imp.)	to grow	**prerásti** (pf.)	to overgrow
solíti (imp.)	to salt	**presolíti** (pf.)	to add too much salt
sladkáti (imp.)	to sweeten	**presladkáti** (pf.)	to oversweeten
plačáti (pf.)	to pay	**preplačáti** (pf.)	to overpay, pay too much
hvalíti (imp.)	to praise	**prehvalíti** (pf.)	to overpraise
živéti (imp.)	to live	**preživéti** (pf.)	to outlive

(e) Duration of action for a certain period of time

sedéti (imp.)	to sit	**presedéti** (pf.)	to sit for a certain period of time
jokáti (imp.)	to sob	**prejokáti** (pf.)	to sob for a certain period of time
strádati (imp.)	to starve	**prestrádati** (pf.)	to starve for a certain period of time
molčáti (imp.)	to be silent	**premolčáti** (pf.)	to be silent for a certain period of time
smrčáti (imp.)	to snore	**presmrčáti** (pf.)	to spend a certain period of time snoring

pred-

Action before, prior to

pakírati (imp.)	to pack	**predpakírati** (pf.)	to prepack
gréti (imp.)	to heat, warm	**predgréti** (pf.)	to preheat
vídeti (imp.)	to see	**predvídeti** (pf.)	to foresee

pri-

(a) Perfectivisation of the simple verb (no change in lexical meaning)

síliti (imp.)	**prisíliti** (pf.)	to force
blížati se (imp.)	**približati se** (pf.)	to approach
godíti se (imp.)	**prigodíti se** (pf.) (arch.)	to occur

(b) Movement towards, approach, arrival

íti (imp.)	to go	**príti** (pf.)	to arrive, come
letéti (imp.)	to fly	**priletéti** (pf.)	to fly up to, approach flying
plúti (imp.)	to sail	**priplúti** (pf.)	to sail (in)to, arrive (of ship)
šépati (imp.)	to limp	**prišépati** (pf.)	to limp up to, arrive limping

(c) Addition to the action

točíti (imp.)	to pour	**pritočíti** (pf.)	to add by pouring
méšati (imp.)	to mix	**priméšati** (pf.)	to admix
líti (imp.)	to pour	**prilíti** (pf.)	to add by pouring
račúnati (imp.)	to calculate	**priračúnati** (pf.)	to add to account, calculations

(d) Attachment to something

lepíti (imp.)	to stick, paste	**prilepíti** (pf.)	to stick on
kŕpati (imp.)	to patch	**prikŕpati** (pf.)	to patch on
šíti (imp.) (arch.)	to sew	**prišíti** (pf.)	to sew on

(e) To obtain something through the action

beráčiti (imp.)	to beg	**priberáčiti** (pf.)	to obtain by begging
barantáti (imp.)	to haggle	**pribarantáti** (pf.)	to obtain by haggling
igráti (imp.)	to play	**priigráti** (pf.)	to win (money) by gambling

(f) Limitation of extent of action

rézati (imp.)	to cut	**prirézati** (pf.)	to clip, trim
dušíti (imp.)	to choke, suffocate	**pridušíti** (pf.)	to muffle, deaden
stríči (imp.)	to cut	**pristríči** (pf.)	to trim

pro-

Movement through (something)

sévati (imp.)	to radiate	**prosévati** (pf.)	to shine through (and **presévati**)
dréti (imp.)	to rush, tear along	**prodréti** (pf.)	to break through, make one's way

žéti (imp.) (arch.) to squeeze   **prožéti** (pf.) (arch.) to impregnate, imbue (and **prežéti**)

raz-

(a) Perfectivisation of the action (no change in lexical meaning)

mehčáti (imp.)   **razmehčáti** (pf.)   to soften
bistríti (imp.)   **razbistríti** (pf.)   to clarify, make clear
topíti (imp.)   **raztopíti** (pf.)   to melt, dissolve

(b) Division into parts

lomíti (imp.) to break   **razlomíti** (pf.) to break into pieces
rézati (imp.) to cut   **razrézati** (pf.) to cut into pieces
grísti (imp.) to bite   **razgrísti** (pf.) to bite into small pieces, corrode
tólči (imp.) to beat, break   **raztólči** (pf.) to pulverise, crush

(c) Movement, action in various directions

nêsti (imp.) to carry   **raznêsti** (pf.) to burst, explode
mázati (imp.) to grease, oil   **razmázati** (pf.) to smear, daub all over
letéti (imp.) to fly   **razletéti se** (pf.) to scatter, fly asunder
trésti (imp.) to shake   **raztrésti** (pf.) to scatter, strew

(d) Nullification, annulment of the action

bremeníti (imp.) to load   **razbremeníti** (pf.) to unburden
vézati (imp.) to bind, tie   **razvézati** (pf.) to untie
mótati (imp.) to wind   **razmótati** (pf.) to unwind
bŕzdati (imp.) to bridle   **razbŕzdati** (pf.) to unbridle

(e) Intensity of the action

kúhati (imp.) to cook   **razkúhati** (pf.) to overcook
gréti (imp.) to warm, heat   **razgréti** (pf.) to make very hot
rásti (imp.) to grow   **razrásti se** (pf.) to branch out, grow luxuriantly
prasketáti (imp.) to crackle   **razprasketáti** (pf.) to begin crackling very loudly

u-

(a) Perfectivisation of the verb (no change in lexical meaning)

braníti (imp.)	**ubraníti** (pf.)	to defend
gásniti (imp.)	**ugásniti** (pf.)	to go out
krotíti (imp.)	**ukrotíti** (pf.)	to tame
sídrati (imp.)	**usídrati** (pf.)	to anchor

(b) Movement away, down

bežáti (imp.)	to run	**ubežáti** (pf.)	to escape
têči (imp.)	to run	**utêči** (pf.)	to run away, escape
íti (imp.)	to go	**uíti** (pf.)	to run away, escape
dréti (imp.)	to rush, hurry	**udréti se** (pf.)	to sink down
sésti (pf.)	to sit down	**usésti se** (pf.)	to sink, cave in

(c) Decrease in size as a result of the action (reflexive verbs)

kúhati (imp.)	to cook	**ukúhati se** (pf.)	to become smaller, shrink as a result of cooking
sušíti (imp.)	to dry	**ususíti se** (pf.)	to dry up
pêči (imp.)	to bake	**upêči se** (pf.)	to become smaller as a result of baking

(d) Error in completing the action (reflexive verbs)

téhtati (imp.)	to weigh	**utéhtati se** (pf.)	to make a mistake in weighing
mériti (imp.)	to measure	**umériti se** (pf.)	to make a mistake in measuring
račúnati (imp.)	to calculate	**uračúnati se** (pf.)	to miscalculate
štéti (imp.)	to count	**uštéti se** (pf.)	to miscount

v-

(a) Movement into, towards, inclusion in

plúti (imp.)	to sail	**vplúti** (pf.)	to sail into
lomíti (imp.)	to break	**vlomíti** (pf.)	to break into
račúnati (imp.)	to calculate	**vračúnati** (pf.)	to take into account
korákati (imp.)	to step, march	**vkorákati** (pf.)	to march in
klesáti (imp.)	to sculpture, chisel	**vklesáti** (pf.)	to engrave
pisáti (imp.)	to write	**vpisáti** (pf.)	to register, inscribe

(b) Movement up

státi (imp.)	to stand	**vstáti** (pf.)	to get up

vz-

(a) Perfectivisation of the verb (no change in lexical meaning)

rohnéti (imp.)	**vzrohnéti** (pf.)	to fume, rage
kalíti (imp.)	**vzkalíti** (pf.)	to germinate
dramíti (imp.)	**vzdramíti** (pf.)	to rouse, wake

(b) Movement upwards

letéti (imp.)	to fly	**vzletéti** (pf.)	to fly up
íti (imp.)	to go	**vzíti** (pf.)	to rise, ascend
plúti (imp.)	to sail	**vzplúti** (pf.)	to surface
kipéti (imp.)	to boil	**vzkipéti** (pf.)	to boil over

(c) Beginning of the action or state

plamtéti (imp.)	to flare up	**vzplamtéti** (pf.)	to begin to flare up
ljubíti (imp.)	to love	**vzljubíti** (pf.)	to take a fancy to, fall in love with
tléti (imp.)	to glow, smoulder	**vztléti** (pf.)	to begin to glow, smoulder

za-

(a) Perfectivisation of the simple verb (no change in lexical meaning)

kričáti (imp.)	**zakričáti** (pf.)	to cry out
čutíti (imp.)	**začutíti** (pf.)	to feel
ščítiti (imp.)	**zaščítiti** (pf.)	to protect

(b) Movement behind or to the rear

toníti (imp.)	to sink	**zatoníti** (pf.)	to go down behind, set (of sun)
tláčiti (imp.)	to squeeze, press	**zatláčiti** (pf.)	to tuck in
íti (imp.)	to go	**zaíti** (pf.)	to set (of sun)

(c) Movement into

vêsti (imp.)	to lead, guide	**zavêsti** (pf.)	to tempt, seduce (into)
brêsti (imp.)	to wade	**zabrêsti** (pf.)	to wade into
víti (imp.)	to wind	**zavíti** (pf.)	to wrap up
grísti (imp.)	to bite	**zagrísti** (pf.)	to bite into

(d) Beginning of the action

ihtéti (imp.)	to sob	**zaihtéti** (pf.)	to begin to
díhati (imp.)	to breathe	**zadíhati** (pf.)	to begin to breathe

filozofírati (imp.)	to philosophise	**zafilozofírati** (pf.)	to begin to philosophise
vládati (imp.)	to reign	**zavládati** (pf.)	to begin to reign

(e)　An error, a mistake, loss because of the action

delíti (imp.)	to divide	**zadelíti se** (pf.)	to divide incorrectly, make a mistake in dividing
špekulírati (imp.)	to speculate	**zašpekulírati** (pf.)	to lose by speculation
kóckati (imp.)	to play dice	**zakóckati** (pf.)	to gamble away
íti (imp.)	to go	**zaíti** (pf.)	to go astray
govoríti (imp.)	to say	**zagovoríti se** (pf.)	to let slip

(f)　To do something for a long time, too long (reflexive verbs)

klepetáti (imp.)	to chatter	**zaklepetáti se** (pf.)	to chatter for a long time
sedéti (imp.)	to sit	**zasedéti se** (pf.)	to sit for too long, a long time
govoríti (imp.)	to speak	**zagovoríti se** (pf.)	to talk for a long time, too long

(g)　To cover, fill up, fill in

zídati (imp.)	to build	**zazídati** (pf.)	to wall in
šíti (imp.)	to sew	**zašíti** (pf.)	to sew up
mêsti (imp.)	to snow heavily	**zamêsti** (pf.)	to snow in, cover with snow
dímiti (imp.)	to smoke (fish)	**zadímiti** (pf.)	to fill with smoke

6.43.1　Compound prefixes (doubly prefixed verbs)

In some cases compound prefixes (consisting of two simple prefixes) are used to form perfective verbs from which imperfect counterparts may or may not be derived by suffixation, e.g.

> **spáti** (imp.) 'to sleep'; **zaspáti** (pf.) **zaspávati** (imp.) 'to fall asleep'; **pozaspáti** (pf.) 'to fall asleep one after the other'
>
> **glédati** (imp.) 'to look'; **preglédati** (pf.) **pregledováti** (imp.) 'to examine, inspect'; **spreglédati** (pf.) **spregledováti** (imp.) 'to overlook'

In these cases an additional prefix has been added to an already prefixed verb and either further modifies the lexical meaning of the prefixed verb or gives a more precise meaning.

The compound prefixes found in Slovene are:

izpod-/spod-, izpre-/spre-, izpo-/spo-, predpo-, predpri-, prena-, preo(b)-, poza-, poraz-, proiz-, razpo-, sodo-, sopod-, sou-, sov-, vzpo-, vzpod-

Examples:

spodbudíti (pf.)	**spodbújati** (imp.)	to stimulate, spur
izpopolníti (pf.)	**izpopolnjeváti** (imp.)	to improve, perfect
predpostáviti (pf.)	**predpostávljati** (imp.)	to presuppose
prèdpripráviti (pf.)		to prepare in advance
prenapolníti (pf.)		to overfill
preobremeníti (pf.)	**preobremenjeváti** (imp.)	to overburden
preosvetlíti (pf.)		to over expose
proizvêsti (pf.)	**proizvájati**	to produce
razposadíti (pf.)	**razposájati** (imp.)	to plant in several places
vzpostáviti (pf.)	**vzpostávljati** (imp.)	to restore, re-establish
vzpodbôsti (pf.)	**vzpodbádati** (imp.)	to goad, prompt
sòdoživéti (pf.)	**sòdožívljati** (imp.)	to experience together with
sòpodpisáti (pf.)	**sòpodpisováti** (imp.)	to countersign
sòudeležíti se (pf.)	**sòudeleževáti se** (imp.)	to take part in together with
sovpásti (pf.)	**sovpádati** (imp.)	to coincide

6.43.2 Prefixed perfective verbs without a simple (non-prefixed) imperfective form

These are perfective verbs consisting of a prefix plus **-preti, -četi, -uti**. From these verbs imperfective counterparts are created by suffixation e.g.

Perfective	*Imperfective*	
zapréti	**zapírati**	to shut
odpréti	**odpírati**	to open
upréti se	**upírati se**	to resist
začéti	**začénjati**	to begin
pričéti	**pričénjati**	to begin
obúti	**obúvati**	to shoe, put shoes on someone
sezúti	**sezúvati**	to remove someone's shoes

6.44 IMPERFECTIVE VERBS

Imperfective verbs are either simple verbs (see **6.2.3**) or are derived from perfective verbs by suffixation. This imperfectivisation is primary in the case of simple non-prefixed perfective verbs (see **6.2.3**) and secondary in the case of prefixed perfective verbs, e.g.

(a) Primary

kupíti (pf.)   **kupováti** (imp.)   to buy

(b) Secondary

pisáti (imp.)   to write: **podpisáti** (pf.) – **podpisováti** (imp.)   to sign

One should note, however that imperfective verbs are not derived from all prefixed perfectives by means of suffixation. For example, the prefixed perfectives **zajádrati** 'to sail into', **podkováti** 'to shoe (a horse)' do not have corresponding lexical imperfective counterparts. In these cases, the simple imperfective verbs **jádrati** 'to sail', **kováti** 'to forge' are used as their imperfective counterparts.

6.45   SUFFIXATION

When suffixation occurs this may be accompanied by a consonantal alternation in the root (i.e. jotation, loss of original palatalisation, see **1.9.1** and **1.9.2**), a change in vowel quality, a change of stress or a combination of these things. In Slovene the following suffixes are used to form imperfective verbs: -a-, -áva-, -va-, -ová-/-evá-. Of these the most productive are -va-, -ová-/-evá-,-a-.

6.45.1   The suffix -a-

The suffix -a- is used to form imperfectives from the following perfective verbs.

(a) Verbs in -iti. In these cases the imperfective verbs very often show jotation of the root final consonant and sometimes a qualitative change -o- > -a- in the root vowel, e.g.

izkrivíti	**izkrívljati**	to distort
potopíti	**potápljati**	to immerse
zamísliti si	**zamíšljati si**	to imagine
zgostíti	**zgóščati**	to thicken
zanemáriti	**zanemárjati**	to neglect
pogasíti	**pogášati**	to extinguish
odgovoríti	**odgovárjati**	to answer
osvojíti	**osvájati**	to conquer
zapustíti	**zapúščati**	to bequeath, abandon
osúmiti	**osúmljati**	to suspect
ohladíti	**ohlájati**	to cool
ukaníti	**ukánjati**	to dupe
razšíriti	**razšírjati**	to widen

vlomíti	**vlámljati**	to break in
zgubíti	**zgúbljati**	to lose
naročíti	**naróčati**	to order
ogrozíti	**ogróžati**	to threaten
sprehodíti se	**sprehájati se**	to take a walk

In the case of a few verbs the root of the prefixed perfective verb ends in -č or -ž (which arose as a result of palatalisation), while the imperfective verb restores the original velar consonant (depalatalisation) and shows a change in the quality of the root vowel.

Note: The simple perfective verb **skočíti** also forms its imperfective this way.

Perfective	*Imperfective*	
natočíti	**natákati**	to pour
izložíti	**izlágati**	to unpack
namočíti	**namákati**	to soak
skočíti	**skákati**	to jump

Note: The simple perfective verbs **póčiti** 'to burst', **píčiti** 'to sting', **tŕčiti** 'to collide' also form their imperfectives this way, but there is no change in the quality of the root vowel, i.e. **pókati**, **píkati**, **tŕkati**.

(b) Verbs in -**sti**, -**či**. In the case of verbs in -**sti** the -**s**- is replaced in the imperfective form by the original final consonant of the root, i.e. -**d**- or -**t**- (see **6.12.2**). However, if the -**s**- in the infinitive was the original final consonant of the root then it is not replaced. Verbs in -**psti**, -**bsti** simply drop the final -**sti**. There may be a qualitative change in the root vowel.

Examples

Perfective	*Imperfective*	
zbôsti	**zbádati**	to prick, sting
zaprêsti	**zaprédati**	to spin
odplêsti	**odplétati**	to unravel
pomêsti	**pométati**	to sweep up
pásti	**pádati**	to fall
otrésti	**otrésati**	to shake off
iztêpsti	**iztépati**	to beat
zagrêbsti	**zagrébati**	to bury
docvèsti	**docvétati**	to finish blooming
nagnêsti se	**nagnétati se**	to pile up
izjésti	**izjédati**	to corrode, eat into
zasésti	**zasédati**	to occupy

(c) Verbs in -**či**. In the case of perfective verbs in -**či** the -**č**- is replaced in their imperfective counterparts by the velar consonant that originally appeared in the root, i.e. -**g**- or -**k**-. In a few cases it is replaced by -**z**-.

Examples

Perfective	Imperfective	
zaséči	zaségati	to seize
prestréči	prestrézati	to block, parry
pripêči	pripékati	to scorch, burn
ustréči	ustrézati	to satisfy, suit
odtêči	odtékati	to leak out
izrêči	izrékati	to utter
vpréči	vprégati/vprézati	to harness
uléči se	ulégati se	to lie down
pomôči	pomágati	to help

(d) Prefixed forms of the verbs **tréti** 'to crush', **vréti** 'to boil', **mréti** 'to die', dréti 'to flay', **zréti** 'to look at' and prefixed forms of **-préti**: these verbs replace **-reti** with **-irati** in the imperfective verb.

Examples

Perfective	Imperfective	
zatréti	zatírati	to suppress
zavréti	zavírati	to brake
prezréti	prezírati	to disregard, to overlook
odpréti	odpírati	to open
prodréti	prodírati	to break through
umréti	umírati	to die

(e) Prefixed forms of the verbs **živéti** 'to live', **védeti** 'to know', e.g.

Perfective	Imperfective	
zavédeti se	zavédati se	to realise
izživéti se	izživljati se	to enjoy
preživéti	preživljati	to spend, pass

(f) Prefixed forms of the verbs **péti se** (imp.), 'to climb, go up'; **kléti** 'to swear'. In the imperfective forms of these verbs the **-e-** is replaced by **-enja-/-inja-** respectively, which contain the **-n-** of the original root.

Perfective	Imperfective	
napéti	napénjati	to strain
odpéti	odpénjati	to unbuckle
pripéti	pripénjati	to pin, fasten
prekléti	preklínjati	to curse
zakléti se	zaklínjati se	to vow

(g) Prefixed forms of the literary verb **žéti** (imp.) 'to squeeze'. In the imperfective verbs the **-m-** which occurred in the original root also appears before the suffix **-ati**, e.g.

ožéti (pf.)	ožémati (imp.)	to squeeze
zažéti (pf.)	zažémati (imp.)	to squeeze
prižéti (pf.)	prižémati (imp.)	to clasp

(h) Semelfactive perfective verbs in **-niti.** In the imperfective verb the suffix **-niti** is replaced by **-ati** and any final consonant that was lost from the original root (i.e **-b-, -p-, -t-, -k-**) appears again before the suffix **-ati.** Again, a qualitative change in the root vowel or jotation may take place.

Examples

Perfective	Imperfective	
zéhniti	**zéhati**	to yawn
mígniti	**mígati**	to beckon, wink
kríkniti	**kríkati**	to cry out
kreníti	**krétati**	to move
žvížgniti	**žvížgati**	to whistle
pritísniti	**pritískati**	to press
utoníti	**utápljati**	to drown
spotakníti	**spotíkati**	to trip up
odkleníti	**odklépati**	to unlock
síkniti	**síkati**	to hiss
ogníti se	**ogíbati se**	to avoid

Note: The verb **vrníti** (pf.) and its prefixed perfective derivatives form their imperfective counter-parts in -(v)ráčati, e.g.

prevrníti – prevráčati	to overturn, overthrow
zavrníti – zavráčati	to reject
obrníti – obráčati	to turn round
odvrníti – odvráčati	to divert, avert

(i) Prefixed forms of the archaic imperfective verb **súti** 'to pour'. In the modern language **súti** has been replaced by **sípati** and this is the form found in the imperfective prefixed counterparts, e.g.

| **zasúti** (pf.) | **zasípati** (imp.) | to fill in by pouring |
| **vsúti** (pf.) | **vsípati** (imp.) | to pour in |

(j) Prefixed forms of the imperfective verbs **žgáti** 'to burn' and **zváti** 'to call'. In the case of both verbs an **-i-** is inserted between the initial two consonants (i.e. **zv-, žg-**) in the imperfective forms.

Examples

Perfective	Imperfective	
zažgáti	**zažígati**	to set on fire
ožgáti	**ožígati**	to singe, scorch

pozváti	pozívati	to call
odzváti se	odzívati se	to respond

(k) Perfective prefixed forms of the imperfective verbs **bíti** 'to beat', **píti** 'to drink', **víti** 'to wind'. In these cases the suffix is added to the present tense bases **-bij-**, **-pij-**, **-vij-**.

Examples

Perfective	Imperfective	
nabíti	**nabíjati**	to load; affix
vpíti	**vpíjati**	to absorb
zavíti	**zavíjati**	to wrap up

(l)   Prefixed forms of the verbs **státi** (imp.) 'to stand' and **dáti** (pf.) 'to give', which have imperfectives in **-ájati**.

Examples

Perfective	Imperfective	
nastáti	**nastájati**	to arise, originate
ostáti	**ostájati**	to stay, remain
vstáti	**vstájati**	to get up
predáti	**predájati**	to hand over
prodáti	**prodájati**	to sell
izdáti	**izdájati**	to betray

Note: The simple perfective verb **dáti** also forms its imperfective this way, i.e. **dajáti**.

6.45.2   The suffix **-áva-**

This suffix is used to form imperfective verbs from the following perfective verbs:

(a) Verbs in **-niti**. In the imperfective verbs the suffix **-niti** is replaced by **-ávati**.

Examples

Perfective	Imperfective	
izbégniti	**izbegávati**	to avoid
prekúcniti	**prekucávati**	overturn
spodŕsniti	**spodrsávati**	to slip, slide

(b) Verbs in **-riti**, e.g.

Perfective	Imperfective	
odobríti	**odobrávati**	to approve
pokoríti	**pokorávati**	to subdue

(c) Prefixed forms of the verb **leteti** (imp.) 'to fly', e.g.

Perfective	Imperfective	
odletéti	**odletávati**	to fly away
zletéti	**zletávati**	to fly up

(d) Verbs in **-psti**, e.g.

iztêpsti (pf.)   **iztepávati** (imp.)   to beat out

Note: This verb also has an alternative imperfective **iztépati**.

6.45.3 The suffix **-va-**

This suffix is used to form imperfective verbs from the following verbs:

(a) Perfective verbs in **-ati** (whether prefixed verbs or simple verbs), e.g.

Perfective	Imperfective	
končáti	**končávati**	to finish
néhati	**nehávati**	to stop, cease
ménjati	**menjávati**	to change
sréčati	**srečávati**	to meet
razkopáti	**razkopávati**	to dig up
razgíbati	**razgibávati**	to flex
vsípati	**vsipávati**	to pour in

(b) Prefixed verbs in **-eti** with a present tense in **-im**, **-iš**; **-ejem**, **-eješ**; **-ojem**, **-oješ**

Perfective	Imperfective	
zgoréti	**zgorévati**	to burn down
omedléti	**omedlévati**	to faint
odštéti	**odštévati**	to subtract
razgréti	**razgrévati**	to heat
opéti	**opévati**	to praise in song

(c) Prefixed forms of the following verbs: **míti** (arch.) 'to wash'; **líti** 'to pour'; **šíti** (arch.) 'to sew'; **kríti** 'to cover'; **ríti** 'to dig'; **bíti** 'to be'; **žíti** (arch.) 'to live'; **počíti (se)** 'to rest'

Perfective	Imperfective	
prelíti	**prelívati**	to spill
umíti	**umívati**	to wash

zašíti	**zašívati**	to sew up
pokríti	**pokrívati**	to cover
zaríti	**zarívati**	to dig in
prebíti	**prebívati**	to reside
užíti	**užívati**	to enjoy
odpočíti se	**odpočívati se**	to rest

(d) Prefixed verbs in **-uti** with the meaning 'to put on or take off shoes', e.g.

Perfective	*Imperfective*	
obúti	**obúvati**	to put on
sezúti	**sezúvati**	to take off

6.45.4   The suffixes **-ová-/-evá-**

These suffixes are very productive. The suffix **-evá-** replaces **-ová-** after the consonants **č, ž, š, c, j**. They form imperfective verbs from the following verbs:

(a) Simple and prefixed perfective verbs in **-ati**, e.g.

Perfective	*Imperfective*	
plačáti	**plačeváti**	to pay
pričakáti	**pričakováti**	to expect
podpisáti	**podpisováti**	to sign
zmágati	**zmagováti**	to conquer
izbóljšati	**izboljševáti**	to improve
zmánjkati	**zmanjkováti**	to lack
zmajáti	**zmajeváti**	to shake
raziskáti	**raziskováti**	to research
navézati	**navezováti**	to tie, fasten
končáti	**končeváti**	to finish
obdélati	**obdelováti**	to cultivate

(b) Simple and prefixed perfective verbs in **-iti** and some verbs in **-niti**:

Perfective	*Imperfective*	
kupíti	**kupováti**	to buy
navdúšiti	**navduševáti**	to enrapture
premísliti	**premišljeváti**	to reflect
prezráčiti	**prezračeváti**	to ventilate
utrdíti	**utrjeváti**	to fortify
namígniti	**namigováti**	to hint
vzdígniti	**vzdigováti**	to lift
nategníti	**nategováti**	to stretch

(c) A few isolated verbs, e.g.

Perfective	Imperfective	
oskrbéti	oskrbováti	to supply
pregrísti	pregrizováti	to bite through

6.45.5 Alternative imperfective suffixes

In some cases perfective verbs have two or even three imperfective counterparts formed with different suffixes. Such alternative derivatives are a result of the historical development of the Slovene literary language, whereby different dialects favour one or other type and both have been allowed in the amalgamative development of the literary language. It should be noted that in the modern language forms -ováti/-eváti tend to be favoured, e.g.

Perfective	Imperfective	
sréčati	srečeváti; srečávati	to meet
ménjati	menjeváti; menjávati	to change
opazíti	opážati; opazováti	to notice
razkrínkati	razkrinkováti; razkrinkávati	to unmask
iztegníti	iztegováti; iztézati, iztégati	to extend
ohladíti	ohlajeváti; ohlájati	to cool
končáti	končeváti; končávati	to finish
odletéti	odletávati; odlétati	to fly away
prekúcniti	prekuceváti; prekucávati	to overturn

6.46 SUPPLETIVE ASPECTUAL PAIRS

There are few aspectual pairs where suppletion occurs, i.e. where the aspectual counterparts are derived from different roots. In Slovene they include the following verbs:

Perfective	Imperfective	
rêči	govoríti; práviti	to say
povédati	govoríti	to tell
naredíti; storíti	délati; počéti; počénjati	to do
vréči	metáti	to throw
vzéti	jemáti	to take

6.47 VERBS OF MOTION

There are twelve recognised basic verbs of motion in Slovene. They are unusual in that they have two imperfective forms. They are usually classified as determinate/indeterminate pairs. The determinate member expresses movement in one direction (linear, goal-oriented movement), while the indeterminate member denotes frequentative movement or movement in more than one direction. It should be noted, however, that the basic distinction between the two forms is lost in many instances in the modern language. These verbs are often neutralised because of the changed meaning of the indeterminate member (see **6.47.2**).

The two imperfective forms of the basic verbs of motion are given below with their core meanings.

Determinate	Indeterminate	
nêsti	**nosíti**	to carry
peljáti	**vozíti**	to lead, drive
jáhati	**jézditi**	to ride
gnáti	**goníti**	to drive, chase
têči	**tékati**	to run
letéti	**létati**	to fly
bežáti	**bégati**	to flee
lésti	**lazíti**	to climb
íti	**hodíti**	to go
vléči	**vlačíti**	to drag
brêsti	**brodíti**	to wade
vêsti	**vodíti**	to lead

6.47.1 Perfective forms of the verbs of motion and their imperfective counterparts

There are approximately three hundred prefixed verbs of motion in use in the modern language. The prefixes used with the verbs of motion are: **do-, iz-, na-, nad-, o-, ob-, od-, po-, pre-, pro-, pri-, raz-, s(n)-, u-, v-, vz-, z-, za-**. Basically these prefixes indicate the direction of the movement, e.g. **v-** 'into'; **iz-** 'out of' etc. They may sometimes, however, give the verb a figurative or idiomatic meaning e.g. **otêči** 'to swell'; **ponosíti** 'to wear out'. Most of the above mentioned prefixes are used with most of the determinate imperfectives to form perfective verbs. The only exceptions are **bežáti** and **brêsti**, which are rarely prefixed. These new prefixed perfectives then form new imperfective counterparts by suffixation (although not all prefixed forms of determinate verbs form imperfective counterparts). The only prefixed determinate verbs which do not form new imperfectives by suffixation are **bežáti, brêsti** and **jáhati**. The prefixed determinate verbs **íti, nêsti, peljáti, gnáti, letéti, vêsti** form their imperfective counterparts with the prefixed forms **-hájati, -nášati, -peljeváti, -gánjati, -letávati, -vájati** respectively, e.g. **odíti – odhájati** 'to go away'; **prinêsti – prinášati** 'to bring'; **izpeljáti – izpeljeváti** 'to derive'; **odgnáti – odgán-jati** 'to drive away'; **preletéti – preletávati** 'to fly across'; **prevêsti – prevájati** 'to translate'.

Prefixed forms of the determinate verb **têči** form their imperfective counterparts with the corresponding prefixed indeterminate form of the verb, e.g. **odtêči – odtékati** 'to flow away'. Prefixed forms of **vléči** form their imperfective counterparts with **-vlačeváti**, e.g **zavléči – zavlačeváti** 'to protract'. Although the verb **lésti** is often prefixed (e.g **prelésti, odlésti, prilésti** 'to crawl across, away, up to') imperfectives are not derived from these forms.

The indeterminate verbs of motion are also sometimes prefixed to form perfective verbs, e.g. **odvozíti** 'to carry off, away', **prijézditi** 'to come on horseback', **prebrodíti** 'to ford', **obhodíti** 'to go around, patrol', **ponosíti** 'to wear out', **zabégati** 'to run', **zvodíti** 'to lead, take', **dogoníti** 'to finish herding', **prelazíti** 'to cross', **prelétati** 'to cross quickly'. Imperfective forms are rarely derived from most such perfectives. However, they can be derived sometimes from prefixed forms of **vozíti, hodíti** and **nosíti** with **-vážati, -hájati** and **-nášati**, e.g. **prevozíti – prevážati** 'to transport, convey'; **obhodíti – obhájati** 'to go round'; **znosíti – znášati** 'to carry'.

6.47.2 The use of the basic verbs of motion

These twelve aspectually unique verbs with two imperfective forms can cause difficulties for foreigners.

Slovene grammars distinguish between determinate (unidirectional) and indeterminate (multidirectional) imperfectives. The determinate member expresses single, durative, linear, goal-oriented actions, whereas the indeterminate member is frequentative and goal-oriented for regularly repeated actions or lacks any goal. Determinate imperfectives are, however, used to denote repeated action if supported by a suitable adverb. In the modern Slovene language these distinctions are sometimes lost or neutralised, with one member of the pair acquiring additional meanings.

The basic use of these verbs is illustrated in the following examples:

(a) **jáhati** (det.) – **jézditi** (indet.) 'to ride' (on horseback)
   The basic distinction between these two imperfectives has been lost. The verb **jáhati** is now the only form used.

Note: In some dialects **jézditi** is the only form used.

   Vsák dán jáham do párka in nazáj
   Every day I ride to the park and back

   Ne jáhaj kónj
   Do not ride the horses

   Òn jáha brez sêdla
   He rides without a saddle

   Bova jáhala próti vási
   We (d.m.) will ride towards the village

(b) **brêsti** (det.) – **brodíti** (indet.) 'to wade'

The basic distinction between these two verbs has been neutralised and they are used in the same contexts. The form **brêsti** tends to mean 'to wade' and the form **brodíti** tends to mean 'to wander':

Kitájski kmétje cél dán brêdejo po vôdi, ko séjejo ríž
Chinese peasants wade in water all day when they sow rice

Brêde v težávah
He is in difficulties

Otròk brêde/bródi po vôdi
The child is wading in the water

Otròk brêde/bródi z žlíco po júhi
The child is playing with his soup with his spoon (i.e he does not want to eat it)

Mísel na bég mu nèprestáno bródi po glávi
The thought of escape continually goes (i.e wanders) through his head

(c) **letéti** (det.) – **létati** (indet.) 'to fly'

The basic distinction between these two forms has been largely neutralised. **létati** tends to mean 'to run about':

Ptíč letí
A bird flies

Žerjávi letíjo na júg
The cranes are flying south

Dívje gosí letíjo v klínu
Wild geese fly in a V-formation

Pilót letí vsák téden na prógi Lóndon-Paríz
The pilot flies every week on the London to Paris run

Letála mórajo kàr nàjveč letéti, da so rentabílna
The planes must fly as much as possible to be profitable

Čàs letí hítro
Time passes quickly

Metúlj léta od cvéta do cvéta
A butterfly flies from flower to flower

Kdór visôko léta, nízko páde
Pride comes before a fall

(d) **gnáti** (det.) (present **žênem**) – **goníti** (indet.) 'to drive'

The basic distinction is largely neutralised; **gnáti** is the more usual form, while **goníti** has the additional meaning 'to go on about':

Kávboji žênejo kráve na pášo
The cowboys drive the cows to pasture

Kmétje nikóli ne žênejo kráv na pášo pred zôro
The peasants never drive the cows to pasture before dawn

Vôda žêne turbíne
Water drives the turbines

Glád žêne ljudí v obúp
Hunger drives people to despair

Znáno je, da diréktorji žênejo délavce, da trdó délajo
It is known that the directors urge the workers to work hard

Jánez védno góni êno in ísto
Janez always goes on about the same thing

Gônil je koló
He was pedalling a bike

Note: The verb **gnáti se** means 'to try, strive' and the verb **goníti se** means 'to be on heat', e.g. **Ána se žêne za nôvo slúžbo** 'Ana is trying to find a new job'; **Máčka se góni** 'The cat is on heat'.

(e) **bežáti** (det.) – **bégati** (indet.) 'to flee, run (away)'
The verb **bégati** is used in the sense 'to run to and fro', usually in confusion, otherwise it is replaced by the indeterminate verb **tékati** 'to run'. It also has the additional meaning 'to confuse, baffle':

Tá matemátična ugánka me béga
This maths puzzle baffles me

Ôgenj je izbrúhnil in Ána je pánično bégala po dvoríšču
A fire broke out and Ana ran about the yard in panic

Ne béži, saj ní nevárnosti
Don't run away, there is no danger

Živál béga po klétki
The animal is running around the cage (i.e confused and wants to get out)

Vsák dán begúnci bežíjo iz Bósne
Everday refugees flee from Bosnia

Zméraj, kàdar vídim psà, bežím
Everytime I see the dog I run away

(f) **têči** (det.) – **tékati** (indet.) 'to run, flow'
The verb **tékati** implies 'to run to and fro (in confusion)'. The verb **têči** is the normal verb 'to run, flow':

Ràd têčem
I like running

Vsák dán têčem v slúžbo
Everyday I run to work

Têče žé véč lét
He has been running for several years

Skózi Ljubljáno têče Ljubljánica
The Ljubljanica flows through Ljubljana

Téka od ênega zdravníka do drúgega, pa ji nobêden ne móre pomágati
She dashes from one doctor to another and not one can help her

Hrôščki tékajo sèm ter tjà
The beetles are running hither and thither

O čém têče beséda?
What are you talking about?

(g) **lésti** (det.) – **lazíti** (indet.) 'to crawl, creep'
These verbs may preserve the distinction between one and many directions. The verb **lésti** tends to mean 'to crawl, climb' using legs, while **lazíti** tends to mean 'to crawl without legs' and also means 'to crawl many times'. Another meaning of **lazíti** is 'to chase after' or 'to gad about'; **lésti** has the additional meaning 'to slip':

Pólž, káča, mrávlja léze
A snail, a snake, an ant crawls

Gosénica léze po lístu
The caterpillar is crawling across the leaf

Gosénice lázijo po môji soláti
Caterpillars are crawing about my salad

Káj lázi tàm po trávi?
What is that crawling in the grass?

Ne lézi čez ográjo
Do not climb over the fence

Tíger léze proti svôji žŕtvi
A tiger crawls towards its victim

Otròk je lézel na drevó
The boy climbed the tree

Ôkno léze
The window slips

Nèprestáno lázi za njó
He keeps on chasing after her

Njegóva mláda žêna bo hítro lézla po drúžbeni léstvici
His young wife will quickly climb the social ladder

Kjé si lázil vsò nóč?
Where have you been gadding about all night?

(h) **vléči** (det.) – **vlačíti** (indet.) 'to drag, pull, haul, lug'
The verb **vléči** implies single direction, but can have a general meaning. The verb **vlačíti** means many directions and repetition, but also implies difficulty and long duration:

Vòl vléče plúg
The ox draws the plough

Otròk vléče máter za krílo
The child is pulling at his mother's skirt

Vsák dán vléčem vozíček v trgovíno
Everyday I take a trolley to the shop

Včéraj sem dvákrat vlékla dŕva iz gózda
I hauled wood from the forest twice yesterday

Cél fébruar so vláčili dŕva iz gózda
The whole of February they hauled wood from the forest

Zakáj pa vláčiš tóliko prtljáge?
Why are you lugging so much luggage with you?

Krílo se ji vléče po tléh
Her skirt drags on the ground

Vléčejo ga za nós
They are making a fool of him

(i) **nêsti** (det.) – **nosíti** (indet.) 'to carry, take'
The verb **nêsti** may be used instead of the perfective verb **odnêsti** and means one direction. The verb **nosíti** implies repetition of the action and also has the meaning 'to wear':

Natákar žé nêse víno
The waiter is bringing the wine

Včéraj sem nêsla písmo na pófto
Yesterday I took a letter to the post-office

Kám nêseš knjíge?
Where are you taking the books?

Béžal je, kàr so ga nêsle nôge
He ran as fast as his legs could carry him

Nêsla je aparát v popravílo
She took the appliance to be mended

Pogósto móram nêsti knjíge v knjížnico
I often have to take books to the library

Kóliko čása žé nósiš očála?
How long have you been wearing glasses?

Kdó bo nôsil poslédice?
Who will bear the consequences?

Stárši želíjo, da njíhovi otrôci nê bi nosíli tako têžkih tórb v šólo
The parents do not want their children to carry such heavy bags to school

Mládi nósijo módna oblačíla
Young people wear fashionable clothes

Učênci so učíteljici vès dán nosíli daríla
The pupils took presents to the teacher all day long

Note: If an adverb of frequency in **-krat** is used then in the last example the verb **nêsti** would replace **nosíti**, i.e. **Pétkrat so učênci nêsli daríla učíteljici** 'The pupils took presents to the teacher five times'.

(j) **íti** (det.) [present **grém**] – **hodíti** (indet.) 'to go'
The distinction between determinate and indeterminate action is largely kept, but in some instances it is lost. The verb **hodíti** also has the meaning 'to go out with someone':

Kakó gréš v kíno – z ávtom? Nè, grém péš
How are you going to the cinema – by car? No, on foot

Vsáko jútro grém mímo téga drevésa
Every morning I pass this tree

Ob pétkih zvečér grém ráda v kíno
On Friday evenings I like going to the cinema

Mój bràt ràd hódi v kíno
My brother likes to go to the cinema

Ko gré vlák skózi tunél, je tréba zapréti ôkna
When the train goes through a tunnel, you have to close the windows

Tjà bomo šlì z letálom, vráčali se bomo pa z vlákom
We will go there by plane, but we will return by train

Šèl je mímo, ne da bi nas poglédal
He went by without giving us a glance

Z njím je šlà věčkrat plésat
She went dancing with him frequently

Iz dímnika gré dím
Smoke is coming from the chimney

Daljnovòd gré po dolíni
The power line goes through the valley

Ne mára hodíti
He does not like to walk

Ne mórem věč hodíti, se lahkó málo usédem?
I can't walk any more, may I sit down for a little?

Njéna hčérka hódi v gimnázijo
Her daughter goes to the grammar school

Bolník šè hódi z bérglami/ob bérglah
The patient still walks with crutches

Nikár ne pójdi v klét, ker straší
Do not go into the cellar on any account because it is haunted

Vsák dán grém/hódim v gledalíšče
Everyday I go to the theatre

Note: In this latter example **grém** emphasises 'what I do' while **hódim** implies 'it is my hobby'.

Ne hôdi po trávi
Do not walk on the grass

Márko in Iréna sta hodíla pét mésecev, potém pa sta se razšlà
Marko and Irena went out together for five months and then they parted

(k) **peljáti** (det.) – **vozíti** (indet.) 'to drive, take, convey'
The verb **vozíti** tends to have a more general meaning than **peljáti** which implies 'taking/driving someone/something somewhere'. They are, however, at times interchangeable.
   The reflexive forms of these verbs differentiate between actually being the driver (**vozíti se**) and just using transport (**peljáti se**). The verb **vozíti** also has the additional meaning 'to get on with':

Znáš vozíti ávto? Sevéda, žé pét lét vózim?
Do you know how to drive? Of course, I have been driving for five years now

Ávto bom pêljal na sêrvis
I will take the car in for a service

Ob nesréči so skúšali ugotovíti, kdó je vôzil
At the accident they tried to establish who was driving

Pêlji ráje po srédnjem pásu; míslim, da je hitréjši
Drive in the middle lane; I think that it's quicker

Ne vôzi ávta, ker je nevárno
Do not drive a car, because it is dangerous

Ali se ráda vóziš/pélješ z aviónom?
Do you like flying/travelling by plane?

Pêlji nas na izlèt
Take us on an outing

Pri nàs ôče vózi ávto
In our family father drives the car

Ávtobus vózi vsáko úro
A bus goes every hour

Zdàj péljem hčérko v glásbeno šólo
I am taking my daughter to music school now

Kám ste se peljáli čez víkend?
Where did you go during the weekend?

Vózimo se žé trí úre, pa smo prišlí šelè do Postójne
We have been driving for three hours and we have only just reached
 Postojna

Kakó vóziš z njó?
How do you get on with her?

Vsì Slovénci vózijo prehítro
All Slovenes drive too fast

Ávtobus je pêljal z žéléznǐske postáje proti sredíšču mésta
The bus drove from the railway station towards the centre of town

(l) **vêsti** (det.) – **vodíti** (indet.) 'to lead'
 The verb **vêsti** is no longer used in the modern language, where it is
 replaced by **peljáti**. In the modern language **peljáti** and **vodíti** are often
 interchangeable. The verb **vodíti** also has the additional meanings 'to
 conduct, manage, be in the lead':

Vsák dán péljem psà na sprehòd
Everyday I take the dog for a walk

Vodìč vsák dán pélje turíste na grád
The guide takes tourists to the castle everyday

Otrôci so pogósto vodíli domóv svôje prijátelje
The children often brought their friends home

Césta pélje/vódi mímo šóle
The road leads past the school

Vráta vódijo/péljejo v klét
The door leads to the cellar

Kám me vódiš/pélješ?
Where are you taking me?

Delegácijo vódi znán polítik
A well-known politician leads the delegation

Olímpija vódi za štíri tóčke
Olimpija lead by four points

Òn vódi trí zbôre
He runs three choirs

6.48 PLACE OF STRESS IN VERBS

The following comments are a guide to place of stress, but not an exhaustive treatment. Full details on stress in verbs can be found in the Slovene Academy's *Slovar slovenskega knjižnega jezika*.

(a) Present tense
Most verbs retain the stress of the infinitive in the present tense, e.g.

délati	to do	–	**délam**
končáti	to finish	–	**končám**
vídeti	to see	–	**vídim**
govoríti	to speak	–	**govorím**
kupováti	to buy	–	**kupújem**
odštévati	to subtract	–	**odštévam**

A certain number of verbs in **-ati**, **-iti** allow alternative stresses in the infinitive. The most common of these verbs are:

čákáti	to wait	**klícáti**	to call	**jókáti**	to sob
sáhníti	to dry up	**kázáti**	to show	**páhníti**	to push
písáti	to write	**dáhníti**	to breathe	**pláčáti**	to pay
mákníti	to move	**plésáti**	to dance	**šálíti se**	to joke
skákáti	to leap	**plázíti**	to creep	**vézáti**	to tie
gáníti	to arouse	**zíbáti**	to swing	**lóčíti**	to separate
bráníti	to defend	**brúsíti**	to whet	**céníti**	to value
kópáti	to bathe	**cépíti**	to chop	**méšáti**	to mix
čútíti	to feel	**drémáti**	to doze	**drámíti**	to rouse
stréljáti	to shoot	**drážíti**	to irritate	**škrípáti**	to creak

hrániti	to feed	**vprášati**	to ask	**hváliti**	to praise
zídáti	to build	**klátiti**	to knock	**máhati**	to wave
dájáti	to give		down	**razgŕniti**	to spread out
króžiti	to circle	**pomágati**	to help	**krúšiti**	to crumble
pláníti	to rush	**pólniti**	to fill	**slútiti**	to anticipate,
kúríti	to heat	**kúpiti**	to buy		suspect
máhniti	to wag, wave	**stópiti**	to step	**slúžiti**	to serve
lótiti se	to tackle	**ljúbiti**	to love	**obŕniti**	to invert
poklé-		**pogŕniti**	to cover	**páziti**	to observe
kníti	to kneel	**pláviti**	to float	**strážiti**	to keep watch
lúpíti	to peel	**strášiti**	to scare	**čúditi se**	to wonder
sóditi	to judge	**blóditi**	to roam	**vábiti**	to invite
méniti	to think	**prázniti**	to empty	**tŕditi**	to affirm
sovrážiti	to hate	**vŕniti**	to return	**pozábiti**	to forget
mlátiti	to thresh	**réšiti**	to solve	**mótiti**	to disturb
napótiti	to direct	**plášiti**	to frighten	**seznániti**	to acquaint

Note: The verbs **drážiti** and **stópiti** also have homonyms with one fixed stress, i.e. **dražíti** 'to make dearer' and **stopíti** 'to melt'.

In the modern language there is a tendency to stress such verbs on the root in the infinitive. In the present tense the stress is always on the root, i.e. **píšem, pláčam, zídam, tŕdim, kúpim, slúžim**.

A certain number of verbs have mobile stress, i.e. final stress in the infinitive, but root stress in the present tense, e.g.

hodíti	to go	–	**hódim**
iskáti	to look for	–	**íščem**
zakleníti	to lock	–	**zaklénem**
jemáti	to take	–	**jêmljem**
peljáti	to drive, lead	–	**péljem**

Other common verbs and their prefixed derivatives with mobile stress are:

česáti	to comb	**prosíti**	to ask	**razuméti**	to understand
močíti	to wet	**nosíti**	to carry	**lomíti**	to break
metáti	to throw	**molíti**	to pray	**hotéti**	to want
skloníti	to bow	**lagáti**	to lie	**skočíti**	to jump
klesáti	to sculpture	**točíti**	to pour out	**tesáti**	to hew
vozíti	to drive, ride	**posláti**	to send	**ženíti se**	to get married
oráti	to plough	**brodíti**	to wade	**zobáti**	to peck
goníti	to drive	**dovolíti**	to allow	**kloníti**	to yield
klepáti	to sharpen	**selíti**	to move	**kresáti**	to strike sparks

kreníti	to set out	**ogníti se**	to avoid	**odkleníti**	to unlock
upogníti	to bend	**sejáti**	to sow	**toníti**	to sink
smejáti se	to laugh				

(b) The -l participle

For the majority of verbs the stress of the -l participle is fixed and the same as that of the infinitive, e.g. **délati – délal, délala, délalo**, etc.

A certain number of verbs, however, are stressed on the root in the masculine singular form but on the vowel preceding -l in the other forms. To this category belong the following three types (i) verbs with alternative stresses in the infinitive, (ii) verbs with mobile stress, (iii) second conjugation verbs in **-áti/-ím**, e.g.

(i)	**odlóčiti**	to decide	–	**odlóčim – odlóčil, odločíla, odločíli**
(ii)	**kreníti**	to start, set out	–	**krénem – krênil, kreníla, krenílo**
(iii)	**držáti**	to hold	–	**držím – dŕžal, držála, držálo**

Note: The -l participle of the verb **biti** 'to be' is always stressed on the final syllable, i.e. **bíl, bilà, bilò/biló, bilì/bilí** etc.

(c) The past participle passive

Most past participles have the same stress as the infinitive, e.g. **prodáti** 'to sell'

prodáti	to sell	–	**prodán**
zastrelíti	to shoot	–	**zastreljèn**

Exceptions are (i) verbs with alternative stresses in the infinitive, (ii) verbs with mobile stress, (iii) verbs in **-sti, -či** with an open vowel **ê, ô** in the infinitive root.

Verbs in categories (i) and (ii) are stressed on the root, while verbs in (iii) are normally stressed on the final **-èn**, e.g.

(i)	**opázíti**	to observe	–	**opážen**
(ii)	**zlomíti**	to break	–	**zlómljen**
(iii)	**pomêsti**	to sweep	–	**pometèn**
	spêči	to bake	–	**spečèn**
	prebôsti	to pierce	–	**prebodèn**
but	**pretrésti**	to shake	–	**pretrésen**
	izdólbsti	to excavate	–	**izdólben**

(d) Present participle active and gerunds

The present participle active and the present gerund are always stressed on **-oč, -eč**, e.g. **nesóč**, 'carrying'; **gledajóč** 'watching'; **vabèč** 'inviting'.

Present gerunds in **-aje, -e** are always stressed **-áje, -é**, e.g. **kazáje** 'pointing', **ležé** 'lying'. Past gerunds are stressed on the syllable preceding the suffix **-(v)ši**, e.g. **pozabívši** 'having forgotten'.

(e) The supine
The place of stress of the supine is the same as that of the infinitive for most verbs, e.g.

kupováti – kupovàt   to buy
mériti – mérit   to measure

However, in verbs with alternative stresses in the infinitive, in verbs with a mobile stress or verbs in **-áti/-ím** the stress of the supine is always on the root, e.g.

		Present		*Supine*
zídáti	to build	– **zídam**	–	**zídat**
točíti	to pour out	– **tóčim**	–	**tôčit**
držáti	to hold	– **držím**	–	**dŕžat**

(f) The imperative
The majority of verbs have the same stress in the imperative as in the infinitive, e.g.

délati   to do – **délaj, délajte, délajta**
dvígniti   to lift – **dvígni, dvígnite, dvígnita**

In certain verbs, however, there is a mobile stress in the imperative, whereby the second person singular form is stressed on the root and the other forms on the suffixes **-íva, -íta, -ímo, -íte**.

To this type belong (i) verbs with a mobile stress in the 'infinitive/present tense', (ii) verbs with alternative stresses in the infinitive, (iii) verbs in **-êsti, -ôsti**, (iv) verbs stressed in **-íti/-ím, -éti/-ím**, (v) verbs in **-áti/-em**, (vi) verbs in **-áti/-ím**, e.g.

(i)	**peljáti**	to drive	– **pêlji, peljíte**
	točíti	to pour out	– **tôči, točíte**
(ii)	**zídáti**	to build	– **zídaj, zidájte/zídajte**
	slúžíti	to serve	– **slúži, služíte/slúžite**

Note: These verbs also allow fixed stress in all forms and in the colloquial language this stress is favoured.

(iii)	**plêsti**	to knit	– **plêti, pletíte**
	bôsti	to butt	– **bôdi, bodíte**
(iv)	**dušíti**	to choke	– **dúši, dušíte**
	vrtéti	to rotate	– **vŕti, vrtíte**
(v)	**bráti**	to read	– **bêri, beríte**
(vi)	**držáti**	to hold	– **dŕži, držíte**

7 ADVERBS

7.1 FORMATION OF ADVERBS

Adverbs may be divided into two basic groups

1. adverbs derived from adjectives,
2. adverbs derived from other parts of speech.

7.2 ADVERBS DERIVED FROM ADJECTIVES

Adverbs derived from adjectives are mostly identical with the nominative singular neuter form of the adjective in **-o/-e**. The stress is normally the same as that in the neuter adjective form (e.g. **vesélo** 'happily'; **vróče** 'ardently'; **gládko** 'smoothly'; **dívje** 'savagely', etc) but in a few instances the adverb is stressed on the final **-ó**, e.g.

Adj.	Adverb		Adj.	Adverb	
lépo	lepó	beautifully	láhko	lahkó	easily
hládno	hladnó	coolly	tŕdo	trdó	rigidly
tôplo	topló	warmly	mêhko	mehkó	softly
húdo	hudó	badly			

Sometimes an adverb has alternative stresses in which case the form with final stress is used for stylistic purposes, e.g. **gládko/gladkó** 'smoothly'.

Occasionally an adverb formed from an adjective has the suffix **-oma** as well as or instead of a form in **-o**: e.g.: **nágloma/náglo** 'hurriedly'; **popólnoma** 'completely'; **nemúdoma/nemúdno** 'promptly'; **nenádoma/nenádno** 'suddenly'

Note: In the latter two examples the adjectival suffix **-n-** is also lost if **-oma** is used.

An adverb in **-o** derived from an adjective may be preceded by the preposition **po** and then has the meaning 'in the manner of, in the style of'. In this sense it is also used to indicate that someone speaks a certain language, e.g.

po gospôsko	in a lordly manner
po kršćánsko	in a Christian way
Tújec govorí po slovénsko	The stranger speaks Slovene
po vólčje tulíti	to howl like a wolf

7.3   ADVERBS DERIVED FROM OTHER PARTS OF SPEECH

Adverbs may be derived from (a) nouns, (b) prepositional constructions, (c) verbs, (d) numerals, e.g.

(a)   Adverbs are derived from the (archaic) oblique cases of nouns, e.g. **dávi** 'this morning'; **gôri** 'above'; **láni** 'last year'; **jeséni** 'in Autumn'; **méstoma** 'in places'; **domóv** 'home(wards)'; **domá** 'at home'.

(b)   Adverbs are derived from a preposition plus noun/adjective/pronoun/ adverb, e.g. **vkùp** 'together'; **včásih** 'sometimes'; **naglás** 'aloud'; **začása** 'in good time'; **pozími** 'in winter'; **pokônci** 'upright'; **opóldne** 'at midday'; **navzkríž** 'crosswise'; **zakáj** 'why'; **potém** 'then'; **povsèm** 'entirely, completely'; **potíhem** 'silently'; **zmláda** 'in one's youth'; **zlépa** 'amicably'; **zgŕda** 'in an unfriendly way'; **odspôdaj** 'below, beneath'.

(c)   Adverbs from verbs are normally derived from the present gerund or from participle forms, in which case the adverb is identical with the nominative singular neuter form of the participle, e.g. **nèhoté** 'unintentionally'; **mímogredé** 'in passing'; **nèvedé** 'unwittingly'; **grozéče** 'threateningly'; **pričakujóče** 'expectantly'; **nèpričakováno** 'unexpectedly'.

Note: Occasionally the suffix **-oma/-ema** is used to derive adverbs from verbal roots, e.g. **zdŕžema** 'continuously'; **skrívoma** 'secretly'.

(d)   Adverbs from numerals are formed with the suffixes **-krat**; **-ič**, e.g. **pŕvič** 'firstly'; **trétjič** 'thirdly'; **dvákrat** 'twice'.

7.4   TYPES OF ADVERB

Adverbs may be divided into the following types (a) adverbs of time, frequency and duration, (b) adverbs of place, (c) adverbs of manner, (d) adverbs of degree, (e) interrogative adverbs, (f) negative adverbs, (g) indefinite adverbs.

7.5   ADVERBS OF TIME

Adverbs in this category indicate the point in time when something happens (e.g. **včéraj** 'yesterday'; **zdàj** 'now'), frequency (e.g. **zméraj** 'always'; **dnévno** 'daily') and duration (e.g. **vékomaj** 'forever').

The interrogative adverbs of time are: **kdáj** 'when'; **odkléj** 'since when, how long'; **dokléj** 'till when, how long'. Both **odkléj** and **dokléj** are, however, very literary forms and are normally replaced by **od kdáj** and **do kdáj**.

The major adverbs of time used in response to **kdáj** are the following: **zdàj/-sedàj** 'now'; **tedàj** 'then'; **nékdaj** 'formerly, once upon a time'; **nekóč** 'once upon a time'; **níkdar/nikóli** 'never'; **kàdarkóli** 'whenever'; **zjútraj** 'in the morning'; **dávi** 'this morning'; **navsezgódaj** 'early in the morning'; **dopóldne** 'before moon'; **opóldan/opóldne** 'at noon'; **popóldne** 'in the afternoon'; **podnévi** 'by day'; **drévi** 'tonight, this evening'; **dánes** 'today'; **nocój** 'tonight'; **zvečér** 'in the evening'; **ponôči** 'at night'; **opólnoči** 'at midnight'; **sinóči** 'last night'; **predsinóčnjim** 'the night before last'; **včéraj** 'yesterday'; **jútri** 'tomorrow'; **predlánskim** 'two years ago'; **predvčérajšnjim** 'the day before yesterday'; **pojútrišnjem** 'the day after tomorrow'; **dándánes** 'nowadays'; **zgódaj** 'early'; **začása** 'in good time'; **pôzno** 'late'; **spomládi** 'in Spring'; **jeséni** 'in Autumn'; **poléti** 'in Summer'; **pozími** 'in Winter'; **létos** 'this year'; **láni** 'last year'; **védno/zméraj/zmérom/vsèlej** 'always'; **prècej** 'immediately, instantly'; **istočásno/istodôbno/obênem/hkráti** 'simultaneously'; **kmálu** 'soon'; **prekmálu** 'too soon'; **préj** 'earlier, sooner'; **zdávnaj** 'long ago'; **prihódnjič** 'next time'; **zádnjič** 'the other day'; **nèdávno** 'recently'; **màrsikdàj** 'often'; **rédko(kdàj)** 'rarely, seldom'; **dnévno** 'daily'; **mésečno** 'monthly'; **tédensko** 'weekly'; **létno** 'yearly'; **običájno** 'usually'; **prvôtno** 'originally'; **posmŕtno** 'posthumously'; **prezgódaj/predčásno** 'prematurely'; **nemúdoma** 'instantly, promptly'; **naênkrat/máhoma/nenádoma** 'suddenly'; **nenéhno/nenéhoma** 'continually'; **včásih** 'sometimes'; **nazádnje/navsezádnje** 'eventually'; **pràvkar/préjle/rávnokar/málopréj** 'just now, just this moment'; **pogósto/pogóstoma/čésto** 'often'; **takój** 'immediately'; **vékomaj** 'for ever and ever'; **žé** 'already'; **šè** 'still'; **začásno** 'temporarily'; **sčásoma** 'eventually'; **kônčno** 'finally'; **poznéje** 'later'; **préj ali sléj/préj ali poznéje** 'sooner or later'; **slédnjič** 'at last'; **vnapréj** 'beforehand'; **nàjprej** 'first'; **tóčno** 'on time; punctually'; **ponóvno** 'repeatedly'; **trájno** 'permanently'.

Adverbs used in response to **dokléj/do kdáj** are: **dozdàj/dosléj** 'up till now'; **dotléj** 'up till then'; **doklèr** 'as long as'; **doklèr ne** 'until'.

Adverbs used in response to **odkléj/od kdáj** are: **posléj/odsléj** 'henceforth, from now on'; **odtléj** 'from then on, since then'. In the modern language **posléj/odsléj** and **odtléj** are replaced by **od zdàj** and **od tedàj**.

Examples of the usage of adverbs of time

Kdáj prídeš? Jútri	When will you come? Tomorrow
Nemúdoma poklíči domóv	Phone home immediately
Do kdáj mísliš ostáti v Ljubljáni?	How long do you intend to stay in Ljubljana?
Doklèr nísi polnoléten, ne móreš volíti	You cannot vote until you are of age
Od zdàj ne bóš šlà nikámor vèč sáma	From now on you will go nowhere on your own
Zádnjič se mi je mudílo	The other day I was in a hurry
Sčásoma smo postáli prijátelji	In time we became friends

Máloprej si govóril drugáče	A moment ago you were saying otherwise
Kúpna móč nenéhno narášča	Purchasing power continually grows
Vstála je zgódaj	She got up early
Vŕnil se bo pôzno	He will return late

7.6 ADVERBS OF PLACE

Adverbs of place indicate position (e.g. **tàm** 'there'; **spôdaj** 'below') and direction (e.g. **domóv** 'home(wards)'; **navkréber** 'uphill'.

The interrogative adverbs of place are **kjé** 'where'; **kám** 'whither, to where'; **kód** 'where' (this adverb denotes the surface area over which an action occurs); **od kód** 'whence'.

The adverbs of place used in response to **kjé** are: **tù/tùle/túkaj** 'here'; **tàm/tàmle** 'there'; **kjèr** 'where'; **nekjé** 'somewhere'; **nikjér** 'nowhere'; **kjèrkóli** 'wherever'; **posébej** 'apart'; **domá** 'at home'; **zdóma** 'out, not at home'; **zgór/(od)zgôraj** 'above, upstairs'; **dôli/(od)spôdaj/(od)spód/odzdôlaj/zdôlaj** 'beneath, below, downstairs'; **zád(aj)/odzád(aj)** 'behind'; **znótraj/nótri** 'inside'; **odznótraj** 'within'; **sprédaj** 'in front, ahead'; **zúnaj/odzúnaj** 'outside'; **dáleč** 'far'; **blízu** 'near'; **drugjé** 'elsewhere'; **póleg/zráven** 'alongside'; **povsód** 'everywhere'; **vzdólž** 'along'; **préko** 'beyond'; **vmés** 'in between'; **naspróti** 'opposite'; **skúpaj** 'together'; **počéz** 'across'.

Adverbs of place used in response to **kám** are: **sèm** 'hither, to here'; **tjà** 'thither, to there'; **nékam** 'to somewhere'; **drugàm** 'elsewhere'; **nikámor** 'to no place'; **kámor** 'where, whither'; **kámorkóli** 'wheresoever'; **domóv** 'home'; **gôr/navzgôr/kvíšku** 'up(wards)'; **dôl/navzdôl** 'down(wards)'; **vstrán** 'aside'; **navzvèn/vèn** 'out(wards)'; **nóter/navznóter** 'in(wards)'; **napréj** 'forwards, ahead'; **pròč** 'away'; **nazáj** 'backwards'; **málokàm** 'anywhere, to few places'; **na(s)próti** 'towards'; **dálje** 'onwards'; **mímo** 'past'.

Adverbs of place used in response to **kód** are: **tód** 'to here, in this direction'; **ponekód** 'somewhere'; **nikóder** 'nowhere'; **kóder** 'to where'; **kóderkóli** 'to wherever'.

Adverbs of place used in response to **od kód** are always preceded by the preposition **od**: **od blízu** 'from near'; **od zgôraj** 'from above'; **od spôdaj** 'from below'; **od drugód** 'from elsewhere'; **od tàm** 'from there'.

Examples of the usage of adverbs of place

Kjé je gledalíšče? Tàm na drúgi stráni céste
Where is the theatre? There on the other side of the street

Nikjér níma mirú
There is no peace anywhere

Kód se gré na grád?
Which way is it to the castle?

Odkód prihája òn?
Where does he come from?

Ali gréš vèn?
Are you going out?

Nikámor ne grém
I am not going anywhere

Kám potúješ? Domóv
Where are you travelling to? Home

Na hríbu je trdnjáva, spôdaj têče réka
On the hill is a castle, a river runs down below

Ob césti stojí híša, naspróti je spomeník
The house is by the road, opposite it stands a memorial

Na désni stráni stojí pôšta, tik zráven je trgovína
On the right is the post office, right next to it is a shop

7.7 ADVERBS OF TIME AND PLACE BEGINNING WITH **màrsi-/mnógo-** 'MANY A . . .'; **málo-/rédko-** 'HARDLY . . .'

The forms in **mnógo-** are considered very literary and not normally used in the spoken language. In the modern language the following forms are found: **màrsikjé/mnógokjé**, **màrsikód/mnógokód** 'many a place'; **màrsikàm** 'to many a place'; **màrsikdàj/mnógokdàj** 'many a time'; **málokdàj/rédkokdàj** 'hardly ever, rarely, seldom'; **málokàm/rédkokàm** '(to) hardly anywhere'; **málokjé/rédkokjé** 'hardly anywhere'

Examples of usage

Màrsikjé so tlà močvírna
In many a place the ground is marshy

Màrsikdàj se je zamíslil
Many a time he became sunk in thought

Zahájal je màrsikàm, nàjrájši pa v gostílno
He frequented many a place, most of all the pub

Málokdàj je bolán
He is hardly ever ill

Rédkokdàj je domá
He is hardly ever at home

Málokàm/Rédkokàm gré
He hardly goes anywhere

Málokjé tóčijo bóljše víno
Hardly anywhere do they serve better wine

Rédkokjé se takó dôbro počúti kot pri njíh
There is hardly anywhere that he feels as good as he does at their place

7.8 ADVERBS OF MANNER

Adverbs of manner denote the way something is done (e.g. **okórno** 'clumsily'), the way it is done and the feelings of the person doing it (e.g. **zaskrbljêno** 'anxiously') and the circumstances in which something is done rather than how it is done (e.g. **nèzakoníto** 'illegally').

The interrogative adverb of manner is **kakó** 'how'.

Examples of adverbs of manner are: **takó** 'thus'; **natánko** 'accurately'; **udóbno** 'comfortably'; **prevídno** 'carefully'; **pomótoma** 'inadvertently'; **molčé** 'in silence'; **glasnó** 'loudly'; **namérno** 'intentionally'; **zamàn** 'in vain'; **zastónj** 'gratis, free'.

Examples of usage

Ustrelíla ga je namérno
She shot him deliberately

Vsè dopóldne smo zamàn čákali nánjo
All morning we waited for her in vain

Vzdíhnila je glasnó
She sighed loudly

Slabó se počútim
I'm not feeling well

Móštvo je igrálo ofenzívno
The team played an attacking game

Srdíto ga je poglédal
He looked at him angrily

Kakó ste nášli nášo híšo? Čísto lahkó
How did you find our house? Very easily

Pràv si izračúnal
You have calculated correctly

7.9   ADVERBS OF DEGREE

Adverbs of degree give more information about the extent of an action or the degree to which it is performed. They also often modify other adverbs, adjectives, pronouns and numerals, e.g. **popólnoma/povsèm** 'completely'; **docéla** 'entirely'; **délno/déloma** 'partly'; **domála/skôraj** 'almost'; **málo** 'somewhat'; **precèj** 'much; rather, quite'; **zeló** 'very'; **kàr** 'tolerably, fairly'; **kàrsedá** 'extremely'; **pràv** 'very, really'.

Examples of usage

docéla pozabíti	to forget entirely
Nesréče je déloma krív	He is partly to blame for the accident
Domála vsì so túkaj	Almost everyone is here
Skúpaj sta délala skôraj desét lét	They (d.) worked together for almost ten years
Bíl sem málo presenéčen	I was somewhat surprised
Položáj je precèj jásen	The position is quite clear
Razmére so se povsèm spremeníle	The circumstances have entirely changed
Njén móž je popólnoma glúh	Her husband is completely deaf
domála pléšast	almost bald
Čévlji so šè kàr dôbri	The shoes are still fairly good
Premíka se kàrsedá previdno	He moves extremely cautiously
Pràv blízu dóma smo žé	We are already very close to home
Rána zeló krvaví	The wound is bleeding a lot
Skôraj nìč ne vémo o tém	We know almost nothing about this
Hrána v tém hotélu ní pràv pocéni	The food at this hotel is not very cheap
Pràv sramôtno se je obnášal	He behaved really disgracefully

7.10   INTERROGATIVE ADVERBS

The interrogative adverbs of time (**kdáj** 'when'; **odkléj** 'since when'; **dokléj** 'till when'), place (**kjé**; **kám**; **kód** 'where'; **od kód** 'whence') and manner (**kakó** 'how') have already been mentioned (see 7.5, 7.6, 7.8). The remaining interrogative adverbs are:

(a)   The interrogative adverbs of cause and reason: **zakáj/káj/čemú** 'why'

(b)   The interrogative adverbs of quantity, frequency and duration: **kóliko** 'how much, how many'; **kólikokrat** 'how often'; **kólikič** 'how many times'; **kakó dólgo** 'how long'.

7.11 INTERROGATIVE ADVERBS OF CAUSE AND REASON: zakáj/káj/čemú 'WHY'

The normal interrogative adverb of cause or reason is **zakáj**, e.g. **Zakáj si jézen na nàs?** 'Why are you angry with us?'

The adverb **čemú** is normally used to enquire about intention or purpose but is sometimes also used instead of **zakáj**, e.g. **Čemú ti bó knjíga, če ne znáš bráti?** 'Why do you want a book if don't know how to read?'; **Čemú ste prišli sèm?** 'Why have you come here?'; *but* **Povéj, zakáj/čemú se nísi ožênil** 'Tell me why you did not marry'.

The form **káj** is used expressively instead of **zakáj**, e.g. **Káj me takó začúdeno glédate?** 'Why are you looking at me in such astonishment?'

Káj may also be used to enquire about an intention, e.g. **Káj ti bó knjíga, če ne znáš bráti?**

7.12 INTERROGATIVE ADVERBS OF QUANTITY, FREQUENCY AND DURATION

(a) **kóliko** 'how many, how much'
This adverb may stand alone or be used with the genitive case, e.g.

Kóliko brátov imáš?	How many brothers do you have?
Kóliko stáne kilográm móke?	How much does a kilogram of flour cost?
Kóliko denárja imáš?	How much money do you have?

(b) **kólikokrat** 'how often, how many times'
This adverb requires an answer using an adverbial numeral in **-krat**, e.g. **Kólikokrat si bíl tàm? Pétkrat/velíkokrat** 'How many times have you been there? Five times/frequently'.

(c) **kólikič** 'how many times'
This adverb requires an answer using an adverbal numeral of time in **-ič**, e.g.

Kólikič je žé poročêna, ali nè trétjič? How many time has she been married, is this not the third time?

(d) **kakó dólgo** 'how long', e.g. **Kakó dólgo boš ostál túkaj?** 'How long will you stay here?

7.13 NEGATIVE ADVERBS

The negative adverbs are **nikjér** 'nowhere'; **nikámor** 'to nowhere'; **od nikóder** 'from anywhere/nowhere'; **níkdar/nikóli** 'never'; **nikár** 'on no account'; **nikákor** 'not at all, in no way, by no means'; **nobênkrat** 'not once'.

These adverbs are used in negated sentences with the negative particle **ne**.

Examples of usage

Nikjér ne nájdem kljúča
I can find the key nowhere

Nikámor ne móreš pobegníti
There is nowhere you can escape to

Pomóč ní prišlà od nikóder
Help did not come from anywhere

Tó nikákor šè ní dokáz
This is no proof at all/This is in no way proof

Ali si spét zamúdil? Nikákor nè, šè ní ósem
Are you late again? Not at all, it is not eight yet

Med vôjno se nobênkrat nísva vídela
We did not see each other once during the war

Téga ne bóm nikóli pozábil
I shall never forget this

Téga mi nísi níkdar oménil
You never mentioned this to me

The adverb **nikár** is usually used to strengthen a prohibition, e.g. **O tém nikár nikómur ne právi** 'On no account tell anyone about this'.

7.14 INDEFINITE ADVERBS

The indefinite adverbs are: **kjé/nekjé** 'somewhere'; **kàm/nékam** 'to somewhere'; **kakó/nekakó** 'somehow'; **kdàj** 'sometime'; **nékdaj/nekóč** 'once (upon a time), sometime'; **kód/nekód** 'somewhere; **drugjé/drugód** 'elsewhere'.

The difference between the forms with **ne** and those without is that the forms without **ne** denote any arbitrary concept, i.e. 'somewhere or other, somehow or other, sometime or other' whereas the forms with **ne** denote a particular place, time or manner that is either unnamed or unknown, i.e somewhere, somehow, sometime.

Also included among indefinite adverbs are those compounded with the particles **-kóli** or **-sibódi**: **kjèrkóli/kjèrsibódi** 'anywhere, wherever'; **kámorkóli** 'to somewhere or other'; **kóderkóli** 'anywhere, to wherever'; **kàkorkóli** 'somehow or other'; **kàdarkóli** 'whenever'.

Examples of usage

Móral se je kjé ustáviti	He had to stop somewhere
but **Nekjé je otròk dobíl jábolka**	The child got the apples somewhere
Ali boš kàm odpotovàl?	Will you be going somewhere?
but **Presélil se je nékam na Štájersko**	He moved to somewhere in Styria
Pót boš žé kakó nášel	You will find the path somehow
but **Nekakó smo se vèndar rešíli iz težáv**	Somehow, however, we got out of the difficulties
Prídi šè kdàj	Come again sometime
but **Z máterjo sva šlà nekóč na tísti hríb**	We once went to that mountain with mother
nékdaj môčna vôjska	a once mighty army
Ne hôdi po gózdu, lahkó se kód zgubíš	Don't go through the forest, you could lose yourself somewhere there

The adverb **nekód** is used with the preposition **od**, e.g.

Od nekód píha
There is a draught from somewhere

Njegóve mísli so drugód
His thoughts are elsewhere

Òn ní od tód, je od drugód
He is not from here, he is from elsewhere

but

Sédi sèm, drugjé ní prostóra
Sit here, there is no room elsewhere

Ávtobus se ne ustávlja kjèrkóli/kjèrsibódi, ámpak samó na postájah
The bus doesn't stop just anywhere, but only at bus stops

Domá ne strpí, móra v kíno, kavárno ali kámorkóli
He cannot stand being at home, he has to go to the cinema, a cafe or somewhere

Kláti se po pólju, gózdu, kóderkóli
He roams about the field, the forest or anywhere

Skúšal se je rešíti kàkorkóli
He tried to save himself somehow

Ker so bilí sosédje, jo je lahkó vídel kàdarkóli
Because there were neighbours, he could see her anytime

7.15 ADVERBS GOVERNED BY PREPOSITIONS

Adverbs of time and place are very often governed by prepositions, e.g.

Do kdáj?	Until when?
od tàm	from there
krùh od včéraj	yesterday's bread
Počákajmo do jútri	Let us wait until tomorrow
Od túkaj do dóma je dáleč	It is far from here to home
pridélek od létos	this year's harvest
Nísem ga vídel žé od predsinóčnjim	I haven't seen him since the night before last

7.16 THE COMPARATIVE OF ADVERBS

The comparatives of adverbs derived from adjectives have for the most part two forms. One form is identical with the nominative singular neuter form of the comparative adjective, e.g. **hitréjše** 'quicker'; **čistéjše** 'more cleanly'; **močnéjše** 'more strongly'; **hújše** 'worse'; **víšje** 'higher'; **nížje** 'lower'; **globóčje** (styl.) 'more deeply'. The alternative form, if one exists, has either no -š- following -j- and thus ends in -je, e.g. **hitréje, čistéje, močnéje** or no -j- following a -č-, -ž-, -š-, and thus ends in -če, -že, -še e.g. **húje, více, níže, globóče** (styl.).

The forms in -je, -še, -že, -če are typical of the literary language, whereas the forms in -jše and -šje/-žje/-čje are typical of the spoken language.

The comparatives of some adverbs like the comparatives of some adjectives are apparently irregular because of jotation, the loss of a final suffix or the use of a suppletive form. The following is a list of the most common irregular comparative forms. Where alternative forms are given the first form is the more commonly used:

Adverb		*Comparative*
dragó	dearly	**dráže, drážje**
grdó	badly, nastily	**gŕše**
lepó	beautifully	**lépše**
trdó	hard, firmly	**tŕše**

globôko	deeply	**glóblje**
krátko	briefly	**krájše**
lahkó	lightly, easily	**láže, lážje**
blízu	near	**blíže, blížje**
nízko	low(ly)	**níže, nížje**
sládko	sweetly	**slájše**
dáleč	far	**dljè** 'farther' [i.e. with reference to physical distance]
dôbro	well	**bólje, bóljše** 'better'
ózko	narrowly	**óžje**
širôko	widely	**šírše**
tánko	thinly	**tánjše**
tího	quietly	**tíše, tíšje**
visôko	highly	**víše, víšje**
težkó	heavily	**téže, téžje**
rádo	gladly	**ráje, rájši**
dólgo	lengthily	**dálj** [colloquially also **dljè**]

Two other important comparative forms that should be noted are **vèč** 'more' and **mànj** 'less', which both end in a consonant.

7.17 ANALYTICAL COMPARATIVES

It is possible to form the comparative degree of an adverb by using the forms **bôlj** 'more' and **mànj** 'less' with the simple adverb, e.g. **bôlj vróče** 'hotter'; **bôlj obláčno** 'cloudier'; **mànj razlóčno** 'less clearly'; **bôlj pámetno** 'more sensibly'.

Comparative constructions

(a) The construction '**čím** + comparative adverb, **tèm** + comparative adverb' This construction is used to translate English constructions of the type 'The sooner the better', e.g.

čím préj, tèm bólje	the sooner the better
čím bòlj zgódaj, tèm bólje	the earlier the better
Čím níže sva prihájala, tèm bòlj je biló vróče	The lower down we went the hotter it became

(b) The construction '**bôlj ali mànj** + adjective' is used to translate English 'more or less', e.g. **Stvár je bôlj ali mànj jásna** 'The matter is more or less clear'.

(c) The construction '**védno/zmérom/zméraj/čedálje/vsè** + comparative adverb' is used to translate English constructions of the type 'nearer and nearer', 'more and more', e.g.

Hrúp je prihájal zmérom/védno blíže	The noise was coming nearer and nearer
Grmí čedálje močnéje	The thunder is getting heavier and heavier

7.18 THE SUPERLATIVE OF ADVERBS

The superlative of adverbs may be formed in two ways:

(a) By using the prefix **nàj-** plus the comparative forms of the adverb, e.g. **nàjblíže** 'nearest'; **nàjdlje** 'farthest'; **nàjhúje** 'worst'; **nàjkrájše** 'shortest'; **nàjmanj** 'least'; **nàjhitréje** 'most quickly'; **nàjbolj** 'best'.

(b) By using the superlative forms **nàjbolj** or **nàjmanj** plus the positive form of the adverb, e.g. **nàjbolj zgódaj** 'earliest'; **nàjmanj razlóčno** 'least clearly'; **nàjbolj lógično** 'most logical'.

English constructions of the type 'as soon as possible' which express the greatest possible degree are translated in Slovene either by the adverb **kàr** plus the superlative form of the adverb or by the adverb **kàrsedá** plus the positive form of the adverb, e.g. **kàr nàjhitréje** 'as quickly as possible'; **kàr nàjmanj** 'the least possible'; **kàrsedá prevídno** 'as cautiously as possible'.

It should be noted that **kàrsedá** is a very literary form and **kàr** is more normal in conversation.

7.19 THE PREFIX pre-

The prefix **pre-** is used with the positive form of adverbs to express an extreme or excessive degree, e.g. **premrzló** 'very cold'; **pretemnó** 'very dark'; **prenahítro** 'too quickly'; **predáleč** 'too far'.

7.20 PREDICATIVES

Certain adverbs and a few nouns used (undeclined) with an adverbial function occur in the predicate of impersonal sentences. In Slovene grammar these words are called predicatives. They may be:

(a) modal predicatives, i.e. express some modal relation such as possibility or necessity, e.g. **móžno** 'possible'; **mogóče** 'possible'; **tréba** 'necessary'

(b) statal predicatives, i.e. express physical or mental state, e.g. **már** 'care for'; **všéč** 'like'; **pràv** 'right'; **dólgčas** 'miss; bored'; **nápak** 'mistaken'; **žàl** 'sorry'; **škóda** 'a pity, a waste'; **stráh** 'afraid'; **srám** 'ashamed'; **mràz** 'cold'; **grôza** 'dreadful, terrible'.

In Slovene predicatives are normally used with the link verb **bíti** 'to be'. If the impersonal construction is in the past tense then the neuter singular form of the verb 'to be', i.e. **biló** is used even when the predicative is seemingly a masculine or a feminine noun.

The use of these predicatives is illustrated in the following sentences:

móžno/mogóče

Ní mi mogóče/móžno príti	I cannot come

tréba

Vesél je, da mu ní tréba živéti v méstu	He is glad that he doesn't have to live in town
Ní mi tréba tvôjega denárja	I don't need your money

már

Za polítiko mi ní már	I am not interested in politics
Már ti je	Much do you care
Tó ti ní nìč már	This is none of your business
Káj ti je tó már?	What is that to you?

všéč

Darílo jim je všéč	They like the present
Všéč ji je njegóv glás	She likes his voice
Modêrne slíke mu níso všéč	He doesn't like modern paintings

pràv

Mêni je pràv, če je têbi	It's alright with me if it's alright with you
Imáš pràv	You are right
Po môjem ní pràv, da púščaš otrôka sámega	In my opinion it is not right that you leave the child on his own
Če ti je pràv ali nè	Whether you like it or not
Pràv ti je	It serves you right
Tá klobúk mi je pràv	This hat fits

Note: **pràv** is also used with the verb **príti** 'to come' in the sense 'to come in handy'; e.g. **Tá vŕvica utégne poznéje pràv príti** 'This string may come in useful later'; **Vsè pràv príde** 'Every little helps'.

dólgčas

Zeló mi je dólgčas	I am bored
Dólgčas mi je po njéj	I miss her

nápak

Ne bi biló nápak (záte), če bi tó stóril	It wouldn't be amiss were you to do that

žàl

Zeló mu je žàl za vsè húdo, ki ga je povzróčil	He is very sorry for all the harm he has caused
žàl ji je zánj	She is sorry for him

škóda

Té obléke je škóda za domá	It is a pity/a waste to wear these clothes at home
Škóda ga je	He wastes his talents

stráh; **srám**; **mràz**; **grôza**

Stráh nas je	We are frightened
Srám ga je izrážati svôja čústva	He is ashamed to express his feelings
Mràz mi je biló	I was cold
Grôza me je téga	I dread this

The adverb **lahkó** 'eas(il)y' is also widely used in a predicative function in Slovene. It is used with the personal forms of full meaning verbs to convey the meaning 'can, may be able to' (see also **6.39**), e.g.

Lahkó tó bêreš?	Can you read this?
Lahkó ga obíščete, kàdar hóčete	You can visit him when you like
Tó vam lahkó pové léktor	The lektor can tell you this
Če ga nújno potrebújete, vam ga jàz lahkó posódim	If you need it urgently I can lend it to you
Ali vas lahkó nékaj vprášam?	May I ask you something?

Two other indeclinable words which occur only in the predicate are **kós** (+ dat.) 'equal to' and **bót** 'quits, even'. They do not occur in impersonal sentences, however, but are used instead after the personal forms of the verb **bíti** 'to be', e.g.

kós

Nísem ti kós	I am no match for you
Nísmo kós tému délu	We are not up to this work
Nalógi ní bilà kós	She was not equal to the task

bót

Zdàj sva bót	Now we are quits
Nékaj dodáj, pa si bóva lepó bót	Add something and then we will be quits

8 PREPOSITIONS

Most Slovene prepositions have a relatively constant meaning and a clear English equivalent. However, some prepositions are extremely elusive in their meaning and purely idiomatic in use. For example **ob** + loc. can be translated as: 'at, beside, by, along, next to, against, in, over, on'.

In Slovene each preposition governs a noun, pronoun or numeral in an oblique case i.e. acc./gen./dat./loc./instr. Most prepositions govern only one case, (e.g. **do** + gen. 'before, as far as', **pri** + loc. 'at') but some prepositions govern two cases (e.g. **v** + acc./loc. 'in', **na** + acc./loc. 'on') or uniquely three cases (e.g. **za** + acc. 'for'; **za** + instr. 'behind'; **za** + gen. 'during').

All Slovene prepositions precede the word they govern. Apparent exceptions are the adverbial prepositions **naspróti** 'opposite'; **navkljúb** 'in spite of'. These normally precede the noun or pronoun governed, but sometimes follow a pronoun. In these instances they are considered to be adverbs (see **8.4** and **8.9.16**)

In Slovene prepositions may also be used with adverbs, e.g. **do jútri** 'until tomorrow', **od dáleč** 'from afar', **od sedàj napréj** 'from now on', **vsák dán rázen jútri** 'every day except tomorrow'.

In the spoken language prepositions may be used in elliptical (incomplete) constructions with understood complements, e.g. **Jánez je za** 'Janez is for' (i.e. for the proposal made).

8.1 THE REPETITION OF PREPOSITIONS

Prepositions are not normally repeated when governing two nouns in the same clause, e.g.

v Ljubljáni in drúgih méstih   in Ljubljana and other towns
Ôna je prišlà z očétom in máterjo   She came with her father and mother

Less normal and only for emphasis would be: **V Ljubljáni in v drúgih méstih;
Ôna je prišlà z očétom in z máterjo**.

However, if a second noun would normally be governed by a variant form of the first preposition (i.e. **k/h**; **z/s**, see **8.3.2**) then the preposition must be repeated, e.g. **Ôna je prišlà z očétom in s sêstro** 'She came with her father and sister'.

The mandatory repetition of the preposition always takes place if it governs two clitic or stressed forms of the personal pronouns in the same clause, e.g.

Z njím in z njó smo se peljáli v Ljubljáno	We drove to Ljubljana with him and her
Izbrál je daríla záme in záte	He chose presents for me and for you
Govoríla je o mêni in o njíh	She was speaking about me and about them

The mandatory repetition of the preposition also takes place where two nouns governed by the same preposition appear in different clauses, e.g.

Lahkó se zanêsete ne samó na Jáneza, tèmveč túdi na njegóvo sêstro	You can rely not only on Janez but also on his sister

If a noun is governed by two prepositions in the same clause then the noun must be repeated if the prepositions govern two different cases. Alternatively and better still, the second noun may be replaced by a pronoun, e.g. **pred rábo in po rábi** 'before and after use' or **pred rábo in po njéj**.

Note: The construction **pred in po rábi** is incorrect but is encountered in colloquial speech.

8.2 TYPES OF PREPOSITIONS

Slovene prepositions are single words with the exception of **nègledé na/nè gledé na** 'irrespective of, regardless of, notwithstanding' and certain secondary prepositions (see **8.6** and **8.7**). They may be subdivided as follows: (a) Primary or underived prepositions (b) Adverbial prepositions (c) Nouns used as prepositions (d) Derived prepositions (e) Secondary prepositions.

8.3 PRIMARY PREPOSITIONS

The primary prepositions govern the following cases. Only the principal meanings are given here. Other meanings and translations are to be found in the examples given to illustrate each preposition.

Genitive: **brez** 'without'; **do** 'to, as far as'; **iz** 'out of'; **z/s** 'from, off'; **od** 'from, since'; **za** 'during'; **(i)zmed** 'from among, out of'; **(i)znad** 'from above'; **izpod/spod** 'from below'; **izpred/spred** 'from in front of'; **izza** 'from behind'; **zarádi** 'on account of, because of, owing to'

Dative: **k/h** 'to, towards'

Accusative: **med** 'between'; **na** 'on, to'; **nad** 'above'; **ob** 'by, against'; **po** 'for'; **pod** 'under, beneath'; **pred** 'before, in front of'; **raz** 'from, off'; **za** 'behind, for'; **v** 'to, into'

Locative: **na** 'on, in, at'; **ob** 'by, at, on'; **o** 'about'; **po** 'after, over, by, along'; **pri** 'in, at, with'; **v** 'in, at'

Instrumental: **z/s** 'with'; **med** 'between'; **nad** 'above'; **pod** 'underneath'; **pred** 'before, in front of'; **za** 'behind'

Note: The forms **(i)zmed, (i)znad, izpod, izpred/spred, izza** are derived from two primary prepositions, i.e.. **iz** + **med, nad, pod, pred, za**. They are, however, included here because they are only used as prepositions and not as adverbs. Similarly **zarádi** is derived from the prepositions **za** and **rádi**. The use of **rádi** in the sense **zarádi** is, however, nowadays considered incorrect.

8.3.1 Stress in primary prepositions

Primary prepositions are normally unstressed. Exceptions are monosyllabic prepositions used with the clitic accusative forms of the personal pronouns (all persons in the singular and the third persons dual and plural), e.g. **záme** 'for me'; **záte** 'for you'; **zánj** 'for him/it'; **zánje** 'for them'; **zánju** 'for them (d.)'; **prédme** 'in front of me'; **nánjo** 'on her'; **óbnjo** 'against her'; **vánj** 'in him/it'.

8.3.2 Variants of primary prepositions

(a) The preposition **z** 'with, from' has a written variant **s**. The preposition **z** is written as **z** before words beginning with a voiced obstruent, a sonorant or a vowel, but is written as **s** before words beginning with a voiceless obstruent, e.g.

z brátom	with the brother
z Bléda	from Bled
z míze	from the table
z očétom	with the father
but	
s sêstro	with the sister
s stréhe	from the roof

(b) The preposition **k** is written as **h** if it occurs before words beginning with **k** or **g**, e.g.

k oróžju	to arms
k mízi	to the table
k bratráncu	to the cousin
but	
h gôri	to the mountain
h grádu	to the castle
h kováču	to the blacksmith
h kônju	to the horse

(c)   The preposition **ob** + loc. 'at, during' used in a temporal sense has a variant **o** when used with the names of religious holidays, e.g.

o božíču   at Christmas
o véliki nôči   at Easter
o bínkoštih   at Whitsun

Such phrases are now considered archaic and are normally replaced by alternative constructions, e.g. **za bôžič, na božíčni dan, za véliko nóč, za bínkošti**.

(d)   The preposition **v** has the stressed variant **va-** when used with the accusative clitic forms of the personal pronouns, i.e. **váme, váte** etc.

8.4   ADVERBIAL PREPOSITIONS

Adverbial prepositions are adverbs that may function as prepositions. The majority of adverbial prepositions take the genitive case; only a few take the dative or the accusative.

(a)   *Genitive*:   **blízu** 'near'; **mímo** 'past, by'; **naspróti** 'opposite, against'; **okóli, okrog** '(a)round, near'; **ónstran, ónkraj** 'beyond, on the other side of'; **póleg** 'by'; **prek(o)** 'over'; **rázen** 'except'; **srédi** 'in the middle of'; **tik** 'close by'; **tóstran** 'on this side of'; **vpríčo** 'in the presence of, in full view of'; **vštric** 'alongside, next to'; **vzdólž** 'beside, alongside'; **zúnaj** 'outside of'; **znótraj** 'inside of'

Note: The preposition **nasróti** is also used with the dative case in the meaning 'opposite'.

The preposition **srédi** has an alternative form **sréd** but this is now considered archaic. The preposition **vpríčo** has an alternative, now archaic, form **spríčo**. These two forms are often used nowadays in journalese instead of **zarádi** with the meaning 'because of, on account of', e.g.

Vpríčo/spríčo pománjkanja dokázov so ga oprostíli
Because of the lack of evidence they acquitted him

(b)   *Dative*:   **kljúb/navkljúb** 'in spite of, notwithstanding'; **proti** 'against, towards'; **nasróti** 'against'

The form **navkljúb** is nowadays rare and normally replaced by **kljúb**, e.g.

Kljúb dežjù smo šlí na izlèt   In spite of the rain we went on the outing

However, **navkljúb** is still found if its meaning is stressed, e.g.

Navkljúb težávam smo končáli žétev
In spite of all the difficulties we completed the reaping

Note: **navkljúb** may follow a pronoun, but then is normally considered an adverb, e.g. **Vsèmu navkljúb smo se iméli dôbro** 'In spite of everything we had a good time'.

In the modern language **naspróti** would normally be replaced by **proti** + dat. in the sense 'against' e.g. **zločín (nas)proti národu** 'A crime against the people'.

In older literature and now considered archaic we find the prepositions **vzlíc/navzlíc** + dative used in the sense **kljúb**.

(c) *Accusative*: **skóz(i)** 'through'; **zóper** 'against'; **čez** 'over, across, through'; **niz** 'down'

The preposition **niz** is now considered archaic and in the modern language it is replaced by **vzdólž** + genitive, e.g. **plúti vzdólž réke** 'to sail down the river'.

8.5   NOUNS USED AS PREPOSITIONS

These all take the genitive case: **dnò** 'at the bottom of'; **kônec** 'at the end of'; **kraj** 'beside, by'; **krog** 'round, about'; **vrh** 'on the top of, over, besides, moreover'.

When **vrh** has the meaning 'moreover' it also has a variant form **povŕh(u)**, e.g.

Včéraj je deževálo in biló je vetróvno, vrh/povŕh(u) vsèga pa je zvečér začéla pádati šè tóča

Yesterday it rained and it was windy and moreover in the evening it began to hail

The preposition **kônec** when used in a temporal or spatial meaning is now somewhat archaic and it is normally replaced by **na kôncu** + gen. (spatial) and **ob kôncu** + gen. (temporal). Another variant is the instrumental form **kôncem** which is used in a temporal sense, e.g. **Knjíga bo izšlà kôncem mája** 'The book will be published at the end of May'.

The preposition **kraj** is also now considered archaic as is its variant **pokràj** and normally replaced by the prepositions **ob, zráven**.

The preposition **krog** too is now considered archaic and replaced by the adverbial prepositions **okrog, okóli**.

8.6   DERIVED PREPOSITIONS

Derived prepositions in Slovene are formed from primary prepositions plus a noun or adverb, e.g. **namésto** 'instead of'; **vsled** 'owing to, on account of'; **zavóljo** 'on account of, because of, owing to'; **zastrán** 'on account of, because of'; **ízven** 'outside of'.

These prepositions all take the genitive case. In the modern langugage **zastrán** is considered archaic and **vsled** too is archaic and its use disapproved of. In the modern language both are replaced by **zarádi**.

The only two prepositions derived from a verb are **gledé** + genitive 'as regards' and **nègledé na** + accusative 'in spite of, regardless of'.

8.7 SECONDARY PREPOSITIONS

Secondary prepositions are nouns governed by a preposition which are followed either by the genitive or by another preposition, e.g. **s pomočjó** + gen. 'with the help of'; **v iménu** + gen. 'in the name of'; **v zvézi z** + instr. 'in connection with'; **z ozírom na** + acc. 'with regard to'.

8.8 THE MEANINGS OF PREPOSITIONS

With regard to their meaning and function prepositions may be classified as follows:

1. Spatial prepositions
2. Temporal prepositions
3. Prepositions with causal meanings
4. Prepositions denoting purpose or intention
5. Prepositions expressing means and manner
6. Prepositions expressing concessive meanings
7. Prepositions expressing quantifying relationships
8. Prepositions expressing comparison

8.9 SPATIAL PREPOSITIONS

8.9.1 Spatial prepositions denoting movement to(wards) a place

v/na + accusative
These prepositions are used to denote respectively movement 'to/in(to)' and 'on(to)/to' a place, e.g.

v:	**Grém v mésto**	I am going to town
	Položil sem knjígo v predál	I put the book in the drawer
	Ôna je sédla v naslanjáč	She sat down in the chair
	Vŕgel je kámen v vôdo	He threw a stone into the water
	Vstopíla je v sôbo	She entered the room
	Prišlí so v híšo	They came to the house
	íti v bolníšnico/gostílno/ mesníco/Ljubljáno	to go to the hospital/inn/butcher's/ Ljubljana
na:	**Dála je klobúk na glávo**	She put the hat on her head
	Máček je splézal na drevó	The cat climbed onto the tree

Bómba je pádla na híšo	A bomb fell on the house
Potováli smo na Dúnaj	We were travelling to Vienna

8.9.2 Nouns governed by **na** + acc. 'to/in(to)' a place

The preposition **v** + acc. is the preposition normally used to express movement 'to/in(to)' a place in Slovene and **na** + acc. normally denotes movement 'on(to)'. However, certain common nouns and some proper nouns are governed by **na** and not **v** with the meaning 'to/in(to)'. These include the following:

(a) Common nouns

aerodróm 'aerodrome'; **akademíja** 'academy'; **ambasáda** 'embassy'; **avión** 'plane'; **ávtobus** 'bus'; **balkón** 'balcony'; **bórza** 'exchange'; **césta** 'road'; **dežéla** 'country'; **dirkalíšče** 'racecourse'; **dvoríšče** 'courtyard'; **drážba** 'auction'; **ekspedícija** 'expedition'; **fakultéta** 'faculty'; **gimnázija** 'grammar school'; **gradbíšče** 'building site'; **hodník** 'hall'; **igríšče** 'playground'; **izlèt** 'outing'; **jézero** 'lake'; **kmetíja** 'farm'; **komité** 'committee'; **koncêrt** 'concert'; **konferénca** 'conference'; **kongrés** 'congress'; **konzulát** 'consulate'; **letalíšče** 'airport'; **mêja** 'border'; **mórje** 'sea'; **njíva** 'field'; **obála** 'coast, seaside'; **obísk** 'visit'; **oddélek** 'department'; **ôtok** 'island'; **parkiríšče** 'parking area'; **páša** 'pasture'; **perón** 'platform'; **plés** 'dance'; **podróčje** 'region, sphere'; **podstréšje** 'attic'; **pogrèb** 'funeral'; **pokopalíšče** 'cemetery'; **policíja** 'police'; **pólje** 'field'; **pólotok** 'peninsula'; **postája** 'station'; **postajalíšče** 'stop'; **póšta** 'post office'; **predávanje** 'lecture'; **predstáva** 'performance'; **prireditev** 'show'; **razstáva** 'exhibition'; **séja** 'meeting'; **sejmíšče** 'fairground'; **sestának** 'meeting'; **skedènj** 'barn'; **smetíšče** 'rubbish tip'; **smúčanje** 'skiing'; **smučíšče** 'ski slopes'; **sodíšče** 'court'; **sprehòd** 'walk'; **sprejèm** 'reception'; **stádion** 'stadium'; **stráža** 'guard, sentry duty'; **svátba** 'wedding'; **tékma** 'match'; **televízija** 'television'; **trávnik** 'meadow'; **tréning** 'training'; **tŕg** 'square'; **univêrza** 'university'; **veleposláništvo** 'embassy'; **vlák** 'train'; **vógel** 'corner'; **vŕt** 'garden'; **žága** 'saw mill'.

Common nouns governed by **na** + acc. also include points of the compass, e.g. **séver** 'North'; **júg** 'South'; **vzhòd** 'East'; **zahòd** 'West'; **séverovzhòd** 'north east'; **júgozahòd** 'south west'

Examples of the use of **na** *'to/in(to)'*

Prepeljáli so ga na ôtok	They took him to the island
Na tréning hódi dvákrat tédensko	He goes to training twice a week
Hitéla je na vlák	She hurried to the train
Šlí smo na sestának	We went to the meeting
Pogrébni sprevòd je zavíl na pokopalíšče	The funeral procession turned into the cemetery

Vpísal se je na medicínsko fakultéto	He enrolled in the faculty of medicine
Vsò navláko so odpeljáli na smetíšče	They took all the rubbish to the tip
Ko je vstópal na vlák, je sprevódnik zažvížgal	As he got in the train the conductor blew the whistle
Dvé móštvi sta prihájali na stádion	The two teams entered the stadium
Gréva na jézero lovìt ríbe	Let us (d.) go to the lake to fish
izvážati na zahòd	to export to the West
Letálo se je usmérilo na séver	The plane headed towards the North

(b) Place names governed by **na**

These include the names of islands, peninsulas, archipelagos, climatic zones, foreign countries, regions in Slovenia, towns, mountains and lakes.

(i) Islands, peninsulas, archipelagos

Since **ôtok** 'island' is governed by **na** + acc. so too are the names of islands. Similarly the nouns **pólotok** 'peninsula' and **otóčje** 'archipelago', which are derived from it, are likewise governed by **na** + acc., e.g. **Krím** 'The Crimea'; **Grenlándija** 'Greenland'; **Islándija** 'Iceland'; **Balkán** 'The Balkans'; **Kréta** 'Crete'; **Cíper** 'Cyprus'; **Kanárski otóki** 'The Canaries'; **Apenínski pólotok** 'The Appenine Peninsula'; **Ístrski pólotok** 'The Istrian Peninsula'; **Havájsko otóčje** 'The Hawaian Archipelago'; **Británsko otóčje** 'The British Isles', e.g. **potovati na Krím/Kréto/Islándijo/Filipíne/Británsko otóčje/Kanárske otóke** 'to travel to the Crimea/Crete/Iceland/the Philippines/the British Isles/the Canaries.

It should be noted, however, that the islands of New Zealand and the place name **Ístra** 'Istrian Peninsula' are governed by the preposition **v** as is the name 'England' which is thought of as a country and not an island, e.g. **potováti v Ánglijo/Nôvo Zelándijo/Ístro** 'to travel to England/New Zealand/Istria'

(ii) The climatic zones: **Árktika** 'Arctic'; **Antárktika** 'Antarctic', e.g. **ekspedícija na Árktiko** 'an expedition to the Arctic'

(iii) Foreign countries and the names of regions in Slovenia which are feminine adjectives in -ska, -ška, e.g. **Madžárska** 'Hungary'; **Kitájska** 'China'; **Japónska** 'Japan'; **Póljska** 'Poland'; **Hrváška** 'Croatia'; **Dolénjska** 'Lower Carniola'; **Gorénjska** 'Upper Carniola'; **Štájerska** 'Styria'; **Primórska** 'The Littoral'; **Koróška** 'Carinthia', e.g. **Grém na Kitájsko/Koróško** 'I am going to China/Carinthia'; **Létos sem šlà na Hrváško** 'This year I went to Croatia'

(iv) Mountains and towns in Slovenia

These are mountainous regions and certain towns, e.g. **Ptúj**,

Jeseníce, Blégoš, Péca, Póhorje, e.g. **potováti na Ptúj/Póhorje** 'to travel to Ptuj/Pohorje'

(v) The foreign place names **Dúnaj** 'Vienna' and **Himalája** 'The Himalayas', e.g. **Odpráva na Himalájo** 'An expedition to the Himalayas'; **Odpotovàl je z letálom na Dúnaj** 'He flew to Vienna'

(vi) The names of lakes
Since the noun **jézero** 'lake' is governed by **na** + acc. so too are the names of lakes, e.g. **potováti na Bléd/Plítvice/Bajkálsko jézero/ Bohínjsko jézero** 'to travel to Lake Bled/Plitvice/Lake Baikal/Lake Bohinj'

Note: If the accompanying verb denotes motion into the depths of a lake then the preposition **v** is used instead of **na**, e.g. **Réka se izlíva v Bajkálsko jézero** 'The river flows into Lake Baikal'; **Pádel je v jézero** 'He fell in the lake'.

8.9.3   Spatial prepositions denoting location

v/na + locative
These prepositions are used to denote respectively location 'in, inside of, at' and 'on, on top of' e.g.

v: **Ostála je v híši**	She stayed in the house
Písmo je biló v škátli v mansárdi	The letter was in a box in the attic
Sedéli smo v galeríji	We were sitting in the gallery
V šóli se téga še níso učíli	They still haven't studied this in/at school
Kupíla je krùh v pekárni	She bought bread in/at the baker's shop
na: **Na mízi stojí kozárec**	A glass is standing on the table
Slíka visí na sténi	The picture hangs on the wall
Na stréhi gnézdijo štórklje	Storks are nesting on the roof

If a noun or a place name is governed by **na** + accusative in the sense of movement 'to or into' then it will also be governed by **na** + locative in the sense 'in, inside of, at', e.g.

Sréčala sta se na pόšti	They met at the post office
Zborovánje je biló na stádionu	The rally was held in/at the stadium
Na vŕtu ne stréžemo	There is no service in the garden
Njegóv bràt je profésor na ekonómski fakultéti	His brother is a professor in the Faculty of Economics
Déla na njívi	He is working in the field
Mladόst je prežível na Kitájskem	He spent his youth in China
Zméraj dežúje na Británskem otóčju	It always rains in the British Isles
Na zahόdu so se pojávili tèmni obláki	Black clouds appeared in the West

8.9.4 Individual nouns governed by either **na** + acc./loc. or **v** + acc./loc.

A few nouns may take either **v** or **na** + acc./loc. The choice depends on certain semantic nuances.

(a) **šóla** 'school'
If the word school denotes the type of school or school/class in general then **v** is used, e.g.

Dánes je biló v šóli zabávno It was amusing in school/class today
Hódim v srédnjo šólo I go to secondary school

If, however, the name of the school is indicated or the idea of the school as a total institution is understood then **na** is used, e.g.

Hódim na Stáneta Žágarja/Ledíno I go to the Stane Žagar/
  Ledina school

Na šólo se je vpisálo 50 nôvih Fifty new pupils enrolled in
  učêncev the school

(b) **bánka** 'bank'
When **bánka** means the building then **v** is used, e.g.

Móram v bánko I must go to the bank
V bánki je zaposlênih 20 ljudí Twenty people are employed in the
  bank

Note: Colloquially we find **na bánko** and **na bánki** in such examples. When, however, **bánka** is used to mean the account held at the bank, then colloquially **na** is used, e.g. **Dánes sem položíla 5000 tólarjev na bánko** 'Today I deposited five thousand tolars in the bank'.

(c) **óbčina** 'municipal office/municipality'; **skúpnost** 'community offices, community'
These two nouns are governed by **na** if they denote the foundation, institution or building itself or a meeting of the organisation, e.g.

Grém na óbčino, da uredím dokumênte
I am going to the municipal offices to put my papers in order

Na krajévni skúpnosti so razprávljali o problému begúncev
At the meeting of the local community they discussed the problem of refugees

If, however, they denote the region they are governed by **v**, e.g.

V óbčini Ljubljána Cénter živí Fifty thousand inhabitants live in
  50000 prebiválcev the municipality of Ljubljana
  Centre

Živímo v skúpnosti, ki spoštúje We live in a law abiding community
  zakóne

(d) **póstelja** 'bed'

When **póstelja** is used in the sense 'sleep' (i.e. to go to/to be in bed) then it is governed by **v**, e.g.

Dánes zvečér grém zgódaj v pósteljo	I am going to bed early this evening
Otròk spí v svôji póstelji	The child is sleeping in his own bed

In the concrete meaning of 'a bed' **póstelja** is governed by **na**, e.g.

Ôna je priklénjena na pósteljo	She is bedridden
Ulégel se je na pósteljo	He lay down on the bed
Poglavár je lêžal na smŕtni póstelji	The chieftain was dying

(e) **zràk** 'air'

When used in the sense of 'fresh/open air' **zràk** is governed by **na**, e.g.

Grém na zràk	I am going out for some air
Otrôci so se igráli na zráku	The children were playing outside/in the fresh air

Otherwise it is governed by **v**, e.g.

Zdrúžene držáve Amêrike imájo vojáško premóč v zráku	The U.S.A has military superiority in the air
Rakéta je poletéla v zràk	The rocket flew up into the air

(f) **nebó** 'sky'

When used with the names of heavenly bodies **nebó** is governed by **na**, e.g.

Sónce je žé visôko na nébu	The sun is already high in the sky
Sónce se je dvígalo na nebó	The sun rose in the sky

In other instances **nebó** is governed by **v**, e.g.

Gôre se dvígajo v nebó	The mountains rise up into the sky
Glédal je v nebó, kákšno bo vrême	He looked up at the sky to see what the weather would be like

Note: When **nebó** is used in the plural in the sense 'heaven' it is also governed by **v**, e.g. **Dôbri ljudjé bodo šlí v nebésa** 'Good people will go to heaven', **Bíl je v devêtih nebésih, kot bi zadél glávni dobítek na loteríji** 'He was in seventh (lit. ninth) heaven, as if he had won first prize in the lottery'.

(g) **mórje** 'sea, seaside'

In the sense 'seaside' or 'to sea, at sea' **mórje** is governed by **na**, e.g.

Odpotováli sta na mórje	They (f.d.) went away to the seaside
izlèt na mórje	a trip to the seaside

víkend na mórju	a weekend at the seaside
Vsáko léto potújemo na Sredozémsko mórje	Every year we travel to the Mediterranean
vihár na mórju	a storm at sea
Ládja je odplúla na odpŕto mórje	The ship sailed out to the open sea

In other instances **mórje** is governed by **v**, e.g.

Žénska je utoníla v mórju	The woman drowned in the sea
Réka se izlíva v mórje	The river flows into the sea
Vŕgla je stekleníco v mórje	She threw the bottle into the sea

(h) **vás** 'village, countryside'
In the sense 'countryside' **vás** is governed by **na**, e.g.

Grémo na vás	We are going to the countryside
Môja sêstra živí na vási	My sister lives in the country

In the concrete sense of 'a village' **vas** is governed by **v**, e.g.

Tekmoválci stanújejo v olímpijski vási	The competitors live in the Olympic village

(i) **dežêla** 'country(side), land, province'
In the sense 'country(side)' **dežêla** is governed by **na**, e.g.

Njén stríc imá híšo na dežêli	Her uncle has a house in the country
Poléti se bomo preselíli na dežêlo	In summer we will move to the country

When used with the meaning 'land, province' **dežêla** is governed by **v**, e.g.

V dežêli vzhajajóčega sónca žénske nósijo kimóno	In the Land of the Rising Sun (i.e. Japan) women wear kimonos
Nékaj gnílega je v dežêli Dánski	There is something rotten in the state of Denmark

(j) **grád** 'castle'
When 'motion towards' or 'presence at' is indicated, **grád** is governed by **na**, e.g.

Turísti gredó na grád	The tourists are going to the castle
Na Ljubljánskem grádu je dánes precéj turístov	There are a lot of tourists at Ljubljana castle today

If, however, one specifically wishes to indicate the interior of the castle **v** is used, e.g.

V grádu straší	The castle is haunted
Vojáki so vdŕli v grád	The soldiers burst into the castle

(k) **odbòr** 'committee'

When considered as a group of people **odbòr** is governed by **v**, e.g.

Izvóljen je bíl v odbòr	He was elected to the committee
Nájin prijátelj je v odbôru	Our (d.) friend is on the committee

If, however, **odbòr** denotes the place of the committee meeting it is governed by **na**, e.g.

Na odbôru so skleníli pomémbne stvarí	At the committee they resolved important issues
Šèl bom na odbòr	I will go to the committee meeting

(l) **hríb** 'hill, mountain'; **gôra** 'mountain'

In the general sense of 'mountains' (i.e. mountainous region) these two nouns are governed by **v**, e.g.

Prebíli so počítnice v gôrah	They spent their holidays in the mountains
Pozími hódim v gôre/hríbe na smúčanje	In winter I go to the mountains for skiing
Ljudjé, ki živíjo v hríbih, so zdrávi	People who live in the mountains are healthy

If, however, a specific mountain is denoted then **na** is used, e.g.

Na gôri se je zbrálo 10 planíncev	Ten climbers assembled on the mountain
Prídiga na gôri	The Sermon on the Mount
Hítro móram na gôro, ker bo lahkó dèž	I must get to the mountain quickly, because it may rain

Note: **v** is used with **hríb** in the sense 'uphill', e.g.

Težkó hódi v hríb	He walks uphill with difficulty
Tjà ne mórem, je prevèč v hríb	I cannot get there, it is too uphill

(m) **úlica** 'street'

This noun is normally governed by **na** when it denotes 'where someone is or lives' or 'motion out onto', e.g.

Grém vèn na úlico	I am going out onto the street
Na úlicah je velíko ljudí	There are a lot of people on the street
Stanúje na Čôpovi úlici številka 5	He lives at number 5 Čop Street
Študènti so šlí na úlice	The students went out onto the streets

The preposition **v** is, however, used when the location of a building is indicated, e.g.

Òn imá delávnico v májhni, zakótni úlici   He has a workshop in a small, remote street

Note: The preposition **v** is also used in the figurative phrase **Pogájanja so zašlà v slépo úlico** 'The negotiations led nowhere (i.e. went up a blind alley)'.

(n) **zbòr** 'meeting, gathering, assembly: choir, chorus, company'. In the meaning 'choir, company', **zbòr** is governed by **v** but in the meaning 'meeting' it is governed by **na**, e.g.

Môja sêstra je bilà sprejéta v   My sister was accepted into
  cerkvéni zbòr   the church choir
Profésorjeva nečákinja je solístka v The professor's niece is the
  balétnem zbôru   soloist in a ballet company
Nàš delegát je govoríl na zbôru   Our delegate spoke at the
                                          meeting
Povabíli so me na zbòr   They invited me to the meeting

(o) **svét** 'world'
When **svét** means the world we live in it is governed by **na**, e.g.

Pét milijárd ljudí živí na svétu   Five billion people live in the
                                          world
Móramo si prizadévati za mír na   We must strive for peace in the
  svétu   world
glávna industríjska síla na svétu   the main industrial power in the
                                          world

If, however, **svét** is used figuratively, i.e. it means 'the world of . . .' or 'life' or 'circumstances' it takes **v**.

novósti v svétu známosti   innovations in the world of
                                          science
Dánes živímo v drugáčnem svétu   Today we live in a different world
íti v svét   to go out into the world

8.9.5 Spatial prepositions denoting movement from or out of a place

iz/z/s + genitive
These prepositions denote respectively movement 'out of/from' and 'down from, from (off), off' a place. They are respectively the opposites of the prepositions **v**, **na**, i.e. **v** + acc./**iz** + gen.; **na** + acc./**z/s** + gen., e.g.

iz: **Peljáli smo se iz mésta v hríbe**   We drove from the town to the
                                          mountains

Pótnik je izstópil iz ávtobusa	The passenger got off the bus
Márica je prišlà iz šóle vsà razbúrjena	Marica arrived from school all excited
Tína je vzéla svínčnik iz púšice	Tina took a pencil from the pencil case
Iz kúhinje prihája prijéten vónj	A pleasant smell is coming from the kitchen

(cf. **peljáti se v mésto** 'to drive to town'; **vstopíti v ávtobus** 'to get on a bus'; **správiti svínčnik v púšico** 'to put a pencil in a pencil case'; **íti v šólo** 'to go to school', etc.)

z/s:
Otròk je pádel z drevésa	The boy fell from the tree
Snéla je plášč s kljúke	She took her coat from the hook
Knjíga je pádla s políce	The book fell from off the shelf
Véter mu je odnésel klobúk z gláve	The wind blew his hat from off his head
Letálo je poletélo z letalíšča	The plane took off from the airport

(cf. **splézati na drevó** 'to climb a tree'; **obésiti plášč na kljúko** 'to hang a coat on a hook'; **postáviti knjígo na políco** 'to put a book on a shelf'; **dáti klobúk na glávo** 'to put a hat on one's head', etc.)

The oppositions **v/iz** and **na/z, s** are consistently observed. Very often they are used together to denote the starting and finishing points of a movement, e.g.

| Ôče je nemírno hôdil iz kóta v kót | The father walked restlessly from corner to corner |
| Ptíč je skákal z véje na véjo | The bird hopped from branch to branch |

If a noun or place name is governed by **na** + acc., when the preposition has the meaning 'to, into', then it will be governed by **z/s** with the meaning 'from, out of', e.g.

Razlágal je, da se je pràvkar vŕnil s tréninga	He explained that he had just returned from training
Prihája z Jeseníc	He comes from Jesenice
Vŕnil se je z otóka Cípra	He returned from Cyprus
S sévera je píhala búrja	A storm was blowing from the north
Nàš dopísnik poróča z razstáve v Lóndonu	Our correspondent is reporting from the exhibition in London
Gôste so preselíli z vŕta v dvoráno	They moved the guests out of the garden into the hall

In the case of those nouns which can take either **v** or **na** (see **8.9.4**) then the respective use of **iz** or **z/s** will reflect the same semantic nuances, e.g.

mórje

iz/v: **Policíst je vlékel trúplo iz mórja** — The policeman dragged the body from the sea

Vŕgel je kámenček v mórje — He threw a stone into the sea

z/na: **Prihájamo z mórja** — We have come from the seaside

Odpótovali so na mórje — They set off for the seaside

svét

iz/v: **Na rádiu 'Ljubljána' obstája oddája 'Iz svetá glásbe'** — On radio Ljubljana there is a broadcast 'From the World of Music'

novósti v svétu znánosti — innovations in the world of science

z/na: **Konferénce so se udeležíli predstávniki z vsèga svetá** — Representatives from the whole world took part in the conference

Prizadévamo si za mír na svétu — We are striving for peace in the world

8.9.6 Extensions of the spatial meanings of v; na; iz

A number of meanings of **v**, **na** and **iz** may be regarded as extensions of their spatial meanings.

v + acc. denotes:

(a) The target of an action:
stréljati v tárčo — to shoot at a target
udáriti kóga v obràz — to strike somebody in the face

(b) The place where some state or characteristic occurs:
zredíti se v obràz — to put on weight in the face
rdèč v obràz — red in the face

(c) The object towards which an emotion is directed:
zaljubíti se v púnco — to fall in love with a girl
verováti v Bogá — to believe in God
zaúpati v kóga — to trust in someone
úpanje v uspèh — hope of success

(d) The change from one state to another (usually in the construction **iz** + gen. **v** + acc.):
preračúnati iz tólarjev v márke — to convert tolars into marks
prevájati iz angléščine v slovénščino — to translate from English into Slovene
Iz púnčke se je spremeníla v doráslo mládo žénsko — She changed from a little girl into a young lady
Polétje se je prevésilo v jesén — Summer turned to Autumn

(e)   Inclusion within a sphere, group or object:

Tó ne spáda v môjo stróko   This does not fall within my field of expertise

vzéti v račún   to take into account

stopíti v stránko   to join a party

(f)   The object of the action denoted by the verb:

lésti v dolgóve   to incur debts

vméšati se v délo   to interfere in an affair

správiti sôbo v réd   to tidy a room

spustíti se v bòj   to enter a battle

v + loc. denotes:

(a)   Membership of a body or group:

bíti v vládi   to be in the government

otròk v družíni   a child in the family

(b)   The sphere of activity someone is engaged in:

délati v administráciji, v turízmu, v   računálništvu   to work in administration, in tourism, in computers

(c)   The circumstances in which an action takes place:

rêči v jézi   to say in anger

Vájeni so délati v vročíni   They are used to working in the heat

Plés v dežjù   Singing (lit. dancing) in the rain (film title)

Note: **po dežjù** is also used in the sense 'in the rain', e.g. **Ràd hódim po dežjù** 'I like walking in the rain'.

(d)   The sphere to which the verbal action is limited:

zmágati v téku   to beat in a race

napredováti v znánju   to progress in knowledge

(e)   The condition or state where the verbal action takes place:

živéti v pokóju   to be retired

Reševálci so bilì v velíki nevárnosti   The rescuers were in great danger

na + acc. denotes:

(a)   The target of an action or noun:

stréljati na sovrážnika   to fire at the enemy

Pès lája na póštarja   The dog is barking at the postman

ôkno na vŕt   a window looking on to the garden

vráta na balkón   the door to the balcony

(b)   Transfer or transition to another position or state:

prenêsti odgovórnost na drúge   to place the responsibility on others

Bolézen se prenáša z žívali na   človéka   The disease is transferred from animal to man

(c)   The aim of an intellectual, emotional or physical activity:

Ôče je jézen na sína	The father is angry with his son
Òn mísli na prihódnost	He is thinking of the future
Opozoríli smo ga na napáke	We warned him about the mistakes
Čákamo na ávtobus	We are waiting for the bus
spomíni na vôjno	memories of the war

(d)   The physical restriction of some characteristic:

hròm na obé nôgi	lame in both legs
slép na êno okó	blind in one eye
glúh na lévo uhó	deaf in the left ear

na + loc. denotes:

(a)   The physical restriction of some characteristic:

Profésor je bolán na pljúčih	The professor has lung trouble
Ôna je bólna na sŕcu	She has heart trouble

(b)   The activity taking place when used with the verb **bíti** 'to be' and certain other verbs:

bíti na lôvu	to be out hunting
bíti na stráži	to be on guard duty
Njegóv bràt je na délu v Némčiji	His brother is working in Germany
Ponesréčil se je na smúčanju	He had an accident when skiing

iz + gen. 'of, out of'

(a)   This construction may indicate the material source of something, e.g.

izdélati kípec iz brôna	to make a statue out of bronze
zíd iz kámna	a stone wall
pŕstan iz zlatá	a gold ring
vênec iz tŕnja	a crown of thorns
krùh iz béle móke	bread made from white flour

(b)   It has a figurative meaning with words like **móda** 'fashion', **fórma**, e.g.

Móštvo je precéj iz fórme	The team is very much out of form
Tá obléka je žé iz móde	This dress is already out of fashion

8.9.7   Prepositions denoting spatial proximity or contact

(a)   **pri/ob** + loc.; **ob** + acc.
These prepositions denote the place where an action occurs or immediate spatial proximity or contact. They may also denote the physical circumstances which accompany an action. These prepositions have several translations in English. It should be noted that **pri** + loc. and not **v/na** denotes location for human objects.

(b) **pri** + loc.:'at, on, by, beside, among, with'

Òn stanúje pri stárših	He lives with his parents
bíti pri frizêrju	to be at the hairdresser's
Délam pri strícu	I work at my uncle's
Tó je naváda pri Italijánih	It is a custom among Italians
gréti se pri ôgnju	to warm oneself by the fire
Òn je pri telefónu	He is on the telephone
	(colloquially **na telefónu**)
Obstál je pri vrátih	He stopped by the door
Smúčar je pádel pri sestópu	The skier fell on the descent
bítka pri Verdúnu	the Battle at/of Verdun
klóp pri studênčku	a bench beside the small well
bíti pri máši	to be at Mass

Note: pri + loc. is also used to denote something is a part of something/someone, e.g.

zobjé pri grábljah	the teeth of a rake
ovrátnik pri srájci	the collar of a shirt
Rôka pri človéku je drugáčna kot pri ópicah	The hand of a man is different to that of a monkey

(c) **ob** + loc.:'in, at, by, beside, along, over, against, next to'

Ob lépem vreménu je vsè mésto na úlicah	Everyone is out on the streets in fine weather
sprehájati se ob mesečíni	to walk in the moonlight
Slonél je ob drevésu	He was leaning against a tree
Ob zídu stojí omára	A wardrobe stands by the wall
svetílnik ob mórju	a lighthouse by the sea
drévje ob césti	the trees beside the road
Stojíta drúg ob drúgem	They (d.) are standing next to one another
Mèč mu visí ob bóku	His sword hangs at his side
Želéznica je speljána ob réki	The railway runs along the river
ob pŕvi prilóžnosti	at the first opportunity
Pogovárjali so se o problému ob kozárcu vína	They talked about the problem over a glass of wine

(d) **ob** + acc.'against, over, beside, by, at'
With the accusative **ob** denotes either

(i)   movement towards and contact with something that is an obstruction or hindrance

(ii) movement to within a very close distance of something/someone, e.g.

Udáril sem z glávo ob zíd	I struck my head against the wall
Postávila je koló ob zíd	She placed her bike against the wall
Spotáknil se je ob kámen	He tripped over a stone

Dèž bíje ob šípe	The rain beats against the window panes
Púško je polóžil óbse	He placed the gun at his side

8.9.8 Other spatial prepositions denoting spatial proximity

These all take the genitive case and include: **kraj** 'near, by'; **blízu** 'near, close to'; **zráven** 'near, close to, by the side of'; **póleg** 'by the side of, next to'; **tik** 'close to, right next to'; **vštric** 'abreast with, alongside, next to'; **vzdólž** 'along-(side), next to'

Of these **kraj** is very literary. The prepositions **zráven** and **póleg** are synonymous but **póleg** is very formal. In normal conversation **zráven** (or **pri** + loc.) would be preferred. The prepositions **tik** and **vštric** tend to mean 'right next to'. **tik** is very literary and **vštric** has the additional meaning of 'to the left or right of' and is used with verbs of motion. **Vzdólž** means 'proximity along the length of something'.

Examples of usage

kraj:	**Híša stojí kraj gózda**	The house lies near the forest (More usual here would be **ob gózdu**)
blízu:	**vás blízu Ljubljáne**	a village near Ljubljana
zráven:	**Stála je zráven ávta in čakála**	She stood next to the car and waited
póleg:	**Póleg híše je vŕt**	There is a garden next to the house
	Stál je póleg mêne	He stood next to me
tik:	**Usédla se je tik njêga**	She sat down next to him
vštric:	**Hodíla je vštric očéta**	She was walking next to her father
vzdólž:	**Vzdólž réke rástejo topôli**	Poplars grow alongside the river
	stôli vzdólž zidú	the chairs along the wall

8.9.9 Spatial prepositions denoting movement away from or towards

(a) **od** + gen.
   This preposition expresses movement away from an object or person, or distance from an object. One should note that **od** + gen. and not **iz/z** is used for human objects, e.g.

Odmáknil sem pósteljo od ôkna	I moved the bed away from the window
pót od postáje	the road leading from the station
nèdáleč od Ljubljáne	not far from Ljubljana
Prihájam od očéta	I have come from my father
Ríbič je odrínil čóln od bréga	The fisherman pushed the boat away from the bank
Vráčam se od máme	I am returning from my mother's

Further meanings of **od** + *gen.*:

(i) Separation from an object:

ločíti mesó od kostí	to separate the meat from the bone
odmakníti se od polítike síle	to distance oneself from power politics

(ii) Choice or selection from among:

êden od učêncev	one of the pupils
Izbrála sem ênega od nàjlépših daríl	I chose one of the most beautiful presents
nàjlépša od deklét	the most beautiful of the girls

(iii) Origin or starting point of something:

písmo od stríca	a letter from uncle
Tá nasvèt sem dobíl od prijátelja	I got this advice from a friend

(iv) The object of which something is a part:

kljúč od omáre	the key of/to the cupboard
držáj od kladíva	the handle of the hammer (also possible **držáj kladíva**)

(b) **do** + gen.

This preposition indicates movement towards or as far as an object, e.g.

Sprémil te bom do póšte	I'll accompany you to the post office
césta od postáje do bólnice	the road from the station to the hospital
Prispéli smo do kônca potí	We reached the end of the journey
do róba póln kozárec	a glass filled to the brim
Dvé vozóvnici do Cêlja, prósim	Two tickets to Celje, please

Note: The prepositions **od** and **do** are often used together to denote the starting and finishing point of a movement or the distance between two points, e.g. **Vlák vózi od Ljubljáne do Dúnaja** 'The train runs from Ljubljana to Vienna'; **Od Ljubljáne do Kránja je 25 kilométrov** 'It is twenty five kilometres from Ljubljana to Kranj'.

(c) **k (h)** + dat.

This preposition governs the person or object towards which or whom a movement is made. It should be noted that **k (h)** + dat. and not **v/na** is used for human objects, e.g.

Grém k odvétniku	I am going to the lawyer
Míha je bíl poklícan k tábli	Miha was called to the blackboard
Poklíčite Darínko k telefónu	Call Darinka to the phone (colloquially **na telefón**)
Obŕnil se je k ôknu	He turned towards the window
Stèza pélje h gózdu	The path leads to the wood
Grém k máši	I am going to Mass

Further meanings of **k** (**h**) + *dat.*:

(i) addition, supplementation:

pripisáti obrésti h glávnici	to add interest to the capital
pripómbe k zakónskemu osnútku	annotations to the bill
prispévek k míru	a contribution to peace
režisêrjev prispévek k predstávi	the director's contribution to the performance

(ii) membership of a group:

Zájec spáda h glodávcem	The hare belongs to the rodent family
Prištévajo ga k nàdrealístom	They number him among the surrealists

Note: Instead of **k** + dat. one may also use **med** + acc. in these examples.

(d) **proti** + dat.

This preposition like **k** expresses motion towards, but usually indicates general direction towards. It also expresses movement towards/against something moving in the opposite direction.

íti proti séveru	to go towards the North
mêja proti Itáliji	the border facing Italy
plúti proti obáli	to sail towards the shore
íti proti sovrážniku	to advance towards/against the enemy
plávati proti tóku	to swim against the current

Further meanings of **proti**

proti + dat. may also denote 'resistance towards, enmity, opposition', e.g.

nastopíti proti rásni diskrimináciji	to oppose racial discrimination
Arsenál je igràl proti Milánu v evrópskem pokálu	Arsenal played Milan in the European Cup
Tá snóv je odpórna proti ôgnju	This material is fireproof
obstójnost bárve proti sónčni svetlôbi	the resistance of a colour to sunlight
pritožíti se proti odlóčbi	to appeal against a ruling
cepíti proti kôzam	to vaccinate against smallpox
storíti kàj proti pravílom	to do something in contravention of the rules
tabléte proti glavobôlu	headache tablets

8.9.10 Prepositions denoting the position of an object in relation to another object or movement to that position

These are the prepositions: **nad** 'above, over'; **za** 'behind'; **pod** 'below, under'; **pred** 'before, in front of'; **med** 'between'. They take either the accusative or the instrumental case. When used with the accusative these prepositions denote movement to these positions, When used with the instrumental they denote the location of an object in relation to another object, e.g.

nad + acc.:	**Slíko sem obésil nad klavír**	I hung the picture above the piano
	Balón se je dvígnil nad obláke	The balloon rose above the clouds
nad + instr.:	**Letálo króži nad méstom**	The plane is circling above the town
	Nad Slovénijo je nízek zráčni pritísk	There is a trough of low pressure over Slovenia
za + acc.:	**Sédla je za volán**	She sat behind the steering wheel
	Céstni razbójnik se je skríl za drevó	The highwayman hid behind a tree
	sésti za mízo	to sit down at a table
za + instr.:	**Tó so naredíli za njegóvim hŕbtom**	They did this behind his back
	Za šólo je igríšče	There is a playground behind the school
pod + acc.:	**Pès je zlézel pod mízo**	The dog crawled under the table
	Pod skodélico je položil króžniček	He put a saucer under the cup
pod + instr.:	**Métla je pod mízo**	The broom is under the table
	Góbe rástejo pod drevésom	Mushrooms grow beneath the tree
pred + acc.:	**Čévlje postávi pred vráta**	Put your shoes in front of the door
	Položil je knjígo pred máter	He placed the book in front of his mother
pred + instr.:	**Čakáli bomo pred gledalíščem**	We will wait in front of the theatre
	Manekénka je stála pred ogledálom	The model stood in front of the mirror
med + acc.:	**Lúna se skríje med obláke**	The moon is disappearing between the clouds
	Prométni policíst se je prerínil med gledálce	The traffic policeman forced his way through the spectators
med + instr.:	**Òn je bíl zapŕt med štírimi sténami**	He was locked up within four walls
	próga med Ljubljáno in Tŕstom	the line between Ljubljana and Trieste

8.9.11 Extensions of the spatial meanings of **nad; za; pod; pred**:

nad + acc.: This denotes movement towards or against with hostile intent:
íti nad sovrážnika   to march against the enemy

nad + instr.: This denotes the object of certain verbs expressing mental or emotional states:

rohnéti nad žêno	to fume at one's wife
maščeváti se nad sovrážnikom	to take one's revenge on the enemy
zamísliti se nad vsebíno romána	to be absorbed by the contents of a novel

za + acc.: This denotes (a) the destination of some form of transport (b) contact with an object as a result of a physical action:

(a) **ládja za Dúbrovnik** 'the boat for Dubrovnik'; **ávtobus za Máribor** 'the bus for Maribor'

(b) **vléči za lasé** 'to drag by the hair'; **Prijéla ga je za rámo** 'She took him by the shoulder'

za + instr.: This denotes (a) something behind which a feeling, emotion or state of mind is hidden (b) sequence (c) an object pursued or followed:

(a) **Za njegóvimi besédami je čutíla ironíjo** 'She sensed irony behind his words'; **Za njegóvim cinízmom se skríva obúp** 'Despair is hidden behind/beneath his cynicism'

(b) **Helikópterji drúg za drúgim vzlétajo in pristájajo** 'Helicopters take off and land one after another'

(c) **gnáti se za čím/kóm** 'to chase something/someone'; **težíti za nèdosegljívim** 'to pursue the unattainable'

pod + acc.: This denotes coming to be subordinate to, dependent on:

príti pod pritísk jávnega mnênja	to come under the pressure of public opinion
Pólk je prišèl pod povêljstvo nôvega polkóvnika	The regiment came under the command of a new colonel

pod + instr.: This denotes (a) the state of being subordinate, dependent on (b) metaphorical concealment (c) the circumstances which accompany an action:

(a) **Pod sebój imá desét délavcev** 'He has ten workers under him'; **Orkéster igrá pod taktírko známega dirigénta** 'The orchestra plays under the baton of a famous conductor'

(b) **Káj razúmeš pod tó besédo** 'What do you understand by that word?'; **Òn potúje pod tújim im22énom** 'He is travelling under another name' (also possible **s tújim imónom**); **Pod**

> **pretvézo, da pomága, je vzél denár od stránke** 'Under the pretext of helping, he took money from the customer'; **Izkoríščal ga je pod krínko prijáteljstva** 'He exploited him under the guise of friendship'

(c) **Òn déla pod stálnim pritískom** 'He works under constant pressure'; **Ponesréčenca so operírali pod narkózo** 'The victim was operated on under anaesthetic'

pred + acc.:   This expresses precedence in classification:
Angléški tekmoválec se je uvŕstil pred evrópskega prváka
The English competitor was ranked above the European champion
Na razpredélnici je Arsenál prišèl pred Leeds
Arsenal came ahead of Leeds in the league table

pred + instr.:   This denotes (a) precedence in classification and (b) something negative which it is necessary to avoid:

(a) **Argentína je zmágala pred Nizozémsko in Itálijo** 'Argentina was victorious ahead of Holland and Italy'

(b) **Tù smo várni pred dežjèm** 'We are safe from the rain here'; **skrívati se pred radovédnimi ljudmí** 'to conceal oneself from curious people'; **Teló se bráni pred mikróbi** 'The body protects itself against microbes'

8.9.12 Prepositions indicating movement from a position that denotes the location of an object in relation to another object

These prepositions all take the genitive case and include: **(i)znad** 'from above'; **izza** 'from behind'; **izpod/spod** 'from below, underneath'; **izpred/spred** 'from in front of'; **(i)zmed** 'from among':

(i)znad:	**Iznad stréh se víje dìm**	Smoke rises from above the roofs
izza:	**Ávto je pripêljal izza ovínka**	A car appeared from around the corner
	Sónce je pokúkalo izza oblákov	The sun peeked out from behind the clouds
izpod/spod:	**Privlékel je tórbo izpod póstelje**	He dragged the bag out from under the bed
izpred/spred:	**Ávtobus odpélje izpred hotéla**	The bus leaves from in front of the hotel
	izgíniti izpred očí	to disappear before one's eyes

izmed: **Izmed vsèh oblék sem izbrála**   From among all the dresses I
   rdéčo   chose the red one

8.9.13   Prepositions denoting movement across, through, over or along

(a) **skóz(i)** + acc. 'through'
The use of this preposition usually implies that there is some form of obstruction, e.g.

preríniti se skózi gnéčo   to push one's way through a crowd
Skózi meglò so vídeli obríse stôlpnic   They could see the outlines of the skyscrapers through the mist

díhati skózi nós   to breathe through one's nose
glédati skózi ključávnico   to look through a keyhole
odíti skózi zádnja vráta   to leave by the backdoor
vréči skózi ôkno   to throw out of the window

(b) **čez** + acc. 'across, over, through'
This preposition implies movement across or over without obstruction, e.g.

skočíti čez járek   to leap over a ditch
íti čez móst   to cross a bridge
nosíti srájco čez hláče   to wear a shirt over one's trousers

(c) **prek(o)** + gen. 'over, through'
This preposition expresses movement towards another side. In many instances it is synonymous with **čez**, e.g.

skočíti preko ográje   to leap over a fence
Ôna je obésila tórbo preko ráme   She hung her bag over her shoulder
nosíti srájco preko hláč   to wear a shirt over one's trousers

Note 1: skózi, čez and preko may all be used in the sense 'via, by way of', e.g. **potováti v Zágreb skózi/čez Nôvo mésto** or **preko Nôvega mésta** 'to travel to Zagreb via Novo mesto'.

Note 2: In the spoken language čez replaces skózi in phrases like **čez vráta/ôkno** 'through the door/window'.

(d) **po** + loc. 'along, about, through, over, around'
This preposition denotes indeterminate movement across or over a surface, or movement along the length of something, e.g.

sprehájati se po párku   to walk around the park
Pôtok têče po dolíni   The stream runs through the valley
Hodíli smo po sejmíšču   We walked around the used car fair
   rábljenih avtomobílov
Vojáki so stópali po stŕmi   The soldiers marched along the steep
   stèzi   path

Ptíce skáčejo po véjah	The birds are hopping about the branches
Po lícih so se ji vsúle sólze	Tears poured down her cheeks

Note: **po** + loc. may also denote location at various points. In this case it is used with the locative plural of nouns, e.g. **Snég leží po gôrah** 'Snow lies on the hills'; **Tá rastlína ráste po prisójnih légah** 'This plant grows in places exposed to the sun'.

8.9.14   Prepositions denoting location around an object

okóli/okrog + gen. '(a)round'
These two prepositions are synonymous, e.g.

sedéti okóli/okrog míze	to sit round a table
zavézati si rúto okóli/okrog vratú	to tie a scarf around one's neck
Zêmlja króži okóli sónca	The earth revolves around the sun
smehljáj okóli njegóvih úst	the smile round his mouth
Césta kmálu zavíje okrog hríba	The path shortly winds round a hill

8.9.15   Prepositions denoting location or movement to a position on the near or far side of something

These prepositions include: **ónstran**, **ónkraj** 'on/to the far side of, beyond'; **tóstran** 'on/to this side'. They all take the genitive case, but are now considered archaic. In the modern language **ónstran**, **ónkraj** are replaced by **na drúgi stráni** (location) and **na drúgo strán** (motion), while **tóstran** is replaced by **na téj stráni** (location) and **na tó strán** (motion).

Examples of usage

híša ónstran jézera	the house on the far side of the lake
úpanje na sréčo ónkraj grôba	hope for happiness beyond the grave
Presélil se je ónstran réke	He moved to the far side of the river
Splézal je tóstran visôke ográje	He climbed over to this side of the high fence
Tóstran gózda je speljána trímska stèza	There is a running track on this side of the forest

8.9.16   Other spatial prepositions

(a) **zúnaj, ízven** + gen. 'outside (of)':

Òn stanúje zúnaj/ízven Ljubljáne	He lives outside Ljubljana
Híša je ízven méstnega obzídja	The house is outside the town walls
ízven streljája	out of range
Ôna imá délo zúnaj híše	She has work outside the house

(b) **znótraj** + gen. 'inside of, within'

híše znótraj méstnega obzídja	the houses within the town walls
nèsoglásja znótraj stránke	disagreements within the party

(c) **mímo** + gen. 'past'

Sáva têče mímo Zágreba	The Sava flows past Zagreb
Šlà je mímo cérkve	She walked past the church

(d) **dnò** + gen. 'at the bottom of'

Dnò mórja je zaklád	There is treasure at the bottom of the sea

(e) **kônec** + gen. 'at the end of'

Kônec pólja je gozdìč	There is a small grove at the end of the field

(f) **vrh** + gen. 'on top of, over'

Vrh stréhe je štórkljino gnézdo	There is a stork's nest on the top of the roof
Vrh obléke je nosíla plášč	She wore a coat over her dress

Note: **dnò**, **kônec** and **vrh** are now archaic literary forms and would be replaced by **na dnú, na kôncu, na vŕhu** in the modern language. In the second example given for **vrh**, **čez obléko** or **povŕh obléke** would nowadays be normal.

(g) **naspróti** + gen./dat. 'opposite'

Ládja se je zasídrala naspróti rtíča/rtíču Dôbre náde	The ship anchored off the Cape of Good Hope
Stanújemo naspróti gostílne/gostílni	We live opposite the pub
Sedím nasróti têbe	I am sitting opposite you

Note: **nasróti** may follow a pronoun in the dative case but is then considered to be an adverb, e.g. **Sedím têbi/ti nasróti** 'I am sitting opposite you'.

(h) **srédi** + gen. 'in the middle of, among'

Srédi mésta je velíko trgovín	There are many shops in the middle of town
Obstál je srédi céste	He stopped in the middle of the road
Míza stojí srédi sôbe	A table stands in the middle of the room
Híša stojí srédi drévja	A house stands among the trees

(i) **raz** + acc. 'from off of'
This preposition is now considered archaic and is replaced in the modern language by **z** + gen.: **Skôčil je raz kônja** 'He leapt from his horse'.

(j) **niz** + acc. 'down'
This preposition is now considered archaic and is replaced in the modern language by **po** + dat.:

Sólza polzí niz njéno líce	A tear runs down her cheek

Rímska césta je šlà niz réko do mésta	The Roman road ran down the river as far as the town

8.10 TEMPORAL PREPOSITIONS

8.10.1 Prepositions denoting 'time when'

(a) **ob** + loc. 'at, on'

  (i) This preposition is used in telling the time in response to the questions **kdáj** 'when?' or **ob katéri úri?** 'at what time?', e.g. **ob ênih, ob dvéh, ob sêdmih** 'at one, two, seven o'clock'.

Note: The number 'one' is used in the plural in this construction.

  Another rarely used alternative construction here is **ob** + the locative of the ordinal numeral and the noun **úra** 'hour', e.g. **ob trétji úri** 'at three o'clock'.

Note: In the case of 'one' the cardinal numeral is used with **úra**, e.g. **ob êni úri** 'at one o'clock'.

  For precise time involving the half hours the construction '**ob** + **pôl** + the loc. of the next following cardinal numeral' is used, e.g. **ob pôl ênih, ob pôl dvanájstih** 'at half past twelve, at half past eleven'.

  If the time phrase used is equivalent to English 'at five thirty' etc., then **ob** is used with the undeclined form of the cardinal number, e.g. **ob êna trídeset, ob pét trídeset** 'at one thirty, at five thirty'.

  For precise times involving the quarter hours or minutes **ob** is used with the undeclined form of the time phrase, e.g.

ob četŕt na trí	at a quarter past two
ob trí četŕt na štíri	at a quarter to four
ob desét čez šést	at ten past six
ob desét do sêdmih	at ten to seven
ob êna čez trí	at one minute past three
ob dvé do štírih	at two minutes to four

  If, however, the equivalent of English 'at one forty, at two twenty five' is used then **ob** takes the loc. plural of the hour + **in** + the nominative of the numeral indicating the minutes, e.g.

ob desêtih in pétindvájset	at ten twenty five
ob ôsmih in desét	at eight ten
ob sêdmih in četŕt	at seven fifteen

  (ii) This preposition is used to denote recurrent points in time in the sense 'on', e.g.

ob práznikih	on festive days
Tréning imámo ob četŕtkih	We have training on Thursdays

Ob nedéljah hódita ôče in máti na sprehòd	Mother and father go for a walk on Sundays

(iii) This preposition is used to mean 'at' with parts of the day, e.g.

ob pŕvem svítanju	at first light, dawn
ob sónčnem zahódu	at sunset
ob mráku	at dusk
Kám gréš ob téj pôzni úri?	Where are you going at this late hour?

(iv) This preposition is used to mean 'at, on, during' in phrases such as the following:

ob vulkánskem izbrúhu	during the volcanic eruption
ob kôncu vôjne	at the end of the war
Prišlà sva ob ístem čásu	We arrived at the same time
Ob téj priléžnosti ti vsè pojásnim	On this occasion I'll explain everything to you
ob môji vrnítvi	on my return
Ob slovésu so vsì jokáli	Everyone wept at the farewell
Ob vsáki priléžnosti jo obíšče	He visits her at every opportunity

(b) **v + loc.** 'in, within, at'

(i) This preposition expresses 'time when', when it is used with weeks, months, years, centuries, specific periods in time, stages in life or a stage in an activity or event, e.g.

Sréda je trétji dan v tédnu	Wednesday is the third day in the week
v jánuarju	in January
Umŕl je v zrélih létih	He died at a ripe old age
v létu Gospódovem	in the year of Our Lord
v zádnjih desêtih létih	in the last ten years
Román se dogája v devetnájstem stolétju	The novel is set in the nineteenth century
v prázgodovíni	in prehistory
V čásu kúge je umŕlo velíko ljudí	At the time of the plague many people died
V stárosti se je ukvárjal s fotografíranjem	In his old age he took up photography
v dôbi pubertéte	in puberty
v pretêklosti	in the past
v prihódnosti	in the future
V drúgem pólčasu je Arsenál vôdil s trémi góli	In the second half Arsenal led by three goals
V drúgem krógu volítev je zmágal nàš kandidát	Our candidate won in the second round of the elections

(ii) This preposition denotes 'within a certain period', e.g.

Shújšala boš za desét kilográmov v tréh mésecih	You will lose ten kilograms within three months
Tó bom narédil v dvéh úrah	I will do this within two hours

(c) **na** + acc. 'on, to, for, per, towards'

(i) This preposition means 'on' with reference to specific days or festivals, e.g.

Na pústni tôrek smo pêkli krôfe	On Shrove Tuesday we made doughnuts
Na božíčni dán smo iméli lépo kosílo	On Christmas Day we had a lovely meal

(ii) This preposition means 'per, every' in phrases indicating the frequency or repetition of an action within temporal units that follow one another regularly, e.g.

Na vsáke trí tédne bràt obíšče sêstro	The brother visits his sister every three weeks
Vídim ga tríkrat na léto	I see him three times per year
Ávtobus vózi na vsáke pól úre	A bus leaves every half hour

Note: In the phrases with **vsáke** it is possible to omit **na**.

(iii) This preposition denotes length of time or time subsequent to the completion of an action, e.g.

Obsodíli so ga na pét lét zapôra	They sentenced him to five years in prison
Spòr se je zavlékel na léta	The quarrel dragged on for years
Nastávila je budílko na šêsto úro	She set the alarm for six o'clock

(iv) This preposition denotes temporal approach, e.g.

Úra gré na pólnoč	It is getting on for/towards midnight
trí četŕt na ósem	a quarter to eight
Vŕnil se bom na jesén	I'll return towards Autumn

(d) **pri** + loc. 'at, in'
This preposition expresses coincidence in time in a number of contexts and is synonymous with **ob** + loc., e.g.

pri večérji	at dinner
pri poúku	at the lesson
pri bélem dnévu	in broad daylight
V šólo je šèl pri šéstih létih	He went to school at the age of six (also possible: **s šéstimi léti**)
člôvek pri šéstdesetih	a man in his sixties

(e) **za** + gen. 'during, in'
This preposition is used in phrases such as:

za čása Napóleona	during the time of Napoleon
Za mládih dní je težkó žível	He had a hard time in his youth

(f) **med** + instr. 'during, between'

(i) This preposition expresses the time during which an action takes place, e.g.

Stríc bêre časopís med kosílom	Uncle reads his newspaper during the meal
Med tédnom zgódaj vstája	He gets up early during the week
Med počítnicami velíko potúje	He travels a lot during the holidays
Takó je biló med vôjno	That's the way it was during the war

(ii) This preposition expresses the period between two points in time, e.g.

otrôci med pêtim in desêtim létom	children between five and ten years of age
Prišlà je na obísk med pêto in šêsto úro	She came to visit between five and six o'clock

(g) **preko** + gen. 'during'
This preposition expresses time during which something happens, e.g.

Kavárna je preko dnéva zapŕta	The coffee shop is closed during the day
Preko zíme se zêmlja spočíje	During the winter the earth rests

Note: In both these examples **preko** could be replaced by **čez** + acc., i.e. **čez dán/zímo**.

8.10.2 Prepositions denoting time limits

(a) **do** + gen. 'until'
This preposition indicates 'until a point in time', e.g.

Kóliko dní je šè do práznikov?	How many days are there until the holidays?
Úra je pét do dvanájstih	It is five to twelve
Bíl je pri zavésti do zádnjega trenútka	He was conscious until the very last moment
Vztrájali bomo do kônca	We will persevere until the very end
otrôci do pêtega léta stárosti	children under five (i.e. until they are five)

(b) **od** + gen. 'since, from'

(i) This preposition indicates the starting point in time, e.g.

Nísva se vídela od mladósti	We (d.) haven't seen each other since our youth
Žé od začétka mu nísem zaúpal	I distrusted him from the very beginning
Òn je bolán od sréde	He has been ill since Wednesday

(ii) This preposition can also denote the date when some publication appeared, e.g.

časopís od tôrka	Tuesday's newspaper (Note: a better construction would be **tôrkov časopís**, i.e. with a possessive adjective)
urédba od pŕvega márca 1965	the decree of the first of March 1965

Note: The prepositions **od** + gen. and **do** + gen. are often used together to denote the starting and finishing points of an action, e.g. **Vstópnice prodájajo od enájste do trínajste úre** 'The tickets are on sale from eleven to one o'clock'; **od zôre do mráka** 'from dawn to dusk'.

(c) **iz** + gen. 'since, from, of'
This preposition indicates a temporal starting point, e.g.

spomíni iz nekdánjih dní	memories of by-gone days
Poznám ga iz šólskih lét	I have known him since my school days

This prepositional construction is also used with **v** + acc. to indicate the repeated starting and finishing points of an action, e.g.

Živímo iz dnéva v dán	We live from day to day
Bolník je iz léta v léto slábši	The patient gets worse from year to year

(d) **z** + gen.
This preposition is used with the gen. form **dné** to denote the day of origin of a document or message, e.g.

písmo z dné pêtega septêmbra	a letter dated the 5th September
poročílo z dné trétjega márca	a bulletin dated the 3rd March

(e) **z/s** + instr. 'from, on, at'
This preposition denotes the time at which an action begins, e.g.

Z danášnjim dném veljájo nôvi predpísi	The new regulations are valid from today
Délati bo začél s pŕvim márcem	He will begin work on the 1st March
Bráti se je naučíla s pêtimi léti	She learnt to read at the age of five (also possible **pri pêtih létih**)

8.10.3 Prepositions denoting sequence in time

(a) **pred** + instr. 'before, ago'
This preposition denotes precedence in time, e.g.

Domá bóm pred poldnévom	I'll be home before mid-day
Pred dvéma létoma sem žível v méstu	Two years ago I lived in town
léta 45 pred nášim štétjem	45 B.C.
nóč pred bítko	the night before the battle
Bilí ste túkaj pred máno	You were here before me

(b) **izpred** + gen.
This preposition indicates coming from a time preceding a specific point in time, e.g.

víno izpred sêdmih lét	a seven-year-old wine
Vráčajo se razmére izpred vôjne	Pre-war conditions are returning

(c) **po** + loc. 'after, in'
This preposition denotes the time which is followed by an event or action, e.g.

Po tréh tédnih se vŕnem	I'll return in three weeks time
Ôče počíva po kosílu	Father rests after dinner
pŕva léta po osvobodítvi	the first years after the liberation
Prišlì so po dvanájsti	They came after twelve

(d) **za** + instr. 'after'
This preposition indicates sequence in time, e.g.

Za dnévom príde nóč	Night follows day
Za tôrkom je sréda	Wednesday follows Tuesday
Takó je šlò úro za úro, dán za dném, léto za létom	Thus it went on hour after hour, day after day, year after year

(e) **za** + acc. 'for'
This preposition denotes the amount of time taken to complete an action, e.g.

Déla imá za trí dní	He has enough work for three days
Odpotováli so za vès téden	They have gone away for the whole week
najéti híšo za vsè polétje	to rent a house for the whole summer
Obíšče nas za nôvo léto	He will visit us for the New Year

8.10.4 Prepositions denoting temporal approach

These prepositions are **proti** + dat., **k/h** + dat. and **pod** + acc. 'towards'. In the modern language **proti** is the preposition most commonly used in this sense.

proti + dat.: **Prišèl bo proti večéru**	He will arrive towards evening
Biló je proti ôsmi úri	It was getting on for eight o'clock

	Račúne poravnámo proti kôncu léta	We settle our accounts towards the end of the year
	Zaspál je proti jútru	He fell asleep towards morning
k/h + dat.:	Délo gré h kôncu	The work is coming to an end
	Napàd pričakújejo k jútru	They are expecting an attack towards morning
pod + acc.:	Pod jesén se začnêjo zbírati lástovke	The swallows begin to assemble towards Autumn

8.10.5   Other temporal prepositions

(a) **čez** + acc. 'in, during, after'

(i) This preposition denotes the time during which an event or action takes place, e.g.

| Sôva se čez dán skríva | An owl hides away during the day |
| Prihája samó ob nedéljah, čez téden ga ní | He only comes on Sundays, during the week he is not here (Note: also possible here **med tédnom**) |

(ii) This preposition denotes the time after which something will be done, e.g.

| Vŕnem se čez desét minút | I'll be back in ten minutes |
| Pláčo za tá mésec boš dobíl čez štíri dní | You will receive your wages for this month in four days time. |

Note: The use of this preposition in telling the time, e.g. **Úra je dvé čez pólnoč** 'It is two minutes after midnight'.

(b) **skózi** + acc. 'during'
This preposition is synonymous with **čez** + acc. and **preko** + gen. (but not common) in the sense that it can denote time during which an action takes place, e.g.

| Skózi/čez polétje živí ob mórju | During the summer he lives by the seaside |
| Takó konzervírana hrána se skózi zímo/preko zíme ne pokvári | Food preserved this way does not go off during the winter |

(c) **srédi** + gen. 'in the middle of'

| Srédi dnéva je bíl že piján | He was already drunk in the middle of the day |
| Preselíli so se srédi lánskega léta | They moved in the middle of last year |

Zbúdil se je srédi nočí	He woke in the middle of the night
Tó se je zgodílo srédi bélega dné	This happened in broad daylight
Zmótil me je srédi déla	He disturbed me in the middle of my work

(d) **ízven/zúnaj** + gen. 'outside (of)'
These prepositions are synonymous although **zúnaj** is used less frequently and is more colloquial, e.g.

Zdravník sprejéma bolníke ízven urádnih úr	The doctor receives patients outside office hours
zúnaj/ízven sezóne	out of season
ízven délovnega čása	outside working hours

(e) **okrog/okóli** + gen. 'about, around'
These synonymous prepositions denote approximate time, e.g.

okóli/okrog nôvega léta	around New Year
Príde okóli/okrog enájstih	He will come at about eleven o'clock
okrog léta 1905	in about 1905

(f) **blízu** + gen. 'close to'

blízu smŕti	close to death
Môja žéna je blízu poróda	My wife is close to delivery
Vàš móž je žé blízu trídesetih	Your husband is already close to thirty

8.11 PREPOSITIONS WITH CAUSAL MEANINGS

(a) **zarádi/zavóljo/spríčo/vsled** + gen. 'because of'
These prepositions express the cause of an action over which the subject has no control. Of these the modern language prefers **zarádi**. The preposition **zavóljo** is very literary, **spríčo** is colloquial and **vsled** archaic and its use not approved of, e.g.

Zarádi meglè in nèprimérne hitrósti se je zgodílo vèč nesréč	Because of the fog and inappropriate speed a lot of accidents happened
Izpustíli so ga zarádi pománjkanja dokázov	They released him because of a lack of evidence
Nàjbóljši igrálec zarádi poškódbe ní nastópil na tékmi	Because of injury the best player did not play in the match
Opravíčila je odsôtnost zarádi bolézni	She justified her absence because of illness
V gostílno zahája zavóljo lépe natákarice	He goes to the inn because of the beautiful waitress

| Spríčo pománjkanja dokázov so ga oprostíli | They acquitted him because of the lack of evidence |
| Vsled bolézni ní prišlà | She didn't come because of illness |

(b) **od** + gen. 'because of, from, by, with, out of'

This preposition denotes the physical and emotional cause of something, e.g.

bíti zadét od stréle	to be struck by lightning
rána od nôža	a knife wound
Vès se trése od jéze	He is shaking with anger
opíkan od komárjev	bitten by mosquitoes
razjéden od čŕvov	wormeaten
od sónca ožgán obràz	a sunburnt face
modríce od udárcev	bruises from the blows
umírati od kôz	to die of smallpox
Od tvôjega klepetánja me žé bolíjo ušésa	My ears ache from your prattling
jókati od bolečíne	to weep with pain
Od strahú je omedléla	She fainted out of fright
Očí se mu svétijo od radovédnosti	His eyes gleam with curiosity
Od njêga imám samó škódo	I have nothing but grief because of him (better here would be **zarádi njêga**)

(c) **iz** + gen. 'out of, by, in'

This preposition like **od** + gen. denotes the emotional cause of something, but not the physical cause, e.g.

tát iz naváde	a thief by habit
Tó je naredíla iz radovédnosti	She did it out of curiosity
Odšèl je iz protésta	He left in protest
storíti kàj iz strahú/iz zavísti/iz usmíljenja/iz lákomnosti/iz gôle hudobíje	to do something out of fear/envy/pity/greed/pure mischief
Iz tŕme ní šèl	He didn't go out of stubbornness

(d) **za** + instr. 'of, with'

This construction is used to express the physical cause of an action or state and is found with verbs meaning 'to be/fall ill with' or 'to die of', e.g.

Bolúje za jétiko	He has tuberculosis
Zboléla je za rákom	She fell ill with cancer
V srédnjem véku so ljudjé pogósto zbolévali za kúgo	In the middle ages people often caught the plague
Umírali so za kôzami	They died of smallpox

(e) **za** + acc. 'for, over'
This preposition expresses the reason why something happens, e.g.

Zapŕli so ga za vèleizdájo	They imprisoned him for treason
kázen za zločín	punishment for a crime
razjezíti se za vsáko malénkost	to get angry over every trifle
Za tíste beséde ti bo žàl	You will regret those words
Bíl je kaznován za svôjo brezbrížnost	He was punished for his carelessness

(f) **po** + loc. 'for, through'
This preposition expresses the reason for an action or state, e.g.

Tó se je zgodílo po tvôji krívdi	This happened through your fault
Bléd sloví po svôji lepôti	Bled is famous for its beauty
Njén móž je znán po grobósti	Her husband is well known for his rudeness

(g) **skózi** + acc. 'because of'
The use of this construction is not considered good style and normally it would be replaced by **zarádi** + gen., e.g.

Tá organizácija je postála pomémbnejša skózi krítike nasprótnikov
This organization became more significant because of the criticisms of its opponents

(h) **nad** + instr. 'with, for, in'
This preposition expresses the reason for an emotion indicated by a verb or verbal noun, e.g.

jókati nad kóm	to weep for someone
zgrážati se nad čím/kóm	to be disgusted with something/someone
Razočárani smo bilí nad sodélavci	We were disappointed in our fellow workers

(i) **na** + acc. 'at, to'
This preposition expresses the cause of a response, e.g.

Ozŕl se je na njegóv krík	At his cry he looked round
Oglásil se je na tŕkanje	He responded to the knock
Odgovoríti móram na nékaj klícev	I have to reply to some calls

(j) **k** + dat. 'on'
This preposition expresses the reason when used with the verb **čestítati** 'to congratulate', e.g.

Čestítam k diplómi/k uspéhu/k rôjstnemu dnévu	I congratulate you on your degree/success/birthday

Normally, however, **čestítati** is used with the preposition **za** + acc.

(k) **pri** + loc. 'because of, given'

This construction may express the circumstances that cause an action or event, e.g.

Pri tólikih stróškíh konkurénca ní mogóča	Given such large costs competition is impossible

(l) **pod** + instr. 'under'

This construction may express the circumstances which cause an action, e.g.

Opotéka se pod têžkim breménom	He is staggering under a heavy burden
Pod radovédnimi poglédi sosédov je vsà zardéla	Under the inquisitive gaze of the neighbours she blushed

8.12 PREPOSITIONS DENOTING PURPOSE OR INTENTION

(a) **zarádi** + gen. 'for'

This construction denotes the purpose for which an action is intended, e.g.

Járke so skopáli zarádi obrámbe mésta	They dug ditches for the town's defence
Ostál je samó zarádi dôbrega vtísa	He stayed only to create a good impression

(b) **za** + acc. 'for'

This construction indicates the purpose for which something is designed or for which an action is performed, e.g.

stáva za denár	a bet for money
bòj za obstánek	the struggle for existence
prôstor za kadílce	smoking area
honorár za člának	fee for an article
pripráviti mesó za pečênje	to prepare meat for roasting
spêči kokóš za večérjo	to roast a chicken for dinner
omárica za pŕvo pomóč	first aid cupboard

(c) **za** + instr. 'for'

This construction indicates the target or aim of an action, e.g.

Òn teží za bogástvom	He strives for riches
Beráč je stíkal po smetéh za hráno	The beggar rummaged through the rubbish for food
lòv za zakládom	the search for treasure

(d) **po** + acc. 'for'
This preposition denotes the object which someone goes to get, e.g.

íti po zdravníka	to go for the doctor
Po káj si prišèl?	What have you come to get?
Skôči v lekárno po zdravílo	Pop into the chemist's for the medicine
séči v žèp po denár	to reach in one's pocket for money

(e) **po** + loc. 'for'

(i) This construction denotes the object which a verbal action seeks to reach, e.g.

Pès je hlástnil po múhi	The dog snapped at the fly
hlástniti po ponúdbi	to snap at an offer
Kmèt je ségel po pálici	The peasant reached for his stick

(ii) This construction indicates the purpose for which the action is performed, e.g.

íti v mésto po oprávkih/po nakúpih	to go into town on business/ to do some shopping

(f) **k** + dat. 'for'
This preposition expresses purpose in the following phrases:

zbráti se k posvetovánju	to meet for a deliberation
k dežjù se priprávlja	It is getting ready to rain

(g) **proti** + dat. 'against'
This construction follows a noun or verb and indicates the intention to avoid something negative, e.g.

zdravílo proti grípi	medicine against flu
tabléte proti glavobôlu	headache tablets
bòj proti rásnemu razločevánju	the fight against racism
cepíti proti dávici	to innoculate against diphtheria

(h) **v** + acc. 'for'
In certain phrases this prepositional construction denotes the purpose of an object or action, e.g.

večérja v část gôsta	a dinner in honour of a guest
maškaráda v koríst slépih	a fancy dress ball in aid of the blind (Note: also possible **za koríst**)
rêči kàj v opravičílo	to say something by way of an apology (Note: also possible **kot opravičílo**)

(i)   **na** + acc. 'for, to'
      This construction indicates purpose in the following phrases:

píti na zdrávje kóga	to drink to the health of someone
klíc na pomóč	a cry for help

8.13   PREPOSITIONS EXPRESSING MEANS AND MANNER

The means, instrument, tool or resource with which an action is carried out is expressed by the following prepositions:

(a)   **z/s** + instr. 'with'

pisáti s svínčnikom	to write with a pencil
pokríti strého z opéko	to tile a roof
umíti se z mŕzlo vôdo	to wash in cold water
igráti se z žógo	to play with a ball
hodíti z bérglami	to walk with crutches

(b)   **na** + acc. 'with, by'

délati na rôko	to do by hand
na pŕste računáti	to count on one's fingers
vídeti na lástne očí	to see with one's own eyes
mlín na véter	a windmill
igráti na klavír	to play the piano
motór na bencín	a petrol engine

(c)   **na** + loc. 'with, from'

kúhati na ólju	to cook with oil
učíti se na napákah	learn from one's mistakes

(d)   **v** + acc. 'in, on, with'

zavít v odéjo	wrapped in a blanket
brísati si rôke v predpásnik	to wipe one's hand on an apron

(e)   **pod** + acc. 'under'

operírati pod narkózo	to operate under anaesthetic
opazováti pod mikroskópom	to observe under a microscope

(f)   **po** + loc. 'by'

posláti po póšti/železnici/zráku	to send by post/train/air
sporočíti po rádiu/telefónu	to inform by radio/telephone
hodíti po pŕstih	to walk on one's toes

The manner in which an action is carried out is expressed by the following prepositions:

(a) **v** + acc. 'in'

zavpíti v èn glás	to cry out in one voice

(b) **na** + acc. 'at, by'

znáti na pámet	to know by heart
kričáti na vès glás	to cry at the top of one's voice

(c) **po** + loc. 'according to, by'

po málem	little by little
po nakljúčju	by chance
ravnáti se po pravílu	to conform to the rule
igráti po poslúhu	to play by ear
po pravíci ali po krivíci	rightly or wrongly

(d) **v** + loc. 'in'

plesáti v párih	to dance in pairs
živéti v pričakovánju	to live in expectation
posnéti v bárvah	to photograph in colour
Véter píha v súnkih	The wind blows in gusts
plačáti v obrókih	to pay in instalments (nowadays usually **na obróke**)
íti v gósjem rédu	to walk in single file

(e) **z/s** + instr. 'with, in, at'

govoríti s hrípavim glásom	to speak in a hoarse voice
vozíti s prevelíko hitróstjo	to drive at too great a speed
premágati nasprótnike z lahkôto	to defeat one's opponents easily
prodájati z izgúbo	to sell at a loss

(f) **skózi** + acc. 'through'

žvížgati skózi zobé	to whistle through one's teeth
Govôri razlóčno in nè skózi nós	Speak clearly and not through your nose
smejáti se skózi sólze	to laugh through tears

(g) **od** + gen. 'by'

živéti od déla/trgovíne	to live by work/trade

8.14   PREPOSITIONS EXPRESSING CONCESSIVE MEANINGS

(a) **kljúb** + dat. 'despite, in spite of'
This is the most common concessive preposition:

uspéti kljúb vsèm težávam	to succeed despite all difficulties
íti na sprehòd kljúb dežjù	to go for a walk in spite of the rain
Kljúb tému ostáneva prijátelja	In spite of this we (d.) remain friends

(b) **navzlíc** + dat. 'despite, in spite of'

Navzlíc vsèm razočáranjem je ostál idealíst	In spite of all disappointments he remained an idealist

Note: This preposition is nowadays often used in the media.

(c) **vzlíc** + dat./**póleg** + gen. 'despite, in spite of'
These two prepositions are now archaic and in the modern language are replaced by **kljúb**:

Vzlíc brádi sem ga spoznál	In spite of the beard I recognised him
Póleg vsèh slabósti je dóber člôvek	In spite of all his failings he is a good man

(d) **ob** + loc./**pri** + loc. 'despite, in spite of'

Ob/pri vsèm bogástvu je nesréčen	In spite of all his wealth he is unhappy

(e) **nè gledé na/nègledé na** 'in spite of, notwithstanding, regardless of'

Nègledé na razlíčnost mnênj je sodelovánje mogóče	Notwithstanding the difference of opinions cooperation is possible
nègledé na poslédice	regardless of the consequences
Sprejét je bíl nègledé na tó, da je mlád	He was accepted despite the fact that he was young

8.15   PREPOSITIONS EXPRESSING QUANTIFYING RELATIONSHIPS

(a) **za** + acc. 'for'
This preposition expresses quantity, measure, amount, e.g.

príti za êno úro	to come for one hour
prodáti za 3000 tólarjev	to sell for 3000 tolars
Za èn dán mi posódi knjígo	Lend the book to me for one day
umakníti se za korák	to take a step back
povéčati za štírikrat	to increase fourfold

(b) **v** + acc. 'with'

This preposition indicates size in relation to a building, e.g. **híša v trí nadstrópja** 'a three-storeyed house' (nowadays more usually **s trémi nadstrópji**);

(c) **okóli/okrog** + gen. 'around, about'

This preposition expresses approximation when used with numbers or dates, e.g.

Prídi okóli desêtih	Come about twelve
Biló je okóli/okrog léta 1930	It was about 1930
temperatúra okrog níčle	a temperature around zero

(d) **od** + gen. 'from'

This construction denotes the starting point of an amount or quantity, e.g.

Té stvarí stánejo od stó dólarjev navzgòr	These things cost from one hundred dollars upwards

(e) **do** + gen. 'to'

This construction denotes the limit of an amount or quantity, e.g.

zapòr do trí dní	imprisonment for three days
štéti do desét	to count up to ten
Téhtnica je do tisočínke gráma natánčna	The scales are exact to within one thousandth of a gram
Goróvje se vzpénja do trí tísoč métrov	The mountains rise to 3000 feet

(f) **preko** + gen., **čez** + acc. 'over'

These two prepositions express excessive amount or measure, e.g.

Profésor imá preko šéstdeset lét	The professor is over sixty years old
píti preko mére	to drink excessively
Vôda mi séga čez pás	The water is over my waist
Njén bràt méri čez dvá métra	Her brother is over two metres tall

(g) **po** + acc. 'in, each'

This preposition has a distributive meaning, e.g.

Študênti so prihájali êden po êden/po dvá/po štírje	The students came in ones/twos/fours
Púnce so prihájale êna po êna/po dvé/po štíri	The girls came in ones/twos/fours
Jájca so bilà na tŕgu po êno márko	The eggs cost one mark each at the market

(h) **po** + loc. 'at, in'

This construction expresses amount or measure, e.g.

prodájati po nízki céni	to sell at a low price
Po čém je víno?	How much is the wine?
jemáti zdravílo po kápljicah	to take medicine in drops
prodájati zemljíšče po parcélah	to sell a piece of land in plots

8.16 PREPOSITIONS EXPRESSING COMPARISON

(a) **zráven** + gen. 'in comparison with'

Zráven drúgih je bíl právi velikán	He was a true giant in comparison with others

(b) **póleg** + gen. 'in comparison with'

Póleg njêga je kàkor pritlíkavec	He is like a dwarf compared with him

(c) **gledé na** + acc. 'in comparison with'

Gledé na préjšnje stánje je tó naprédek	This is an improvement compared to the previous state of affairs

(d) **ob** + loc. 'in comparison with'

Ob njêm sem kàkor pritlíkavec	I am like a dwarf compared with him

(e) **naspróti** + dat. 'in comparison with'

Márčevske céne so nasproti decêmbrskim zeló pádle	Prices in March fell sharply in comparison with those in December

(f) **proti** + dat. 'in comparison with'

Môje skrbí so májhne proti tvôjim	My worries are small compared to yours

8.17 OTHER IMPORTANT PREPOSITIONS

(a) **brez** +gen. 'without'
This preposition denotes the absence or lack of something, e.g.

otròk brez stáršev	a child without parents
bíti brez déla	to be without work
íti v kíno brez dovoljênja	to go to the cinema without permission
prebíti nóč brez spánja	to spend the night without sleep
brez izjéme	without exception

(b) **ob** + acc. 'without'
This construction expresses the loss of something positive or valuable, e.g.

Kráva je ob mléko	The cow has no milk
Ali si ob pámet?	Are you out of your mind?
bíti ob slúžbo	to have no job
Prepróga je šlà ob bárvo	The carpet has lost its colour

(c) **rázen** + gen. 'except, apart from'

Rázen dvéh razbítih ôken je bilà híša nèpoškodována	Except for two broken windows the house was undamaged
Prišlí so vsì rázen stríca	Everyone came except uncle
Ne zná drúgega jezíka rázen máternega	He does not know any language apart from his mother tongue

(d) **za** + acc. 'for, instead of'
This construction denotes substitution, e.g.

| **zaménjati ênosôbno stanovánje za dvósôbno** | to exchange a one-room flat for a two-room flat |
| **Predsédnika ní biló. Zánj je podpísal tájnik** | The President was not there. The secretary signed for him |

(e) **namésto** + gen. 'instead of'

Pójdi tjà namésto mêne	Go there instead of me
Namésto pêtih sta prišlà samó dvá	Instead of five only two came
Namésto knjíge sem kúpil bonbóne	I bought sweets instead of a book

(f) **zóper** + acc. 'against'
This preposition denotes opposition, disagreement, physical resistance to, e.g.

izrêči se zóper deklarácijo	to speak out against a declaration
protestírati zóper nôve zakóne	to protest against the new laws
Tó se je zgodílo zóper njegóvo váljo	This happened against his will
Tó je zóper običáje	This is contrary to custom
Ljúdstvo se je dvígnilo zóper vodítelje	The people rose against their leaders

(g) **o** + loc. 'about, concerning, on'

govoríti o kóm	to speak about someone
Káj mísliš o včérajšnji predstávi?	What do you think about yesterday's performance?
Nímam informácij o tém	I have no information about this
predávanje o zgodovíni póštnih známk	a lecture on the history of postage stamps

(h) **z/s** + instr. 'with'
This construction denotes (a) the presence of a quality or property, (b) accompaniment, (c) reciprocity with certain reflexive verbs, e.g.

(i)   **kònj z dólgo grívo** 'a horse with a long mane'; **púnca s čŕnimi kítami** 'a girl with black pigtails'

(ii) **Na obísk je prišèl njén sín z družíno** 'Her son came to visit with his family; **Pêljal se je v dvigálu s tájnico** 'He travelled in the lift with the secretary'; **jésti s kolégi** 'to eat with one's colleagues'

(iii) **Dogovóril sem se s predsédnikom** 'I conferred with the president'; **O tém se ne bóm prepíral s tebój** 'I will not quarrel with you about this'; **popólnoma se strínjati s kóm** 'to fully agree with someone'

(i)   **póleg** + gen. 'besides, apart from, in addition to'

Póleg dôbrih lastnósti je iméla túdi slábe	In addition to good qualities she also had bad ones
Rastlína potrebúje póleg vláge túdi sónčno svetlôbo	Apart from moisture a plant also needs sunlight

(j)   **gledé** + gen./**gledé na** + acc. 'with regard to, in respect of'

predpísi gledé dohodníne	regulations with regard to income
Gledé téga imám nékaj pomíslekov	I have some doubts with regard to this
preizkús materiála gledé na odpórnost	the testing of material with regard to its resistance
océniti délo gledé na njegóvo umétniško vrédnost	to value a work in respect of its artistic worth

(k)   **vpríčo** + gen. 'in the presence of'

Vpríčo otrók ne bi sméli takó govoríti	They should not talk that way in the presence of children
Vpríčo drúgih so lepó ravnáli z njó	They treated her well in the presence of others

Note: In the media **vpríčo** is sometimes used instead of **zarádi** 'because of', e.g. **Vpríčo nastálega položája je biló tréba nékaj ukreníti** 'Because of the situation that had arisen something had to be done'.

(l)   **povŕh(u)/vrh** + gen. 'in addition to'

Bilà je lépa, vrh téga pa túdi bogáta	She was beautiful and in addition also rich
Ker je vôzil piján, so mu povŕh(u)/vrh drúgega vzéli vozníško dovoljênje	Because he drove while drunk, in addition to everything else they took away his driving licence

(m) **za** + acc. 'as, for'
This construction is used with certain verbs to denote the function a person fulfils, e.g.

poklícati kóga za príčo	to call someone as a witness
veljáti za poštenjáka	to pass for an honest man
Izdája se za zdravníka	He passes himself off as a doctor
najéti kóga za pomočníco	to hire someone as an assistant
vzéti kóga za možá	to take someone as a husband
izvolíti kóga za predsédnika	to elect someone as president

(n) **po** + loc. 'for, by, of, about, from, in accordance with, of'
This prepositional construction has many different meanings:

(i) It expresses the object of a mental or emotional activity, e.g.

potréba po spánju	a need for sleep
pohlèp po denárju	a craving for money
žêlja po popólnosti	a desire for perfection
Hrepenél je po vestéh svôje družíne	He yearned for news of his family
hrepenéti po míru	to yearn for peace
povprášati po znáncu	to enquire about an acquaintance

(ii) It denotes a criteria for judgement, e.g.

spoznáti kóga po hóji/glásu	to recognise someone by/from their walk/voice
postáviti se v vŕsto po velikósti	to form a queue according to height

(iii) It is used after a noun to denote trade or kinship, e.g.

mehánik po poklícu	a mechanic by trade
Slovénec po ródu	A Slovene by birth

(iv) It can indicate the source of a sense or perception, e.g.

Diší po médu	It smells of honey
Smrdél je po žgánju	He stank of drink
okús po ánanasu	the taste of pineapple

8.18   PREPOSITIONS GOVERNING PREPOSITIONAL PHRASES

A distinctive feature of Slovene is that the prepositions **za, do, od** may govern a prepositional phrase.
In the case of **za** the prepositional phrase remains unchanged, e.g.

vlák za v Máribor	the train for Maribor
prepróga za pred pósteljo	the rug for the bedside

Íščemo délavca za k strôju	We are seeking a machine operator
zbudíti otrôka za v šólo	to wake the child for school
knjíge za na razstávo	the books to be sent to the exhibition
Prídi za čez polétje k nàm	Come to us for the summer

In the case of **do** and **od** the noun in the prepositional phrase governed by them takes the genitive case, e.g.

v vôdi do nad kolén	above the knees in water
Vôda séga do pod kolén	The water reaches to below the knees
zapét do pod bráde	buttoned up to the chin
zavíhati rokáve do nad komólca	to roll up one's sleeves above the elbow
Poznáva se od pred vôjne	We have known each other since before the war

Note: The following time phrases where the prepositional phrase remains unchanged following do: **Predpís je veljál do pred krátkim** 'The rule held good until recently'; **do pred krátkim** 'until recently'; **Do pred trémi dnévi se šè ní védelo** 'It was still not known until three days ago'.

9 CONJUNCTIONS

9.1 TYPES OF CONJUNCTIONS

Slovene conjunctions are divided into the following two types:

(a) Coordinating conjunctions which are used to link words, word groups or clauses of equal importance, e.g.

ôče in sín	father *and* son
Tó so beséde, a nè dejánja	These are words *but* not actions
Máma je prišlà domóv in začéla kúhati	Mother came home *and* began cooking

(b) Subordinating conjunctions, which join a subordinate clause to a main clause in order to develop some aspect of what is said in the main clause, e.g.

Ní mógel príti, ker je bíl bolán	He could not come *because* he was ill
Večérja mi ní téknila, čepràv je bilà izvŕstna	I didn't enjoy the dinner, even *though* it was excellent

Conjunctions may consist of one word (simple conjunctions), e.g. **pa** 'but'; **in** 'and' or two or more words (complex conjunctions), e.g. **medtém ko** 'while'; **kljúb tému da** 'although, despite'. Complex conjunctions may be divided into the following two types:

(a) Those formed from an adverb + a simple conjunction, e.g. **takó da** 'so that'; **čèš da** 'as if to say'.

(b) Those formed from a preposition + demonstrative pronoun and a simple conjunction, e.g. **namésto téga da** 'instead of'; **kljúb tému da** 'although'; **s tém da** 'but'.

Certain conjunctions consist of two parts. Either (a) the same conjunction occurs before both the linked words or clauses, e.g. **bódi(si) . . . bódi(si)** 'either . . . or', e.g.

Ptíce si délajo gnézdo bódisi v grmóvju bódisi v véjah
Birds make their nests either in bushes or in branches

or (b) the conjunction is a correlative conjunction consisting of two distinct parts, the second being necessary to complete the first, e.g. **ne samó . . . àmpak túdi** 'not only . . . but', e.g.

Péter ní samó nadárjen, àmpak túdi príden
Peter is not only gifted, but also hard working

Some conjunctions are synonymous in meaning, e.g. **ko/če** 'if', **in/ter** 'and'. In these instances one form is the normally used form and the other higher style, rarer or even archaic. For example in the sentence **Prídi in/ter pogléj** 'Come and look' the form **ter** would be less commonly used than **in**.

Certain conjunctions may also fulfil various functions. For example the coordinating conjunction **pa** may be connective or adversative, while the subordinating conjunction **da** may be causal, explanatory or concessive.

9.2 COORDINATING CONJUNCTIONS

These conjunctions link together two clauses or words of the same grammatical type. They may be subdivided into the following types: connective, intensifying, explanatory, consecutive, causal, adversative and disjunctive conjunctions.

9.2.1 Connective conjunctions

The connective conjunctions are (a) **in/ter/pa** 'and', and (b) the negative connective conjunctions **níti . . . níti** or **ne . . . ne** 'neither . . . nor'.

(a) **in** is neutral, **ter** is literary and **pa** is colloquial, e.g.

Pozábil je tórbo in/ter/pa dežník	He forgot the bag and the umbrella
Sezídali so híšo ter so jo pokríli s skódlami	They built a house and covered it with shingle
Ôkno zaprí, pa vráta túdi	Open the window and the door too

To avoid the multiple use of **in**, the forms **ter** or **pa** are used instead of the second **in**, e.g.

Vzêmi čévlje in copáte ter/pa májico in srájco	Take shoes and slippers and a vest and shirt

Note: The use of **in** is compulsory in certain phrases, e.g. **nikjér in nikóli** 'never ever'; **stáro in mládo** 'old and young'; **krátko in málo** 'briefly'; **čez dŕn in stŕn** 'across country'; **skóz in skóz/čéz in čéz** 'thoroughly'; **bôlj in bôlj** 'more and more'.

(b) The negative conjunctions **níti . . . níti**, **ne . . . ne** are used with a negated verb as follows:

níti òn níti njegóva sêstra	neither he nor his sister
Níti ga nísem vídel níti ga nísem slíšal	I neither saw him nor heard him
Ne zná ne bráti ne pisáti	He knows neither how to read nor write

Note: It is also possible to use **ne . . . níti**, e.g. **Níma ne bráta níti sêstre** 'He has neither a brother nor a sister'.

9.2.2 Intensifying conjunctions

These conjunctions express a greater degree or extent of something in the second clause than that expressed in the first clause. They include the following:

ne samó/lè . . . àmpak/tèmveč/màrveč túdi;   not only but also
  takó . . . kàkor/kot
žé . . . káj šelè   let alone

Examples of usage

Dobíl je ne samó večérjo, àmpak túdi prenočíšče
He got not only a dinner, but also a place to stay for the night

Dobíla je ne samó smučí, tèmveč túdi drsálke
She got not only skis but also skates

Zánjo bi bilà to ne lè sréča, màrveč túdi část
For her this would be not only good fortune but also an honour

Note: **ne samó . . . àmpak túdi** is the conjunction normally used. **Ne lè** in the first clause and **tèmveč túdi** in the second clause are less common, while **màrveč túdi** in the second clause is very rare and very literary.

Žé hódi težkó, káj šelè têče
He walks with difficulty, let alone run

Žé ráhel ugóvor težkó prenêse, káj šelè krítiko
He finds it difficult enough to stand gentle contradiction let alone criticism

Note: If the main clause is negated then **žé** is omitted and **káj šelè** used alone, e.g. **Tákrat níso poználi Amêrike, káj šelè Avstrálijo** 'At that period America was unknown, let alone Australia'; **Od strahú ní môgla naredíti níti koráka, káj šelè zbežáti** 'Out of fear she could not even take a step, let alone run away'

S fílmom so bilí zadovóljni takó gledálci kot krítiki
Not only the viewers but also the critics were pleased with the film

Izrékam vam sožálje takó v svôjem imému kàkor túdi v iménu svôje družíne
I am expressing my condolences to you not only in my name but also in the name of my family

9.2.3 Explanatory conjunctions

These conjunctions introduce a clause which defines more precisely or corrects the previous clause: **tó je** 'that is (to say), namely'; **in sícer/in tó** 'and what is more'.

Examples of usage

Jóže se je vŕnil prepôzno, tó je šelè ob enájstih zvečér
Jože came back very late, that is to say only at eleven o'clock in the evening

Telefoníral mi je zvečér, in sícer/in tó ob ôsmih
He telephoned me this evening and that was at eight o'clock

V šólo prihája od dáleč, in tó s kolésom
He comes to school from far away and what is more he comes by bike

9.2.4 Consecutive conjunctions

These conjunctions introduce a clause denoting the consequence or result of the action in the main clause. They include: **zató/zatórej/pa/tórej/takó/tedàj** 'therefore, consequently, thus, accordingly'.

Zató is the conjunction normally used in this sense, while **zatórej** is its emphasised equivalent. **Pa** in the second clause expresses the logical conclusion or consequence of what is stated in the first clause.

Examples of usage

Prosíli so me, zató sem jim pomágal
They asked me, therefore I helped them

Nihčè nóče popustíti, zatórej sporazúma ne bó
Nobody wants to yield, therefore there will be no agreement

Na céstah je polédica, pa/zató/zatórej se promèt odvíja počási
The roads are slippery, therefore the traffic is moving slowly

Tórej used instead of **zató(rej)** is stylistically marked. It is normally used in the second clause when this indicates a conclusion that is reached from the premises in the first clause, e.g.

Míslim, tórej sem
I think therefore I am

Nímaš čása, tórej ne prídeš
If you do not have the time, then you will not come

Ní pazíla na úlice, takó se je izgubíla
She did not pay any attention to the streets and therefore she got lost

Dólgo se nísmo vídeli, tedàj si imámo dôsti povédati
We have not seen each other for a long time and therefore we have a lot tell
    each other

9.2.5 Causal conjunctions

These conjunctions include: **zakáj/kájti/sàj**, 'for, since, because'; **sícer (pa)/ drugáče** 'otherwise'; **nàmreč** 'because'.

Zakáj and **kájti** are very literary forms and are normally replaced by the subordinating conjunctions **ker** or **zató ker** (see **9.3.2**). **Sícer** indicates that something has been prevented because of the action in the main clause. **Sícer pa** emphasises the reason for the main statement.

Examples of usage

Nobêden ne spí, kájti napàd pričakújejo vsák trenútek
Nobody is asleep because they are expecting an attack at any minute

Vozíli smo prevídno, kájti césta je bilà spólzka
We drove carefully since the road was slippery

Nihčè ní prišèl v šólo, zakáj vsì smo bilí bólni
Nobody came to school because we were all ill

Mój ôče je dóber šofêr, sàj v dvájsetih létih ní imél nobêne prométne nesréče
My father is a good driver for he has not had an accident in twenty years

Poznáš jo, sàj je hodíla s tebój v šólo
You know her because she went to school with you

Psà smo oddáli, sícer bi nam požŕl vsè kokóši
We gave the dog away otherwise he would have eaten all the chickens

Pohíti, sícer boš prišèl pôzno
Hurry, otherwise you will arrive late

Za kônec tédna navádno kàm odídemo, sícer pa smo zméraj domá
We usually go away for the weekend, otherwise we are always at home

Ne bóm mógel príti, nímam nàmreč čása
I will not be able to come because I haven't got time

Ne mudí se mu, drugáče bi žé odšèl
He is not in a hurry, otherwise he would have left already

9.2.6 Adversative conjunctions

These conjunctions express contrast or opposition. They include: **pa/tóda/ àli/vèndar/vèndarle/a/àmpak/tèmveč/màrveč** 'but'; **samó/lè/samó da/lè da** 'although, but, except that'.

The conjunctions **pa, tóda, vèndar(le), a** introduce a clause that contrasts in meaning with the main clause. One of the clauses is usually affirmative and the other negative. **Pa**, **tóda** and **vèndar** are more common than **a** which is a literary form; **àli** is now rarely used, e.g.

Obljúbil je, beséde pa ní dŕžal
He promised but he didn't keep his word

Ràd bi šèl v kíno, pa ne smé
He would like to go to the cinema, but is not allowed to

Ráde bi šè ležále, pa mórajo vstáti
They would like to stay in bed, but they have to get up

Tó so beséde, a nè dejánja
These are words but not deeds

Obláčno je rés, a/vèndar(le) je vsèêno vróče
It is true that it is cloudy, but it is nevertheless warm

Note: If **tóda** was used in this last example it would change the word order, i.e **Obláčno je rés, tóda vsèêno je vróče.**

Natočíla mu je póln kozárec, tóda sáma ní píla
She poured out a full glass for him, but didn't drink herself

Rékel je, da bo pomágal, tóda obljúbe ni izpólnil
He said he would help, but didn't keep his promise

Težáve níso velíke, vèndar obstájajo
The difficulties are not great, but they exist

Novínarji so jo spraševáli, vèndarle ní bilà priprávljena odgovárjati
The journalists questioned her but she was not prepared to answer

The conjunctions **àmpak**, **tèmveč**, **màrveč** are used to introduce an affirmative subordinate clause, which contrasts with a negated main clause. The conjunction **àmpak** is the form used colloquially, **tèmveč** is literary and neutral and **màrveč** is literary and high style, e.g.

Ne jókaj, àmpak/tèmveč/màrveč stísni zobé	Don't cry, but grit your teeth
Ne píše za mladíno, àmpak za odrásle	He doesn't write for young people, but for grown-ups
Tá novíca je ní pomiríla, tèmveč šè bòlj vznemírila	This news did not allay her fears, but made her even more worried

The conjunctions **lè**, **lè da**, **samó**, **samó da** introduce subordinate clauses that denote some restriction on what is said in the main clause, e.g.

Govorí lepó, lè málo tího
He speaks well, although quietly

Vsì bodo dobíli nôvo stanovánje, samó/lè jàz nè
Everyone will get a new flat except for me

Naj gré, lè/samó bojím se, da bo prepôzno
Let him go, but I fear that it will be too late

Note: **samó** is more commonly used than **lè**.

Vláki prihájajo, lè da/vèndar/samó z zamúdo
Trains are arriving but with delays

The adversative conjunction **vèndar** may be accompanied by the use of **sícer** at the beginning of the first clause. This introduces a restriction to the statement, contradicted by the statement in the second clause, e.g.

Sícer zná, vèndar ne razúme dôbro
He may well know, but he does not understand well

Sícer je mlád in nèizkúšen, vèndar zeló spréten
He may be young and inexperienced, but he is skilful

9.2.7 Disjunctive conjunctions

These conjunctions express a choice and include the following: **ali** 'or'; **ali pa** 'or else'; **ali . . . ali(pa)/bódi(si) . . . bódi(si)/bódisi . . . ali/nàjsibó . . . nàjsibó/ nàjsi . . . nàjsi/nàjsibó . . . ali** 'either . . . or'; **če . . . ali/naj . . . ali** 'whether . . . or'.

Examples of usage

Jàz ali tí, êden móra odnéhati
You or I – one of us has to give way

Dàj mi kávo ali pa čáj
Give me coffee or else tea

Ali délaj ali pa pójdi
Either work or else go

Ali mi pomágaj, kot sem te prôsil, ali pa me pústi pri míru
Either help me as I asked you to or leave me in peace

Naj príde bódisi jútri bódisi v tôrek ali srédo
Let him come either tomorrow or on Tuesday or Wednesday

Ne vém, če je rés ali nè
I do not know whether it is true or not

Naj bo lépo ali slábo vrême, v vsákem priméru bomo šlí na izlèt
Whether the weather is good or bad we will go on the outing

Kúpim si televízor, nàjsibó holándski ali pa japónski
I am going to buy a television set, either a Dutch one or a Japanese one

Nàjsi bogatáš nàjsi révež, vsák móra umréti
Whether rich or poor everyone has to die

9.3 SUBORDINATING CONJUNCTIONS

Subordinating conjunctions introduce subordinate clauses dependent on main clauses and may be subdivided into the following types: explicative, causal, conditional, concessive, consecutive and contrastive conjunctions and conjunctions of comparison, manner, purpose, time and place.

9.3.1 Explicative conjunctions

The explicative conjunctions are (a) **da** 'that', and (b) **naj** 'that'.

(a) The conjunction **da** is used after the verbs belonging to the semantic sphere of 'saying, seeing, thinking, knowing, observing, remembering, feeling, requesting, warning', etc. Unlike English 'that' however, this **da** is never omitted.

Examples of usage

Ali ne vídiš, da se žé daní
Can you not see that dawn is breaking

Opazíla je, da sta se pobótala
She observed that they had made up

Strokovnjáki míslijo, da bó nôvo zdravílo zeló učinkovíto
The experts think that the new medicine will be very effective

Právijo, da je bogáta
They say she is rich

Zatŕdil je, da o tém nìč ne vé
He stated that he knows nothing about this

Rékel mi je, da se kmálu vŕne
He told me that he would return soon

Opozóril ga je, da je naprávil napáko
He warned him that he had made a mistake

Prósimo obiskoválce, da se ne dotíkajo razstávljenih predmétov
Visitors are requested not to touch the exhibits

Ne zaníkam, da mi ugája
I do not deny that I am pleased

Priznáva, da téga ne vé
He admits that he does not know this

Mínka je obljubíla, da príde ob sêdmih
Minka promised to come at 7 o'clock

Prodajálka je odgovoríla, da téga blagá nímajo
The shop assistant replied that they did not have this material

Strínjam se, da je táko ravnánje nèprimérno
I agree that such behaviour is unbecoming

Spómnil se je, da so posláli po zdravníka
He remembered that they had sent for the doctor

Note: **da** may also be used following a noun, e.g. **Déjstvo, da je proizvódnja pádla, káže na résen položáj v továrni** 'The fact that production has fallen indicates the serious situation in the factory'.

(b)   The conjunction **naj** is used in subordinate clauses with reference to the object/indirect object in the main clause to express 'wish, desire, request or demand'. In these instances it is usually translated by the English infinitive or by 'should'.

Examples of usage

Prôsil ga je, naj ne gré na zabávo
He asked him not to go to the party (i.e. that he not go . . .)

Nagovárjajo me, naj se umáknem
They are trying to persuade me to withdraw (i.e . . . that I should withdraw)

Dál mi je známenje, naj ga počákam
He signalled for me to wait for him

9.3.2   Causal conjunctions

These conjunctions explain the cause or reason for the statement in the main clause. They include **da** 'that = because'; **ker/ko** 'because, since'. The conjunction **da** is used after main clauses expressing 'feelings', **ker** is the usual causal conjunction following other verbs, while **ko** (pronounced **kə**) is used more frequently in the spoken language.

Note: **ker** may sometimes be preceded by **zató** for emphasis.

Examples of usage

Kesá se, da je takó ravnál
He regrets that he behaved that way

Žàl mu je, da se je spozábil
He is sorry that he lost his temper

Vesél sem, da si me obískal
I am pleased that you have visited me

Bojím se, da ní takó, kot míslite
I fear that the situation is not as you think

Veselí se, da se bo peljála z njím
She is pleased that she will be travelling with him

Ker ga je domá zéblo, je šèl v kavárno
Since it was cold at home he went to the café

Ní mógel príti, ker je bíl bolán
He could not come because he was ill

Odložíla je slušálko, ker se nihčè ní oglásil
She put down the receiver because no one answered

Ne móre bráti, ko pa níma očál pri sêbi
He cannot read because he does not have his glasses with him

9.3.3   Conditional conjunctions

These conjunctions explain the condition for the realisation of the statement in the main clause. They include: **če/ko/ako/da/naj** 'if'; **samó da/da lè** 'provided that, on the condition that'.

The most common conjunction with the meaning 'if' is **če**, while **ako** is now archaic. **ko** is an alternative to **če** in clauses containing the conditional mood, i.e used with **bi**. The conditional conjunction **da** is a very literary form used instead of **če**. The conjunction **naj** is used expressively in the meaning 'if only'.

Examples of usage

Če si láčen, ti dám krúha
If you are hungry I will give you some bread

Če bi globôko kopáli, bi prišlí do vôde
If they dug deep, they would come across water

Užáljen je, če se ne mótim
He is offended if I am not mistaken

Če bo dèž, ne pójdem
If it rains I will not go

Ko bi/če bi se fànt vsáj málo učíl, bi narédil izpít
If the boy had studied just a little he would have passed the exam

Naj te kdó slíši, pa bo zaméra
Should anyone hear you they will take offence

Vsè bi biló lahkó drugáče, da nísem bilà takó lahkomíselna
Everything could have been different if I had not been so thoughtless

Tó bi tí zmôgla, ako bi hotéla
You could do it if you wanted to

The conjunction **če že** may sometimes be found instead of **če** and then expresses some reservation about the condition, e.g.

Naj gredó, če žé hóčejo, àmpak míslim, da tó ní dôbra idéja
Let them go if that is what they want to do, but I don't think that it is a good idea

In the media and colloquially one very often finds **v kólikor** used instead of **če** but this is not considered good style, e.g.

V kólikor me ne bó domá, me poklíči v slúžbo
If I am not at home call me at work

Držáva bo braníla plóvbo po Zalívu, v kólikor jo bo Irán ogrózil
The state will protect shipping in the Gulf if Iran threatens it

Restricted condition is expressed by the conjunctions **samó da/da lè** with the meaning 'provided that':

Samó da dobím denár, pa ti bom pomágal
Provided I get the money, then I will help you

Da ga lè nájdem, pa mu povém resníco
Provided that I find him, then I will tell him the truth

9.3.4   Concessive conjunctions

Concessive conjunctions introduce a statement which contrasts with the statement in the main clause or makes it seem surprising. The concessive conjunctions in Slovene are: **čepràv/četúdi/čerávno/da/dasi/dasirávno/dasitúdi/ akorávno/naj/nàjsi/naj túdi/kljúb tému da/kàkor** 'although, even though, even if'.

The most commonly used of these are **čepràv, četúdi, kljúb tému da**. The forms **akorávno, čerávno, dasitúdi** are now considered old fashioned, while **dasirávno, dasi, nàjsi, naj túdi** and **kàkor** are very literary forms. The conjunction **da** is also very literary and only rarely used as a concessive conjunction.

Examples of usage

Príden je, čepràv nè posébno nadárjen
He is industrious, although not specially gifted

Čepràv/kljúb tému da je deževálo, se je oblékel in odšèl
Although it was raining he dressed and left

Prídemo, četúdi bo deževálo
We will come even it it rains

Trepéče, da sám ne vé zakáj
He is trembling even though he himself doesn't know why

Kàkor ga imám ráda, ljubíti ga nê bi môgla
Although I like him, I could never love him

Da je vès zlát, ga nê bi vzéla za možá
Even if he was kindhearted she would not have him as a husband

Naj bi me stókrat vprášal, nê bi mu povédal
Even if he asked me a hundred times I would not tell him

Nàjsi je tá trdítev resníčna, primérna ni
Even though this statement is true, it is not fair

9.3.5   Consecutive conjunctions

Consecutive conjunctions express consequence or result and include **da/takó . . . da** 'so that'; **tóliko . . . da** 'so much so that'.

Examples of usage

Takó sem bíl nervózen, da sem kómaj díhal
I was so nervous that I could hardly breathe

Biló je vróče, da je z ljudí znój kàr líl
It was so hot, that sweat was dripping from people

Grdó píše, takó da njegóve pisáve ní mogóče bráti
He writes so terribly that it is impossible to read his writing

Note: **takó da** may be split, e.g. **Takó grdó píše, da njegóve pisáve ní mogóče bráti.**

Učíl se je tóliko, da je zbôlel
He studied so much so that he fell ill

Note: **tóliko da** plus a negated verb is also used to show the consequence of an action that nearly occurred. It then has the meaning 'almost', e.g.

| Nágnil se je dáleč skózi ôkno, tóliko da ní pádel vèn | He leant right out of the window and almost fell out |
| Tóliko da ní pádel, ko je stópil na banánin olúpek | He almost fell when he stepped on a banana skin |

9.3.6   Contrastive conjunctions

These are the conjunctions **namésto da** 'instead of' and **medtém ko** 'whereas'. They introduce a subordinate clause denoting an opposition to the main clause, with the action in the main clause being realised instead of or in preference to that in the subordinate clause.

Examples of usage

Namésto da bi délal, postópa
Instead of working he loafs around

Pomágaj mu, namésto da glédaš
Help him instead of just watching

Namésto da bi ostál domá, je odšèl
Instead of staying at home he went out

Ôni dobíjo bél krúh, medtém ko mí samó čŕnega
They get white bread, whereas we get only black bread

9.3.7   Conjunctions of comparison

Conjunctions of comparison introduce clauses which denote (a) simple comparison, (b) comparison with a possible, unreal or imaginary event, (c) comparison of the degree of intensity, (d) comparison of quantity or extent.

(a)   The conjunctions of simple comparison are: **kot/ko/kàkor** 'as, like'. The conjunction **kot** is used more frequently than **kàkor**, while **ko** is now archaic in the literary language although still used colloquially.

Examples of usage

Obnášaj se, kot se spodóbi za mládega fánta
Behave yourself as befits a young man

Jàz in Míha sva se grdó glédala kot/kàkor dvá bôjna petelína
Miha and I eyed each other meanly like two fighting cocks

Òn pláva kot/kàkor ríba
He swims like a fish

Fànt je navíhan, kàkor sem bíl jàz v njegóvih létih
The boy is roguish as I was at his age

(b) Conjunctions introducing clauses which denote comparison with possible, unreal or imaginary events are: **kot da/ko da/kàkor da/čèš da/kàkor bi** 'as if'.

Examples of usage

Obnáša se, kot da je òn gospodár
He behaves as if he were the master

Odskôčil je, ko da bi ga káča píčila
He leapt back as if a snake had bitten him

Pláva, kàkor bi bíl ríba
He swims as if he were a fish

Déla se, kàkor da me nê bi poznál
He makes as if he doesn't know me

Zdí se, kàkor da ní rešítve
It seems as if there is no solution

Zamáhne z rôko, čèš da/kàkor da ní nìč
He waved his hand, as if to say nothing was wrong

(c) The conjunctions denoting comparison of the degree of intensity are **čím . . . tèm** 'the more . . . the more / the less'; comparative + **ko** 'the more . . . the more'. When **čím . . . tèm** is used both clauses are structurally parallel and may contain the comparative form of an adjective or an adverb.

Examples of usage

Čím vèč imá, tèm vèč hóče
The more he has the more he wants

Čím préj, tèm bólje
The sooner the better

Čím bôlj ga opazúje, tèm mànj mu je všéč
The more he observes him the less he likes him

The conjunction **ko** preceded by a comparative adverb is used expressively to translate 'the more . . . the more', but appears only in the subordinate clause, which then precedes the main clause, e.g.

Dljè ko je brál, bôlj ga je povést zanímala
The longer he read, the more the story interested him

(d) The conjunctions denoting comparison of quantity or extent are **kàkor . . . takó** 'as . . . so'; **kólikor . . . tóliko** 'the more . . . the more', e.g.

Kàkor boste sejáli, takó boste žéli
As you sow, so will you reap

Kàkor se šíri dolína, takó je bôlj naséljena
As the valley widens, so it becomes more populated

Kólikor vèč imá, tóliko bôlj skopári
The more he has the more miserly he becomes

9.3.8 Conjunction of manner

Nè da plus the conditional mood 'without' acts as a conjunction of manner.
It introduces the subordinate clause which explains the manner in which the
action in the main clause was carried out. It is translated in English by the
construction 'without . . . ing', e.g.

Pláneš v sôbo, nè da bi potŕkal
You dash into the room without knocking

Odšèl je, nè da bi spregovóril besédo
He left without saying a word

Têkla sem, nè da bi glédala na césto
I ran along without looking at the road

Šlà je hítro spát, nè da bi večérjala
She went quickly to bed, without having dinner

9.3.9 Conjunctions of purpose

These conjunctions introduce a subordinate clause, which explains the purpose of the action in the main clause. They include the following: **da/naj** 'so
that, in order to'.

The normal conjunction of purpose is **da**, although **naj** is sometimes used
in the colloquial language instead of **da**. The conjunction **da** is sometimes
preceded by **zató** which then adds emphasis to the statement in the subordinate clause.

Examples of usage

Dála je otrôku igráčo, da nê bi jókal
She gave the child a toy to stop him crying

Ko se je zmračílo, so otrôci šlì domóv, da bi večérjali in šlí spát
When it got dark the children went home to have dinner and go to bed

Povédal sem ti, zató da se boš védel ravnáti
I told you so that you will know how to behave

Sédel je, (zató) da bi se odpočíl
He sat down to rest

Prišèl sem, da se pritóžim
I have come to complain

Pójdi k sêstri, naj/da ti zašíje srájco
Go to your sister so that she can sew up your shirt

Têkla sem, da nê bi zamudíla
I ran so as not to be late

9.3.10   Conjunctions of time

Temporal conjunctions introduce time clauses, which state when something happens by referring to a period of time or to another event. The temporal conjunctions in Slovene include: **ko** 'when'; **kàdar** 'when(ever)'; **kàdarkóli** 'whenever'; **doklèr** 'as long as, while'; **doklèr ne/da** 'until'; **odkàr/da** '(ever) since'; **préden/préj ko/pred tém ko** 'before'; **préj ko . . . (préj)** 'the sooner . . . the . . . er'; **potém ko** 'after'; **bŕž ko/kàkor hítro** 'as soon as'; **kómaj žé/ko; tóliko da . . . žé** 'no sooner, hardly . . . than'; **medtém ko** 'while'; **šelè . . . ko** 'only when, not until'.

(a) **ko; kàdar** 'when'
     The difference between these two conjunctions is that **kàdar** is only used to refer to repeated action, e.g.

     Ko se je prebúdil, je biló sónce žé visôko
     When he awoke, the sun was already high

     Ko prídeš domóv, napíši písmo
     When you get home write a letter

     Naj me obíšče, kàdar hóče
     Let him visit me when(ever) he wants to

     Kàdar je tréba cemênta, ga ní
     When(ever) cement is needed, there is none

(b) **kàdarkóli** 'whenever'

     Kàdarkóli ga sréča, je zméraj vesél
     Whenever he meets him he is always cheerful

(c) **doklèr** 'as long as, while'
     Doklèr is used only with imperfective verbs, e.g.

Doklèr je zákon v veljávi, se ga je tréba držáti
While/as long as the law is in force, one has to obey it

(d) **doklèr ne/da**
In the sense 'until' **doklèr** is always used with the negative particle **ne** but **da** is not, e.g.

Varúj otrôka, doklèr se ne vŕne máti
Look after the child until his mother returns

Nísem odšèl, doklèr ní prišèl
I did not leave until he came

Počákal sem, da se je odkášljal/doklèr se ní odkášljal
I waited until he had cleared his throat

(e) **odkàr/da** '(ever)since'
Odkàr is the conjunction normally used. The use of **da** in this sense is tending to disappear in the modern language, e.g.

Odkàr je ožénjen, ne zahája v gostílno
Ever since he got married, he does not visit the pub

Dežúje, odkàr sem prišèl
It has been raining ever since I arrived

Minúli sta dvé léti, da nísem bíl domá
It is two years since I was home

(f) **préden/préj ko/pred tém ko** 'before'
Of these conjunctions **pred tém ko** is the one that is least frequently used, e.g.

Préden je odšlà, je zapŕla ôkna
Before she left she closed the windows

Vôjne bo kônec, préj ko míne léto
The war will end before the year is out

Pred tém ko je šèl k vojákom, je prídno délal
Before he joined the army he worked hard

(g) **préj ko ... (préj)** 'the sooner ... the ... er'
This is a conjunction of time comparison, e.g.

Préj ko prídeš, préj bomo končáli nalógo
The sooner you come, the sooner we will finish the task

Préj ko začnêmo, préj bomo néhali
The sooner we begin, the sooner we will finish

Préj ko priznáš, bólje bó záte
The sooner you confess, the better it will be for you

(h) **potém ko** 'after'

> **Potém ko je povečérjal, je odšèl v mésto**
> After he had had dinner he went off into town

(i) **bŕž ko/kàkor hítro** 'as soon as'

> **Vŕni se, bŕž ko bo mogóče**
> Return as soon as possible

> **Kàkor hítro je za sílo okréval, se je odprávil na pót**
> As soon as he had recovered sufficiently, he set out on his journey

(j) **kómaj . . . žé/ko; tóliko da . . . žé** 'no sooner, hardly . . . when/before'
Of these two conjunctions **kómaj . . . žé/ko** is the one commonly used, e.g.

> **Kómaj séde, in žé ga spét klíčejo**
> No sooner does he sit down, when they call him again

> **Kómaj se je ožênil, pa se žé ločúje**
> No sooner has he got married than he is getting a divorce

> **Kómaj léžem, žé zazvoní telefón**
> No sooner am I in bed than the telephone rings

> **Kómaj sem se ulégla, ko so me spét poklicáli**
> Hardly had I gone to bed, when they rang me again

> **Tóliko da sem se pokázal, me je žé začél oštévati**
> No sooner had I appeared than he began to rebuke me

(k) **medtém ko** 'while'

> **Medtém ko smo mí délali, so ôni pohajkováli**
> While we worked, they gadded about

(l) **šelè ko** 'not until, only when'

> **Šelè ko se je vrême izbóljšalo, so odplúli**
> Only when the weather improved did they set sail

> **Šelè ko sem ponóvil vprašánje, me je razuméla**
> Only when I repeated the question did she understand me

9.3.11 Conjunctions of place

Conjunctions of place are used in a subordinate place clause when one wishes to refer to the location or position associated with the action in the main clause. They include: **kjèr** 'where'; **kóder** 'where'; **kámor** 'where, whither'; **kjèrkóli** 'wherever'; **do kóder** 'whither, to where'; **od kóder** 'whence, from where', **kóderkóli** 'wherever'.

In the modern language **kóder** is colloquially often replaced by **kjèr**. **kóder** tends to refer to the area throughout which movement takes place as opposed to **kjèr**, which indicates the spot where the event takes place.

Examples of usage

Naj ostáne, kjèr je
Let him stay where he is

Kóder/kjèr je divjál vihár, so híše porúšene
Houses are razed to the ground, where the storm raged

Šlà sva, kámor je kázal kážipót
We (d.) went where the signpost pointed

Ustávlja se v vsáki gostílni, kjèrkóli imájo dôbro víno
He stops at every inn wherever they have good wine

Pès ga je sprémljal, kóderkóli je hôdil
The dog accompanied him wherever he went

Pêlji, do kóder móreš
Drive to where you can

Odšèl je tjà, od kóder ni vrnítve
He went to a place from where there is no return

10 PARTICLES

Particles are indeclinable words which impart additional semantic nuances to other words, word groups or whole clauses. They are mainly a feature of the spoken language, where they are used to introduce additional information, to express a variety of subjective attitudes or assessments, to make justification for statements, to appeal for agreement, to add emphasis, to indicate possibility, etc. Particles imbue individual speech with emotive colour and expressive spontaneity.

They may be divided into two types: (a) primary particles and (b) secondary particles.

10.1 PRIMARY PARTICLES

Primary particles are those whose sole function is that of a particle. They do not derive from other words and cannot be used alone. The primary particles in Slovene are **le** and **kóli**.

(a) **le**

(i) This particle is used preceding a demonstrative pronoun to refer to the last-mentioned noun in the preceding clause and then conveys the English meaning 'latter', e.g.

Nekatéri rodóvi so se razvíli v poljedélce, drúgi v pastírje. Le-tí níso poználi stálne naselítve
Certain races developed into farmers, others into herdsmen. The latter did not have permanent places of abode

(ii) **Le** may be postposed to an adverb or pronoun to single out or intensify the meaning of a word, e.g.

Tále fànt je mój bràt	This boy is my brother
V téjle híši sem jàz gospodár	I am master in this house
Za tóle boste odgovárjali	You will answer for this
Zdàjle bomo glédali film	Now we'll watch the film
Kàj tákega se ti priméri edínole v sánjah	That sort of thing happens to you only in dreams

(b) **kóli**

This particle is postposed and used with pronouns and adverbs to indicate indefiniteness, generalisation, uncertainty, e.g.

Kdórkóli tó tŕdi, láže	Whoever asserts this is lying
Ostáni, kjèrkóli si	Stay wherever you are
Ali imá tó kákršnokóli zvézo z menój?	Does this have any connection with me?

10.2   SECONDARY PARTICLES

Secondary particles are not restricted to the role of particle, but may also function as adverbs or conjunctions. Their semantic classification is problematic but they may tentatively be divided into the following types:

(a)   Interrogative and dubitative particles
(b)   Particles of affirmation and agreement
(c)   Particles of negation and disagreement
(d)   Connective or linking particles
(e)   Emphatic particles
(f)   Particles of possibility or probability
(g)   Particles of surmise and opinion

10.3   INTERROGATIVE AND DUBITATIVE PARTICLES

These particles include the following: **ali**; **a**; **mar**; **káj**; **kajnè**; **kajnèda**; **a nè(da)**; **ne rés**.

(a)   **ali; a**
These particles are used with a verb to introduce a yes-no question. **Ali** is the literary form and **a** the colloquial form, e.g.

Ali prídeš?	Will you come?
Ali ste razuméli?	Did you understand?
A si ga vídel?	Did you see him?

(b)   **mar; káj**
These particles express the speaker's surprise or disbelief:

Mar/káj nísva prijátelja?	Are we not friends?
Mar téga rés ne véste?	Do you really not know this?
Káj žé gréste?	Are you going already?
Káj je rés bolán?	Is he really ill?

(c)   **kajnè; kajnèda; a nè(da); ne rés**
These particles correspond to English 'tag questions' and ask for confirmation that something is true, e.g.

Kajnèda ga imáš ràd?	You like him, don't you?
Saj pójdeš z máno, kajnè?	But you will go with me, won't you?
Kajnè/ne rés/a nè da boš tí túdi prišèl?	You will come as well, won't you?
Kajnèda/a nè da, včéraj smo se sijájno zabávali?	We had a great time yesterday, didn't we?
Ne bóš povédal očétu, kajnè/a nè?	You won't tell father, will you?

Note: After a question **ali káj** or colloquial **a káj** is used to express English 'or what?', e.g. **Si tí zméšan, ali káj/a káj** 'Are you mad, or what?'

10.4 PARTICLES OF AFFIRMATION AND AGREEMENT

Slovene has two words for 'yes': **dà** and **já**: **dà** is the literary form and **já** the colloquial form, e.g.

Si priprávljen? Dà.	Are you ready? Yes.
Je tó vàš sín. Já.	Is that your son? Yes.

Other particles used to express affirmation include: **sevéda/sevé/jásno/kájpak/ kakó da ne** 'of course; **pàč** 'yes'; **pràv** 'okay', e.g.

Ali gréš z máno? Sevéda/sevé	Are you going with me? Of course
Boš prišèl? Kájpak! se je zasméjal	Will you come? Of course, he said with a smile
Tórej mísliš zarés? Kakó da ne	So you really think so? Of course
A prídeš na zabávo? Jásno	Are you coming to the party? Of course

(a) **pàč**

The particle **pàč** may be translated in English as 'yes' or 'no'. It introduces a negation of the statement made and adds a correction, e.g.

Té pravíce nímaš. Pàč, imám jo	You do not have the right. Yes, I do
Nas nísi pričakovàl, kajnè? Pàč, pàč, zató sem šè pokônci	You did not expect us, did you? Yes, yes I did, that's why I am still up
Smo vsì zbráni? Pàč, pàč, Andréja šè ní	Are we all here? No, no, Andrej is still missing

(b) **pràv**

This particle is used to express consent or acceptance of some fact, e.g.

Pràv, pa pojdímo	Okay, let's go
Pràv, kàkor hóčeš	Okay, as you wish
Pràv, če žé móra bíti takó	Okay, if it must be so

10.5 PARTICLES OF NEGATION AND DISAGREEMENT

The particles of negation are **ne** 'no', **níti ne** 'not even' and **nikákor ne** 'not at all, in no way'.

The form **ne** is used either alone or to negate a verb. The form **níti ne** is used to emphasise the negation and is also used colloquially in the sense 'not really'. The form **nikákor ne** indicates that the statement made is inappropriate or groundless, e.g.

Ali je knjíga tvôja? Nè, izposójena	Is the book yours? No it's borrowed
Ne vém	I do not know
Ne bojím se povédati resníce	I am not afraid to tell the truth
Níti minúto se ní obotávljal	He did not hesitate for even a minute
Níti dvájset lét níma	He is not even twenty
Utrújen si, kajnè? Níti ne, sem vájen hóje	You are tired, aren't you? Not really, I am used to walking
Ali si spét zamúdil? Nikákor ne, šè ní ósem	Are you late again? Not at all, it's not eight yet

10.6 CONNECTIVE OR LINKING PARTICLES

These particles may: introduce a related comment (e.g. **in** 'and'; **sàj** 'but'); introduce a sentence that contrasts with the previous sentence or gives another point of view (e.g. **vsèêno** 'nevertheless'); indicate that the fact being mentioned exists because of the fact(s) stated previously (e.g. **zatórej** 'therefore); indicate a stage in a sequence (e.g. **drúgič** 'secondly').

Examples of the use of such particles

Dàj mu kozárec vína. Sàj je žé píl
Give him a glass of wine. But he has already had a drink

In kakó je s tábo?
And how are you?

Pláčal mu je za délo in povŕhu dál nékaj za otrôka
He paid him for the work and moreover gave him something for the child

Túdi nàm se je tó zgodílo
This also happened to us

Izjáva ní resníčna, nasprótno, zlonamérna je
The statement is not true, on the contrary it is a malicious lie

Uspél je, a vsèêno ní zadovóljen
He succeeded, nevertheless he is not satisfied

Tá vidík je resníčen, vèndar ênostránski
This point of view is true, but biased

Novínarji so jo spraševáli, vèndarle ní bilà priprávljena odgovárjati
The journalists questioned her, nevertheless she was not prepared to answer

Poméni se s sosédom, sevéda mírno, brez prepíra
Talk to your neighbour, calmly of course, without quarrelling

Nesréča se je vsèkakor zgodíla zarádi malomárnosti
At any rate the accident happened because of carelessness

Nísmo jim pomágali. Vsèga smo tórej sámi krívi
We did not help them. Therefore we ourselves are to blame for everything

Vsè se draží, kakó naj potemtákem révež žíví
Everything is getting more expensive, consequently how can a poor man live?

Nihčè nóče popustíti. Zatórej sporazúma šè ne bó
Nobody will yield. Therefore there will be no settlement yet

Prosílec ne ustréza, pŕvič ker níma zadôstne izobrázbe, drúgič ker níma délovnih izkúšenj
The applicant is unsuitable, firstly because he is not educationally qualified and secondly he has no work experience

10.7 EMPHATIC PARTICLES

These particles are used to emphasise a word or clause, or to emphasise that only one particular thing is involved in what you are saying. Examples of such particles are: **posébno** 'especially'; **zlásti** 'particularly, especially'; **celó** 'even'; **predvsèm** 'above all'; **rávno** 'just, exactly, precisely'; **samó/edíno/lè** 'only, merely'; **vsáj** 'at least, at any rate'; **žé** 'very'; **splòh** 'then'; **práv** 'right'.

Examples of usage

Posébno tí bi tó móral védeti
You especially should have known that

priméri iz svetóvne knjížévnosti, posébno/zlásti francóske knjížévnosti
examples from world literature, especially French literature

Prepírali so se in celó stêpli
They quarrelled and even came to blows

Tó je môčna pijáča, celó za krêpkega možá
That's a strong drink even for a strong man

Mále ogláse objávlja samó ob délavnikih, predvsèm ob pétkih
He publishes small ads only on weekdays, above all on a Friday

Káj splòh hóče?
What then does he want?

Kdó pa ste splòh ví?
Who are you then?

Rávno tó sem hôtel védeti
That's precisely what I wanted to know

Prišlí so lè tríje
Only three came

Vsè je pogorélo, samó/edíno hlév je ostál
Everything burnt down, only the stable remained

Vsáj êden se me je spómnil
At least one person remembered me

Vsáj prišèl bi, kot si obljúbil
You could at least have come as you promised you would

žé drúgi dán
the very next day

Pràv pred híšo je ustávil ávto
He stopped the car right in front of the house

Žé sáma mísel na tó je záme strášna
The very thought of that I find terrible

10.8 PARTICLES OF POSSIBILITY OR PROBABILITY

These particles are used to indicate whether a situation merely seems to exist or might exist. They include the following:

mordà/mogóče/nemára (arch.)/ **eventuálno/morebíti**	possibly, perhaps, maybe
nàjbrž/verjétno	probably
bŕžčas/bŕžda/bŕžkone (arch.)	most probably

Examples of usage

Zvečér se mordà vídiva
Maybe we'll see each other this evening

Mogóče pa òn tó vé
It is possible that he knows that

Povédala je vsè, morebíti šè vèč, kàkor je tréba
She told everything, perhaps more than was necessary

Stàr je nemára pétdeset lét
He is maybe fifty years old

Posódil bi ti lahkó tísoč tólarjev, eventuálno túdi dvá tísoč
I could lend you 1000 tolars, perhaps even 2000

Pozvonílo je, nàjbrž je póštar
There's the bell, it's probably the postman

Ní šè prišèl, verjétno je zaspál
He has not yet arrived, he has probably overslept

Bŕžčas príde jútri
He will most probably come tomorrow

Tó bo bŕžda držálo
This will most probably hold

Bŕžkone je na sestánku
He is most probably at the meeting

10.9   PARTICLES OF SURMISE AND OPINION

These include particles such as the following: **gotóvo** 'surely'; **mendà** 'surely, presumably'; **bajè** 'allegedly, supposedly'; **recímo/denímo/vzemímo/postávimo** 'suppose, supposing'; **čèš (da)** 'as if'.

Examples of usage

Tó gotóvo ne móre bíti njén bràt
That surely can't be her brother

Če prenêse móst kamión, bo mendà túdi mêne
If the bridge can take the weight of a lorry, it can surely bear my weight

Mendà si tó slíšal
I suppose you've heard this

Bajè so zeló bogáti
Allegedly they are very rich

Dŕžal se je samozavéstno, čèš jàz se ne bojím nikógar
He acted self-confidently as if to say I fear nobody

Recímo, da ne príde
Suppose he doesn't come

Nò, vzemímo, da imáš pràv
And supposing you are right

11 INTERJECTIONS

There are three types of interjection in Slovene:

(a) Emotive interjections. These express a person's feelings, reactions or mood (i.e. surprise, pleasure, pain, horror, disgust, fear, amazement, annoyance, anger, doubt, dismay, sympathy, etc.).

(b) Onomatopoeic interjections.

(c) Appellative (imperative) interjections. These are interjections with which speakers express their will, a wish, a desire or a request by addressing listeners with some sort of call or summons. They are therefore closely related in function to imperative sentences.

11.1 EMOTIVE INTERJECTIONS

Examples of emotive interjections are: **á, é, í, ó, ú, áu, àh, èh, ìh, àj, jój, jéj, ùf, jójme, jáv, ehéj, mm, pfùj, hm, jójna, jèžešna, bógvé, jézus, madónca**. Some of the simple interjections can express more than one emotion and some are synonymous. For example **ó** can express surprise, admiration, pain and resignation and **àj** can express pain or surprise. It should also be noted that simple interjections are often reduplicated in speech.

Some examples of usage

Pfùj, kákšne gŕde beséde	Phew, what obscene language
Àj, kakó skelí	Ow, it smarts
Jáv, jáv, kakó me bolí	Ouch, ouch it hurts
Ùf, téga nísem pričakovál	Ugh! I did not expect this
Madónca, smo utrújeni	Oh boy, are we tired
Jèžešna, kám se tí takó mudí?	Good heavens, where are you off to in such a hurry?
Jézus, ali je tó mogóče?	Jesus, is this possible?
Jójme, kljúč sem izgúbil	Oh dear, I've lost the key
Jéj, jéj, káj bó iz têbe?	Dear, dear, what will become of you?
Àh! Tí si	Ah! It is you
Ú, kakó prídna si bilà	Gosh, you were diligent

11.2   ONOMATOPOEIC INTERJECTIONS

These interjections imitate the sounds made by people, animals, machines or mechanisms or the sounds made by things falling or striking something etc. Very often these interjections lend themselves to reduplication, e.g.

ha ha hà; **hi hi hì**	ha ha ha; hee hee hee
ahčì	atishoo
mijáv	miaow
hòv	woof
mú	moo
bê bee	baa, baa
kukú	cuckoo
réga, réga	croak, croak
íha	neigh
kokokó/kokodák	cluck, cluck, cluck
tík ták	tick tock
škŕt, škŕt, škŕt	snip, snip, snip (of scissors)
cìn, cìn, cìn	ding, ding, ding
štrbúnk	plop, splash
tòk, tòk, tòk	rata tat tat
klòp klòp klòp	clip clop

Note: Onomatopœic interjections often serve as bases for the derivation of verbs, e.g. **Žábe régajo** 'Frogs croak'; **Kokóši kokodákajo** 'Hens cluck'; **Žábe so drúga za drúgo štrbúnkale v vôdo** 'The frogs plopped into the water one after the other'; **Kónjska kopíta klopotájo po kámenju** 'The horses hooves go clip, clop across the stones'; **Máčka mijávka** 'A cat miaows'.

11.3   APPELLATIVE INTERJECTIONS

These interjections are those with which a speaker establishes contact with or tries to attract the attention of a person or animal, e.g. **nò** 'there, well'; **hórùk** 'heave ho'; **dàj/dèj** 'go on, come on'; **óha** 'whoa'; **počák** 'wait'; **pst** 'psst, sh'; **léj** 'look, see'; **ná** 'take it'; **tà tà** 'here boy (to dog)'; **múc múc** 'puss puss'; **hí** 'giddiup'; **čák** 'wait'.

Examples

Pst, ôče spí	Sh, father is asleep
Nò, ne jókaj	There, there, don't cry
Ná knjígo	Take the book then (Note, **ná** is used with the accusative)
Príden kúža, tà tà tà	Good dog, here boy, here boy
Dàj, vstáni	Well get up then

Note: Verbal imperative endings denoting plural and dual are sometimes added to a few of these interjections, e.g.

Déjva, vzemíva šè kós slaníne	Go on, let us (d.) take another piece of bacon
Náte/náta bonbóne	Go on (plur./d.), take some sweets
Léj, kákšna sréča	Look, what good fortune

11.4 GREETINGS

Finally, it should be noted that greetings may also be classified as interjections, e.g. **dober večér** 'good evening'; **sêrvus** 'hello'; **sréčno** 'good luck'; **žívio** 'cheers, hello'; **adíjo** 'goodbye'; **lahko nóč** 'good night'.

In the case of two word greetings only the last word is stressed. Moreover such greetings are often abbreviated, e.g. **dober večér** > **čér**; **lahko nóč** > **nóč**.

12 WORD ORDER

Slovene is characterised by variable word order, which is far freer than word order in English. This freedom, however, is relative and does not mean random word order. Slovene's inflectional system is highly developed so there is little scope for ambiguity and the sequential order of words does not usually change their syntactic or semantic functions. Word order may vary depending on communicative, expressive and stylistic factors and on emphasis.

An exhaustive treatment of word order is not possible in a work such as this and what follows is a general guide to word order in Slovene.

12.1 DECLARATIVE SENTENCES

The normal word order in a simple neutral (unmarked) declarative sentence is 'subject' (= topic or theme) followed by 'verb + object' (= comment or rheme), e.g. **Otròk bêre knjígo** 'The child is reading the book'; **Máti ljúbi otrôka** 'The mother loves the child'.

This word order is, moreover, obligatory in morphologically ambiguous sentences, where nouns have nominative = accusative and are of the same person and number (i.e. the dual of masculine, feminine and neuter nouns, the singular of masculine inanimate nouns and of feminine nouns in a consonant, the plural of feminine and neuter nouns), e.g.

Teléti glédata žrebéti	The calves (d.) are looking at the foals (d.)
Tekmoválke občudújejo zmagoválke	The competitors praise the victors
Pohlèp premagúje stráh	Greed overcomes fear

If the word order in these sentences was changed the meanings would change, e.g. **Stráh premagúje pohlèp** 'Fear overcomes greed'.

In English only the word order 'The child is reading the book' or 'The mother loves the child' is possible and any change in the order either leads to a non-sentence or a change in meaning, e.g. 'The book is reading the child' or 'The child loves the mother'.

In Slovene, however, it is possible to change the word order in such sentences giving any of four possible word permutations, i.e.

1. **Otròk bêre knjígo**   1. **Máti ljúbi otrôka**
2. **Otròk knjígo bêre**   2. **Máti otrôka ljúbi**

3. **Knjígo bêre otròk** 3. **Otrôka ljúbi máti**
4. **Knjígo otròk bêre** 4. **Otrôka máti ljúbi**

In these sentences the subject (s) verb (v) and object (o) do not have to appear in the order svo as in English, because the subject can be distinguished morphologically from the object. The different word order reflects a different communicative point of view or makes the sentence order marked. From a communicative point of view whatever comes first (whether the subject or not) operates as a starting point for the sentence. This initial element is the 'topic' and is the thing about which the speaker wishes to give the listener some piece of information, i.e. the 'comment'. The 'topic' might be known to both speaker and listener (i.e. refers back to something already established or mentioned) or just known to the speaker. Hence in the sentence **Otròk bêre knjígo** the speaker establishes the 'topic', i.e. **otròk** or **otròk bêre**, but the new information, i.e. **bêre knjígo** or **knjígo** is known only to the speaker and could arise from the posed questions: **Káj déla otròk?** 'What is the child doing? ' (i.e. **bêre knjígo**) or **Káj bêre otròk?** 'What is the child reading?' (i.e. **knjígo**).

It should be noted that sentences such as **Knjígo bêre otròk** or **Knjígo otròk bêre** where the object is in initial position and is therefore the topic, often correspond to passive sentences in English, i.e. 'The book is being read by the child' with either the emphasis on 'is being read' or 'by the child'. The use of the passive in English enables the noun 'book' to appear in sentence initial position and mark it overtly as the topic. As far as the other Slovene permutation of this sentence is concerned this again conveys slightly different information, i.e. **Otròk knjígo bêre** conveys the information as to what the child is doing to the book, i.e. that the child *is reading* the book (as opposed to tearing it etc.). Different word order can also create a marked sentence and convey different emphasis. Basically, however, one can state that the order in Slovene sentences is 'topic and comment' with the emphasis on the final part of the comment.

If there is no object in a sentence, the neutral order is 'subject + verb', e.g. **Adriána spí** 'Adriana is sleeping'.

A subject may, however, follow a verb in existential sentences of the following type:

Bíl je králj   There was once a king
Obstája velíko vŕst gób There are many types of mushroom

Here the 'verb + subject' order establishes the existence and subsequent relevance of a new individual/thing, who/which then becomes the 'topic' (= subject, theme) of the next sentence, e.g.

Obstája nevárnost popláv. Popláve so láni naredíle velíko škóde
There is a danger of floods. The floods caused a lot of damage last year

The neutral word order 'subject + verb (+ object)' is normal (a) if both the subject and object are known to the speaker and listener or if the subject is already established as a topic of conversation and (b) if the subject and object are both new in the discourse and the speaker is establishing a topic for discussion. In a declarative sentence (whether simple, complex or compound) the subject, verb or object are often qualified by modifiers such as adjectives, pronouns, adverbs, etc. or by prepositional phrases or relative clauses, e.g.

> **Mój bràt in mládi študènt z rôko v prevézi néžno glédata tvôjo sêstro, ki bêre knjígo v kótu sôbe**
> My brother and the young student with his arm in a sling are looking tenderly at your sister, who is reading a book in the corner of the room

The word order of such a sentence could be changed if the 'topic' (i.e. the known information) was not **mój bràt in mládi študènt z rôko v prevézi**. If the 'topic' was **tvôjo sêstro** the order would be **Tvôjo sêstro, ki bêre knjígo v kótu sôbe, néžno glédata mój bràt in študènt z rôko v prevézi**. Such an order would mean that 'My brother and the student with his arm in a sling' is the new information (answering a question such as 'Who is looking tenderly at my sister?').

It should be noted that the 'topic' need not be a noun (phrase), but could be a verb, adverb, adverbial phrase or a prepositional phrase, e.g.

Nosíti móram očála, ker na obé očési slabó vídim	I have to wear glasses because both my eyes are weak
Pri úri fízike smo spoználi Newtonov zákon	In the physics lesson we got to know Newton's law
Včéraj smo bilì v gledalíšču	We were at the theatre yesterday
Obnávljali so cérkev in odkríli srednjevéške fréske	They were renewing the church and discovered mediaeval frescoes

In real contexts such as discourse or narrative the relative dynamism of the constituents of the sentence means that the 'comment' (i.e. the new information) in one sentence often becomes the 'topic' in the next sentence as is illustrated by the following text:

> **Skózi ôkno vídim nášega soséda. Sôsed gléda nášega psà. Pès, ki se imenúje Rover, je na vŕtu. Vŕt je obdán z leséno ográjo. Ográjo je létos postávil mój móž létos. Móž mi je rékel, da bo dánes prišèl domóv ob pêtih in da bova šlà v kíno. Do kína ní dáleč. Tam predvájajo nòv kávbojski film. Kávbojski filmi mi níso všéč.**
> Through the window I can see our neighbour. The neighbour is looking at our dog. The dog, who is called Rover, is in the garden. The garden is surrounded by a wooden fence. The fence was put up this year by my husband. My husband told me that he would be home at five o'clock today and that we would go to the cinema. It is not far to the cinema. There they are showing a new cowboy film. Cowboy films are not to my liking.

Any change in this text to the conventional neutral order of 'topic and comment' would make the sentence marked in some way or indicate some form of emphasis.

12.2 INTERROGATIVE SENTENCES

There are two types of interrogative sentence in Slovene:

(a) A declarative sentence may be turned into a question by means of interrogative intonation and no change in word order. For example, the four different word orders given for the sentence **Otròk bêre knjígo** (see **12.1**) could all be made into questions by means of intonation. Moreover, two more versions of the sentence with the verb in initial position could also produce questions, i.e. **Bêre knjígo otròk?** and **Bêre otròk knjígo?**

(b) Interrogative sentences are introduced by pronominal or adverbial interrogatives or by prepositional phrases (e.g. **kdó** 'who'; **kjé** 'where'; **kákšen** 'what kind of'; **kakó** 'how'; **s čím** 'with what', etc.) or by the unstressed interrogative particles **ali**, **a**. These interrogatives are normally followed by the verb and then its subject or object. These are then followed by any additional information required by the sentence, e.g.

Ali si žé vídel kengurúja?	Have you seen a kangaroo yet?
Ali/a živí vàš prijátelj v Ljubljáni?	Does your friend live in Ljubljana?
Ali péljejo kmétje sádje na tŕg?	Do the farmers take the fruit to market?
Káj je pripeljálo turíste?	What did the tourists come in?
Kdó gré z máno na sprehòd?	Who is going for a walk with me?
Ob katéri úri se bo jútri vŕnil ôče?	At what time will father return tomorrow?
Kám gre vlák?	Where is the train going?';
Kjé stanúje tvój prijátelj?	Where does your friend live?
Ali gréš popóldne na tékmo?	Are you going to the match this afternoon?
Kjé se je zgodíla nesréča?	Where did the accident occur?

Note: It is also possible for the subject of the verb to appear before the present tense of the verb or immediately before the -l participle in the future and perfect tense or the conditional mood.

Kdáj je profésor spoznál svôjo zmóto?	When did the professor realise his mistake?
Kdáj bodo článi sindikáta oddáli svôje glasóvnice?	When will the trade unionists hand in their votes?
Káj bi vàš bràt narédil, če bi zadél dvá milijóna na loteríji?	What would your brother do if he won two million on the lottery?

Ali so kmétje peljáli sádje na tŕg?	Did the farmers take the fruit to market?
Kdó se je pŕvi povzpél na Tríglav?	Who first climbed Triglav?
Ali učítelj razlága vprašánja?	Does the teacher explain the questions?

Note: **vsè** is used immediately after interrogatives like **kdó** 'who', **káj** 'what' to indicate a number of people or things, e.g.

Káj vsè je biló na mízi?	What/What things was/were on the table?
Kdó vsè je bíl za mízo?	Who/Which people was/were at the table?
S kóm vsè si bíl tàm?	Who/Which people were you there with?

12.3 THE ORDER OF INDIVIDUAL WORDS

(a) Independent words like nouns, verbs, adverbs, adjectives, numerals and pronouns may, as already indicated, change their place in a sentence to reflect a different communicative point of view or a different emphasis. Thus their position within the sentence determines the effect that the speaker wishes to achieve.

(b) Dependent words, however, like prepositions, conjunctions, particles, the short clitic forms of the personal and reflexive pronouns, and the present and past forms of the verb **bíti** 'to be' used as past and future tense auxiliaries follow a much stricter word order.

12.3.1 Independent words

(a) Adjectives and pronouns
The attributive adjective always precedes the noun except in marked expressions, which might occur in emotional speech or poetry, e.g.

nôva knjíga	the new book
nesréčni otròk	the unfortunate child
lépa púnca	the beautiful girl

but

Otròk nesréčni!	Wretched boy! [emotional]
Òj, zêmlja lépa!	Oh beautiful land! [poetic]

This post position in emotional utterances is often the case if the adjective and noun come from the same root, e.g. **lenúh léni** 'lazy devil'; **skopúh skópi** 'mean devil'.

Where more than one adjective modifies a noun, a qualitative adjective precedes a relational adjective, e.g. **nôvi dirkálni ávto** 'the new racing car'.

A possessive adjective will precede a qualitative or relational adjective, e.g. **očétov nôvi ávto** 'father's new car'.

A qualitative adjective will precede a generic possessive, e.g. **velíka ríbja koščíca** 'a large fish bone'.

Possessive pronouns precede an 'adjective + noun', e.g. **náše koló** 'our bicycle'; **náše nôvo koló** 'our new bicycle'.

Other adjectival pronouns precede a 'noun' or 'adjective + noun' or a 'possessive adjective/pronoun + adjective + noun', e.g.

tó (zelêno) jábolko	this (green) apple
tísta (velíka) ríbja koščíca	that (large) fish bone
tísti očétov nôvi ávto	that new car of father's

The pronoun **vès** 'all' precedes all other adjectival pronouns, e.g. **vsì tí náši otrôci** 'all those children of ours'.

Certain adjectives govern the oblique cases of nouns or govern prepositional phrases. When such an adjective is used before a noun, the prepositional phrase or oblique case must precede the adjective, e.g.

na rôko tkáne prepróge	hand woven carpets
dobróte láčni otrôci	children hungry for kindness
částí in sláve žêljen člôvek	a man thirsting for fame and honour

(b) **Adverbs**

The placement of adverbs or adverbial phrases depends on the sequence of the information conveyed, i.e. the topic and comment. In neutral, non-emphatic contexts adverbs of time and place tend to be placed earlier in the sentence and adverbs of manner later, e.g.

Dánes je lép dán	It's a nice day today
Sinóči je deževálo	It rained last night
Spomládi je topló, poléti pa je topléje	It is warm in Spring, but it is warmer in Summer
Povsód po dežêli so se kmétje upírali	Everywhere throughout the land the farmers put up resistance
Zgôraj ga čákajo prijátelji	Friends are waiting for him up above
Imé v člânku je pomótoma izpádlo	The name in the article was omitted by mistake
Ustrelíla ga je namérno	She shot him deliberately

Adverbs of degree occur before the adjective or verb they modify:

Njíhovih obrázov nísem docéla razlóčil	I did not fully discern their faces
Razmére so se povsèm spremeníle	The circumstances have changed entirely
Vročína je bilà skôraj nevzdŕžna	The heat was almost unbearable

The adverb **vrèd** 'together (with), including' always follows the prepositional phrase **z** + instr., e.g. **z obréstmi vrèd** 'including interest'; **s postréžbo vrèd** 'service included'.

12.3.2   Dependent words

(a)   Prepositions
Prepositions always precede the word they govern. The prepositions **navkljúb** (arch.) 'in spite of' and **naspróti** 'opposite' may however in some circumstances follow the word they govern (see **8.4**; **8.9.16**).

(b)   Conjunctions
Coordinating conjunctions stand between the words, phrases or sentences they coordinate (see **9.2**). The conjunction **pa** may, however, come after the first word in the second part of the coordinated elements. This occurs when **pa** has a confrontational role and means 'but, whereas' and not 'and', e.g.

Obljúbil je, beséde pa ní dŕžal	He promised but he didn't keep his word
Êno tékmo so izgubíli, trí pa dobíli	They lost one match but won three

(c)   Emphatic particles
Emphatic particles (see **10.7**) precede the word they emphasise, e.g.

Prišlì so lè tríje	Only three came
Žé sáma mísel na tó je záme strášna	The very thought of this I find terrible

(d)   Clitics
In Slovene the clitics are:

(i)   The short forms of the reflexive and personal pronouns, e.g. **se**, **ga**, **mu**, **jo** etc.

(ii)   The present and future tense forms of the verb **bíti** 'to be' used as auxiliaries in the perfect and future tenses, e.g. **sem**, **si**, **je**; **bom**, **boš**, **bo**, etc.

(iii) The conditional particle **bi**

These clitic forms normally occur in 'second position' in declarative sentences, subordinate clauses and questions. The 'first position' may be occupied by:

1. an independent word such as a noun, pronoun, verb, adverb, numeral or substantivised adjective
2. a noun phrase, verb phrase, adjectival phrase or adverbial phrase
3. a subordinating conjunction
4. a particle, e.g. **naj, ali, a**

Examples of clitics in 'second position'

(1/2)

Têti smo za poróčno darílo kupíli jedílni pribòr
We bought Auntie cutlery as a wedding present

Òn se bojí smŕti
He is afraid of death

Včéraj je bilà šè otròk, zdáj je lépo deklè
Yesterday she was a still a child, now she is a beautiful young lady

Nôčna dežúrna je zjútraj predála délo
The woman on night duty handed over her job in the morning

Z dôbrim znánjem jezíkov boš napredovàl
With a good knowledge of languages you will get on

Kônec mája bomo odpotováli
We will depart at the end of May

Tékel je, da bi ujél ávtobus
He ran to catch the bus

Od jútra do nočí je délal v pisárni
He worked in the office from morning to night

Spêkli bi potíco, a nísmo iméli oréhov
We would have baked a cake, but we didn't have any nuts

Obé sêstri in njúna máti so čakále na postáji
Both sisters and their mother were waiting at the stop

Ob desêtih je slovésni začétek seminárja
The official opening of the seminar is at ten o'clock

Ôni tríje so mŕtvi
Those three are dead

(3/4)

Naj ti povém, kakó se je tó zgodílo
Let me tell you how it happened

Ali si žé bíl na Tríglavu
Have you already been up Triglav?

A me nísi opázil, ko sem šlà mímo têbe?
Didn't you notice me, when I walked past you?

Ne vém, če jo poznáš
I don't know if you know her

Prídem, da ti povém vesélo novíco
I am coming to tell you some good news

Bolník je zatrjevàl, da ne móre pisáti, ker ga bolí rôka
The patient maintained that he wasn't able to write, because his hand hurt

Note: **da**, **ali**, **če** precede **naj** if they are used with it, e.g.

Tó je potrébno, če naj se izógnemo poslédicam	This is necessary if we are to avoid the consequences
Prósim, da naj bi se mi ne smejáli	I ask you not to laugh at me
Ali naj se mu opravíčim?	Should I apologise to him?

12.4   CLITIC ORDER

If two or more clitics occur in 'second position' in a declarative sentence, subordinate clause or question then they must adhere to the following fixed left to right order 1–6.

1. (a) Present tense forms of the verb **bíti** 'to be' (with the exception of **je**), when used as perfect tense auxiliaries, i.e. **sem, si, sva, sta, smo, ste, so**
   (b) The conditional particle **bi**

2. The reflexive pronouns **se, si**

3. The dative clitic forms of the personal pronouns, i.e. **mi, ti, mu, ji, nama, vama, jima, nam, vam, jim**

4. The accusative clitic forms of the personal pronouns, i.e. **me, te, ga, jo, naju, vaju, ju, nas, vas, jih**

5. The genitive clitic forms of the personal pronouns, i.e. **me, te, ga, je, naju, vaju, ju, nas, vas, jih**

6. (a) The third person singular of the verb **bíti** 'to be' used as a perfect tense auxiliary, i.e. **je**
   (b) The future tense forms of the verb **bíti** 'to be' used as a future tense auxiliary, i.e. **bom, boš, bo, bova, bosta, bomo, boste, bodo/bojo**

Examples of clitic order

Skleníli smo, da mu ga bomo posláli	We agreed to send it to him
Čákaj, òn ti bo pokázal písmo	Wait, he will show you the letter
Nìč se ga ne bój	Do not be afraid of him/it at all
Včéraj sem jo sréčal v méstu	I met her in town yesterday

Obràz se mu je zjásnil	His face brightened up
Obnáša se, kot bi nas ne poznál	He behaves as if he didn't know us
Dobíl ga bo, če se bo oglásil pri nàs	He will get it if he calls in to see us
Míslil sem, da si ga kupíla láni	I thought that you bought it last year
V katéro šólo sta ju vpisála?	In which school have you (d.) enrolled them (d.)?
Prinêsli ji ga bomo	We will bring it to her
Mórala si je priznáti, da ji je bilà predstáva všéč	She had to admit to herself that she liked the performance

It should also be noted that the rules of clitic placement are also followed when a modal verb or another verb precede an infinitive and they both have the same subject, e.g.

Začéla se je obláčiti v čŕno	She began to dress herself in black
Ničésar se ne mórem spómniti	I can't remember anything
Pozabíli so ji jo dáti	They forgot to give it to her
Òn mu ga je móral dáti	He had to give it to him

12.5   THE NEGATIVE PARTICLE ne

The negative particle **ne** immediately precedes the verb it negates. In the perfect and future tenses it precedes the auxiliary verb **bíti** 'to be' (i.e. **nísem, ne bóm** etc.) which is then non-clitic. In the conditional moods it nowadays normally precedes the particle **bi**. In this case **nê bi** is non-clitic. In the literary language, however, it can sometimes follow **bi** and then **bi** is treated as a clitic.

Examples

Ali vam nísem rékel, da se nánj ne zanášajte?
Did I not tell you not to rely on him?

Takó obléčen se ne bojím mráza
Dressed like this I am not afraid of the cold

Úpamo, da se ne bóste jezíli, če bomo málo zamudíli
We hope that you will not be angry if we are a little late

Če bi bilà na tvôjem méstu, se nê bi pustíla takóle ponížati
If I were in your place I would not allow myself to be demeaned in such a way

Ôče želí, naj nê bi začéli, doklèr sám ne príde
Father doesn't want them to start before he arrives

Tákega denárja dosléj šè nísem vídel
As yet I had still not seen such a coin

Neródno bi biló, če bi mu ga ne posláli (or . . . , **če mu ga nê bi posláli**)
It would be awkward if we didn't send it to him

Žé včéraj bi se bil vŕnil, ko bi ne bíl zamúdil vláka
He would have returned yesterday if he hadn't missed the train

Ne bómo se pozabíli ustáviti túdi pri klétkah s pápigami
We will not forget to stop also at the parrot cages

Če nê bi bíl v stíski, te nê bi prôsil
If I wasn't in a scrape I wouldn't ask you

Ako bi me poslúšal, se nesréča nê bi zgodíla
If he had listened to me the accident would not have happened

Vêde se, kàkor da bi me ne poznál (or . . . , **kàkor da me nê bi poznál**)
He behaves as if he didn't know me

Note: In the construction equivalent to English 'without . . . ing' the word order is **ne da bi**, e.g.
Pláneš v sôbo, ne da bi potŕkal 'You burst into the room without knocking'.

When the negative particle **ne** is the first word in a declarative sentence or in an imperative construction, it is immediately followed by the verb. If the sentence contains clitics these will immediately follow the negated verb, e.g.

Ne bojím se povédati resníce	I am not afraid to tell the truth
Ne jézi se náme	Do not get angry with me
Ne móreš mu verjéti	You cannot believe him
Ne želí jim pomágati	He doesn't want to help them

Note: If a negated reflexive verb is followed by another reflexive verb then the reflexive pronoun **se** need not be repeated, e.g. **Ne sramújejo se obnášati (se) kot májhni otrôci** 'They are not ashamed to behave like small children'.

12.6 CLITICS IN INITIAL POSITION IN A SENTENCE, CLAUSE OR QUESTION

There are certain occasions when a clitic appears in initial position in Slovene. This occurs in the following instances:

(a) When a subordinate clause precedes a main clause, then the main clause starts with the enclitic, e.g.

Če nê bi iméla gúb, bi bilà vídeti mláda
If she didn't have wrinkles, she would look young

Ker ga je domá zéblo, je šèl v kavárno
Because he felt cold at home, he went to the coffee shop

Ko sem se blížal híši, me je ôče čákal pred vráti
When I approached the house, father was waiting for me in front of the gate

(b) In direct speech the clitic occurs in first position in the reporting clause following the quote. Reporting verbs are those like 'add, ask, boast, suggest, urge, explain', etc.

'Kóliko tó stáne?', je vprášal
'How much does this cost?', he asked

'Jútri grémo v gledalíšče', je obvéstil učítelj učênce
'Tomorrow we are going to the theatre', the teacher informed the pupils

'Prídi k mêni', jo je iz tèmnega kóta poklícal
'Come to me', he called to her from the dark corner

'Šè málo boš mórala potrpéti', je dodál Tóne
'You will have to be patient a little longer', added Tone

'Ali bi mi lahkó posódil lopáto, prósim?', sem prôsil soséda
'Could you lend me a spade please?', I asked my neighbour

'Kakó pa bomo prišlì v klét?', se je pozanímala Sára
'How will we get to the cellar?', enquired Sara

'Kdó pa je numizmátik?', je spraševàl Andréj. 'Tó je nekdó, ki zbíra stàr denár', mu je pojásnil
'What is a numismatist?', asked Andrej. 'That is someone who collects old coins', he explained to him

(c) When the interrogative particle **ali/a** or another optionally deleted but understood element (e.g. **tó** 'this') is deleted from initial position, then the clitic may stand in initial position, e.g.

Si bolán?	Are you ill?
Si ga vídel?	Did you see him?
Ste bilì v Slovéniji?	Have you been to Slovenia?
Se je máma žé vrníla iz bólnice?	Has mum returned from the hospital already?
Ga ne poznáte?	Do you not know him?
Me ne móti	This doesn't disturb me
Me ne zaníma	This doesn't interest me

13 WORD FORMATION

The most widely used means of word formation in Slovene are affixation and various types of compounding. Deaffixation, where a word is truncated, is also encountered and mainly affects verbs. Abbreviation plays only a limited role in Slovene.

13.1 AFFIXATION

In affixation a suffix or a prefix is added to a word's root or base form to create a new word. In some cases more than one suffix or prefix may be added, e.g. **nèprepoznáven** 'unrecognisable' where the root **zna-** is preceded by three prefixes (**ne-, pre-, po-**) and followed by one suffix **-ven**.

13.2 SUFFIXATION

Suffixes may be native suffixes (e.g. **-ka, -arna, -ič** etc.) or loan suffixes (e.g. **-ist, -ant**). In this description of Slovene suffixes only native suffixes will normally be discussed.

Certain suffixes are very productive and widely used (e.g. **-ar, -ica**) while others are non-productive, i.e. rarely found and no longer used to derive new words (e.g. **-aj, -nik**). Suffixes may be simple (e.g. **-ec, -ica**) or compound, i.e. made up of two or more suffixal elements (e.g. **-iček, -ljivost**).

The addition of a suffix may or may not change the category of a word. For example the addition of the suffix **-ec** to the noun **bràt** 'brother' merely creates another noun with a diminutive meaning, i.e.. **brátec** 'little brother'. However, the addition of the possessive suffix **-ov** creates an adjective, i.e. **brátov** 'brother's'.

Suffixes may be relational or expressive. In the case of relational suffixes there is a logical link between the base word and the suffixed word e.g. **dèž** 'rain' – **dežník** 'umbrella' – **dežníkar** 'umbrella maker'. Relational suffixes may also change the category of a word, e.g. **dežníkast** (adj.) 'umbrella-like', **dežníkarski** (adj.) 'umbrella making' (e.g. **dežníkarska obŕt** 'umbrella making craft/trade').

Expressive suffixes indicate an attitude on the part of the speaker towards the designated noun, adjective or verb. Such suffixes may be diminutive (e.g. **otročíček** 'baby, tot'; **májcen** 'tiny'; **jókcati** 'to sob'), augmentative (e.g.

lomástiti 'to rumble, storm; **grozánski** 'huge'), pejorative (e.g. **klepetúlja** 'chatterbox') or affectionate (e.g. **čístkan** 'clean', **spánčkati** 'to sleep (of child)'). An expressive suffix always preserves the word's category.

It is also possible for one suffix to have a variety of meanings, e.g. **-ica** may denote a female or have a diminutive meaning.

As an example of the use of suffixes in Slovene, the various suffixes used with the root **čist(-)** 'clean' are given below:

číst	clean	**čistína**	clarity, purity
čístiti	to clean	**čistínski**	pure
čistílec	male cleaner; purifier; cleanser	**čístka**	purge
čistílka	female cleaner	**čistôta**	cleanliness
čistílen	cleansing, purifying	**čistôča**	cleanliness
čistílnica	refinery	**čístost**	purity
čistílnik	(oil) filter	**číščenje**	cleaning
čistílo	detergent		

13.3 CONSONANTAL ALTERNATIONS

Suffixation is sometimes accompanied by phonological changes, i.e. alternations in stem-final consonants. The consonantal alternations are mainly those brought about by palatalisation (e.g. **rôka** 'hand' – **ročíca** 'little hand'; see **1.9.1**) and jotation (e.g. **govédo** 'cattle' – **govéji** '(of) beef'; see **1.9.2**).

Changes brought about by jotation may then lead to the creation of analogous forms with the same alternations, which are not historically justified, e.g. **grád** 'castle' – **grájski** 'castle's (adj.)' by analogy with **govéd** – **govéji**, **redíti** 'to breed' – **réja** 'breeding', etc.

Other alternations occur as a result of assimilation or dissimilation, e.g.

Assimilative changes

sc	>	šč	:	**drevésce** 'small tree' – **drevéšček** 'Christmas tree'
sk	>	šč	:	**pomôrski** 'naval, maritime' – **pomoršćák** 'sailor'
st	>	šč	:	**góst** 'dense' – **goščáva** 'thicket'
z(nj)	>	ž(nj)	:	**vozíti** 'to drive – **vôžnja** 'ride'
s(nj)	>	š(nj)	:	**prosíti** 'to ask' – **prôšnja** 'request'
n(b)	>	m(b)	:	**pomeníti** 'to signify' – **pomémben** 'significant'

Dissimilative changes

č > š :	**gostáč** 'tenant' – **gostáški** 'tenant's'
k > š :	**otròk** 'child' – **otróški** 'child's, childish'
t > š :	**Hrvàt** 'Croat' – **hrváški** 'Croatian'
c > š :	**déklica** 'young girl' – **deklíštvo** 'maidenhood'

13.4   THE DERIVATION OF NOUNS BY SUFFIXATION (RELATIONAL SUFFIXES)

13.4.1   Suffixes used to derive nouns denoting persons or animals

(a) Masculine nouns denoting persons or animals may be derived from nouns, verbs or adjectives. The suffixes used are the following:

(i) From nouns

-ec	:	**Avstríjec** 'Austrian'; **zemljepísec** 'geographer'; **jezikoslóvec** 'linguist'
-ar	:	**brodár** 'ferryman'; **novínar** 'reporter'; **očálar** (pej.) 'someone who wears spectacles'
-anec	:	**luteránec** 'Lutheran'; **Peruánec** 'Peruvian'
-ik	:	**botánik** 'botanist'; **akadémik** 'academician'; **gráfik** 'illustrator'
-nik	:	**glásbenik** 'musician'; **zdravník** 'doctor'
-an	:	**meščán** 'citizen'; **otočán** 'islander'; **Parižán** 'Parisian'; **državiján** 'citizen'
-až	:	**kočijáž** 'coachman'
-ič	:	**dédič** 'heir'; **ríbič** 'fisherman'
-ač	:	**bradáč** 'someone with a long/large beard'; **brkáč** 'someone with a large moustache'
-ež	:	**prismódež** 'foolish person'; **Angléž** 'Englishman'
-oz	:	**Francóz** 'Frenchman'
-alec	:	**industriálec** 'industrialist'
-ur	:	**nemčúr** 'Germanophile'

(ii) From verbs

-ja	:	**vódja** 'leader'
-ec	:	**jézdec** 'horseman'; **lôvec** 'hunter'; **žánjec** 'reaper'
-lec	:	**brálec** 'reader'; **gasílec** 'fireman'; **prebiválec** 'inhabitant'
-vec	:	**pévec** 'singer'; **brívec** 'barber'; **volívec** 'voter'
-ič	:	**vodìč** 'guide'; **mlatìč** 'thresher'; **gonìč** 'herder'
-ač	:	**baháč** 'boaster'; **jaháč** 'rider'; **vesláč** 'oarsman'
-uh	:	**dremúh** 'sleepyhead'
-avh	:	**dremávh** 'sleepyhead'
-aj	:	**čuváj** 'guard, keeper'; **strežáj** 'servant'
-nik	:	**sodník** 'judge'; **sprevódnik** 'conductor'; **bojévnik** 'combatant'
-telj	:	**gostítelj** 'host'; **gradítelj** 'builder'; **ravnátelj** 'headmaster'
-ček	:	**postréžček** 'porter'
-in	:	**potepín** 'vagrant'
-un	:	**vohún** 'spy'
-ar	:	**kúhar** 'cook'; **zidár** 'stonemason'
-avs	:	**godrnjávs** 'grumbler'

-avt : **zmikávt** 'thief'
-ež : **gúlež** 'swot'; **motovílež** 'clumsy person'

(iii) From adjectives

-ec : **stárec** 'old man'; **hinávec** 'hypocrite'; **góbavec** 'leper'
-ič : **mladìč** 'young one, cub'; **slabìč** 'weakling'
-enič : **mladénič** 'young man'
-uh : **debelúh** 'fat man'; **lenúh** 'idler'
-jak : **divják** 'savage'; **zanesenják** 'enthusiast'; **južnják** 'southerner'
-ček : **ljúbček** 'sweetheart'
-ik : **bolník** 'patient'
-an : **velikán** 'giant'
-jan : **modriján** 'sage'
-in : **dolgín** 'tall person'
-un : **grdún** 'ugly person'
-avš : **grdávš** 'ugly person'
-avž : **grdávž** 'ugly person'
-ež : **duhovítež** 'witty person'

The foreign suffixes **-or, -ant, -ent** normally occur in borrowed words, e.g. **inštrúktor, emigránt, korespondènt,** etc. However, the suffix **-ant** is also found used with native roots, i.e. **zabušànt** 'shirker'; **zafrkànt** 'tease'; **prevaránt** 'deceiver'.

(b) Feminine nouns denoting persons or animals may be derived from nouns, verbs and adjectives. The suffixes used are the following :

(i) From nouns

-inja : **Angléžinja** 'Englishwoman'; **prerókinja** 'prophetess'; **biológinja** 'biologist (f.)'
-nica : **špórtnica** 'sportswoman'
-ica : **prijáteljica** 'friend (f.)'; **lisíca** 'vixen'; **profésorica** 'professor (f.)'
-ka : **cigánka** 'gypsy woman'; **barbárka** 'barbarian (f.)'; **študêntka** 'girl student'; **medvédka** 'she-bear'
-ična : **kraljíčna** 'princess'

(ii) From verbs

-a : **čvéka** 'babbler'; **príča** 'witness'
-ica : **períca** 'laundress'; **rešíteljica** 'saviour, rescuer (f.)'
-nica : **nevédnica** 'ignorant woman'; **naročníca** 'subscriber (f.)'
-ača : **klopotáča** 'rattlesnake'; **lováča** 'prostitute'
-lja : **fŕklja** 'tomboy'
-ilja : **šivílja** 'dressmaker'; **pletílja** 'knitter'
-ulja : **klepetúlja** 'chatterbox'; **blebetúlja** 'windbag'

| -ka | : | **brálka** 'reader (f.)'; **poslušálka** 'listener (f.)'; |
| (-lka, -vka) | | **pévka** 'singer (f.)'; **volívka** 'voter (f.)' |

(iii) From adjectives

| -ica | : | **nágica** 'stripper' |
| -ka | : | **sívka** 'a grey cow' |

13.4.2 Suffixes used to derive nouns denoting objects, substances, etc.

(a) Masculine nouns denoting objects may be derived from nouns, verbs and adjectives. The suffixes used are the following:

(i) From nouns

| -ec | : | **burgúndec** 'Burgundy wine'; **vipávec** 'Vipava wine' |
| -ak | : | **zidák** 'brick' |

(ii) From verbs

-ec	:	**plôvec** 'buoy'
-lec	:	**vlačílec** 'tug'; **grélec** 'hot water bottle'
-vec	:	**ostrívec** 'acute accent'; **štévec** 'meter'
-ač	:	**odpiráč** 'tin opener'
-aj	:	**držáj** 'handle'; **izpuščáj** 'eruption'
-elj	:	**cúcelj** 'baby's dummy'
-nik	:	**hladílnik** 'refrigerator'; **brívnik** 'razor';
(-lnik, -vnik)		**menjálnik** '(transmission) gear'

(iii) From adjectives

-ec	:	**krúhovec** 'breadfruit tree'; **maslénec** 'butter bean'
-ič	:	**belìč** 'farthing'
-ak	:	**krávjak** 'cow dung'
-nik	:	**jábolčnik** 'cider'
-uš	:	**belúš** 'asparagus'
-ež	:	**bélež** 'whitewash'

(b) Feminine nouns denoting objects, substances, etc. are derived from nouns, verbs and adjectives with the following suffixes:

(i) From nouns

| -lica | : | **cvetlíca** 'flower' |
| -ka | : | **amerikánka** 'trout' |

(ii) From verbs

| -ica | : | **bodíca** 'thorn, prickle'; **grebljíca** 'poker' |
| -nica | : | **dovódnica** 'vein'; **nosílnica** 'stretcher' |

-ača	:	igráča 'toy'; brisáča 'towel'; grebáča 'poker'
-lja	:	gréblja 'poker'; žvŕklja 'whisk, beater'
-lka	:	budílka 'alarm clock'; glasílka 'vocal cord'; brizgálka 'syringe'
-ina	:	tekočína 'liquid'

(iii) From adjectives

-ica	:	kíslica 'sorrel'; mŕzlica 'fever'
-ina	:	kislína 'acid'
-ika	:	mladíka 'sprout, shoot'
-ulja	:	krivúlja 'curve'

(c) Neuter nouns denoting objects, substances, etc. are derived from verbs with the following suffixes:

-lo	:	mehčálo 'softener'; bodálo 'dagger'; strašílo 'ghost'; lepílo 'paste, glue'
-vo	:	cepívo 'vaccine, serum'; strelívo 'ammunition'; gorívo 'fuel'

13.4.3 Collective nouns

Collective nouns are either feminine or neuter and may be derived from nouns.

(a) Neuter collective nouns are derived with the following suffixes:

-je	:	otóčje 'archipelago'; kámenje 'rocks'; grmíčje 'shrubbery'
-evje	:	vejévje 'branches'
-ovje	:	hrástovje 'oak forest'; grmóvje 'shrubbery'
-stvo	:	móštvo 'team'; članstvo 'members'

(b) Feminine collective nouns are derived with the following suffixes:

-a	:	gospôda 'gentlemen'; déca 'children'
-ina	:	divjáčina 'game'
-ovina	:	hrastovína 'oak wood'
-ščina	:	duhóvščina 'clergy'
-(j)ad	:	otročád 'children'; divjád 'game'

13.4.4 Nouns denoting a place

Masculine and feminine nouns denoting a place are derived from nouns, verbs and adjectives, while neuter nouns denoting a place are derived from nouns and verbs but not adjectives.

(a) Masculine nouns denoting a place are derived with the following suffixes:

(i) From nouns

-nik : **ríbnik** 'fish pond'; **kúrnik** 'hen coop'; **zélnik** 'cabbage patch'

(ii) From verbs

-njak : **blodnják** 'maze, labyrinth'

(iii) From adjectives

-njak : **opičnják** 'monkey cage'; **ovčnják** 'sheep pen'

(b) Feminine nouns denoting a place are derived with the following suffixes:

(i) From nouns

-nica : **mesníca** 'butcher's shop'; **čuvájnica** 'watchman's hut'; **kováčnica** 'smithy, forge'; **kolesárnica** 'bicycle shed'; **carinárnica** 'customs house'

-ovnica : **kotlóvnica** 'boiler house'

-arna : **čolnárna** 'boathouse'; **cukrárna** 'sugar refinery'

-ija : **kovačíja** 'smithy, forge'; **davkaríja** 'tax office'; **Ánglija** 'England'; **Rúsija** 'Russia'; **planšaríja** 'mountain chalet'

-ura : **intendantúra** 'commisariat'; **prefektúra** 'prefect's office'

(ii) From verbs

-a : **stája** 'fold, pen'

-nica : **čakálnica** 'waiting room'; **spálnica** 'bedroom';

(-lnica/-vnica) **jedíinica** 'dining room'; **pívnica** 'tavern'; **brívnica** 'barber shop'

-(l)na : **prodajálna** 'shop'; **gostílna** 'inn'

(iii) From adjectives

-ica : **čájnica** 'tea room'; **klávnica** 'abbatoir'; **gróbnica** 'tomb, crypt'

-išnica : **noríšnica** 'lunatic asylum'; **bolníšnica** 'hospital'

-ina : **kraljevína** 'kingdom'; **carjevína** 'empire'

(c) Neuter nouns denoting a place are derived from nouns and verbs with the suffix **-išče**, e.g.

(i) From nouns

gnojíšče 'dunghill'; **krompiríšče** 'potato field'

(ii) From verbs

strelíšče 'shooting range'; **igríšče** 'playground'; **gledalíšče** 'theatre'; **drsalíšče** 'rink'

13.4.5 Abstract nouns

Abstract nouns denote a quality or condition or intangible thing rather than a concrete object. They also include philosophical, scientific and artistic concepts, languages and branches of science.

(a) Masculine abstract nouns tend to be loan words with the suffix -izem, e.g. **alkoholízem** 'alcoholism'; **agnosticízem** 'agnosticism'; **cinízem** 'cynicism'.

(b) Feminine abstract nouns are derived from nouns and adjectives with the following suffixes:

   (i) From nouns

-arija	:	**otročaríja** 'childishness'
-ota	:	**grozôta** 'horror'
-ura	:	**advokatúra** 'the legal profession'; **profesúra** 'professorship'

   (ii) From adjectives

-oba	:	**grenkôba** 'bitterness'; **lenôba** 'laziness'
-ica	:	**náglica** 'haste'
-inja	:	**blagínja** 'welfare'
-obija	:	**hudobíja** 'mischief'; **grdobíja** 'dirty trick'
-ina	:	**belína** 'whiteness'; **glob(oč)ína** 'depth'
-ota	:	**gluhôta** 'deafness'; **nagôta** 'nakedness'
-oča	:	**čistôča** 'cleanliness'
-ost	:	**grobóst** 'rudeness'; **hvaléžnost** 'gratitude'; **slabóst** weakness'

(c) Neuter abstract nouns are derived from nouns and adjectives with the following suffixes:

   (i) From nouns

-stvo	:	**cigánstvo** 'gypsydom'; **gostínstvo** 'hotel management'; **gurmánstvo** 'greediness'
-štvo	:	**beráštvo** 'beggary'; **devíštvo** 'virginity'
-evsto	:	**hlápčevstvo** 'servitude'

   (ii) From adjectives

-stvo	:	**bogástvo** 'riches'; **izgnánstvo** 'exile'
-štvo	:	**siromáštvo** 'poverty'; **deklíštvo** 'maidenhood'

13.4.6 Verbal nouns

(a) The vast majority of verbal nouns are neuter and are derived from verbs with the suffixes -nje, -tje (see **6.38**), e.g. **bránje** 'reading'; **gíbanje** 'motion';

hlajênje 'cooling'; **smejánje** 'laughing'; **pletênje** 'knitting'; **mamljênje** 'enticement'; **migljánje** 'twinkling'; **díhanje** 'breathing'; **grétje** 'warming, heating'; **sprejétje** 'acceptance'; **mlétje** 'grinding, milling'.

Other verbal nouns, including those expressing the result of the verbal action may be derived with other suffixes or even by means of deaffixation, i.e. the verbal root alone is used to form the noun. These nouns may be either masculine or feminine.

(b) Other suffixes used to form verbal nouns

    (i) Masculine

-aj	:	**migljáj** 'wink'; **smehljáj** 'smile'
-ljaj	:	**dihljáj** 'breath'; **vzdihljáj** 'sigh'
-ek	:	**domíslek** 'fancy, idea'; **dogódek** 'event, occurrence'
-ček	:	**izkupíček** 'takings'; **dobíček** 'profit, gain'
-ež	:	**drémež** 'doze'; **krádež** 'theft'; **lájež** 'barking'; **vŕvež** 'bustle'

    (ii) Feminine

-a	:	**zmága** 'victory'; **izgúba** 'loss'; **ukána** 'trick, ruse'
-ja	:	**krája** 'theft'; **hója** 'walking'; **kája** 'smoking'; **mólža** 'milking'
-ba	:	**obsôdba** 'sentence'; **enáčba** 'equation'; **brámba** 'defence';
-ura	:	**dresúra** 'training'
-nja	:	**grádnja** 'construction'; **blódnja** 'delirium'; **vôžnja** 'drive, ride'
-ava	:	**izpeljáva** 'execution; derivation'; **izmenjáva** 'exchange'; **zidáva** 'building'
-ezen	:	**bolézen** 'illness'; **ljubézen** 'love'
-tev	:	**spregátev** 'conjugation'; **terjátev** 'demand'; **molítev** 'prayer'; **podražítev** 'price rise'; **osvobodítev** 'liberation'

(c) Verbal nouns formed by deaffixation

    (i) *Masculine*: **cvrkút** 'chirping'; **nadév** 'stuffing'; **mŕk** 'eclipse'; **donòs** 'yield'; **napàd** 'attack'; **prenòs** 'transmission'

    (ii) *Feminine*: **pomóč** 'help'; **zapóved** 'order, command'; **rást** 'growth'; **skŕb** 'care'

13.5   THE DERIVATION OF NOUNS BY SUFFIXATION (EXPRESSIVE SUFFIXES)

13.5.1   Diminutive suffixes

Diminutive nouns are derived from nouns with the following suffixes:

(a)   Masculine nouns

-(e)c	:	**brégec** 'small shore, bank'; **vétrc** 'breeze'; **zóbec** 'small tooth'
-ič	:	**grmìč** 'small shrub'; **snôpič** 'fascicule'
-ek	:	**gúmbek** 'small button'; **ptíček** 'small bird'
-ček	:	**strôjček** 'small machine'; **zvônček** 'small bell'
-iček	:	**čolníček** 'dinghy'; **gozdíček** 'small wood'

(b)   Feminine nouns

-ca	:	**živálca** 'small animal'; **klópca** 'small bench'
-ica	:	**híšica** 'small house'; **nôgica** 'small leg'; **ročíca** 'small hand'
-ka	:	**púnčka** 'small girl'; **nogavíčka** 'small sock'

(c)   Neuter nouns

-ce	:	**méstece** 'small town'; **ústeca** 'small mouth'; **vrátca** 'door';
(plur. **-ca**)		**bêdrce** 'small thigh'

13.5.2   Affectionate/emotive diminutive suffixes

These suffixes have an emotive as well as a diminutive meaning and apply to masculine, feminine and neuter nouns, e.g.

(a)   Masculine emotive suffixes

-če	:	**Tónče** 'dear little Tone'; **Andréjče** 'dear little Andrej'
-i	:	**ôči** 'daddy'
-ko	:	**sínko** 'dear little son'; **déčko** 'little lad'

(b)   Feminine emotive suffixes

-ica	:	**krávica** 'dear little cow'; **barábica** 'little scoundrel'
-ička	:	**bábička** 'granny'; **golobíčka** 'little dove'
-i	:	**mámi** 'mummy'; **múci** 'pussy'

(c)   Neuter emotive suffixes

-ce	:	**čêlce** 'little forehead'; **mescè** 'meat'

13.5.3   Pejorative suffixes

Pejorative nouns of all three genders may be derived from nouns, verbs and adjectives with the following suffixes:

(a) Suffixes used to derive pejorative nouns from nouns

(i) Masculine

-on	:	**beračón** 'beggar'
-ur	:	**nemčúr** 'Germanophile'
-avs/avz	:	**kmetávs/kmetávz** 'peasant'
-ež	:	**barábež** 'scoundrel'

(ii) Feminine

-ulja	:	**klepetúlja** 'gossip'; **blebetúlja** 'blabbermouth (f.)'
-ela	:	**babéla** 'woman'; **hudičéla** 'harridan'
-ura	:	**babúra** 'hag, harridan'; **knjižúra** 'book without literary merit'; **hišúra** 'ugly house'

(iii) Neuter

-šče	:	**bábišče** 'puny old woman'
-še	:	**babšè** 'puny old woman'; **kravšè** 'scrawny old cow'

(b) Suffixes used to derive pejorative nouns from adjectives

(i) Masculine

-uh	:	**debelúh** 'very fat man'; **lenúh** 'idler'; **skopúh** 'miser'
-uhar	:	**lenúhar** 'idler, lazy man'
-avs	:	**robávs** 'brute, tough'; **grdávs** 'unattractive person'

(ii) Feminine

-uhinja	:	**debelúhinja** 'very fat woman'
-uharica	:	**debelúharica** 'very fat woman'

(c) Suffixes used to derive pejorative nouns from verbs

(i) Masculine

-uh	:	**smrdúh** 'smelly person'; **smrčúh** 'snorer'
-ač	:	**čvekáč** 'blabberer'; **gobezdáč** 'blusterer'
-avt	:	**stikávt** 'rummager'

(ii) Feminine

-uhinja	:	**požerúhinja** 'gluttonous woman';
-ulja	:	**smrdúlja** 'smelly woman'

(iii) Neuter

-alo	:	**jezikálo** 'talkative person'; **gobezdálo** 'blusterer'

13.6 THE DERIVATION OF ADJECTIVES BY SUFFIXATION

13.6.1 Adjectives derived from nouns

(a) Possessive adjectives

Adjectives expressing individual, specific possession are derived from masculine and neuter nouns with the suffixes **-ov/-ev** and from feminine nouns with the suffix **-in**:

-ov	:	**brátov** 'the brother's'; **telétov** 'the calf's'; **sosédov** 'the neighbour's'
-ev	:	**stríčev** 'the uncle's'; **delovódjev** 'the foreman's'
-in	:	**sêstrin** 'the sister's'; **hčérin** 'the daughter's; **múcin** 'the cat's'

(b) Adjectives expressing generic possession are derived from the names of people, animals, birds, insects with the suffixes **-ji, -ski, -ški**

-ji	:	**golóbji** 'of pigeons'; **pávji** 'of peacocks'; **lévji** 'of lions'; **čebélji** 'of bees'; **knéžji** 'of a prince, princely'; **princésji** 'of a princess; **žužélčji** 'of insects'
-ski	:	**môški** 'of men'; **délavski** 'of workers'; **režisêrski** 'of directors'; **škorpijónski** 'of scorpions'
-ški	:	**angléški** 'English'; **katóliški** 'Catholic'; **predsédniški** 'chairman's'; **razbójniški** 'of robbers'; **hrváški** 'Croatian'

(c) Relational adjectives

Relational adjectives whose meanings are related to the core meaning of the noun and express type, similitude or the material from which something is made are derived from nouns with the following suffixes:

-anski	:	**božánski** 'divine'; **človečánski** 'humane'; **pomladánski** 'Spring'
-en (= ən)	:	**úmen** 'intelligent'; **božíčen** 'Christmas'; **hrúpen** 'noisy'
-en	:	**čústven** 'emotional'; **grádben** 'building'; **lesén** 'wooden'; **bakrén** 'copper'
-ičen	:	**kémičen** 'chemical'; **simbóličen** 'symbolic'
-even	:	**dežéven** 'rainy'; **krajéven** 'local'
-oven	:	**čaróven** 'magical'; **čekóven** 'cheque'
-in	:	**lúnin** 'lunar'; **púškin** 'rifle'
-ov	:	**ogljíkov** 'carbon'; **citrónov** 'citric'; **premógov** 'coal'
-ev	:	**alumínijev** 'aluminium'; **čéšnjev** 'cherry'
-nat	:	**slámnat** 'straw'; **papírnat** 'paper'; **cévnat** 'tube-like'
-ast	:	**brónast** 'bronze'; **gúm(ij)ast** 'rubber'; **čebúlast** 'bulbous'; **cúnjast** 'ragged'

(d) Adjectives which express the abundance of a feature or property are derived from nouns with the following suffixes:

-av	:	**dlákav** 'hairy'; **solzàv** 'tearful'
-ast	:	**gúbast** 'wrinkled'; **sájast** 'sooty'
-at	:	**bradàt** 'bearded'; **glavàt** 'big-headed, thick-skulled'
-nat	:	**véjnat** 'branchy'; **pródnat** 'gravelly'
-evit	:	**gričévit** 'hilly'
-ovit	:	**duhovít** 'witty'
-evnat	:	**dežévnat** 'rainy'
-iv	:	**črvív** 'maggoty, full of worms'; **ušív** 'lice ridden'

13.6.2 Adjectives derived from verbs

(a) Adjectives may be derived from active and passive participles, e.g. **gníl** 'rotten'; **pozábljen** 'forgotten'; **potŕt** 'dejected'; **uvél** 'withered'; **gorèč** 'burning'; **deróč** 'torrential'; **omíkan** 'civilised'

(b) Other adjectives are formed from verbs with the following suffixes:

-en	:	**negíben** 'immobile'; **kôven** 'malleable'
-len	:	**likálen** 'ironing'; **uspaválen** 'soporific'; **volílen** 'elective'; **hranílen** 'nourishing'
-ven	:	**štéven** 'counting'; **délaven** 'busy, diligent'; **obetáven** 'promising'
-ast	:	**šépast** 'lame'; **spremínjast** 'changeable'
-av	:	**šépav** 'lame'; **hvalísav** 'boastful'
-jiv	:	**deljív** 'divisible'; **izpeljív** 'feasible'
-ljiv	:	**dosegljív** 'attainable'; **prevedljív** 'translatable'

13.6.3 Adjectives derived from adjectives

These adjectives express a greater or lesser or approximate degree of the quality of the original adjective. They are formed with the following suffixes:

(a) Diminutives

-kan	:	**čístkan** 'really clean'
-čkan	:	**bolánčkan** 'sick'; **drôbčkan** 'tiny'
-čken	:	**májčken** 'wee, tiny'
-cen	:	**drôbcen** 'tiny'; **májcen** 'tiny'

(b) Augmentatives

-anski	:	**velikánski** 'gigantic'
-ovit	:	**grozovít** 'dreadful, atrocious'

(c) Approximating adjectives

-ikav	:	bledíkav	
-ičen	:	bledíčen	
-ičast	:	bledíčast	} 'palish, pallid'
-ikast	:	bledíkast	

-kast : debélkast 'somewhat fat'; ruménkast 'yellowish'; grénkast 'somewhat bitter'

-ljat	:	grenkljàt	
-ljast	:	grénkljast	} 'somewhat bitter'

13.6.4 Adjectives derived from adverbs

These are derived with the following suffixes

-nji : sedánji 'present'; zgórnji 'upper'
-šnji : takójšnji 'immediate'; zdájšnji 'current, present'; včerajšnji 'yesterday's'
-šen : precéjšen 'considerable'
-ski : lánski 'last year's'

13.7 THE DERIVATION OF VERBS

For the derivation of imperfective verbs by suffixation see **6.45**.

Verbs may be derived from verbs, nouns, adjectives, pronouns, numerals and interjections, e.g.

(a) Verbs from nouns

korákati 'to pace'; kraljeváti 'to reign'; beráčiti 'to beg'; gladováti 'to go hungry'; gnojíti 'to compost'

(b) Verbs from adjectives

bledéti 'to grow pale'; globíti 'to deepen'; mehčáti 'to soften'; obogatíti 'to enrich'

(c) Verbs from pronouns

tíkati 'to say tí (you)'; víkati 'to say ví (you)'

(d) Verbs from numerals

podvojíti 'to (re)double'; početvériti 'to quadruple'

(e) Verbs from interjections

čívkati 'to cheep'; grúliti 'to coo'; hmkati 'to hem and hum'

(f) Verbs from verbs

(i) Verbs with emotive or diminutive meanings are derived from basic verbs with the following suffixes:

Note: These verbs are often used when talking to children.

-kati	:	**lêžkati**	to lie down
-čkati	:	**stójčkati**	to stand
-cati	:	**jókcati**	to sob
-icati	:	**kotalícati**	to roll
-incati	:	**krulíncati**	to grunt

(ii) Verbs with augmentative or pejorative meanings are derived with the following suffixes:

-astiti	:	**lomástiti**	to burst through noisily
-ihati	:	**sopíhati**	to puff and pant
-avhati	:	**dremávhati**	to have a good doze
-isati	:	**hvalísati se**	to boast exaggeratedly

13.8   THE DERIVATION OF ADVERBS

Adverbs are derived primarily from adjectives with **-o/-e** (see **7.2**). Otherwise in the derivation of adverbs one should note particularly the use of the suffix **-oma/-ema** which is used to derive adverbs from nouns, adjectives, verbs and prepositional phrases.

(a) From nouns

načêloma 'in principle'; **večínoma** 'mostly'; **hípoma** 'instantly'; **cúrkoma** 'in streams'; **stôpnjema** 'by degrees'; **izjémoma** 'exceptionally'; **krížema** 'crosswise'

(b) From adjectives

rédkoma 'rarely'; **tíhoma** 'quietly'; **popólnoma** 'completely, entirely'; **plôskoma** 'flat'

(c) From verbs

krádoma 'stealthily'; **nemúdoma** 'promptly'; **nenéhoma** 'incessantly'; **nehôtoma** 'involuntarily'; **skrívoma** 'secretly'; **nevédoma** 'unwittingly'; **zdŕžema** 'continuously'; **nevzdŕžema** 'incessantly'

(d) From prepositional phrases

sčásoma 'gradually'; **postópoma** 'gradually'; **potíhoma** 'silently'; **medpótoma** 'on the way'

13.9   PREFIXATION

Prefixation is widely used to form perfective verbs from imperfective verbs (see **6.42**), but is less frequently used to derive nouns or adjectives. Such derivation is limited to the following prefixes:

(a) Prefixes used to derive nouns

nad-	:	**nadvláda** 'supremacy, hegemony'
ne-	:	**nèdisciplína** 'indiscipline'
pa-	:	**pákróg** 'ellipse'
pod-	:	**pòdčástnik** 'non-commissioned officer'
pra-	:	**prájêzik** 'proto language'
po-	:	**pòsezóna** 'after season'
pre-	:	**prebòj** 'break-through'
pred-	:	**prèdjéd** 'hors d'oeuvre'
so-	:	**sòdélavec** 'collaborator, co-worker'
laži-	:	**lážidemokracíja** 'pseudo-democracy'; **lážibóg** 'a false god'
med-	:	**mèdígra** 'interlude'
z-	:	**zrastlína** 'growth'
za-	:	**zagóvor** 'advocacy'
proti-	:	**prótisrédstvo** 'antidote'
ob-	:	**obtôžba** 'accusation'
pol-	:	**pólbóg** 'demigod'; **pólmrák** 'twilight'

(b) Prefixes used to derive adjectives

nad-	:	**nàdčlovéški** 'superhuman'
pa-	:	**pákróžen** 'elliptical'
pra-	:	**prázgodovínski** 'prehistoric'
pre-	:	**prelép** 'very beautiful'
pred-	:	**predmésten** 'suburban'
so-	:	**sorazméren** 'proportional'
pod-	:	**podzêmeljski** 'subterranean'
po-	:	**pòbínkošten** 'post Whitsun'
laži	:	**lážiznánstven** 'pseudo-scientific'
proti-	:	**prótipostáven** 'illegal'
med-	:	**mèddržáven** 'interstate'
ob-	:	**obcésten** 'wayside'
pol-	:	**póldívji** 'semi-wild'; **pólslép** 'purblind'
ne-	:	**nèrjavèč** 'rustless'; **nèoficiálen** 'unofficial'; **nèokréten** 'clumsy'; **nèbístven** 'unessential'

Note: **ne-** is a very productive prefix in adjectives and is used to create antonyms.

13.10 COMPOUND WORDS

A compound word is a combination of two or more words, which function as a single word. Compound words are formed in two basic ways (a) by juxtaposition or concatenation, (b) by composition.

13.10.1 Concatenation

In this type of compounding the words of a phrase or syntactic structure are merely linked together to form a new word, which might be a noun, adjective, numeral or adverb. This phenomenon is, however, rare in Slovene.

Examples

očenàš 'the Lord's prayer' (< **ôče nàš** 'Our Father'); **dólgčas** 'boredom' (< **dólg čàs** 'long hour'); **sevéda** 'of course' (< **se vé da** 'it is known that'); **nebódigatréba** 'an univited person' (< **ne bódi ga tréba** 'he is not needed'); **neprídipràv** 'a good for nothing' (< **ne prídi pràv** 'he is of no use'); **pétintrídeset** 'thirty five' (< **pét in trídeset** 'five and thirty'); **bojažêljen** 'bellicose' (< **bôja žêljen** 'desirous of battle'); **navsezgódaj** 'early in the morning' (< **na vsè zgódaj** 'early for everything'); **némanič** 'a penniless person' (< **nema nìč** 'he has nothing')

13.10.2 Composition

In composition two full meaning words are joined together. Nouns, adjectives and verbs may be formed by composition, although the formation of verbs in this way is very limited, e.g.

(a) Nouns

    (i)   When two nouns are joined together a link vowel **-o-/-e-** is used if the first noun ends in a consonant, e.g. **zobozdravník** 'dentist'; **mišelóvka** 'mousetrap'; **nosoróg** 'rhinocerous'; **krvodajálec** 'blood donor'; **volkodlák** 'werewolf'.

Note: **dláka** also loses final **-a** and becomes a masculine noun.

    (ii) If the first noun is a neuter noun in **-o/-e** or a masculine noun in **-o** then no additional link vowel is added, e.g. **drevoréd** 'avenue of trees'; **delokróg** 'sphere of activity'; **morjeplóvec** 'seafarer'; **kínokámera** 'cine camera'; **kolovódja** 'ringleader'; **ávtocésta** 'highway'.

    (iii) If the first noun is a feminine noun in **-a** then this **-a** is replaced by **-o-/-e-**, e.g. **živinozdravník** 'vet'; **slavolók** 'triumphal arch'; **glavobòl** 'headache'; **zemljevíd** 'map'.

(iv) If the first element in composition is an adjective or an adjectival pronoun and the second element a noun, then the adjective takes the link vowels -o-/-e-, e.g. **črnoborzijánec** 'blackmarketeer'; **sámoupráva** 'autonomy'; **svojevóljnost** 'arbitrariness'; **dolgožívost** 'longevity'.

(v) If one of the elements is a verbal root then again a link vowel -o-/-e is used, e.g. **vodomér** 'water gauge'; **vrtoglávica** 'vertigo'; **zemljepís** 'geography'; **tresorépka** 'wagtail'; **brzojàv** 'telegram'.

(b) Adjectives

These are formed from (i) a noun plus verb, (ii) an adjective plus a noun, (iii) two adjectives. Once again a link vowel -o-/-e is used.

In the case of (i) and (ii) the adjectival suffix **-en** is often added to the second element, e.g.

(i) **črvojéden** 'wormeaten'; **miroljúben** 'peaceful'; **slavohlépen** 'ambitious'

(ii) **kratkovíden** 'short sighted'; **dolgočásen** 'boring'; **mladoléten** 'under age'

(iii) **sívomóder** 'greyish blue'; **cerkvénoslovánski** 'church slavonic'; **óbčečlovéški** 'common to mankind'

(c) Verbs

There are very few examples of compounded verbs. They are derived from adjectives plus nouns or prepositional phrases, e.g. **dolgovéziti** 'to be longwinded'; **slepomíšiti** 'to feign'; **udobrovóljiti** 'to put in a good mood'; **obelodániti** (arch.) 'to publish'; **dolgočásiti** 'to bore'; **uravnotéžiti** 'to balance'.

BIBLIOGRAPHY

Albretti, A. (1995) *Colloquial Slovene*, London-New York: Routledge

Albretti, A. (1997) *Slovene. A complete course for beginners*, London: Hodder and Stoughton

Andoljšek, E., Jevšenak, L. and Korošec T. (1973) *Povejmo slovensko*, Ljubljana: Državna založba Slovenije

Bajec, A. (1950–2) *Besedotvorje slovenskega jezika*, vol. I: *Izpeljava samostalnikov*, vol. II: *Izpeljava slovenskih pridevov*, vol. III: *Zloženke*, Ljubljana: Slovenska akademija znanosti in umetnosti

Bajec, A., Kolarič, R. and Rupel, M. (1964) *Slovenska slovnica*, Ljubljana: Državna založba Slovenije

Bajec, A. et al. (1962) (eds) *Slovenski pravopis*, Ljubljana: Državna založba Slovenije

Bajec, A. et al. (1997) (eds) *Slovar slovenskega knjižnega jezika*, Ljubljana: Slovenska akademija znanosti in umetnosti

Berce, S. et al. (eds) (1989) *Angleško-slovenski slikovni slovar*, Oxford-Ljubljana: Clarendon-Cankarjeva založba

Breznik, A. (1982) *Jezikoslovne razprave*, Ljubljana: Slovenska matica

Ceklin, I. and Levstik, N. (1998) *Kaj znam za maturo. Slovenski jezik pregledno in nazorno*, Ljubljana: Zavod Republike Slovenije za šolstvo

Čuk, M., Mihelič, M. and Vuga, G. (1996) *Odkrivajmo slovenščino*, Ljubljana: Filozofska fakulteta

Čuk, M. (1994) *Za začetek. Učimo se slovenščino*, Ljubljana: Filozofska fakulteta

Davis, M.G. (1989) *Aspects of Adverbial Placement in English and Slovene*, Munich: Sagner

Derbyshire, W.W. (1993) *A Basic Slovene Reference Grammar*, Columbus, Ohio: Slavica

Grad, A. and Leeming, H. (1990) *Slovensko-angleški slovar*, Ljubljana: Državna založba Slovenije

Grad, A., Škerlj, A. and Vitorovič, N. (1994) *Veliki angleško-slovenski slovar*, Ljubljana: Državna založba Slovenije

Gradišnik, J. (1993) *Slovensko ali angleško*, Celje: Mohorjeva družba

Gradišnik, J. (1974) *Slovenščina za vsakogar*, Ljubljana: Cankarjeva založba

Hajnšek-Holz, M. and Jakopin P. (1996) (eds) *Odzadnji slovar slovenskega jezika*, Ljubljana: Slovenska akademija znanosti in umetnosti

Jug-Kranjec, H. (1992) *Slovenščina za tujce*, Ljubljana: Filozofska fakulteta

Jurančič, J. (1971) *Slovenački jezik*, Ljubljana: Državna založba Slovenije

Kopčevar, I. and Kopčevar, C. (1971) *Jezikovna vadnica*, Ljubljana: Državna založba Slovenije

Križaj-Ortar, M. (1989) *Učimo se slovenščino*, Ljubljana; Filozofska fakulteta

Lenček, R.L. (1966) *The Verb Pattern of Contemporary Standard Slovene*, Wiesbaden: Otto Harrassowitz

Lenček, R.L. (1982) *The Structure and History of the Slovene Language*, Columbus, Ohio: Slavica

Lenček, R.L. (1996) *Izbrane razprave in eseji*, Ljubljana: Slovenska matica v Ljubljani

Madžarevič, B. (ed.) (1993) *Password. English Dictionary for Speakers of Slovenian*, Ljubljana: Državna založba Slovenije

Markovič, A. (1995) *Učimo se slovenščino (II)*, Ljubljana: Filozofska fakulteta

Orešnik, J. (1994) *Slovenski glagolski vid in univerzalna slovnica*, Ljubljana: Slovenska akademija znanosti in umetnosti.

Pirih, N. (1997) *Slovenščina na koncu jezika*, Ljubljana: Filozofska fakulteta

Plotnikova, O.S. (1990) *Slovenskij jazyk*, Moscow: Moscow University

Povodnik, M.P. (1992) *Oblikoslovje*, Ljubljana-Nova Gorica: Jutro

Povodnik, M.P. (1993) *Skladnja*, Ljubljana-Nova Gorica: Jutro

Priestly, T.M.S. (1993) *Slovene*. In: Comrie, B. and Corbett, G.G., *The Slavonic Languages*, London, New York, pp. 388–451: Routledge

Rehder, P. (1998) *Das Slovenische*. In: Rehder, P., *Einführung in die Slavischen Sprachen*, Darmstadt: Wissenschaftliche Buchgesellschaft

Schlamberger-Brezar, M. (1994) *Učimo se slovenščino (III)*, Ljubljana: Filozofska fakulteta

Skaza, J. (1995), *Pravopis*, Ljubljana: Jutro

Sršen, J. (1992) *Jezik naš vsakdanji*, Ljubljana: Gospodarski vestnik

Stankiewics, E. (1959) 'The vocalic system of modern standard Slovenian', *International Journal of Slavic Linguistics and Poetics*, 1, 2, pp. 70–6: Mouton

Svane, G.O. (1958) *Grammatik der Slowenischen Schriftsprache*, Copenhagen: Rosenkilde und Bagger

Toporišič, J. (1972–3) *Slovenski knjižni jezik*, vols 1–4, Maribor: Obzorja

Toporišič, J. (1982) *Nova slovenska skladnja*, Ljubljana: Državna založba Slovenije

Toporišič, J. (1984) *Slovenska slovnica*, Maribor: Obzorja

Toporišič, J. et al. (eds) (1990) *Slovenski pravopis. I. Pravila*, Ljubljana: Državna založba Slovenije

Toporišič, J. (1991) *Družbenost slovenskega jezika*, Ljubljana: Državna založba Slovenije

Toporišič, J. (1992) *Zakaj ne po slovensko? Slovene by Synthetic Method*, Ljubljana: Filozofska fakulteta

Toporišič, J. (1992) *Enciklopedija slovenskega jezika*, Ljubljana: Cankarjeva založba

Toporišič, J. (1994) *Slovenski jezik in sporočanje I*, Maribor: Obzorja

Verbinc, F. (1994) *Slovar tujk*, Ljubljana: Cankarjeva založba

Vidovič-Muha, A. (1988) *Slovensko skladenjsko besedotvorje ob primerih zloženk*, Ljubljana: Partizanska knjiga

Vincenot, C. (1975) *Essai de grammaire slovène*, Ljubljana: Mladinska knjiga

Žagar, F. (1985) *Slovenska slovnica in jezikovna vadnica*, Maribor: Obzorja

INDEX